The Rough

D0112655

Travel health

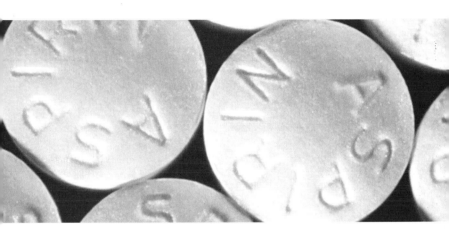

written and researched by

Dr Nick Jones

with additional contributions from
Dr Janet Gray and Dr Charles Easmon

ROUGH GUIDES

NEW YORK • LONDON • DELHI

www.roughguides.com

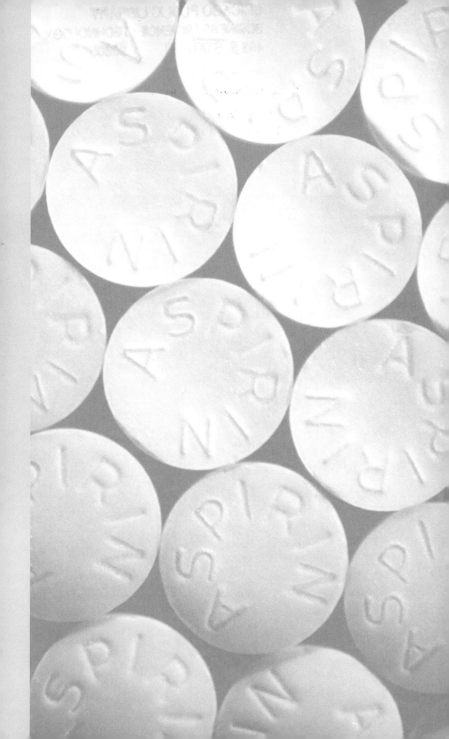

Contents

Introduction

Travel can be fraught with health hazards, even the most minor of which can seriously hamper your enjoyment of a trip. Caught up in the excitement of being away, it's easy to drop your guard in a way that you might not at home, whether it's a simple case of overindulgence in the local cuisine or pulling a muscle in the rush to catch a train. But perhaps the biggest danger to the traveller is the assumption that "it can't happen to me".

By looking at travellers' health from two perspectives – the prevention of illness before it happens, as well as how to cope if things do go wrong – **The Rough Guide to Travel Health** strives to help you avoid the risk, or at least minimize the impact, of illness abroad. **Part 1**, "Being Prepared", steers you through the considerations you need to make before you set out, with detailed advice on the kinds of vaccinations you might require, plus recommendations on what to pack in your medical kit – homeopathic remedies are discussed as well as conventional Western medicines. This section also advises on precautions to help you stay well while you're away, and how to cope with problems like motion sickness and fear of flying in the course of getting there. Detailed advice for travellers with specific needs completes the section, catering for those with diabetes or epilepsy, for example, as well as elderly or pregnant travellers and those on business or taking a gap year.

Part 2, the "A–Z", is an alphabetical listing of the illnesses and other health risks that you may encounter on your travels, with descriptions of the kinds of symptoms you can expect as well as the best treatments. The section opens with step-by-step instructions on "Making a Diagnosis", or assessing your symptoms to determine a likely cause. **Part 3**, First Aid, gives basic practical advice on how to cope with everything from cuts and grazes to broken bones. A regional review of the potential risks forms **Part 4**, "Where in the World?", while **Part 5** comprises a "Directory" of useful sources of further information, much of it online. Lastly, there's a **glossary** of medical terms.

There are a number of "**routes**" into this book. It might help to read through the whole of Part 1 in the planning stages of your trip. If you're far from home and suspect you're coming down with a particular illness, you can turn direct to the A–Z for advice on treatment. If you're less certain what you've got, the section on "Making a Diagnosis" will take you through some basic steps to determine the possible cause. Before you arrive at a particular destination, or on experiencing symptoms, you might look up the relevant part of the world in Part 4 for a short summary of potential health hazards and an idea of what vaccinations you'll need.

REMEMBER This book is intended to be used as a guide only. Designed to offer sensible, generalized advice to the sick traveller, it should not be considered as a substitute for the opinion of a qualified doctor. If you are worried about your symptoms, do not hesitate to seek medical advice.

Whether you're in the planning stages before your trip or you're away and feeling ill, it's not the intention of this guide to replace a visit to a doctor. We are confident, however, that this book can help you make a more informed decision about what to do next, no matter where in the world you're travelling.

1

Being prepared

Planning

Prevention of ill health for the traveller starts long before you reach for your travel sickness pills in the airport departure lounge. **Planning** is key – before so much as investing in a bottle of sunscreen lotion, you need to plan your itinerary carefully, consider your insurance requirements, decide whether preventative measures (eg immunizations and malaria prophylaxis) are necessary and assemble a basic medical kit for emergencies.

Start by asking yourself three basic questions: **where**, **when** and **how** are you going to travel? Don't be under any illusions: travelling can be physically, psychologically and emotionally draining, and your answers may have significant implications for your health, not just on the road but also when you return. Your answers to these questions are **individual** and, as such, will help you to focus on your particular pre-departure needs. The information that follows will help you to prepare for problems if and when they arise.

Insurance

It's a common and ill-considered mistake to subscribe to the "it only ever happens to other people" school of thought. Without adequate medical insurance, you risk spending potentially huge amounts for treatment if you do become ill abroad, as well as having to settle for a potentially inferior level of care to what you

The E111 and reciprocal health-care arrangements

For citizens of European Community countries only, the **E111** is available across Europe and entitles you to the same emergency medical care as the local population. This may be **free of charge** or **discounted** depending on where you are. The E111 is valid in the 25 member states of the EU – Austria, Belgium, Cyprus, Czech Republic, Denmark, Estonia, Finland, France, Germany, Greece, Hungary, the Republic of Ireland, Italy, Latvia, Lithuania, Luxembourg, Malta, the Netherlands, Poland, Portugal, Slovakia, Slovenia, Spain, Sweden and the UK – plus Gibraltar, Iceland, Liechtenstein and Norway. However, as cover is often limited, and **does not include repatriation**, it makes sense to take out a separate travel insurance policy as well.

A number of other countries have **reciprocal health-care arrangements** with the UK, which are not dependent on possession of an E111: Anguilla, Australia, Barbados, British Virgin Islands, Bulgaria, Channel Islands, Falkland Islands, Isle of Man, Montserrat, New Zealand, Romania, Russia, St Helena, Turks and Caicos Islands, Yugoslavia and republics of the former Soviet Union.

At the time of writing, the E111 is available as a paper form – you can get one from post offices throughout the UK, or download it from the UK Department of Health website (⊛www.dh.gov.uk). However, the paper form is due to be replaced by a **European Health Insurance card** by December 2005; details will appear on the Department of Health website. For general information on the E111, obtain a copy of the excellent *Health Advice for Travellers* leaflet, published in the UK by the Department of Health and available free from post offices, doctors' surgeries and some travel agents, as well as on the DOH website.

Rough Guides Ltd offers a low-cost **travel insurance policy**, especially customized for our statistically low-risk readers by a leading British broker, provided by the American International Group (AIG) and registered with the British regulatory body, GISC (the General Insurance Standards Council). There are five main Rough Guides insurance plans: **No Frills**, for the bare minimum for secure travel; **Essential**, which provides decent all-round cover; **Premier**, for comprehensive cover with a wide range of benefits; **Extended Stay**, for cover lasting four months to a year; and **Annual Multi-trip**, a cost-effective way of getting Premier cover if you travel more than once a year. Premier, Annual Multi-Trip and Extended Stay policies can be supplemented by a **"Hazardous Pursuits Extension"** if you plan to indulge in sports considered dangerous, such as scuba diving or trekking. For a **policy quote**, call the Rough Guides Insurance Line toll-free in the UK ☎0800/015 0906 or ☎+44 1392 314 665 from elsewhere. Alternatively, get an online quote at ⊛www.roughguides .com/insurance.

know at home. The basic premise is **never travel uninsured** – buying a policy that's right for your needs will be a great reassurance in you hour of need, ensuring you a greater chance of good and speedy treatment.

Choosing a policy

If you've paid for your trip with plastic, bear in mind that many of the big credit card companies have allied travel insurance policies (though the terms are often pretty limited). Most tour operators and travel agents will try to sell you their own insurance when you book, but you're under no obligation to buy. In fact, it generally pays to **shop around** – look for a policy that covers your individual needs, and try to stick to reputable firms or personal recommendations. It's unwise to base your final decision on **cost** alone, as a policy that's dramatically less expensive than the competition may well have loopholes in its coverage. Read insurance documents carefully to ensure that you understand what the restrictions and exclusions mean to you personally. Always declare **pre-existing ill health** to your insurer or you may jeopardize payments if a claim is later made – most policies will not cover you for an undeclared pre-existing medical condition.

Policies can be taken out for a **single holiday** or on an **annual basis**, the latter being a better deal for frequent or business travellers. Some firms offer discounts on joint policies, worth asking about if you're travelling as a couple. All policies have **exclusions** and many are weighted against the elderly, those with chronic illness (including immunodeficient conditions), or those pursuing what insurers consider dangerous activities (bungee jumping, whitewater rafting, skiing, hang gliding other hazardous sports). If you fall into any of these categories, contact the national representative group for your given interest or disability (details are listed in the relevant sections later in this chapter), or a travel agent specializing in your specific needs – many offer customized and competitive policies, arranged with reputable insurers, that would not normally be available to you on an individual basis. If your policy covers your **children**, clarify the policy's definition of a child (under 12, 16 or 18).

It's essential that your policy includes cover for **repatriation** (air evacuation) on medical grounds. Be sure to **clarify emergency procedures**, too: what to do

Finding insurance online

The **Internet** can be a good resource for finding inexpensive policies, but be aware that many sites relating to travel insurance are primarily promotional. It's a good idea to compare offers from several sites before buying a policy; the relatively impartial sites listed below are a good place to start.

Ⓦ**www.uk-travel-insurance-directory.co.uk**
Packed with valuable information and links, and catering for all types of traveller from the UK.

Ⓦ**www.about-online-travel-insurance.co.uk**
Good, sensible advice on all aspects of travel insurance.

Ⓦ**www.quotetravelinsurance.com**
US-based site offering policy price comparisons from big-name providers.

Ⓦ**www.travelinsurance.com.au**
Discounted packages from all the major Australian providers.

in the event of an accident or serious illness, whether there's a 24-hour telephone advice line and whether you will be required to pay for care initially and claim it back later (to be on the safe side, keep all receipts for treatment). Remember that most policies do not provide cover for your travel companion to return with you, nor do they extend to ongoing treatment on your return home.

Always carry your policy documents and important emergency contact numbers in a safe, but accessible place. Backup photocopies carried by your travel companion are a good idea. Don't forget that as well as covering health-related emergencies, a good travel insurance policy should also cover for cancellation costs, baggage loss or theft, and have a robust personal liability clause in case you are sued for injury to others or damage to their property.

Immunization

Immunization provides immunity against some serious, even fatal, diseases (although the protection afforded is rarely 100 percent). Many immunizations are given as a series of vaccinations over a period of time, so you'll need to visit your doctor or local travel clinic at least two months before your trip, sufficient time both for the maximum immunity to develop and for you to recover from any reactions.

Remember that as epidemic trends and environmental conditions change, so too do **vaccination recommendations**. It's a fluid process and what's good for a particular area in one season does not necessarily extend to the next. Generally speaking, no particular immunizations are required for travellers to the USA, Canada, Europe, Australia and New Zealand, while precautions are more likely for non-European countries encircling the Mediterranean and for Africa, Asia, the Middle East and Central and South America. Your doctor or local travel clinic will have the latest advice, although there are some very good resources on the Internet, too (see Part 4, p.249).

The table below lists the vaccinations you might need before a trip, together with the recommended regimes of administration. See p.64 for children's vaccinations.

Vaccine	No. of doses	Interval between doses	Length of immunity
Anthrax	6	2 weeks between first 3, then 6 months between 3rd and 4th, 4th and 5th, and 5th and 6th	1 year (booster recommended annually)
Cholera (Dukoral)	2	7 to 14 days	Booster recommended every 2 years for those over 6 years old.
(Mutacol)	1	–	Booster recommended every 6 months
Hepatitis A	1–2	Repeat initial dose after 6–12 months for full immunity	10 years
Hepatitis B	3	2nd after 4 weeks, 3rd after 6 months	5–10 years
Combined Hep A and Hep B	3	2nd after 1 month, 3rd after 6 months	10 years
Combined Hep A and typhoid	1	Booster of hep A at 6–12 months	
Influenza	1	1 year (different strains each year)	
Japanese encephalitis	2–3	7–14 days after initial. 3rd dose at 28 days.	Uncertain. Timing of booster depends on initial doses and make of vaccination
Meningococcal meningitis	1	3–5 years	
Rabies	3	2nd after 7 days, 3rd after 21 or 28 days	2–3 years. First booster at 6–12 months, then after 2–3 years thereafter.
Tick-borne encephalitis	2–3	2nd after 4–12 weeks, 3rd after 9–12 months	3 years
TB (BCG)	1	–	15 years+
Typhoid (2 types of vaccination)	1 / 3 (oral)	– / Alternate days	3 years / 1 year
Yellow fever	1	–	10 years

NB: Diphtheria, whooping cough, polio, tetanus, measles, mumps and rubella (German measles) are normally given as standard childhood vaccinations, but may need boosting.

If more than ten years have elapsed since your last tetanus and polio immunizations, you'll need a **booster** before you travel. Always keep a **personal record** of which vaccinations you have been given and when. **Charges** for vaccinations vary from country to country, although some are likely to be state-funded. Rates can be significant, so it's worth shopping around a little. **Yellow fever** is currently the only vaccine that requires **certification**, and production of the certificate is a legal requirement for entry into a number of countries, even if you're only passing through (see Part 3).

If you're exempt from vaccination for any reason, you will require written evidence of this from your doctor. Pregnant women and those with a weakened immune system from concurrent illness should discuss vaccination plans with a doctor before going ahead. For more detailed advice on vaccinations and HIV, see p.56.

Vaccination and immunity

Immunity to a disease can be acquired in two ways. The most common method, known as **active immunization**, stimulates the body to make antibodies to the disease in response to a vaccination or by contracting the infection itself. This usually results in long-term protection. **Passive immunity**, on the other hand, is achieved by inoculation with preparations derived from the blood plasma of individuals who already have immunity to the disease. The duration of protection is shorter, although repeat immunization is possible.

Vaccinations themselves can be divided into three categories: live, inactivated or extracts produced by the micro-organism in question. **Inactivated vaccinations** are mostly produced from dead disease-producing organisms. Achieving adequate immunity frequently requires a series of injections, and the duration of immunity can vary from months to years. **Extract vaccinations**, derived from cellular components of the germs, require an initial series of injections followed by periodic boosters.

Live vaccinations are a weakened form of the disease-causing organism, and include the following:

- ✚ Oral polio
- ✚ Oral typhoid
- ✚ Oral cholera (Mutacol)
- ✚ Yellow fever
- ✚ BCG (TB)
- ✚ Measles
- ✚ Mumps
- ✚ Rubella

Live vaccinations generally produce a long-lasting immunity from a single dose. Try to allow enough time to avoid more than one live vaccination being given at the same time. A gap of three weeks between injections is ideal, but if this is unfeasible, at least make sure the vaccines are injected into different body sites.

Reactions to vaccination

Mild **reactions** are common after vaccination. These include swelling, redness or discomfort at the injection site, slight fever and malaise. As a general rule, it's best to postpone immunizations if you're suffering from an acute illness, particularly one causing fever, because the vaccine itself may produce a fever and your body's response to vaccination may be undermined. Again discuss this with a doctor beforehand. Some vaccinations contain small amounts of antibiotics or are derived from egg proteins (see box below). If you know that you have specific **allergies**, always tell the doctor or nurse before any vaccination. Severe reactions to vaccination, such as anaphylaxis (see p.91), are very rare but also very dangerous.

Although the subject of considerable research, no vaccinations are currently available against malaria and dengue fever. Malaria prophylaxis, discussed on pp.41 & 163–170, needs advanced planning and the most up-to-date advice.

Individual vaccinations

Common **vaccinations** for travellers are covered separately on the following pages, with advice on how soon before your trip you should be vaccinated, the length of immunity conferred by each, and any possible side effects.

Anthrax

There are very few circumstances that merit pre-travel immunization against **anthrax**: only those who will be working with animals, animal products or in agriculture in high-risk areas are likely to need to have it. The vaccine itself remains very hard to come by, however, despite much media attention in recent years. It's usually given in three **doses** over six weeks, followed by boosters at six, twelve and eighteen months. Annual boosters are recommended. **Reactions** (lymph gland swelling, mild fever and itching) are rare.

▶▶ See also Anthrax, p.94.

Cholera

Low efficacy – about fifty percent protection lasting three to six months – and relatively common side effects mean that injected **cholera** vaccinations are now largely obsolete; scrupulous food and drink hygiene provide a far more effective means of avoidance. However if you'll be staying in an endemic area for a prolonged period without easy access to medical care; if you've ever had surgery to your stomach; or if you're a heavy user of antacids or regular anti-stomach ulcer medications, ask your doctor about the two new, highly effective oral vaccinations now on offer (availability varies from country to country). **Dukoral** is an inactivated vaccine administered as two separate doses (three for children aged between 2 and 6), taken a week apart and, completed a minimum of one week before entering a high-risk area. Boosters are recommended every two

> ### Vaccines containing egg proteins
>
> If you're **allergic to eggs** or are a **vegan**, be aware that the following vaccinations are derived from cultures containing egg proteins. The first two are low-risk, but reactions to the others can be severe.
>
> ✚ Measles
> ✚ Mumps
> ✚ Influenza
> ✚ Rabies
> ✚ Yellow fever
> ✚ Tick-borne encephalitis

years for adults, and every six months for children between 2 and 6 years old. It's safe in pregnancy and when breast-feeding, but is not recommended for children under two. **Mutacol** is a live vaccination, given as a single dose which confers a high level of protection as early as seven days post-vaccination. It isn't recommended for children under two. Although it's length of protection has yet to be firmly established, the current recommendation is that boosters should be given every six months.

Trials have indicated that these new vaccinations are highly effective. Reported **side effects** of both vaccines have commonly been abdominal pain, diarrhoea, nausea and vomiting; ironically, both are also thought to confer a degree of immunity against e-coli-induced travellers' diarrhoea. Further references about these vaccinations can be found on the Centre for Disease Control website (see p.276).

Although **certificates of immunization** against cholera are not officially required, customs officers in some countries still demand them from travellers arriving from an infected area (perhaps as a lever to extract money). Countries following this "unofficial" policy include Egypt, Ghana, Kenya, Madagascar, Rwanda and Tanzania. If such problems are anticipated, obtain a letter from your doctor stating that the vaccine is medically contraindicated. Because of the risk of diseases from poorly sterilized equipment, avoid being vaccinated on arrival in the country at all costs.

▶▶ See also Cholera, p.102.

Diphtheria

In developed countries, the **diphtheria** vaccination is a routine childhood immunization. If you're travelling to countries where diphtheria may still be endemic, and if your last booster was more than ten years ago, you certainly should have a further booster before leaving home. If for some reason you have never been immunized, you will require the full three-dose **course** at monthly intervals before departure. **Reactions** are usually mild, consisting of redness and swelling around the injection site, malaise, headache and a transient fever.

▶▶ See also Diphtheria, p.117.

Hepatitis A

The most common method of immunization against **hepatitis A** is a **single dose**, which takes about 10–14 days to make the body produce enough antibodies to confer high levels of immunity. A further vaccine 6–12 months later gives up to ten years' immunity. Adverse **reactions**, usually confined to the first few days, include soreness around the injection site and, less frequently, fever, malaise, fatigue, headache, nausea and loss of appetite.

You can also be immunized against hepatitis A via one of the **combined vaccines** (see opposite).

▶▶ See also Hepatitis A, p.141.

Hepatitis B

Hepatitis B immunization in the UK is currently restricted to those at particular risk because of their lifestyle, occupation or close proximity to a case or carrier, although in some countries (eg France and the USA) it's given as a routine childhood vaccination. The standard **course** is three doses, with the second being administered one month after the first, and the third six months after the first. Immunity length varies, so it's sensible to check antibody levels after the primary course is completed. Boosters are recommended after ten years for those still at risk. Hepatitis B vaccination is generally well tolerated; the most common **reaction** is soreness around the injection site, although, rarely, fever, rash, malaise and influenza-like symptoms can occur.

You can also be immunized against hepatitis B via one of the combined vaccines described below.

▶▶ See also Hepatitis B, p.141.

Combined vaccines

Combined vaccinations save you money as well as reducing the number of needle pricks you have to endure. The main drawback is the disparity between the length of time before a booster is needed for the individual vaccine components – unless meticulous records are kept, things can get very complicated and confusing. The text below details combined preparations most likely to be of use to travellers.

The vaccine against **hepatitis A and B** is estimated to offer protection against hepatitis A and B for ten years. The course comprises three doses of the vaccination, with the second being given one month after the first and the third six months after the first. A booster is recommended after ten years.

The combined vaccine against **hepatitis A** and **typhoid** is given as a single dose to adults at least two weeks before risk of exposure. A booster of hepatitis A may be given between six and twelve months afterwards to confer immunity for up to ten years. People at prolonged risk from typhoid should have a typhoid booster after three years. There is not enough data available to comment on its safety in pregnancy. **Side effects** are reportedly uncommon but include redness, pain and swelling at the injection site and malaise, headaches, nausea, muscle aches, itching and fever.

Influenza

The ever-changing nature of the **influenza** virus means that it's impossible to produce long-term immunity from a single immunization. Thus each year, the flu vaccine (given as a **single dose**) is tailored against the prevalent viral strain, and is recommended to those at highest risk from the disease: the elderly, people with severe asthma or chronic chest problems, those with other chronic illnesses such as diabetes, heart disease or kidney failure, and anyone with a compromised immune system.

The vaccine is generally well tolerated, but should be avoided if you're allergic to **eggs**. Because influenza epidemics occur in the winter months, supplies of the vaccine may be a problem if you need a jab prior to a summer break; if possible, arrange the vaccination as far in advance as possible.

▶▶ See also Influenza, p.147.

Japanese encephalitis

Immunization against **Japanese encephalitis** is recommended for travellers spending a month or more in Southeast Asia and the Far East, especially those staying in rural areas at the end of the rainy season. Bear in mind that as this is not a commonly administered vaccination, your doctor may need to order it specially – allow some extra time for this. There are several different types of vaccination, although the Japanese Biken and the South Korean Green Cross are the commonly used varieties in the UK and USA. The Biken provides protection for up to two years after the initial three-dose **course**; protection after the initial two-dose course of Green Cross lasts for approximately one year, but thereafter boosters are recommended every three years. Neither vaccine is advisable for children aged less than 1 unless the risk is particularly high.

Adverse effects include swelling and pain at the injection site, and rare systemic allergic reactions such as breathing difficulties and itching. These reactions can be delayed for up to two weeks after the vaccine has been given, so it's recommended that an immunization course be *completed* at least two weeks before you travel.

▶▶ See also Japanese encephalitis, p.153.

Meningococcal meningitis

The risk of acquiring **meningococcal meningitis** is greatest for people spending a month or more in an endemic area, in close proximity to the local population. High-risk areas include much of sub-Saharan Africa, as well as Nepal, Bhutan, Pakistan and the area around Delhi.

Note that vaccination (and appropriate documentation) against **meningitis subgroups** A, C, W135 and Y (marketed in the UK as ACWY Vax) is obligatory for those travelling to Saudi Arabia for the hajj and Umrah pilgrimages. If this applies to you, ensure that you make your plans clear to your doctor or travel clinic to avoid being given the standard vaccination against the A and C strains only.

The ACWY vaccine is a **single dose** and should be given at least a week before travelling. Immunity lasts three to five years in adults, less in children. Following vaccination, a high temperature is not uncommon, especially in children, and a local **reaction** at the injection site can last for a few days. The vaccine should be avoided if you already have a fever or if you've previously suffered severe reactions to the vaccine. There is no definitive data regarding the safety of the vaccine in pregnancy, so it's best considered only if there is a true risk of infection, for example following an outbreak.

▶▶ See also Meningococcal meningitis, p.171.

Plague

The risk of the average traveller being exposed to **plague** is extremely low, and routine vaccination is unnecessary. It need only be considered if you're visiting areas where there's an active outbreak and are likely to be in close contact with the locals. However, as it's not commercially available in the US or the UK, it may be hard to get hold of. The current recommended **course** is three doses, with the second administered four weeks after the first and the third six months after the first. The vaccination reduces the incidence and severity of the illness, but the protection afforded appears to be relatively low. Adverse **reactions** are usually infrequent and mild after the first vaccination but are more common or severe after repeat doses. Redness and swelling around the injection site occur in about ten percent of individuals; more general effects include malaise, headache, fever and swollen lymph glands. When possible, try to avoid cholera and typhoid vaccinations being given at the same time.

▶▶ See also Plague, p.179.

Polio

There are two types of **polio** vaccination: the oral, live version and the inactivated injection. In developed countries, the oral version is routinely administered in childhood. If you haven't had a booster within the last ten years, it's advisable to have one before travelling to any area other than Australia, New Zealand, northwestern Europe and the USA. The full three-dose **course** should be taken at monthly intervals if you have not been previously immunized. Because the oral immunization is live and remains so in the gut, it should be deferred if you have diarrhoea or are vomiting and avoided if your immune system is weakened or you are in close contact with someone who is immunosuppressed. In such cases, you may have the inactivated vaccine instead.

Oral polio and oral typhoid vaccinations must be separated by at least three weeks because of potential interaction.

▶▶ See also Polio, p.180.

Rabies

Although cases are relatively rare, **rabies** occurs in all continents except Antarctica and, once the symptoms appear, is almost always fatal. Immunization should be considered by anyone likely to be working with animals and by travellers spending prolonged periods in remote areas where rabies is endemic and where adequate medical treatment may not be readily available.

The three-dose **pre-exposure** vaccination (see overleaf) provides a reasonable level of protection, although it's important to remember that if you're bitten by a rabid animal, you will still require some degree of **post-exposure** treatment with rabies immunoglobulin (RIG). Note, however, that in many developing countries RIG may first of all be hard to come by, and that as it will have been derived locally from human neural tissue, it may carry a risk from other blood-borne infections such as HIV or hepatitis B. If you are bitten by a rabid animal and you have not had pre-exposure prophylaxis, you will require immediate, more involved, post-exposure treatment. Thus:

✚ Pre-exposure vaccine x 3 + BITE = Post-exposure vaccine x 2 on days 0 and 3–7;

✚ No pre-exposure vaccine + BITE = Rabies immunoglobulin (RIG) immediately + post-rabies vaccine x 5 on days 0, 3, 7, 14 and 28 (a sixth is sometimes given on day 90).

Two doses of pre-exposure treatment four weeks apart give acceptable levels of immunity if post-exposure treatment is likely to be immediately available. The full course of three vaccinations should provide protection for two to three years. If you're at continuous risk, you should have a single reinforcing dose after two years.

A localized **reaction** to the vaccine is the most common adverse effect. Headache, fever, muscle aches, vomiting and itchy rashes have also been reported. If you're pregnant, avoid pre-exposure vaccination unless there are exceptional circumstances; get expert advice.

▶▶ See also Rabies, p.182.

The case for pre-exposure rabies vaccination

Given that the rabies vaccine is costly, and that direct contact with the disease is highly unlikely for the majority of travellers, many question the need for **pre-exposure vaccination**. It's important to remember, however, that rabies is untreatable and almost invariably lethal once contracted. Also, consider the cultural place that dogs and other animals hold in many parts of the developing world, where they are either allowed to roam free or used for such things as home security – hence travellers are very likely to encounter them at some point, trekkers to remote areas being particularly at risk. Pre-exposure vaccination, although not eliminating the need for post-exposure treatment, greatly simplifies the course (RIG isn't needed) and reduces the likelihood of reactions to the prolonged treatment course. Additionally, RIG may not be readily available or may have been improperly screened for other diseases (see above). Although post-bite treatment always needs to be initiated as quickly as possible, the immunity of someone who has had the pre-exposure course will be enhanced and a delay in access to post-exposure therapy may be less dangerous. Finally, the pre-exposure course may protect to some degree against unknown or unapparent exposure to the virus (eg handling a piece of wood that has been chewed by a rabid animal).

Tetanus

Tetanus vaccination is part of the normal course of childhood immunizations in most countries. Booster doses after injury are only necessary if ten years have elapsed since the previous immunization. Any adult who has had five doses (that's the normal childhood **course** of three, plus two subsequent boosters) is considered to possess lifelong immunity.

Reactions to the vaccine include pain, redness and swelling around the injection site and, less commonly, malaise, headache, lethargy, muscle aches and fever.

Tick-borne encephalitis

The prophylactic vaccine against **tick-borne encephalitis** is recommended for travellers who'll be hiking, camping or working in the warm, heavily forested parts of central and eastern Europe and Scandinavia in late spring or summer. The initial **course** is two injections administered one to three months apart, which provide protection for around a year; you can also have a third dose between nine and twelve months after the first, which extends the period of protection to three years. Boosters are recommended every three years for those at continued risk. A post-exposure preparation is also available in some countries.

Adverse **reactions** to the vaccine are rare and include local swelling and pain around the injection site, fatigue, limb pain, fever, nausea and headache which may last up to 24 hours, as well as transient itchy rashes. The vaccine is contraindicated if you have an allergy to egg protein.

▶▶ See also Tick-borne encephalitis, p.216.

Tuberculosis (TB)

Some countries have routine vaccination programmes aimed at children and teens for the **single-dose BCG** (Bacillus of Calmette and Guerin) vaccination against **TB**. If you're unsure whether or not you've been vaccinated, a test ("Heaf" test) is available through your doctor to assess your immunity. If you have not been vaccinated and have no natural immunity, BCG vaccination is recommended for trips of more than one month to Asia, Africa or Central and South America, especially for anyone who is likely to be in close contact with native populations in these areas. Because it's a live vaccination, it should be used with caution (only on medical recommendation) in pregnancy or by people with weakened immune systems. The vaccination should be given at least three months before departure.

▶▶ See also Tuberculosis (TB), p.218.

Typhoid

As **typhoid fever** is spread by ingestion of food or drink contaminated with the infected faeces, you're at greatest risk where there is poor sanitation or low standards of personal and food hygiene. Immunization is probably less important for short stays in good accommodation.

Two types of typhoid vaccine are routinely available, an injected and an oral form. The **injected vaccine** provides a three-year protection of between seventy and eighty percent after a single dose. The newer three-dose **oral vaccine** offers similarly reliable levels of immunity, but a repeat three-capsule course is required after one year if you remain at continued risk of infection. The three capsules must be taken on alternate days on an empty stomach with a cool drink. Neither of the vaccines offers full protection, and the need for scrupulous attention to personal, food and water hygiene cannot be over-emphasized.

Reactions to the injected form are uncommon, mild and usually local to the site of injection. The oral vaccine may cause transient nausea, vomiting, abdominal cramps, diarrhoea and an itchy rash. Antibiotics can interfere with the immune response to the oral vaccine, as can gastrointestinal upsets. Also, because it's a live vaccine, the oral form is inadvisable if you have a weakened immune function. Oral typhoid vaccination and oral polio vaccination should be taken at least three weeks apart as they may interfere with each other, impairing immunity. Avoid starting the mefloquine antimalarial within three days of completing the course of oral typhoid.

Neither typhoid vaccine should be given if you have a high fever or have suffered severe reactions to previous doses of the same vaccine. If you're pregnant, you should only be vaccinated if there is high risk of infection – seek expert advice.

▶▶ See also Typhoid, p.221.

Yellow fever

Yellow fever symptoms vary in severity, but the fatality rate in unimmunized, non-indigenous populations can exceed fifty percent. Immunization, which offers high levels of protection against the disease (approaching 100 percent), is recommended for anyone spending time in countries where yellow fever is endemic.

An **International Certificate of Vaccination** against yellow fever is compulsory for entry into some countries, and you should check with the relevant embassy before travelling. The certificate is valid for ten years, beginning ten days after vaccination. Travellers who for any reason can't be vaccinated require a letter of exemption from a doctor if they intend to visit these countries, and should seek further advice from the relevant embassy regarding entry.

A single dose of this live vaccine provides protection for up to ten years. If another live vaccine is required, it should be given either at the same time in a different part of the body, or separated by an interval of three weeks.

Only a few people experience mild **reactions**, including headache, muscle pains, fever, generalized itching and soreness at the injection site. Severe allergic reactions are rare but have been reported. In 2001, reports of a handful of fatalities after the vaccination were published. Scrutiny of the data revealed the risk of a life-threatening event following vaccination to be very low (around one in a million), and a great deal less than the dangers of the disease itself.

Avoid this vaccine if you are suffering from high fever; if you have abnormal immune function; if you know from previous reactions that you're allergic to neomycin, polymyxin or egg protein; if you are HIV positive; and if you are pregnant, unless there is high risk of infection. Infants under 9 months should not be vaccinated unless they are at particularly high risk; seek expert advice.

▶ ▶ See also Yellow fever, p.233.

Travel by air

Airports are innately stressful places, their apparent organized chaos triggering niggling worries that something, somewhere along the line, will go wrong – from lost baggage and flight delays to whether the plane will actually stay in the air. Time pressure is the last thing you need, especially if you're a nervous flier, so always arrive early to allow yourself plenty of time to check in. Once **on board**, with the mayhem of customs checks and departure lounges behind you, the cramped, claustrophobic cabin environment can contribute to further anxiety and feelings of motion sickness, as well as making relaxation or sleep during the flight more difficult.

Flying itself can affect your body in a number of ways, and the physiological changes that take place can affect existing medical ailments.

For online advice on health and flying, visit ⓦwww.aviation-health.org.

Fitness to fly

Flying when you are **unfit** may endanger your life as well as disrupting the flight. If you have any form of chronic or ongoing illness which might be affected by flying, consult your doctor for advice beforehand and check that your travel insurance policy covers you adequately. Below are general recommendations for specific conditions.

For information on flying when pregnant and with small babies, see pp.63 & 70.

Asthma and respiratory illnesses

In-flight medical incidents relating to **asthma** are surprisingly common; asthmatic should try to stabilize symptoms before departure. Carry your normal inhalers and asthma medications in hand baggage on the plane. For those with severe or "brittle" asthma, discuss with your doctor the possibility of starting a course of oral steroids two to three days before the flight.

▶▶ See also Asthma, p.51.

If you suffer from chronic **respiratory disease** (eg emphysema or chronic bronchitis), or have recently had a severe chest or upper airway infection, you should not fly without first consulting a doctor. The use of supplemental oxygen may be helpful for sufferers of chronic lung disease, although this needs to be arranged beforehand with the airline and may incur extra cost. Do not fly under any circumstances if you have a suspected collapsed lung (**pneumothorax**) or have had chest surgery within the previous four weeks.

Heart and circulatory problems

If you suffer from angina, always carry your **nitrate spray** (GTN) or pills with you. The risk of most modern airports' customs area metal detectors affecting your cardiac pacemaker is minimal, but tell airport security that you prefer to be searched manually if in any doubt.

Do **not** fly if you:

+ suffer from poorly controlled **angina**, **heart failure** or **abnormal heart rhythms**.
+ have suffered an uncomplicated **heart attack** or open **heart surgery** within the past three weeks. Those who have suffered complications should wait at least six weeks and then fly only after medical clearance.
+ have suffered a stroke or **subarachnoid haemorrhage** (a type of brain haemorrhage) in the past ten days.
+ have suffered a recent deep-vein thrombosis (**DVT**), unless you are well established on anticoagulant treatment.
+ suffer from **anaemia** – with a haemoglobin level of less than 7.5 g/l you definitely should not fly without oxygen, while with a level less than 10 g/l you need to seek medical advice.
+ have **sickle cell anaemia** and have suffered a sickle cell crisis within the past ten days or have full-blown sickle cell disease. Carriers of the sickle cell trait are at only slight risk in pressurized aircraft but might run into problems on unpressurized flights (generally short-hop, low-altitude flights in small planes).

Diabetes

Insulin-dependent **diabetics** should keep to "home time" with regard to insulin and meals, and always carry sweets or sugary drinks in case of a hypo. A slightly higher than normal blood sugar level is more acceptable in the short term than a low reading during the flight. If you've had previous problems with severe hypoglycaemia, always carry glucagon (a drug that causes a rapid elevation in blood sugar). Carry your insulin with you on the plane; if stowed in the hold it will freeze. Specially designed insulated bags are available to keep your insulin cool in transit. Seek advice from your airline beforehand regarding your needles, which are banned from hand baggage unless cleared in advance.

▶▶ See also Diabetes, p.52.

Neurological disorders

Do not fly if you have been diagnosed with a **brain tumour** without first speaking to your specialist. It is also inadvisable to fly if you have frequent fits – postpone your trip until your condition is controlled with medication. If your **epilepsy** is well controlled, keep to "home time" with regard to medications and avoid missing doses.

▶▶ See also Epilepsy, p.54.

Broken bones and fractures

You shouldn't fly within two days of **breaking a bone**. Tell anyone applying a plaster cast that you plan to fly so they can give you a split cast, in case the limb swells during the flight. Passengers with above-knee plaster casts are usually required to buy an extra seat or travel first-class in order to have sufficient leg room. Do not fly within ten days of sustaining a skull **fracture**, and then only after medical clearance.

Surgery

Allow two weeks after major **surgery** to the abdomen, and four weeks after chest surgery, before embarking on a flight. Because of the damage an intra-ocular air bubble could inflict by expanding at altitude, flying should also be postponed after eye surgery until permitted by a specialist.

Ear problems

Consider delaying your flight if you have suffered a recent **ear infection**, which may have left fluid behind the eardrum. Blockage of the eustachian tube as a result of nasal congestion or a sore throat can lead to ear discomfort and even perforation of the drum as the cabin pressure changes. In rare circumstances, an expanding air pocket behind the eardrum can cause permanent damage to the ear. If you have a cold, use steam and decongestants to help clear your nose and upper airways.

Infectious diseases

Airlines may refuse to board passengers with potentially **infectious diseases**, though more often than not this is left to integrity and responsibility of the individuals. Droplet-borne illnesses can easily infect passengers in close proximity, so consider your fellow passengers before boarding a flight with something contagious.

Gastrointestinal problems

Unless it is known to be caused by a haemorrhoid, you should not fly if you have suffered recent **bleeding from the gut**, as there is an increased risk of further bleeding.

Onboard conditions

Cabin air has a very low humidity, which contributes to **dehydration**. Apart from making you feel thirsty, dehydration causes headaches, nasal congestion, drowsiness and increases the risk of deep-vein thrombosis (DVT) in the legs. It may also cause contact lens discomfort and exacerbate the symptoms of jet

The Valsalva manoeuvre

The difference in air pressure inside and outside the eardrum is equalized by the **eustachian tube**, a narrow passage that runs between the inner ear and the back of the throat. In flight, if the tube is blocked through nasal congestion, the air pocket in the inner ear can expand to cause discomfort and even, in extreme cases, rupture of the eardrum.

The pressure variations caused by altitude changes are most apparent during takeoff and landing; if your ears do become uncomfortable, try the **Valsalva manoeuvre** to reopen your eustachian tube. Pinch your nose to seal the airway, close your mouth and breath out *gently* against the resistance. You'll hear a click in both ears as your eustachian tube unblocks.

Other methods of keeping the eustachian tube clear include sucking sweets, chewing gum and yawning.

lag. Minimize the effects of dehydration by resisting last-minute alcohol binges and top-ups to your sun tan, and make sure that you increase your intake of water or uncarbonated drinks during the flight. Tea, coffee and alcohol all act as diuretics (ie, cause fluid loss), so are therefore best avoided.

In the fit and healthy, the reduction in **oxygen concentration** on board the aircraft has an insignificant effect, but problems can arise for people who have compromised heart or lung function; it may be possible to arrange a personalized oxygen supply from the airline. As a rule, if you suffer from a heart or lung condition that causes shortness of breath at rest, prevents you from walking more than 50m on the flat or ascending twelve steps, don't fly without oxygen, and think hard before flying at all. The reduction in oxygen saturation of haemoglobin, the oxygen-carrying molecule in the blood, can also provoke premature labour in late pregnancy, and may be dangerous to premature babies.

The reduced **cabin pressure** in flight causes the gas inside the body to expand. As a result, abdominal bloating and mild ear and sinus discomfort are common, while the expansion of air pockets inside the body can be dangerous soon after an operation or a fractured skull. Minimize the discomfort from bloating of the gut by wearing loose clothing and avoiding fizzy drinks and wind-producing foods before your flight. **Sinus** or **ear pain** occur more commonly when there is already congestion of your airways after a cold or hay fever.

Tips for comfortable air travel

+ Wear loose, lightweight clothing.
+ Avoid or minimize your intake of tea, coffee and alcohol during the flight.
+ Refrain from last-minute alcohol binges or sunbathing before you fly.
+ Avoid spicy food before flying.
+ Drink copious quantities of water or uncarbonated drinks.
+ Get up and move around or, if this is difficult, do calf-stretching exercises.
+ Carry any medications you are likely to need in hand baggage, including insulin (likely to require prior permission), inhalers and decongestants.
+ Remove contact lenses before flying; alternatively, keep moisturizing eye drops handy.

Plane disinsectization

In order to prevent the transportation of insects from country to country, and thus the possible spread of insect-borne disease, some countries practise aircraft **disinsectization**. This may be done by spraying insecticides while passengers are onboard, by spraying when the plane is empty, by treatment of the interior surfaces of the plane with insecticides or a combination of the three. Despite media concerns about this practice, a WHO report in 1995 concluded that, when performed appropriately, disinsectization does not present a significant risk to human health, although occasional allergic reactions can occur.

Few countries currently require aircraft to be disinsectized but most reserve the right to do so if a threat is perceived. If you want to know the likelihood of your flight being disinsectized, check with your airline.

Immobility and inactivity, particularly on long-haul flights, can lead to uncomfortable swollen ankles and, more dangerously, to a deep-vein thrombosis (**DVT**). Ways in which to minimize the risk of DVT are discussed in Part 2 (see p.111), but the key preventatives are stretching and exercise. Note that the legroom at the seats close to exits and those that face the bulkhead are often better than elsewhere on the plane, and it may be possible to reserve these in advance (some airlines have started to charge for this privilege).

It's common knowledge that air within an aircraft is **recirculated**, but as the air passes through filters which remove potentially harmful bacteria, airborne infection is extremely unlikely. A prolonged period in close proximity to other germy humans is far more problematic, as you run the risk of person-to-person droplet spread; even TB can be spread by this method (see p.218). While there is little that you can do to reduce the risk from other people, act responsibly if you are unwell with an infectious illness and defer your flight.

Fear of flying

Whole books have been written about the fear of flying (**aviophobia** or **aerophobia**), an unwieldy subject to cover in a few short paragraphs. A simple fear of the plane falling from the sky is usually exacerbated by other influences such as claustrophobia, fatigue, peer influence, lack of knowledge about how planes fly and which noises and sensations are normal, anxiety about your destination, adverse media publicity or perhaps a previous traumatic experience, while the increased threat of terrorism since 9/11 has done little to help nervous fliers. The physical conditions in the flight cabin also contribute to the dry mouth, tension headache and nausea often caused by fear.

It's quite normal to suffer a degree of anxiety when flying, but severe, debilitating aerophobia, like any other phobia, is almost always irrational – flying is reportedly 25 times safer than driving. Many of the courses for aerophobics focus on putting the risks of flying in perspective, with emphasis on how the plane flies and how the body reacts physiologically to fear and anxiety – the "knowledge is power" principle. Simply talking through your fears and anxieties with a friend or experienced traveller will also help.

On the bright side, psychologists view aerophobia as one of the easiest phobias to cure, responding well to simple relaxation techniques, cognitive behavioural treatment (CBT), hypnosis and psychoanalysis, among a wide range of different treatment. Resources range from educative, self-help pamphlets to in-depth courses. There are a large number of sites to check out on the Internet (see p.276).

There are various ways to minimize aerophobia:

✚ Learn some self-relaxation techniques, which focus on controlling breathing, progressive muscle relaxation and positive imagery.
✚ Think more about your destination and less about the flight.
✚ Avoid rushing to the airport (it's not helpful if you're in a high state of anxiety before you even check in).
✚ Distraction before and during the flight is a good idea: wander around the airport shops, stretch your legs, buy a compelling book or magazine, listen to your personal stereo, write your journal or watch the in-flight movie.
✚ Let the cabin crew know that you are an anxious flyer.
✚ Don't be upset by turbulence – modern aircraft are easily capable of dealing with the buffeting. When turbulence strikes, imagine you're on a boat that's riding the waves – in fact that's more or less what's happening, though the waves are air pockets.

While some **medications** help to take the edge off anxiety, it's always worth remembering that they're treating the symptoms rather than the cause of the problem. That said, they are particularly useful in cases of mild to moderate aerophobia. **Antihistamines** (see p.38) such as promethazine, which can be readily bought over the counter, have a sedative effect and are also helpful in treating motion sickness. Alternatively, your doctor may prescribe either **diazepam** or **beta-blockers**; the latter are used primarily to treat angina and high blood pressure, but in low doses are a useful treatment for anxiety without being overly sedating or addictive. Diazepam (also widely known as Valium) is losing favour because of its addictive potential, but in low doses it is highly effective in the short-term treatment of anxiety. It is sedating and can impair memory and judgement. Bear in mind, however, that any medication which sedates you may encourage you to sleep right through a long-haul flight, and so increase your risk of a DVT due to the prolonged immobility – it's important to consider the pros and cons carefully, especially if other factors (see p.111) put you at high risk of suffering a DVT.

 There are a number of **alternative treatments** you can use to treat anxiety associated with a fear of flying (for more on homeopathic medicine, see p.45). Of **homeopathic remedies**, Aconite 30c, taken at ten-minute intervals, is highly effective in removing the panicky feelings. Argentum nitricum 30c, taken four times a day before travelling,

Panic attacks

If you do feel panicky, you may start to **hyperventilate** (involuntary rapid, shallow breathing). This can lead to further symptoms associated with anxiety such as shaking, chest and throat tightness, nausea and dizziness. Often simple recognition of the problem and concentrating hard on taking slow, measured breaths and expelling the air from your lungs can reduce the panicky feelings. If this fails, breathing in and out of a paper bag controls hyperventilation and its consequent effects. Simply seal the paper bag with your hands around your nose and mouth and breathe in the air you have just breathed out into the bag. The higher concentration of carbon dioxide you inhale normalizes the pH (acidity) of your blood and will slow down your breathing.

will remove the anticipatory fear in the days before setting off. Other options include **Bach Rescue Remedy** (one of a number of flower essence remedies widely available), which calms you when tearful, moody, shocked or fearful; put five or six drops in a glass or small bottle of water and sip periodically. Because of its alcohol content, always dilute it for children; you might also run into problems taking it into "dry" countries. **Lavender oil** is calming and helps to send you to sleep. Both Rescue Remedy and lavender oil are safe to use in pregnancy.

Melatonin and jet lag

A recent review of the alleviative effects of **melatonin** on jet lag symptoms confirmed what many in the military and business community already knew; that it works if taken correctly. A hormone produced in the pineal gland at the base of the brain, and sold in health shops and over the Internet rather than pharmacies, melatonin is believed to act as the body's timekeeper. Doses of between 0.5mg and 5mg, taken between 10pm and midnight destination time, have been shown to reduce jet lag symptoms, especially in those travelling east over more than five time zones. Unfortunately, however, melatonin production lacks the stringent quality controls usually associated with drugs, and little is currently known about its toxicity or long-term effects. It's not recommended for people with epilepsy, and may interact with the drug warfarin.

The **Internet** has reams of content on melatonin, from detailed reviews to online stores. Bear in mind that much of it, whether for or against, is not at all neutral; for an impartial, scientific review, search for "melatonin" at ⊛www.update-software .com/cochrane/abstract.htm.

Jet lag

Jet travel allows us to cross time zones in a shorter time than our bodies' natural rhythms require in order to adjust. The natural rhythms most susceptible to the effects of **jet lag** are those of sleep, appetite and bowel habits; menstruation pattern can also be disturbed. Estimates vary, but jet lag is usually appreciable after journeys in which five or more time zones (a five-hour or greater time difference) have been crossed. It's worse on eastbound flights, after which time is ahead of your natural body clock.

The most common **symptoms** of jet lag are feelings of exhaustion, insomnia, poor concentration, disorientation, loss of appetite, nausea, mood swings, irrational anger, weakness, headache, blurred vision, dizziness and bowel disturbance (diarrhoea or constipation). The cramped, dry conditions of the aircraft, and the effects of alcohol and caffeine, may exacerbate the symptoms. It can take up to a week for your body to readjust.

There are a few measures you can take to minimize its impact on arrival:

+ If possible, take naps during the flight, especially if it's an eastbound journey. Although you might find antihistamines or a mild tranquillizer helpful in getting some sleep, it's better to avoid using sedating medications while flying as they increase immobility and may contribute to dehydration and DVT risk (see pp.113 & 111). They are better used on arrival to restore normal sleep patterns.

+ Increase your fluid intake during the flight but avoid carbonated drinks, alcohol and caffeine. Equally, avoid dehydrating activities – alcohol binges and sunbathing – before you fly.

+ Take regular walks around the cabin if possible. While seated, tense and relax your calf muscles hourly.

+ If you can, avoid strenuous activities or important decision-making within the first few days of arrival, although it's helpful to adapt normal activities of daily living – sleeping and eating, for example – to local time as soon as possible.

+ Break long-haul flights with an overnight stopover.

 You can **treat jet lag homeopathically** by taking a combined dose of Arnica and Cocculus; take one 30c tablet of each four times a day for three or four days. A mixture of grapeseed extract (two drops) and peppermint (one drop) essential oils in a cool footbath (double the amounts if filling a whole bath) will help to revive you after a long journey, especially if you have to go straight to work from the plane.

For every time zone crossed, allow one day to recover.

▶▶ See also Motion sickness, p.173.

Staying well

Although getting ill whilst travelling is extremely common, most travellers' illnesses are trivial (even if it may not seem so at the time) and not life-threatening. Nonetheless, being unwell on your holiday is miserable for both you and your companions: it disturbs plans, wastes time and money, and frequently makes you wonder why you bothered to leave home in the first place. This is a great shame, as so many of the factors that can affect your health while you're travelling are ultimately **avoidable**, either by immunization or drug prophylaxis, or by taking simple precautions to minimize the risks. The box on p.22 details diseases which can be avoided if the appropriate preventative measures are properly observed.

Food and drink

Most **food- and water-borne illnesses** are spread via the faecal–oral route; or more bluntly, by the fact that the food that you eat or water you drink has been contaminated by faeces. Although the risk exists anywhere you go, you're most likely to contract food- or water-borne illnesses in places where economics keep hygiene standards low. The advice below is therefore tailored mostly to travellers in developing countries.

Try to ensure that your food is cooked thoroughly and eat it straight away. Be especially wary of "street food", which may have been left to stand for a long time – not only is it an easy target for flies, but cooling allows contaminating bacteria to multiply quickly. If you can, check that cooked foods are kept separate from the uncooked ingredients, eliminating the risk of one contaminating the other.

Being prepared box and body

Common travellers' diseases by mode of spread

Mosquito-borne diseases

+ Chikungunya fever   p.102
+ Dengue fever   p.113
+ Eastern equine   p.120
  encephalitis
+ Filarial lymphangitis   p.128
+ Japanese encephalitis   p.153
+ Malaria   pp.163–169
+ O'nyong nyong virus   p.177
+ Rift Valley fever   p.184
+ Ross River virus   p.186
+ Venezuelan equine   p.224
  encephalitis
+ West Nile fever   p.225
+ Yellow fever   p.233

Tick-borne diseases

+ Crimean-Congo   p.109
  haemorrhagic fever
+ Human babesiosis   p.145
+ Human ehrlichiosis   p.146
+ Lyme disease   p.162
+ Q fever   p.181
+ Relapsing fever   p.183
+ Rocky Mountain   p.185
  spotted fever and other
  spotted fevers
+ Tick-borne encephalitis   p.216
+ Tularaemia   p.219
+ Typhus   p.222

Flies, fleas and other bugs

+ African trypanosomiasis   p.88
  (tsetse flies)
+ American   p.92
  trypanosomiasis
  (reduviid bugs)
+ Bartonellosis (sand flies)   p.97
+ Leishmaniasis   pp.156–159
  (sand flies)
+ Loiasis (tabanid flies)   p.129
+ Myiasis (tumbu flies,   p.175
  botflies)

+ Onchocerciasis   p.127
  (black flies)
+ Oropouche virus   p.178
  disease (gnats/midges)
+ Plague (fleas)   p.179
+ Relapsing fever (lice)   p.183
+ Sandfly fever (sand flies)   p.150
+ Scabies   p.193
+ Tungiasis (fleas)   p.220
+ Typhus (lice, fleas)   p.222

Freshwater-borne diseases

See p.21 for diseases contracted by
swallowing contaminated water

+ Dracunculiasis   p.117
+ Hookworms   p.227
+ Leptospirosis   p.160
+ Schistosomiasis   p.194

Diseases spread through animal contact, food and liquid

+ Anthrax   p.94
+ Balantidiasis   p.96
+ Brucellosis   p.100
+ Crimean-Congo   p.99
  haemorrhagic fever
+ Hydatid disease   p.146
+ Q fever   p.181
+ Rabies   p.182

Diseases spread through sexual contact

+ Chancroid   p.200
+ Chlamydia   p.199
+ Genital herpes   p.201
+ Genital warts   p.201
+ Gonorrhoea   p.199
+ Hepatitis B   p.141
+ Hepatitis C   p.144
+ HIV   p.144
+ Syphilis   p.198
+ Thrush   p.212
+ Trichomoniasis   p.200

Meat in developing countries may not have been butchered or prepared using adequate standards of hygiene – always order it "well done" to reduce the risk of worm and other infections from undercooked meat. **Fish** goes off quickly, particularly in hot climates, so should be consumed as soon as possible after being caught. In countries where refrigeration techniques are questionable, avoid eating fish in areas that are a long way from the sea. Some species of fish, notably those found around coral reefs, are poisonous even after being cooked (see Ciguatera, p.103, and Scromboid poisoning, p.196). **Shellfish** are particularly prone to contamination because of the large amounts of potentially polluted seawater they filter during feeding.

Rice, the staple diet throughout much of the world, seems innocuous enough but can be contaminated by specific bacteria that survive boiling water by forming heat-resistant spores and, on cooling, multiply rapidly. The bacteria cause quite severe diarrhoea and vomiting, so where possible avoid rice that has not been freshly cooked.

Unpasteurized milk, or products made from it, can transmit a variety of diseases and should be avoided, particularly by pregnant women. Pasteurized, long-life and boiled milk are all safe.

Bear in mind that contamination may come not from the food itself, or the cleanliness of the hands preparing it, but the **water** used in washing and preparation. This is a particular problem with foods eaten raw, like salads or fruit. In areas of high risk, **salads** are probably best avoided unless you prepare them yourself. This being the case, wash the vegetables thoroughly in iodine solution (see below), soak in vinegar for fifteen minutes then rinse with bottled or boiled water. Try to avoid fruit that you have not peeled or cut yourself; before buying whole melons, check the skin carefully for punctures, as vendors have been known to nick holes in the skin and add possibly contaminated water in order to make the fruit heavier (and hence sell for a higher price).

If the local water is contaminated, so too is **ice** made from it, and cups or glasses **washed** with it – if in doubt, drink directly from the bottle (but clean the bottle-top first). Waterborne infections can also be transmitted during teeth-cleaning, and by water swallowed during showering. Where water purity cannot be guaranteed, drink only bottled or canned drinks (check that the cap seal is intact), boiled water (boiled for at least one minute but ideally for three) or water **sterilized** with an adequate purifying preparation. Iodine is the best form of chemical purifier and is readily available from camping shops and

Tips for your tummy

+ Cook it, boil it, peel it or forget it.
+ No matter how expensive the meal, or how established the restaurant, you're never totally free from the risk of food contamination – food can still be improperly chilled or left out for too long, and waiters and kitchen staff in even the most salubrious restaurants use the toilet and forget to wash their hands.
+ Beware of eateries that appear quiet; their food is less likely to have been freshly prepared and may have been reheated frequently.
+ Treat "Chef's Specials" with caution – they be a way of reusing yesterday's leftovers.
+ Avoid seafood when you're a long way from the sea, and think twice about shellfish in any circumstances.
+ Wet-wipes (a travel essential) are a good way of ensuring that your own hands at least are clean before handling food.
+ Inspect the cleanliness of crockery and cutlery before use.

Illnesses linked to contaminated food and water

✚ Amoebiasis	p.93		✚ Meliodosis	p.170
✚ Balantidiasis	p.96		✚ Oriental liver fluke	p.162
✚ Botulism	p.99		✚ Paragonimiasis	p.178
✚ Brucellosis	p.99		✚ Paratyphoid	p.179
✚ Cholera	p.102		✚ Polio	p.180
✚ Ciguatera	p.103		✚ Schistosomiasis	p.194
✚ Cryptosporidiosis	p.110		✚ Scombroid poisoning	p.196
✚ Fascioliasis	p.124		✚ Travellers' diarrhoea	pp.131–137
✚ Giardiasis	p.137		✚ Typhoid	p.221
✚ Hepatitis A	p.141		✚ Worm infections	pp.226–233

pharmacies. It's important to follow the packet instructions carefully, as heavily contaminated water will require stronger solutions. Remember that iodine is not effective against all microbes, and that it should not be used in pregnancy. A variety of portable **water filters** are available on the market, which offer varying different levels of protection against the disease-causing organisms. If water is heavily contaminated, it might be a good idea to use filters in conjunction with iodination (the iodine should be added after filtration). Always wear gloves to change filter cartridges – they accumulate contaminating organisms – and wash your hands afterwards. A detailed overview of filters can be found at Ⓦwww.cdc.gov.

Insect-borne diseases

Many **insect–borne illnesses** are seasonal, and often simply adjusting the timing of your visit to a region can reduce the risks. However for most travellers, arranging their itinerary around the lifecycle of insect species is not a primary consideration. Only a handful of insect-borne diseases are preventable by drug prophylaxis or immunization (even then, the protection conferred rarely approaches 100 percent), which means that your only real protection against the vast majority is **bite avoidance**. Anyone who has tried to evade being bitten by insects will be well aware that complete success is practically unachievable. Unless you're obsessional to an extreme that could jeopardize the enjoyment of your trip, you may as well accept that you are likely to be bitten at some point. The following recommendations concentrate on **risk limitation** – the fewer the bites, the smaller your chance of contracting infection.

Wear long-sleeved shirts, long trousers and socks and use insect repellent containing **DEET** (see p.152), or an equivalent, on any exposed areas of the body, particularly between dusk and dawn when most mosquitoes feed. Don't wear **perfume**, **aftershave** or **sandals**. At night, sleep under a net and tuck it securely under your mattress. It's a good idea to carry your own net as those provided by hostels and hotels are often damaged and therefore useless. For extra protection, spray the net with an insect repellent such as **permethrin** (see p.151); this can also be sprayed on camping equipment, shoes and clothing, and its repellent effect is retained even after laundering. Insect coils can help, but some contain DDT and therefore should be used with caution. Of other measures, **air-conditioning** markedly reduces mosquito activity, but evidence on the efficacy of ultrasonic repellent devices is lacking.

Ticks and mites are slightly easier to avoid than flying insects. Wear light-shaded, tightly woven clothing so that ticks can be easily spotted before they attach themselves to your skin. Ticks tend to gravitate towards darker recesses of the body, with favourite hiding places being the scalp, armpits and genital area, so tuck trousers into socks to close off the easiest channel to bare skin. Apply permethrin-based repellents to clothing and inspect your skin and clothing carefully at the end of each day, as prompt removal can prevent infection. For removal of ticks, see p.152.

Never walk barefoot, especially in the tropics. Shoes provide protection against insect, snake and spider bites, as well as parasites that enter the body through the skin of the foot. Shaking your boots out before putting them on is a good habit to get into.

▶▶ See also Bite prevention, p.149.

Road accidents

It's sobering to remember that despite the vast numbers of weird and unpleasant illnesses lurking between the pages of this book, **road accidents** are responsible for more deaths and serious injuries to tourists than anything else. Driving on unfamiliar roads or in hazardous conditions, badly maintained vehicles, local driving customs, poor driving, and driving while under the influence of alcohol or drugs are all factors that inflate the statistics. While it's impossible to eliminate all of these risks, there are measures you can take to minimize them.

If travelling by bus, always go with an established, reputable company. Where you sit on the bus is of lesser importance, though if you're really worried about the journey ahead, sit near an emergency exit.

If you're behind the wheel, drive defensively and accustom yourself to local conditions before attempting anything too ambitious. Stay alert by breaking long trips periodically (at least every three hours), and avoid unnecessary night driving. Don't exceed the speed limit, especially when road conditions are unfamiliar. Even if local laws are more relaxed, drink-driving abroad is even more foolhardy than at home, where at least driving conditions are more familiar. As at home, designate a driver and make sure that they don't drink.

If you **rent** a vehicle, check the tyres (including the spare), brakes, headlights and seatbelts before leaving the garage forecourt. Also check who you should contact in the event of an accident or breakdown. If you're renting a cycle or moped, always wear a helmet and check the brakes before starting – moped accidents involving tourists, both minor and severe, are very common.

Fire and water

Perhaps surprisingly, **fire** is another significant cause of death and injury abroad. In many developing countries fire regulations are slack, if they exist at all. If nothing is posted, ask about fire escapes and precautions when you arrive at a hostel or hotel. Never smoke in bed and, especially in dry, hot climates, ensure that cigarettes are properly extinguished. Have a plan of escape in case of emergencies, bearing in mind that the best way to escape a fire and the potentially lethal effects of smoke inhalation is to crawl low under the smoke.

A quick dip may be tempting, but think twice before cooling off. **Drowning** accidents involving travellers are relatively common – remember that **currents** in rivers as well as the sea can be extremely strong, and that you're much less buoyant in fresh water than in salt water. Be aware of your own swimming ability and strength, and avoid taking unnecessary risks. Enquire about local water conditions – strong currents or other potential hazards – before taking the plunge. If you're rafting or canoeing always wear a buoyancy aid and a helmet. A number of **diseases** can be contracted by bathing, even paddling, in fresh water (see p.22), and avoidance is your only means of protection. Don't forget more **visible hazards** like snakes (see p.204), crocodiles (see p.130) and voracious fish (see p.130), and wear sandals whilst on the beach to protect against saltwater hazards (see p.187) such as **weever fish**. Never swim directly after eating, when you feel unwell or when under the influence of alcohol or drugs, and never dive into water without knowing its depth (this can result in a broken neck and paralysis).

Contact with animals

The average traveller is at relatively low risk from illnesses spread by animal contact – agricultural workers and vets are most vulnerable. Nevertheless, there is always the temptation to stroke that cute puppy or play with a pet monkey – think of it as Russian roulette. It's very easy for a playful bite or scratch to draw blood, potentially allowing the animal's saliva (which may be loaded with rabies virus) to make direct contact with your blood.

Sexually transmitted diseases

Sexually transmitted diseases are dealt with more fully in Part 2, but the best way to avoid them is obvious. The second best way is always to use a good-quality condom with any new partner.

▶▶ See Sexually transmitted diseases, p.197.

Environmental factors

Sun exposure, heat, cold, humidity, damp and altitude all have a direct effect on health but also indirectly contribute to disease risks. For instance, mosquito-borne illnesses are usually most common during or after the rainy season; colds, upper respiratory tract infections and asthma tend to be more prevalent in cold, wet conditions; and leishmaniasis occurs in dry, dusty conditions. It may be possible to arrange your travel plans around the seasons to minimize such risks.

▶▶ See also Altitude sickness, p.91; Cold exposure, p.104; Sun exposure, p.207.

Violence

Travellers worldwide are often the targets of **violence**, especially if alone, elderly or female. Listen to what the locals or your guidebook tell you, walk tall, look confident and try to avoid potentially dangerous situations. Be particularly alert when travelling on public transport, especially at night or when there are few people around. If at all concerned about your surroundings, avoid drawing attention to yourself by puzzling over your map in the street. Don't wear expensive jewellery or flaunt cash and credit cards, and keep expensive camera equipment hidden until you intend to use it. Go with your instinct: if the person who gets on the subway makes you nervous, you've nothing to lose by changing carriages. If you are confronted by a mugger, the safest bet is to surrender your valuables without resistance.

Nutrition

During prolonged trips abroad, it's not uncommon to lose a few pounds, usually due to a combination of increased exercise and a change in diet. However, eating a **balanced diet** is important wherever you are and failure to do so can put your health at risk. Aim to eat at least five helpings of fruit and vegetables a day (juice, tinned and dried fruit all count). A good travel tip is if in doubt, go vegetarian.

There are six **basic foodstuffs** which you should include in your diet:

✚ **Water** The basic constituent of life, without which we die remarkably quickly. The average adult needs to drink at least three litres per day, more in hot climates or after heavy exercise (in which case it's worth remembering to add a pinch of salt which is lost in sweat). Many soft drinks in hot countries contain added salt.

✚ **Carbohydrates** Energy foods, particularly important if you are exercising vigorously. Examples include cereals (including rice), bread, sugar, potatoes and other root vegetables.

✚ **Proteins** Body-building food, particularly important after you have been ill and lost weight, and in conditions affecting the liver. Examples include meat, dairy products, fish, eggs, lentils, beans and nuts.

✚ **Fats** Energy foods which act as building blocks for some of the important chemicals manufactured in the body. Eating too little of foods from this group is a much rarer problem than eating too much. Avoid fats if you are suffering from hepatitis. Examples include dairy products, eggs, nuts, any fried food and red meat.

✚ **Vitamins and minerals:** Important in the manufacture of various chemicals within the body and also vital factors in some metabolic processes such as releasing the energy from the food we eat. It is rare to be lacking in vitamins and minerals if you follow a balanced diet, particularly incorporating fresh fruit and vegetables. If you're going to be away for long periods of time and think you'll have trouble keeping a balanced diet, consider taking vitamin and mineral supplements.

Contraception

No matter what your intentions, think carefully about **contraception** before you set out travelling, and arm yourself with whichever of the options below best suits your lifestyle. Holiday romances are common and anxiety about **pregnancy** or **sexually transmitted diseases** (STDs) is the last thing you want on the trip of a lifetime.

Aware of the potential local dangers, many travellers make the dangerous assumption that it's safe to pair up with fellow travellers. Even if you consider yourself to be fairly choosy about whom you spend the night with, don't assume that your partner has similar standards or has been conscientious about using condoms to safeguard against STDs.

Condoms

As a contraceptive, **condoms** are relatively safe if a good-quality brand is used properly – take some with you from home as the local brands may be inferior. Condoms' advantage over other contraception is they also offer some, if not complete, **protection against STDs**. It is worth bearing in mind that the latex in condoms deteriorates when exposed to heat so always keep them out of the sun. Contact with sun oil can destroy a condom in as little as fifteen minutes.

The pill

Despite a lot of media hype, **the pill** or **combined pill** (combined oestrogen and progesterone) is relatively free of side effects, both minor and major, and is the safest available contraceptive in terms of accidental pregnancies (failures are almost always due to a missed pill). The pill offers no protection against STDs, however, so it should be used in conjunction with condoms in the event of sex with a new partner.

There are a number of instances in which the combined pill should be avoided, but most relevant to travellers are any arterial or venous thrombosis, any active liver disease (eg hepatitis) or history of jaundice, and an existing or possible pregnancy.

If you are travelling for any length of time, always take adequate supplies as your brand may be difficult to find abroad. Other considerations that you should take on board as a traveller are set out below.

The mini-pill (progesterone-only pill) is not the best contraceptive choice if you're travelling far afield, as its efficacy is dependent on taking it at a fixed, regular time. That said, it has less effect on the clotting system than the combined pill and, theoretically at least, is safer to use at altitude. Its efficacy is also less affected by other drugs (eg antibiotics) than the combined pill. However as there's very little margin for error when taking the mini-pill (within plus or minus one hour each day), it clearly presents practical problems crossing time zones. If you do use it, you'll need to keep to "home time" in order for it to work properly; if a pill is taken more than three hours late, other contraceptive precautions should be taken for the next seven days. The advice on the pill in the text following relates to the combined pill only.

Missed pills

The traveller's often haphazard lifestyle, with few daily routines and overlong journeys sometimes across time zones, means the risk of **missing pills** is high. In the absence of the pill pack instructions, which usually tell you what to do in the event of a missed pill, follow the advice below:

✚ If you are **less than twelve hours late**, don't worry. Take the delayed pill at once and the rest of the packet as usual. No extra contraceptive measures are necessary.

✚ If you are **more than twelve hours late**, take the most recently delayed pill at once, continue the rest of the packet as normal, discard any previously missed pills and observe the "**seven-day rule**". If there are more than seven pills remaining in the packet, maintain the usual seven-day pill-free break before starting your next pack; if there are fewer than seven pills remaining in the pack, omit the break and start your next pack on the day following the completion of your current pack. If you are in any doubt, use condoms for the next seven days.

The pill, vomiting and diarrhoea

If **vomiting** occurs less than three hours after the pill was taken, you should take a replacement pill (from a spare packet) as the original will not have been in the stomach long enough to be absorbed. If the replacement pill does not stay down, take extra precautions from the onset of the illness and continue for seven days after the illness ends. If this is within seven days of the pill-free week, omit the break and start the next pack on the day following completion of the current pack. **Diarrhoea** is generally not regarded as a major problem unless it is particularly severe. If so, observe the seven-day rule (see above).

Other drugs

Many drugs, **antibiotics** in particular, can reduce the effectiveness of the pill. Take alternative precautions while on any course of antibiotics and for seven days afterwards, following the rules above for the pill-free week.

Time zones

It's particularly difficult to keep track of pill-taking on long-haul flights to completely different **time zones**. This problem may be even more difficult to work out during pill-free weeks and may lead to a pregnancy caused by a prolonged pill-free interval (this is the usual cause of pill failures). The easiest way around this is to have two watches, one set at home time, at least until you get used to the local time. Once established on local time, gradually readjust your pill-taking to your usual time (no more than an hour change each day). If confusion arises, err on the side of taking the pill early rather than late.

Flying

A rare side effect of pill-taking is the development of a blood clot in the leg (**DVT**), lung or brain. There is a slightly increased risk of this during long-haul **flights**, but this does not mean that you cannot fly if you take the pill. Minimize the risk by staying hydrated during the flight (avoid excess caffeine and alcohol) and take some exercise while you're in the air. For more on DVT, see p.111.

Altitude

High **altitudes** and the pill both increase blood thickness and predispose to clot formation in the blood vessels. The effect is additive and therefore other forms of contraception should be considered if you are planning to trek or climb above 4000m (especially if you smoke). The use of acetazolamide as a preventative for mountain sickness (see p.43) also increases the risk of clot formation.

Regulating menstruation

By taking the next packet straightaway, and ignoring the pill-free week, bleeding can be averted. You may feel uncomfortable about skipping a period, but this is not dangerous. In fact, there is no reason why the pill should not be taken continuously for three packets with a bleed occurring on withdrawal of the last packet.

Injectable contraception

Injectable contraception has both positive and negative implications in terms of travel. First, the fact that the **injections** are given every twelve weeks means that there is less reliance on memory for full efficacy – all you have to remember is the date of your next injection. However, this is a drawback if you plan to be away for more than twelve weeks, or if you are away when the injection is due. Most people are unwilling to, nor should they, self-administer the injection, and are therefore reliant on someone else (usually a doctor or nurse)

Emergency contraception

You are most at risk of becoming pregnant after unprotected sex in the first half of your menstrual cycle. Many people are already aware of the availability of the **"morning-after pill"** and in some countries it is available without prescription from pharmacies. However, don't use it as a regular form of contraception; if you have sex infrequently, always carry condoms.

Two types of post-coital pill are currently available, one containing progesterone only (**Levonelle 2**), and the other a combined pill containing oestrogen and progesterone (**Schering PC4**). Both must be started within **72 hours** of unprotected sex and are more effective if the first dose is taken as soon as possible. Both involve two doses of tablets, with the second dose twelve hours after the first.

Although reasonably reliable if taken promptly, neither type of pill is 100 percent effective. Your period may be late after treatment (you may also experience a mild bleed within a couple of days after taking the pills), but if you miss it completely do a pregnancy test.

Neither type of pill should be taken if you have severe liver disease or porphyria. The combined type may cause nausea, vomiting and headache and should not be used if you have had a previous thrombosis or suffer regular migraines. If you vomit within three hours of taking the pills, you need to take a replacement dose as the pills will not have been adequately absorbed. As with the combined pill, the efficacy of both types of post-coital pill may be reduced by interactions with other drugs (eg antibiotics). Always read the pack instructions carefully.

Following post-coital contraception, always use condoms as contraception until your period arrives.

▲ Thai anti-AIDS poster

to do this. You may need to carry supplies of the drug with you and even consider needles and syringes if you're heading for wilder parts. The effects of the injections on **menstruation** are also important – if you decide to travel within three to six months of the first injection, you may find the irregularity and unpredictability of the bleeding difficult to manage.

Other advantages of injectable contraception are that it is unaffected by vomiting or diarrhoea, and that it has little or no interaction with other drugs – as the injectable contraceptive contains the same hormone as the mini-pill, it shares its advantages. A disadvantage is that it offers no protection against sexually transmitted diseases, although using a condom at the same time will reduce this risk.

The medical kit

Deciding what **medical provisions** to take away with you and what to leave behind can be tricky, and depends on where you're going, for how long and how cautious you choose to be. Some people travel with their rucksack half full of medications and therapeutic equipment, including drips and even bags of intravenous fluids, while others hike in solitude in remote regions without so much as a sticking plaster.

This section aims to provide the forward-looking traveller with a little more information and advice on the kind of medications and equipment that might be of use on a global trip. While it's not the intention of this book to encourage using potentially dangerous drugs inappropriately, when access to medical advice is difficult, it's often better to start treatment for potentially serious conditions than to wait for help.

In developed countries, many drugs are available only on **prescription** and are therefore only obtainable through a doctor. For long trips, your family doctor or travel clinic may be willing to prescribe one or two items of particular use (don't visit them with a "shopping list"). Perhaps more relevant and useful to the traveller is the knowledge that the same drugs can be bought directly **over-the-counter** in many, usually less developed countries, without a prescription; there are potential hazards, however – see the box opposite. Unfortunately, it goes without saying that any drug can have both good and bad effects on your body, so always use them sensibly and responsibly. Don't use any drug without first weighing up the potential risks and benefits. Remember that drugs can interact with each other so always tell your doctor what other medicines you're taking. Never exceed the recommended dosages.

If you are **pregnant** (see p.72 on drugs that are safe in pregnancy), **breast-feeding**, have ongoing **medical problems** or take **other medications** (interactions between drugs can occur), it's best to seek trained advice before taking any medication – in the absence of a doctor, qualified pharmacists can help. Although side effects are generally uncommon, stop taking the medication if a reaction occurs. Alcohol interacts with only a handful of drugs, but avoiding it when taking medications is a good general rule.

It's estimated that as much as ten percent of the global drug trade consists of counterfeits. In late 2003, the WHO raised concerns about the sale of **fake or substandard drugs**, most notably in Vietnam, Laos, Cambodia, China, Myanmar and Thailand. Some 2800 illegal medicine sellers are thought to be trading in Cambodia alone, whilst there are approximately 1000 unregistered medicines. In Thailand, substandard medicines are believed to account for 8.5 percent of the total market.

The commonest drugs to be counterfeited are antibiotics, antimalarials and antituberculosis drugs. However, as these fakes are as likely to be doled out by doctors as by street-corner vendors, the only way to be sure of avoiding them is to buy your medicines from reputable sources in your home country. If you do need to take medicines prescribed abroad, ask about their origin.

The following section covers drugs and medications that might be useful to the traveller in certain situations. It's worth re-emphasizing that drugs should always be used responsibly. If you experience doubts or side effects, or the condition you are treating does not improve, always seek medical advice. We've listed each drug by its **generic name** because this is how it will be known internationally; what's more, most drugs are cheaper if you ask for them in their generic form. Generic American drug names are given in brackets; we've suggested alternatives where there's no direct US equivalent. Drugs marked with an **asterisk** (★) may be available by prescription only.

Basic advice on children's preparations and doses is given on p.63, and there's a summary of recommended items to include in your medical kit on p.65.

Painkillers (analgesics)

Paracetamol (**acetaminophen** in the USA) is cheap, effective and safe in normal dosage. Note that it's very dangerous to exceed the recommended dosage, as even a relatively small overdose can cause irreparable liver damage. It's useful for bringing down high temperatures, as well as for general pain relief. Side effects are rare and it is safe to use in pregnancy.

Adult dosage: 1–2 x 500mg tablets 4–6hrly to a max of 4g (or 8 tablets) a day. US dosage of acetaminophen is 1–2 x 300mg tablet (total daily dose should not exceed 4g).

Aspirin is cheap and effective but can cause indigestion and damage to the lining of the stomach; to reduce such risks, only take it after food. Aspirin has anti-inflammatory properties, and is therefore particularly useful for sprains, joint pains etc; it also reduces high temperatures. You can take aspirin in conjunction with paracetamol, but it can interact with other drugs so always check the labels of other medications or consult a pharmacist. Allergic reactions are relatively common, and asthmatics should avoid aspirin because it can exacerbate their symptoms. Those with a stomach or duodenal ulcer, pregnant women, breast-feeding mothers, children under 12 and haemophiliacs should not use aspirin or NSAIDs.

Adult dosage: 300–900mg every 4–6hr after food to a maximum of 4g a day.

Ibuprofen, **naproxen**★ and **diclofenac**★ are members of a group of drugs collectively known as **NSAIDs** (non-steroidal anti-inflammatory drugs). NSAIDs are particularly useful in the treatment of soft-tissue injuries and joint pains. Their side effects (gastrointestinal discomfort, diarrhoea, nausea and rashes are the most common) and limitations are generally the same as for aspirin. Ibuprofen is generally recognized as having the fewest side effects of the three but is also probably the weakest painkiller, whilst diclofenac is perhaps the strongest but also the most likely to cause side effects. NSAIDs should be avoided by asthmatics, pregnant women and by people with kidney problems (unless used under medical supervision).

Adult dosage (all after food): ibuprofen 1–2 x 200mg tablet three times a day; naproxen 1–2 x 250mg tablet, twice daily; diclofenac 1–2 x 25mg tablet three times a day.

Combined analgesics usually contain a combination of paracetamol or acetaminophen with a codeine-related drug. They are generally regarded as stronger than the single components, but also tend to produce more side effects. In the UK, **co-proxamol**★, **co-dydramol**★ and **co-codamol** all contain paracetamol and another painkiller – dextropropoxyphene in the case of co-proxamol, codeine phosphate in the latter two. In the US, there are a wide variety of trade names for these drugs; **Tylenol** with codeine and **Phenaphen** with codeine are two common examples. Note that in the US, combined analgesics with codeine are available on prescription only.

Combined analgesics are safe if the normal dosage is not exceeded although all can cause nausea, mild drowsiness and constipation. They should be used as a stronger alternative to paracetamol, but not in addition to it.

Dosage: the same as for paracetamol.

Antibiotics

Antibiotics specifically treat **bacterial** infections, by either killing or weakening the bacteria – in effect, assisting the body's immune system. They have no pain-relieving properties, nor do they directly relieve any other symptoms or have any effect on viral or fungal infections. In most developed countries they are available on prescription only, and there's great variation in the spectrum of action and cost of different antibiotics.

All antibiotics have some, usually mild, **side effects**, and allergic reactions are relatively common. A rare but serious side effect is pseudomembranous enterocolitis (see p.181), which manifests as severe, often bloody, diarrhoea and requires urgent medical treatment.

Drug information on the web

ⓦwww.bnf.org
This UK site is arguably the best web-based resource for drug information, with a comprehensive list of drugs and their indications, side effects, interactions and safety in pregnancy, breast-feeding etc.

ⓦwww.nlm.nih.gov/medlineplus/druginformation.html
Easy to use, comprehensive US-based drug information site, which also has a useful disease encyclopedia and a Spanish-language option.

Antibiotic resistance

Many people wrongly look upon **antibiotics** as the panacea, the universal remedy. Since the discovery of penicillin by Alexander Fleming in 1928 and the subsequent development of therapeutic antibiotics in the 1930s and 1940s, doctors have contributed in no small way to this misapprehension.

It's not difficult to see how it happened. Before antibiotics, millions were dying from illnesses that had no effective treatment. Suddenly doctors were equipped with a useful and potent means of controlling these previously lethal diseases, and antibiotics were soon prescribed for any infection. Only in recent decades have the consequences of irresponsible, albeit perhaps ignorant, prescribing become apparent.

Bacteria reproduce rapidly, and because of **mutation**, an ongoing evolving process, subsequent generations genetically differ from their predecessors. Bacteria with weak characteristics do not survive while those with beneficial mutations survive longer and give rise to more offspring. Thus, using an incomplete course of antibiotics will kill the weaker bacteria but may allow the stronger ones to survive – "survival of the fittest" at its most basic level. Bacterial populations have therefore evolved that are capable of resisting treatment with antibiotics.

To do your bit in preventing the evolution of so-called "**superbugs**", use antibiotics wisely and responsibly:

+ Decide whether your condition really needs antibiotic treatment. If in doubt, wait or seek medical advice.
+ With the help of this book, try to choose the antibiotic that is most appropriate for your complaint.
+ Always complete the suggested course.
+ If you have antibiotics left over, don't leave them in inexperienced hands; donate them to the local clinic.

Your doctor may hesitate to prescribe antibiotics on a purely prospective basis; there is growing concern over the increasing incidence of **bacterial resistance** through antibiotic overuse (see box, above). Always finish a course of antibiotics, as incomplete treatment can lead to a failure in eradicating the bugs, and also encourages resistance. Take special care if you use the oral contraceptive pill, as many antibiotics reduce its efficacy (see Contraception, p.29). All antibiotics increase the risk of **thrush**, so consider getting some simultaneous antifungal treatment; see p.215 for alternative suggestions.

Amoxicillin★ is the most widely prescribed broad-spectrum antibiotic worldwide. Among its many uses is the treatment of chest, ear, mouth and urinary tract infections. It's inexpensive and has minimal side effects, mainly nausea, diarrhoea and rashes. As it's derived from penicillin, it should not be taken by people with penicillin allergy.

Standard adult course: 1–2 x 250mg tablet three times a day for seven days.

Penicillin V (phenoxymethylpenicillin) has a similar side-effects to amoxicillin, but a narrower spectrum of action. It remains a useful option, most notably for tonsillitis.

Standard adult course: 1–2 x 250mg tablets four times daily for seven to ten days.

Co-amoxiclav★ (amoxicillin with **clavulanate** in the US) contains amoxicillin and clavulinic acid, making it much more expensive than amoxicillin but able to fight a broader spectrum of bugs, including bacterial skin infections and infected animal bites. It has much the same range of uses and side effects as amoxicillin (diarrhoea is common). Again, it's not suitable for penicillin-sensitive people; in rare cases, co-amoxiclav can cause jaundice.

Standard adult course: 1–2 x 250/125mg tablet three times a day for seven days.

Flucloxacillin★ (in the US, close equivalents are **dicloxacillin** or **cloxacillin**) is another penicillin-based antibiotic that's particularly useful in treating skin infections like boils and abscesses, as well as wound infections. Common side effects are similar to those of co-amoxiclav.

Normal adult course: 1–2 x 250mg tablet four times daily for seven days.

Erythromycin★ is the most commonly prescribed broad-spectrum alternative to amoxicillin. It's the main option for people with penicillin allergy and its uses are broadly similar to amoxicillin. In addition, it can be used to treat some diarrhoeal illnesses and legionnaires' disease (see p.155). Common side effects include nausea, vomiting, abdominal discomfort and diarrhoea. It should not be taken if you have liver disease, and care should be taken when using it with other medications as it can interfere with the metabolism of other drugs.

Adult course: 1–2 x 250mg tablet four times a day before or with meals for seven days.

Metronidazole★ is a versatile antibiotic used to treat mouth and vaginal infections as well as amoebic, protozoal and giardial infections. It can also be used in the treatment of pseudomembranous colitis. Side effects include an unpleasant taste in the mouth, nausea, vomiting, gastrointestinal disturbances, rashes and itching. **Avoid alcohol** during, and for two days after, a course (it can cause the very unpleasant reactions of extreme nausea and facial flushing). Metronidazole should only be used under medical supervision in pregnancy, breast-feeding and in cases of liver disease.

The adult course is usually 1–2 x 200mg tablet three times a day for seven days, although longer courses are sometimes necessary for certain conditions.

Trimethoprim★ is a commonly prescribed treatment for urinary tract infections, and may also be used to treat travellers' diarrhoea. In the US it usually appears in combination drugs, mixed with **sulfamethoxazole**; this combination should be avoided if you're allergic to sulphur. Trimethoprim-only US brands include Trimpex and Prolorim. Trimethoprim should be avoided in cases of kidney impairment, pregnancy and porphyria (a rare and complex illness). Side effects are uncommon but include nausea, vomiting, itching and rashes.

Normal adult course: 2 x 100mg tablet twice daily for seven days.

Ciprofloxacin★ is a powerful antibiotic that's particularly effective against the common bacterial causes of travellers' diarrhoea (salmonella, shigella and campylobacter), and can also treat chest and urinary tract infections. It's less commonly prescribed in the UK, however, because of its expense and increased incidence of side effects, which include nausea, vomiting, abdominal pain, diarrhoea, headache, dizziness, sleep disorders, itching and increased sensitivity to the sun. Tendon inflammation, and even rupture, is an uncommon side effect, and it may also impair the performance of skilled tasks and enhance the effects of alcohol. It should be avoided if possible in pregnancy, while breast-feeding, and by people with epilepsy, liver or kidney impairment. Like erythromycin, it can interact with a number of other drugs, so be sure to inform your doctor if you're taking anything else.

Adult course (for travellers' diarrhoea): 1–2 x 250mg tablet twice daily for up to three days.

Tetracycline antibiotics are not as widely prescribed as amoxicillin or erythromycin, but the general group (which includes **doxycycline**; see p.42) still has many uses, particularly in treating more unusual infections such as brucellosis, leptospirosis, Lyme disease and Q fever, as well as pelvic inflammatory disease and sexually transmitted infections. Side effects mainly affect the gastro-intestinal tract (indigestion, nausea, vomiting, diarrhoea) although rarely they can have adverse effects on the blood and the liver, and can also cause photosensitivity reactions. They must be used with care in cases of liver disease, kidney disease, myasthenia gravis and SLE and should not be used in children under 12, pregnancy or breast-feeding women.

Dose and frequency of administration vary with each drug within the tetracycline group.

Chloramphenicol★ is a potent antibiotic, but has now been largely superseded by safer alternatives. It's still used, usually in critical situations, for certain types of meningitis and for typhoid, but as it can cause serious blood disorders it should really only be used under medical supervision (hence no dosage instructions appear below). It should not be used in pregnancy, whilst breast-feeding or if you have porphyria.

However, chloramphenicol eye drops or ointment are safe and useful if you're prone to recurrent conjunctivitis (see p.123).

Drops should be applied every 2hr until 48hrs after the eye has settled. Ointment should be applied to the inner surface of the lower eyelid 3–4 times a day for five days. If the problem persists, seek medical advice.

Fusidic acid★ and **framycetin sulphate★** are antibiotic creams used to treat localized skin infections (impetigo, infected hair follicles etc). There are no direct US equivalents, but the similar mupirocin can be used in the same way. All three can cause local redness, itching and swelling, though this is rare.

Adult dosage: apply three times daily for up to five days.

Gentamycin★ drops are an effective treatment for outer ear infections (see p.119). They should not be used if the eardrum is perforated, as potentially toxic side effects can affect the inner ear (seek advice if in doubt). **Gentisone HC** combines the antibiotic with a mild steroid to reduce inflammation. Occasional local skin reactions can occur. There is no direct US equivalent to gentamycin-based topical treatments, although **Corticosporin Otic Solution** is a good alternative.

Dosage: 2–3 drops applied 3–4 times daily for up to fourteen days.

Antihistamines

The unsung heroes of the rucksack, **antihistamines** have multiple uses, are relatively cheap and are generally available without a prescription. They work by suppressing the body's **allergic** ("histamine") response, and their range of action includes the relief of hay fever, skin rashes, itching, insect bites and motion sickness. Almost all antihistamines have **side effects**, principally drowsiness, so take care if you're driving or doing anything that requires coordination or concentration. Other side effects include headache, slowness of movement, difficulty passing urine, dry mouth, blurred vision and gastrointestinal disturbances (usually constipation). Antihistamines should be used with caution if you have epilepsy, prostatic problems, glaucoma and liver disease, and avoided if you suffer from porphyria. They also interact with a variety of other drugs (alcohol among them), so be sure to read the pack instructions carefully.

Chlorpheniramine is cheap and effective in treating allergies, itching and insect bites. It's relatively sedating compared to newer antihistamines (eg loratadine).

Adult dosage: 1 x 4mg tablet every 4–6hr to a maximum of 24mg over 24hr.

Loratadine (Clartin in the US) is similar to chlorpheniramine in its range of action, but is generally regarded as less sedating. It's not recommended in pregnancy or if you're breast-feeding.

Adult dosage: 1 x 10mg tablet daily.

Promethazine (prescription-only in the US) can be used for the same purposes as chlorpheniramine and loratadine, but is especially useful as a preventative against motion sickness – and may even help when you are experiencing symptoms. It is sedating, so much so that it's used as a premedication for surgery – driving or using machinery is inadvisable when taking it.

Adult dosage: for long journeys, 1 x 25mg the night before; shorter trips, 1 x 25mg 1–2hr before. Maximum of four tablets over 24hr.

Cinnarizine is used primarily as a preventative for motion sickness, and is less sedating than promethazine. There is no direct US equivalent; **meclizine** is a suitable alternative.

Adult dosage: 2 x 15mg tablet 2hr before journey, then 1 x 15mg every 8hr.

Creams containing the antihistamines mepyramine and diphenhydramine (eg **Anthisan** and **Caladryl** preparations) are particularly helpful in treating insect bites. They should not be used on broken skin or if you have eczema. Caladryl can cause increased sensitivity of the skin to the sun.

Apply 2–3 times a day for up to three days.

Antidiarrhoeals

The priority in treating **diarrhoea** is preventing or counteracting dehydration (see p.113) – the so-called "blocking drugs" available on the market are of secondary value. Prevention of dehydration is particularly important in children and the frail elderly. A number of commercial **rehydration preparations** are available, which replace the salts lost through acute diarrhoea. They can usually be easily obtained anywhere in the world, but be sure to follow the brand instructions carefully and rehydrate the sachets with safe water only.

The following drugs should be used only in conjunction with other rehydration measures. Remember that they treat your symptoms only, and not the underlying cause. Playing strictly by the book, they should not be used unless the cause of the diarrhoea is known (their use in the treatment of dysentery or diarrhoea caused by pseudomembranous colitis can lead to serious complications). Never use these drugs if you have symptoms such as fever or severe abdominal pain, or if you're passing blood in your stools.

Antidiarrhoeals are relatively expensive and, although there are many different varieties, none appears to have an edge over the others. Overzealousness can lead to constipation, so take it easy. They should not be used to treat children.

 Arsenicum album 30c, given every hour until improvement, is a highly effective homeopathic remedy for diarrhoea.

Loperamide is very commonly used and is a highly effective blocker. Side effects include abdominal bloating, pain and skin rashes.

Dosage: 2 x 2mg tablet initially followed by one x 2mg after every loose stool to a maximum of 16mg over 24hr for no more than five days.

Bismuth subsalicylate (**Pepto–Bismol**) has a mild but direct effect on the bugs causing diarrhoea as well as slowing down gut activity and relieving nausea and indigestion. It is useful in high doses for mild to moderate cases of traveller's diarrhoea.

Dosage: 4.2g daily.

Laxatives

Increasing your intake of dietary fibre (lentils, brown rice, beans, peas, fruit etc) and fluid is the kindest way to alleviate constipation, but if this fails, then generally the simplest and cheapest **laxatives** are adequate for most travellers' needs.
Senna is known as a "stimulant laxative" as it promotes muscular contraction in the bowel to force out the gut contents. It is not recommended for anyone suffering nausea, vomiting, abdominal pain or bowel obstruction. Its side effects include abdominal cramps.

Dosage: 2–4 tablets at night (start with two) until normal bowel function resumes.

Lactulose works by retaining fluid in the bowel, thereby softening the stool. It should not be used in cases of bowel obstruction and can cause flatulence, cramps and abdominal discomfort.

Normal adult dosage: 15ml once or twice daily.

Homemade oral rehydration solution

To one litre of safe (ie boiled, sterilized etc) water, add half a level teaspoon of salt and eight level teaspoons of sugar. A little fruit juice or mashed banana provides potassium, which is often depleted by serious diarrhoea and vomiting, as well as improving the taste. The amount you need to take depends on how much fluid you're losing, but as a rough guide, drink 200–400ml after every loose stool until the diarrhoea settles.

Antisickness drugs

Antisickness drugs (**antiemetics**) are extremely useful, but are usually available only on prescription. Ideally, they should be used only when the cause of the vomiting is known; however, many family doctors are sympathetic to the potential plight of the traveller and will issue a prescription if requested. A rare but unpleasant **side effect** of most antiemetics is **dystonia**, a condition of acute muscle spasm, usually of the facial and neck muscles. It is unusual in short-term use, however, and usually settles without treatment.

Don't forget that **ginger**, **acupressure bands** and some antihistamines, notably **promethazine** (see p.38), can be used to treat sickness and do not require a prescription. Of homeopathic remedies, one **Phosphorus** 30c tablet given hourly settles vomiting quickly; try **Arsenicum album** (same regime) if the nausea is associated with diarrhoea. Stop the medication once the vomiting has settled. As homeopathic remedies don't have to be swallowed (they dissolve in the mouth), they are ideal when vomiting is frequent and uncontrollable.

Domperidone, available in tablet or suppository form, is an effective treatment for nausea and vomiting. It is less likely than other antiemetics to cause dystonia or drowsiness, but must be used with care if you're pregnant, breast-feeding or have kidney disease. Domperidone is not available in the US.

Dosage: 1–2 x 10mg tablet every 4–8hr until symptoms settle.

Metoclopramide is a cheap, effective and much used antiemetic. However, it has a greater tendency to cause dystonia than domperidone, particularly in children and young women. It may also cause muscle stiffness, tremors, drowsiness, restlessness and diarrhoea. It should be avoided if you are breast-feeding or suffer from epilepsy, or kidney and liver impairment. It can be used in pregnancy under medical supervision but, like all drugs in pregnancy, is best avoided if possible.

Dosage: 1/2–1 x 10mg three times a day.

Motion sickness

Motion sickness arises not from gut problems but as a result of confusion between signals sent to the brain by the eyes and from the balance apparatus in the inner ear. As such it responds to different drugs, including the antihistamines promethazine and cinnarizine (see p.38).

 Homeopathically, a combination of **Cocculus** 30c, **Nux vomica** 30c and **Petroleum** 30c should prove effective. Take one tablet of each remedy half an hour before travelling, and repeat if the slightest sign of nausea develops.

Hyoscine hydrobromide (also known as **scopolamine hydrobromide** in the UK and USA) is effective, cheap and available both in tablet and patch form. Common side effects include dry mouth, blurred vision, dizziness, constipation and difficulty passing urine. It should be avoided if you suffer from glaucoma and used only with caution in pregnancy, breast-feeding and a number of rarer medical conditions (eg myasthenia gravis, paralytic ileus, pyloric stenosis and prostatic enlargement). Read the pack instructions carefully.

Adult dosage: 1 x 300mcg tablet 30min before travelling and every 6hr thereafter if required.

Antimalarials

The type of **antimalarial** medication you take depends primarily on where you intend to go, and for how long. Patterns of resistance can change rapidly, so always seek up-to-date advice. None of the antimalarials currently available offers complete protection against malaria, and avoiding being bitten by mosquitoes (see p.149) is your only guarantee – all levels of antimalarial measures relate to **risk limitation** rather than elimination.

Side effects can be troublesome (see pp.164–167), and the protection conferred is not instantaneous, so start the course in good time before entering an endemic area (at least two weeks for mefloquine, one week for chloroquine, doxycycline and proguanil, and one to two days for Malarone). Because of the complicated life cycle of the malaria parasite and the long incubation period of the disease, antimalarials should be continued for at least four weeks after you leave an endemic area (Malarone is the exception, needing only to be continued for one week). In the UK, chloroquine and proguanil are licensed for long-term malaria prophylaxis, whereas doxycycline is licensed for up to two years, mefloquine up to one year, and Malarone for only 28 days within a malarial area.

Combination drugs containing **pyrimethamine** are occasionally used in malaria prophylaxis (Maloprim), and in the treatment of falciparum malaria (Fansidar). They have been largely superseded now and are only used when the first-choice drugs are contraindicated or unavailable. There is no evidence that homeopathy works in a protective way against diseases, so homeopathic "vaccination" against diseases, especially malaria, is not recommended.

Chloroquine is steadily becoming less effective because of increasing worldwide drug resistance. It can be taken alone, but is now more commonly used in conjunction with proguanil. Check with your doctor if you have a medical condition that precludes you from taking it. Side effects include gastrointestinal disturbances, headache, convulsions, visual disturbances, de-pigmentation or loss of hair, and skin reactions. Mild side effects are quite common, severe are rare.

Dosage: 300mg once a week on a full stomach (usually 2 x 150mg tablets).

Proguanil is used almost exclusively in conjunction with chloroquine in the UK, Australia, New Zealand and many European countries. It is not available in the US. Although it can be used in pregnancy and by those with kidney disease, discuss with a doctor beforehand. Side effects include mild stomach upsets, diarrhoea, mouth ulcers and (rarely) skin reactions and hair loss.

Dosage: 200mg once daily (usually 2 x 100mg tablets) .

Despite much adverse publicity, **Mefloquine★** remains a good antimalarial, but as effective alternatives have become available, its long list of side effects have caused it to lose favour. In the US, it's one of only a handful of drugs for which the FDA require doctors, by law, to issue a medication guide setting out potential risks when prescribing. Most **side effects** occur in the first week or two after commencing the drug, and include the following: nausea, vomiting, diarrhoea, dizziness, loss of balance, headache, somnolence, sleep disorders, anxiety, depression, hallucinations, convulsions, ringing ears, visual disturbances, circulatory disorders, muscle pain and weakness, joint pains, rashes, itching, hair loss, malaise, fever, fatigue, loss of appetite, and disturbances in liver function, blood composition and heart conduction. Several studies have shown that side effects are more likely in women.

Despite extensive media coverage, the serious psychiatric disturbances attributed to mefloquine are, in practice, rare. It should not be taken in early pregnancy (current evidence suggests that it is safe later on), if you are breast-feeding, nor if you have had serious psychiatric illness, convulsions, or hypersensitivity to quinine. It should also be avoided if you have liver or kidney impairment, heart conduction disorders and epilepsy. It is not recommended for children under three months.

Dosage: 1 x 250mg tablet each week on a full stomach. (A dose of half a tablet twice weekly may reduce the incidence of gastrointestinal side effects.)

Doxycycline* is an antibiotic which is increasingly prescribed as an effective alternative to mefloquine, and is also useful in areas where mefloquine resistance exists. It reduces the efficacy of the contraceptive pill, however, and should be used only after consultation with a doctor if you have liver impairment. It should not be taken at all if you suffer from porphyria, or if you are pregnant or breast-feeding. **Side effects** include nausea, vomiting, diarrhoea, gullet irritation and ulceration, rashes (including hypersensitivity to sunlight in approximately two percent of cases), and it may predispose to vaginal thrush. More rarely, headache and visual disturbances, pancreatitis and pseudomembranous colitis can occur, all of which need medical attention. Doxycycline should be taken after meals with a glass of water; to reduce the risk of gullet ulceration, avoid taking it last thing at night.

Dosage: 100mg daily after food.

Malarone*, a combination of **proguanil hydrochloride** with **atovaquone**, is the newest addition to the armoury against malaria. As such, less evidence is available on its side effects or long term effects, but initial studies indicate that it is very effective, and has relatively few reported side effects. The main drawback is that it's expensive and is only licensed for use for 28 days within a malarial area (the initial 1–2 days and 7 days on returning are additional); in practice it's probably safe to take for longer. Note that blood levels of atovaquone are reduced by tetracycline antibiotics, so if you're taking these your protection may be diminished.

Dosage: 1 tablet (250/100mg) daily.

Antifungal treatments

Clotrimazole and **miconazole creams** are cheap and effective in treating most fungal skin infections; make sure, however, that you continue the treatment regime for two weeks after the lesions have healed – stopping as soon as symptoms disappear is the main reason why antifungals fail to eradicate infections.

Apply twice daily until two weeks after the lesions have healed.

Vaginal thrush (see p.213) is best treated with **clotrimazole** or **miconazole** pessaries (known as suppositories in the US).

Of the number of different makes of vaginal pessary to choose from, the most convenient is one-off treatment using a 500mg pessary of clotrimazole or 1.2g of miconazole, inserted last thing at night.

Tranquillizers

Many doctors are reluctant to prescribe **tranquillizers** because of their addictive potential. If you do take tranquillizers for whatever reason, avoid using them for more than a week at a time.

Temazepam★ is frequently prescribed for sleep problems. Side effects include clumsiness, drowsiness and lightheadedness the next day.

Adult dosage: 1 x 10mg at night.

Diazepam★ can be used in the short term as a relief for anxiety (eg aerophobia). Its side effects are similar to temazepam.

Dosage: depends on the prescribing doctor but, in most cases, 2mg every 8hr is sufficient.

Altitude sickness

Acetazolamide★ is a useful preventative for acute mountain sickness. It is not recommended for prolonged use, however, and if taken concurrently with the oral contraceptive pill, there is an increased risk of blood clots (eg DVTs).

Dosage: Half a 250mg tablet twice daily.

Note that nifedipine, dexamethasone and furosemide (see overleaf) should only be used under medical supervision.

Suggested medical kit

Medications or equipment you might want to include:

+ **Painkillers** Paracetamol or ibuprofen
+ **Antibiotics★** Amoxicillin or erythromycin; also consider ciprofloxacin
+ **Antihistamines** Chlorpheniramine or loratadine; Anthisan cream
+ **Antidiarrhoeals**
+ **Antifungals** Clotrimazole cream
+ **Oral rehydration fluid**
+ **Antisickness drugs★** Metoclopramide or domperidone
+ **Motion sickness** Hyoscine hydrobromide or promethazine; acupressure bands
+ **Antimalarials** Dependent on the latest recommendations for the country of destination
+ **Antacids**
+ **Condoms**
+ **Sunscreen** Any factor 15+ that protects against UVA and B
+ **Sticking plasters/Band-Aids**
+ **Steristrips**
+ **Crepe bandage**
+ **Scissors**
+ **Tweezers**
+ **Thermometer**
+ **Antiseptic** A dry spray, rather than a cream, is best in hot climates
+ **Sterile gauze and cotton wool**
+ **Safety pins**
+ **Insect repellent**
+ **Aftersun lotion**
+ **Tampons**
+ **Wet-wipes**
+ **Sterile syringes and needles**
(★ available only on prescription)

Nifedipine★ is normally used for the treatment of high blood pressure and angina, but it can be used as a **prophylactic** against mountain sickness, or as a **treatment** in acute episodes. Side effects include faintness (caused by low blood pressure), headache, flushing, dizziness, lethargy, nausea, ankle swelling (unhelpfully, these are all symptoms of altitude sickness as well) and rashes. It should not be taken if you are pregnant or if you suffer from porphyria. If you suffer from heart problems, discuss this with a doctor before using nifedipine.

Recommended dosage: 20mg three times a day.

Dexamethasone★ is a strong steroid used to reduce brain swelling in altitude sickness. It should be used in emergencies only and not for more than two days without medical advice. It buys time for descent only, and further ascent must not be attempted once the symptoms have settled. The side effects of steroids are numerous and can be serious, but short-term use is usually safe.

Standard starting dosage is 4mg four times daily. It's important not to stop taking dexamethasone abruptly; reduce dosage gradually, for example by 2mg every other day (depending on the length of the course).

Furosemide★ is a strong diuretic, useful for acute episodes of altitude sickness when breathing is impaired by an accumulation of fluid in the lungs. Used as a short-term, emergency treatment, side effects are likely to be minimal, although expect to pass urine more often.

Dosage: 40–80mg daily.

 Coca 30c, given four times a day, is a homeopathic remedy worth trying as a preventative for altitude sickness.

Other useful medical items

A few other items you might consider packing include:

✚ **Antiseptic cream**, lotion or dry spray.

✚ **Steroid creams**: hydrocortisone reduces local swelling and itching (eg insect bites). Although only a mild steroid, and, as such, available without prescription, hydrocortisone should be used with discretion because long-term use can cause thinning of the skin. Generally speaking, it should not be used for more than fourteen days at a time. It should not be used for untreated bacterial, viral and fungal infections, and contact with the eyes should be avoided.

✚ **Magnesium sulphate paste** is not an antibiotic, but can be useful in treating boils and minor skin infections.

✚ **Antacids**: Most brands provide good symptomatic relief after hastily gobbled, fried or spicy foods. Follow the instructions on the bottle or packet. The absorption of some drugs can be impaired by concurrent use of antacids.

✚ **Sunscreen or sunblock**: Broadly speaking, sunscreens should have a sun protection factor of 15+, protect from both UVA and UVB, and be water-resistant (see p.210 for more information).

Homeopathy

Homeopathy was developed around 200 years ago by a German doctor, Samuel Hahnemann (1755–1843), who challenged the medical wisdom of the time with his insistence on developing a more natural and gentle system of healing for his patients – an alternative to the heavy metals, strong herbal purges and bloodletting favoured by his contemporaries. Today, homeopathy, like other forms of complementary therapies, has become very popular in the UK, Europe and the US. It's seen as a gentler alternative to powerful antibiotics and other modern drugs, without their attendant side effects.

Throughout this book, homeopathic alternatives to many preventions and treatments have been provided (note that these suggestions, provided by a trained homeopath, should not be taken as replacements for the conventional medical advice given in this book and that they don't necessarily reflect the views of the author). Look for this symbol:

How it works

Coined by Hahnemann, the word "homeopathy" derives from the Greek meaning "similar suffering". Central to it is the idea that "**like cures like**", meaning that a substance capable of causing certain symptoms in a well person can be used to cure the same symptoms in a sick person. For example, the conventional ("allopathic") approach to treating diarrhoea is to take a substance which causes constipation; to treat the same complaint homeopathically, you take a very tiny dose of something that has the power to cause diarrhoea if given to a healthy person. In other words, a substance has the opposite action if used in a tiny dose.

All homeopathic medicines are prepared in licensed laboratories under strict quality control according to a method laid down by Hahnemann himself. Through a process known as "**dilution and succussion**", substances are diluted to the point where no material evidence remains; the idea behind this is to release the true healing nature and potential of the original substance. The varying levels of dilution are known as **potencies** (6c, 30c etc). Homeopathic remedies are derived from a variety of natural materials, including poisonous plants, snake venoms, heavy metals and chemical salts, but because of the high dilution, they're perfectly safe even for pregnant women and children. Remedies are sold in tablet, granule, liquid or powder form, the former being most convenient when you're travelling.

Choosing the right remedy

Treatment in homeopathy is **individualized**. Thus, it's the symptoms that make your condition atypical that determine which particular remedy to choose. For example, if you have a cold, it's not the fact that you have a runny nose – which is common to all colds – that's important, but the nature of the discharge in your particular case (eg bloody, clear, profuse, purulent and so on).

Ideally, homeopathy also takes into account your **mental and emotional symptoms**. If you have diarrhoea, and are restless and anxious in an uncharacteristic way, this would form part of what's known as your "**symp-tom picture**", which would then be matched to a homeopathic remedy, or "**drug picture**". However in order to give homeopathic first aid advice within this book, we've suggested remedies which have been found to be generally useful for particular conditions. When trying to decide which remedy you need, look for recent changes to normal habits, mood and body patterns as well as obvious symptoms.

Taking the remedy

Rather than being swallowed with water, homeopathic tablets should simply be allowed to dissolve in the mouth, as they are absorbed through the mucosal lining. For remedies to work effectively, take them with a "**clean mouth**", ie don't eat, drink or smoke for 10–15 minutes before or after each dose. As remedies can be **antidoted** by peppermint and menthol, it's also wise not to take them too soon before or after brushing your teeth; note that non-mint toothpastes are widely available. Avoid the antidotes of camphor, coffee, eucalyptus and cannabis completely for the days during treatment. Tea, moderate amounts of alcohol and tobacco don't usually affect remedies.

Storage

It's important to **store** homeopathic medicines carefully; a small padded toilet bag is a good option. The effectiveness of your remedies will be prolonged if you avoid exposing them to:

✚ direct sunlight
✚ strong heat – it's not necessary to refrigerate remedies, but try to keep exposure to great heat to a minimum.
✚ strong smells – especially those in chest rubs and decongestants, like camphor, eucalyptus, menthol and peppermint.

Note that although X-ray scanners were once thought to interfere with homeopathic remedies, there's no clear evidence to support this. However if you're a frequent flyer, you may still want to ask for remedies to be inspected by hand, something that most customs officials will be amenable to (make sure the tablets are clearly labelled, however).

Although homeopathic remedy bottles display an expiry date these days, most remedies do not appear to lose their activity over time if stored properly.

Homeopathic first aid

If you see no improvement after a day of taking remedies, **stop**, review the symptoms again and look for another remedy, or else seek medical advice. Don't continue to take a remedy that isn't working – in treating an acute illness using homeopathic first aid, the *right* remedy will work quickly.

Homeopathic first aid remedies

The list below outlines the most common remedies used in **homeopathic first aid for travellers**. Next to each is a brief description of the remedy's uses – look under the relevant illnesses in Part 2 for more detail on recommended

Think about seeing a **homeopath, herbalist** or **acupuncturist** before you set out on a long journey, especially if you have a background of (even niggling) health problems – sun headaches, irritable bowel syndrome, period problems or back pains – which you don't want to be suffering from when you're a long way from home.

You can also buy some of the most common remedies in UK high-street chemists such as Boots and Superdrug, as well as at health food stores, or from the homeopathic pharmacies detailed below, both of which will mail remedies worldwide. You might want to invest in one of the many **homeopathic first-aid kits** on the market, most of which contain 30c strength tablets of the remedies you're most likely to need to treat common travel-related illnesses.

Homeopathic pharmacies

Ainsworths

36 New Cavendish St, London W1M 7LH ☎020/7935 5330, ✆www.ainsworths.com.

Helios

89–97 Camden Rd, Tunbridge Wells, Kent TN1 2QR ☎01892/537254, ✆www.helios.co.uk.

Homeopathic practitioners

For information about finding a homeopath, contact the following governing bodies for the profession. The former represents homeopaths that also have conventional medical qualifications.

The British Homeopathic Association

Hahnemann House, 29 Park St West, Luton LU1 3BE ☎0870/444 3950, ✆www.trusthomeopathy.org.

The Society of Homeopaths

4a Artisan Rd, Northampton, NN1 4HU ☎01604/621400, ✆www.homeopathy-soh.org.

dosages and the like. The names in brackets show how each medicine may appear on the pharmacy label.

Try to obtain a 30c potency of each remedy; if this isn't available, a 6c will be fine, but as this is weaker, doses will need repeating a little more often than a 30c potency.

✚ **Aconite** (Acon.) For fevers, shock, panic and anxiety.

✚ **Allium cepa** (All-c.) Head colds and hay fever.

✚ **Apis mellifica** (Apis mel.) Bites, stings and allergic reactions.

✚ **Argentum nitricum** (Arg. Nit.) Fear of flying, and anxiety before travelling.

✚ **Arnica** (Arn.) Bruises, shock and swelling after injury or surgery. Also useful for jet lag.

✚ **Arsenicum album** (Ars. alb.) Diarrhoea and vomiting.

✚ **Belladonna** (Bell.) Fevers, sun headaches and localized inflammations.

✚ **Calendula** (Calend.) Promotes healing of grazes, and good for wounds that may be going septic. Also useful for nappy/diaper rash.

✚ **Cantharis** (Canth.) Urinary tract infections.

✚ **Coca** Altitude sickness.

✚ **Cocculus indicus** (Cocc.) Travel sickness and jet lag.

+ **Colocynthis** (Coloc.) Diarrhoea, colic and menstrual cramps.
+ **Cuprum metallicum** (Cupr.) Cramps in the limbs.
+ **Eupatorium perfoliatum** (Eup. perf.) Febrile illnesses, such as dengue fever; also influenza.
+ **Ferrum phos** (Ferr-p.) Colds and the first signs of mild inflammatory complaints (chest, throat).
+ **Gelsemium** (Gels.) Flu-like colds, and shock.
+ **Glonoin** (Glon.) Pounding headaches, especially after spending too much time in the sun.
+ **Hypericum** (Hyp.) Helps heal injuries to areas rich in nerves (tongue, lips, fingers and toes); also very useful for a bruised coccyx, eg after a long bumpy journey.
+ **Ignatia amara** (Ign.) Emotional shock and loss.
+ **Ledum pal** (Led.) Heals deep, or dirty, wounds and bites. Can be considered as an anti-tetanus remedy.

Alternative first aid kit

The following alternative items will make good additions to your medical kit.

+ **Bach Rescue Remedy** will keep you calm in times of stress. The **Walnut** Bach remedy will help you adapt to changing circumstances, while the **Crabapple** variety helps clear your system of drugs (all sorts – allopathic, recreational, alcohol etc). For all three, sip two or three drops diluted in a glass of water.
+ **Lavender essential oil** is not only relaxing and calming but stimulates healing and has antibacterial and antispasmodic properties. Apply undiluted to bruises, insect or animal bites and minor burns, and mix one or two drops into after-sun cream to treat sunburn. You can also place a couple of drops on your pillow and sniff regularly during a migraine – this also helps to calm you down and makes you sleep.
+ **Tea tree essential oil** is a powerful antiviral, antibacterial and antifungal that's great for treating thrush, athlete's foot and other fungal skin infections – put three or four drops in a small bowl of warm water for applying or soaking. Dropped into hot water for inhaling, it can help to ease colds, chest infections. Mix a few drops with almond (or any base) oil to make a good chest rub – you can also get it as a cream. If you're pregnant, don't use tea tree oil – try lavender instead.
+ **Grape seed extract** is widely available in liquid or tablet form, and acts as an antiparasitic and natural antibiotic. It can be useful during colds, flu and chest infections, as well as acting as a daily prophylactic or as a treatment against intestinal infections.
+ **Lactobacillus acidophilus** are the so-called "friendly bacteria" that repopulate your intestines after you've had diarrhoea or taken a course of antibiotics. We produce them naturally, but you can also take a top-up, available in tablets, capsules and powder. Taking them during a course of antibiotics helps to prevent an attack of thrush afterwards, and they also help to settle the stomach when you're adjusting to unfamiliar food and water.
+ **Calendula** cream is great for grazes, cuts and wounds. You can also buy it as a **tincture** (a solution of the drug in alcohol); place three or four drops in a small bowl of water for bathing. A combined cream of calendula and hypericum is a good alternative.

- **Mercurius** (Merc. viv. or Merc. sol.) Sore throats.
- **Natrum mur** (Nat–m.) Head colds and cold sores.
- **Nux vomica** (Nux–v.) Hangovers, colic and any form of overindulgence.
- **Opium** (Op.) Travellers' constipation.
- **Petroleum** (Petr.) Travel sickness (particularly if you are averse to the smell of petrol).
- **Phosphorous** (Phos.) Persistent, dry or tickly coughs, vomiting and nosebleeds.
- **Podophyllum** (Podo.) Diarrhoea, tummy upsets.
- **Pulsatilla** (Puls.) Thick mucousy colds and coughs, and homesickness.
- **Pyrogen** (Pyrog.) Septic wounds.
- **Rhus toxicodendron** (Rhus tox.) Strains, sprains and overlifting. Also useful for herpes attacks, chicken pox, and for local skin allergies to certain plants, particularly poison ivy.
- **Silica** (Sil.) Useful for ejecting foreign bodies from the system – splinters, sea urchin spines, bee stings and the like.
- **Sulphur** (Sulph.) Useful for vaginal thrush and itchy fungal skin complaints.
- **Tabacum** (Tab.) Sea sickness.
- **Veratrum album** (Verat. alb.) For severe tummy upsets, dysentery, painful periods.

Further information

@**www.weleda.co.uk**
The website of this natural medicine company has some background on homeopathy as well as a useful remedy finder.

@**www.drlockie.com**
Comprehensive site, with detailed advice on finding the right first-aid remedy, as well as disease information, homeopathic news and links.

@**www.homeopathyhome.com**
Interesting articles, chatrooms and discussion groups, as well as addresses of suppliers of homeopathic goods in the UK.

@**www.homeopathy-uk.com**
Huge web directory of homeopathy-related sites worldwide.

▲ Medicinal herbs, China

Travellers with specific needs

The elderly, the disabled, families with children, pregnant women and sufferers from chronic illness all have **specific needs** to consider in the planning stages of a trip, as do those who travel frequently on business, or who plan on working abroad during a "gap" year. The key is not to overextend yourself, to recognize your limits and plan your trip within them. Pre-considerations such as immunizations, travel insurance and a medical kit are particularly important. As those indulging in adventure pursuits such as trekking or scuba diving are at risk of being injured or of suffering the effects of poor sanitation, active travellers also have much to consider before setting off and whilst away.

The traveller with asthma

Travel can increase your chances of exposure to some of asthma's many **triggers**: cold, damp, exercise, air pollution, altitude, dust, cigarette or wood smoke, air conditioning, upper respiratory tract infections, and anxiety. Given the right conditions, anyone can develop the symptoms of asthma. Smog in cities, crop-harvesting in arid, dusty countryside and local pollen-emitting flora all conspire to cause wheezes and coughs in the unsuspecting traveller.

Symptoms and treatment

The wheeze of asthma does not come from the throat but the chest, and is characteristically worse on breathing out. You may feel tight-chested and have a dry, tickly cough, which is usually worse at night and can be the only symptom. If symptoms are severe, it may be difficult to breathe, or speak in complete sentences.

Mild asthma can be treated fairly easily using **inhalers**. Those with a history of asthma should already be aware of the correct technique and the necessary dosages, but the advice in the box below is included as a guide for new users. Asthma can be controlled either with a beta sympathomimetic inhaler alone (eg salbutamol or terbutaline), or in combination with a steroid inhaler (eg beclomethasone or fluticasone). The former are more useful for the active treatment of symptoms, whereas the latter are regarded more as a preventative.

Medicalert

Medicalert provide medical emergency ID for those with conditions such as epilepsy or asthma or for those allergic to common drugs such as penicillin. Contacts are:
UK: 1 Bridge Wharf, 156 Caledonian Road, London N1 9UU ☎0800/581420, ⓦwww.medicalert.co.uk.
USA: 2323 Colorado Avenue, Turlock CA 95382 ☎888/633-4298 (24hr) or ☎ 209/668-333 from outside the US, ⓦwww.medicalert.org.
Australia: Level 2, 216 Greenhill, Eastwood, SA 5063 ☎08/8274 0361 or 1800/882222, ⓦwww.medicalert.com.au.

Inhaler technique

If you've never suffered asthma symptoms before, it is unlikely that you will develop a serious case of it whilst abroad – but this is not to say that mild symptoms won't benefit from treatment. The first-line treatment for wheeze is a **beta sympathomimetic inhaler**, which is available on prescription in most developed countries. Some people find inhalers difficult to use; it helps to think in terms of getting the drug to where it will do its work, ie the lungs. To use the inhaler, start by taking a deep breath in, then breathe out all the way. At the end of expiration, place the inhaler between your lips and start a slow, deep inhalation; the inhaler should be discharged **during** the deep breath in. Hold your breath for at least ten seconds to allow the drug time to act, then repeat the exercise. Seek medical advice if symptoms persist.

During an asthma attack, the beta sympathomimetics can be taken as two puffs every four hours, and the steroid dose may be doubled (it's usually two puffs twice daily) to two puffs four times a day until symptoms subside.

If you want to try homeopathy as a means of treating asthma, you must consult a homeopath well before departure (see p.47).

Being prepared

If you are an asthma sufferer, you should:

✚ Be aware of the **signs and symptoms** of worsening asthma. In particular, understand the importance of monitoring changes in your peak flow rate.
✚ Be aware of correct **inhaler technique**.
✚ Know how to **regulate the doses** of your inhalers during acute episodes (increase the frequency of both treaters and preventers).
✚ If your asthma is **poorly controlled** or you have previously suffered **severe attacks**, discuss with your doctor whether you need to take oral steroids with you.
✚ Vaccination against **influenza** is highly recommended, particularly if you're flying to an area with high risk.
✚ **Seek medical help** sooner rather than later. Asthma is more difficult to treat the longer symptoms are left, so don't let your symptoms get out of control.

The traveller with diabetes

As a **diabetic** it's very important to discuss travel plans with your doctor or diabetic nurse well in advance of your departure, so that your diabetes can be optimally controlled before you leave. Ensure that you can recognize symptoms of high and, more importantly, low blood sugar and that you understand how your drugs or insulin work. Be aware of what to do if your blood sugar goes too high or too low and how to adjust your treatment during illness (eg diarrhoea and vomiting or high fever).

Although not essential, those who are insulin-dependent would be wise to travel with someone who's aware of the potential problems associated with diabetes, and is able to deal with them. Either way, it's essential to wear dog tag or bracelet **ID** (see p.51) if your diabetes is insulin-controlled.

Always carry an **emergency supply of sweets** in case of hypos.

Medications and insulin

Take ample supplies of insulin, medications and testing equipment with you, as they might be difficult to replace or top up when abroad. It may be possible to obtain information as to equipment availability from the national diabetic association of wherever you're heading; contact the national association (see p.54) in your country of origin for advice on this.

When crossing time zones, remain on your **home time** for insulin injections and carbohydrate intake until arrival. Thereafter, injections can be adjusted in two-hourly increments until they are in line with local time. If the time between successive injections is extended rather than shortened, a smaller, interim dose may be necessary. If the time between injections is shorter, a small, temporary reduction in dose may be necessary (of the order of four to eight units depending on your individual daily dose); discuss such adjustments with your doctor before leaving. When making adjustments, **underdose your insulin rather than overdose** – in the short term, it's safer to have blood sugar levels that are slightly too high rather than too low. If you use oral hypoglycaemic tablets, you don't need to alter your dose times when crossing time zones. It may take a few days to adjust fully to the local time and it is advisable to check blood glucose readings regularly (at least twice daily) during this period.

Take care over the storage temperature of your insulin – extremes of heat and cold can damage it.

Managing your blood sugar

Strenuous **exercise** drops the body's blood sugar level, so try to plan ahead and eat a carbohydrate-rich snack thirty to sixty minutes beforehand. This may need to be repeated during periods of extended exercise.

Insulin requirements during **illness** (ie when your body is under stress) increase, and it may be necessary to temporarily increase your usual daily dosage while unwell. Continue as normal during diarrhoeal and other illnesses, but monitor blood glucose regularly and try to eat easily digestible carbohydrates. Be particularly wary of dehydration. If vomiting occurs continue your insulin injections as normal, but monitor your blood sugar regularly and seek medical advice. **Infections** are a common complication of diabetes, so be particularly vigilant when travelling, especially if your glucose levels are running high. Use antibiotics early if infection is suspected, and don't delay in seeing a doctor. Carry the address and telephone number of your doctor at home in case you or someone else need to make urgent contact. Vaccination against **influenza** is highly recommended if you're travelling to an area with a seasonal risk.

Insulin, syringes and flying

Given the increased threat of terrorism in recent years, most airlines now refuse to allow sharp objects in cabin baggage. Exceptions are possible for diabetics requiring insulin, however, provided you have a **letter from your doctor** stating the need to carry needles on board an aircraft. Doctors may charge for writing these letters, so it's sensible to ask that the wording makes continued long-term need for insulin clear.

Note that **insulin** must always be kept in insulated bags in your hand baggage, as subzero temperatures in the aeroplane hold can damage it.

Travellers with specific needs: Diabetes

National diabetes associations

USA
American Diabetes Association
1701 North Beauregard St, Alexandria, VA 22311 ☎1-800/342-2383, ⊕www
.diabetes.org.

UK
Diabetes UK
10 Queen Anne St, London W1M 0BD ☎020/7323 1531, ⊕www.diabetes.org.uk.

Australia and New Zealand
Diabetes New Zealand
PO Box 12441, Thorndon, Wellington, New Zealand ☎03/499-7145 or ☎0800/342-
238, ⊕www.diabetes.org.nz.

Because long-term diabetes can impair **pain** perception, minor blisters on your feet can develop into more severe ulcers without you knowing. For this reason, take particular care to inspect your feet regularly and carry plenty of dressings, antiseptic and protective "corn plasters".

The traveller with epilepsy

Once your fits are well controlled by medication, **epilepsy** does not exclude you from very much, especially travelling, but there are a number of considerations to take into account before you go and while on the road.

Advice on first aid for a fit appears in Part 3, p.243.

Being prepared

It may be difficult and even dangerous to travel alone, especially if your epilepsy is poorly controlled. Even if your fits are infrequent, it's sensible to travel with someone who knows about your condition and how to deal with a fit if you have one. Always inform your travel agent and airline that you have epilepsy from the outset. Some airlines require special medical certification for epileptics, indicating that the condition is stable enough for flying.

Be aware of conditions or activities which may increase the **risk of fits**: missed medications, fatigue, heat, infections, dehydration, over-rehydration, alcohol, severe diarrhoea, recurrent vomiting, low blood sugar caused by missed meals, stress, menstruation and strobe lights. Although it might be easy to avoid potentially hazardous situations at home, it can be more difficult when you are on the move. Pay particular attention to railway platforms, hotel balconies, roads, cliff edges and around water, camp fires and barbecues. As a sufferer of epilepsy you will already know which **activities** are ill advised, and remember that if you do any of them, it may not be just yourself you are subjecting to risk. Scuba diving and rock climbing are definitely out, while other activities must be viewed in the context of fit frequency and severity. Water sports can be safe provided someone who is aware of your epilepsy accompanies you. Treat horse riding and cycling with the same caution, and always wear protective headgear. There is no international consensus regarding **driving** restrictions for people with epilepsy: generally a licence may be granted after a fit-free period of two years, but your travel insurer may impose further restrictions (for advice on insurance, see p.2).

Most of the travel **immunizations** available are perfectly safe for epileptics, although seek expert advice about antimalarials (chloroquine and mefloquine should be avoided), and bear in mind that the influenza vaccination interacts with phenytoin. See below for a list of drugs relevant to the traveller which may interact with anti-epileptic medication.

Medications

Although flying itself should not increase the risk of fits, disturbed sleep and taking **medications** irregularly can. Try and keep to "home time" when taking medications, but if dose times need to be adjusted, do so gradually. Carry spare medication in your hand luggage, and clearly write down the name of your medication (the precise preparation – this is one instance where the trade name can be important), the strength of dose you take and its regularity in case you need to replace it while you're away. Remember to store the information in a safe place. Before departure, ask your doctor about the merits of taking rectal diazepam on your trip – it can be used in emergencies to stop a fit.

It may not always be possible to obtain the drug you take, so if you are travelling to countries where this may be the case, carry plentiful supplies or have a reliable contingency plan for obtaining medications from home. Some drug export companies can arrange to send supplies abroad for you (contact your national epilepsy association).

Although many drugs interact with anti-epileptic medications, the ones of particular relevance to the traveller are:

✤ **Carbamazepine★**
   Alcohol
   Co-proxamol
   Doxycycline
   Erythromycin
   Oral contraceptive pill

✤ **Phenytoin★**
   Aspirin (and possibly other anti-inflammatories)
   Antacids
   Metronidazole
   Trimethoprim
   Doxycycline
   Ciprofloxacin
   Chloramphenicol
   Fansidar (sometimes used in the treatment of falciparum malaria)
   Maloprim (occasionally used for malaria prophylaxis)
   Oral contraceptive pill

✤ **Valproate**
   Aspirin
   Erythromycin

★*These anti-epileptics increase your vitamin D requirements.*

National epilepsy associations

USA
Epilepsy Foundation of America
4351 Garden City Drive, Landover MD 20785 ☎301/459-3700 or ☎1-800/332-1000, ⓦwww.epilepsyfoundation.org.

UK
British Epilepsy Association
New Anstey House, Gate Way Drive, Yeadon, Leeds LS19 7XY ☎01132/108800, ⓦwww.epilepsy.org.uk.

Australia and New Zealand
Epilepsy Association Australia
GPO Box 9878, plus the name of the state capital you live in ☎1300/366162, ⓦwww.epilepsy.org.au.
Epilepsy New Zealand
Box 1074, Hamilton ☎07/834 3556 or ☎0800/202122 (toll-free), ⓦwww.epilepsy .org.nz.

Travelling with immunodeficiency

Immunodeficiency essentially means that your body's ability to fight off infections is compromised and, as such, you are more vulnerable to infections of any kind. Illnesses which lead to immunodeficiency include leukaemia, lymphoma and HIV infection; you're also at risk after a splenectomy, after chemotherapy, and if you're on high-dose steroids. If you are immunodeficient, focus foreign travel plans around this important and inescapable fact, as you may face considerable risks in developing countries where standards of hygiene are poor and medical care may be inadequate.

You must declare your condition to your insurer, as failure to do so will invalidate any claims made arising from immunodeficiency; see p.3 for more on **insurance** for those with pre-existing conditions. The importance of ensuring your policy has adequate cover for rapid repatriation in the event of an emergency cannot be overstated.

Finally, depending on the cause of your immunodeficiency and its extent, you may also need to consider the suitability of "live" **vaccinations** (see p.6), as these depend on the body being able to form an effective immune response. If in doubt, seek the advice of your specialist before being vaccinated. Vaccination against **influenza** is highly recommended if you're travelling to an area with a seasonal risk.

Travelling with HIV

While any traveller is at risk of infection, those with HIV are more susceptible because of damage to their immune system. **Caution** and **careful planning** are essential if you're intending to visit developing countries where sanitation is poor and medical care may be limited through lack of expertise or funding.

As HIV depletes the ability to fight off infection, it stands to reason that travellers with HIV are at higher risk of contracting an illness than most travellers. There is an increased frequency and severity of most illnesses, but particularly gastrointestinal infections, TB, syphilis and leishmaniasis. However if you are in good health and with a CD4 count (the white cells in the blood which protect against infection) greater than 200, you do not need to take special precautions, although remember that a previously healthy CD4 count could drop while you are away.

For those with CD4 counts below 200, it would be unwise to make an unnecessary trip to areas with poor sanitation. It's best to discuss the risks with your doctor before booking a long trip. Being obsessional about the standard food and drink precautions helps (see pp.21–24); avoid unpasteurized dairy products in particular.

Medications

Complex treatments have been developed which retard the progress of HIV, and carrying the drugs with you when travelling can present logistical problems. A **doctor's letter** stating your need for the drugs is necessary to avoid difficulties with customs officials, but if they suspect that you have HIV, this in itself can cause problems in some countries. Always bring ample supplies of prescribed drugs with you because replacements may be difficult to find, not to mention expensive. Some anti-HIV drugs increase sensitivity to UV light, so it's important to use high-factor sunscreen and avoid strong sunlight where possible.

Vaccinations

"Live" vaccinations (see p.6) should generally be avoided altogether (exceptions are listed in the box below). After **inactivated immunization** there may be a transient increase in the level of HIV in the blood and a consequent decrease in the CD4 count. Those with HIV also have a greater chance of getting a reaction to immunization, as well as a weaker response, or lower level of immunity.

Visa requirements

While most countries do not officially deny entry to HIV travellers who are not intending to work or study, you could, rather ambiguously, be refused entry on account of carrying a "communicable disease". Although you do not have to declare that you are HIV positive, the medications in your luggage might give the game away. No countries insist on **screening** for HIV in casual travellers, although many (including the USA and the UK) will require a test for

---

HIV vaccination advice

The UK Department of Health has issued the following advice on the vaccination of anyone with HIV infection:

✚ Anyone who is HIV positive, with or without symptoms, can receive the following **live vaccines**: oral cholera (Mutacol), measles, mumps, rubella (MMR), oral polio (inactivated vaccine may be a better option for those with symptoms).*

✚ It is also safe to be given the following **inactivated vaccines**: cholera, diphtheria, haemophilus influenza type b, hepatitis A, hepatitis B, influenza, meningococcal meningitis, pertussis (whooping cough), pneumococcal infections (eg pneumonia), inactivated polio, rabies, tetanus and injected typhoid.

✚ If you are HIV positive, you should **not receive** BCG (TB) or oral typhoid; get expert advice on whether yellow fever can be tolerated.

These are not a standard requirement for travelling although those with HIV may lose previous immunity to these illnesses.

longer term immigrants such as students and those seeking work. They'll refuse entry if the test is positive. If you're planning to work or study abroad, contact the appropriate embassy to clarify their policy on HIV tests.

Sex

Sexual encounters with a new partner while travelling are common, yet despite the considerable risks to themselves and others, some people still don't use condoms. Although not offering complete protection, proper use of good-quality condoms greatly reduces the risk of contracting, and passing on, sexually transmitted diseases. **Act responsibly** if you have sex with a new partner, male or female, and always use high-quality condoms, preferably brought with you from home.

Discrimination

Some cultures remain prejudiced against HIV because of enduring associations with sexual behaviour and drug taking, and it's possible that you will suffer **discrimination** when seeking medical help. There is not very much that you can do about this other than to anticipate it and ensure that your insurance cover will bring you home if the going gets rough.

▶▶ See also HIV, p.144.

The elderly traveller

Age is no longer an obstacle to exotic travel. In fact, many people do not have the opportunity to travel seriously until retirement or the children have left home. However, there are a few points that the older traveller ought to consider before setting out.

First, weigh up carefully the **risks** of travelling, particularly if you suffer from a chronic illness. Although you're not necessarily more vulnerable to common travel illnesses, it will take your body longer to restore itself back to normal should you get ill. Be aware of how particular climates or environments (altitude, heat, pollution, long flights) may affect existing medical conditions.

▶▶ See also Altitude, p.91; Cold exposure, p.104; Fitness to fly, p.14; and Heat exposure, p.139.

The usual **pre-trip preparations** are particularly important for the mature traveller. Ensure you have the relevant immunizations and carry your personal medical details and any medications in a readily accessible place. Make sure that you have adequate travel insurance coverage and consider whether your levels of fitness are suitable for your planned activities – a foreign country is not the place to test your limits. Avoid overextending yourself by building more time for rest breaks into your itinerary.

Carry any necessary spares (spectacles, hearing-aid batteries etc) with you, as these may be difficult to obtain at your destination. Inform your travel agent or airline beforehand if you are likely to require assistance boarding the aircraft or carrying luggage. When flying or travelling in one position for any prolonged period, consider taking low-dose aspirin or wearing special support stockings to reduce the risk of a DVT (see p.111).

The elderly are regarded as more vulnerable by petty criminals so it's important to look streetwise and avoid risky areas.

▶▶ See Influenza (p.147).

The disabled traveller

There is no reason why anyone with a **disability**, major or minor, temporary or permanent, should be excluded from travelling abroad. True, the logistics may seem daunting at times, and planning must be thorough as well as flexible, but a positive, focused attitude goes a long way.

National associations and further information

As travel-related information can be hard to find on the websites listed below, we've given some navigation hints.

UK

Age Concern

1268 London Rd, London SW16 4EJ ☎020/8679 8000, ⊛www.ace.org.uk.
See factsheet 26 under "popular links", or enter "travel" in the search facility.

Help the Aged

St James's Walk, Clerkenwell Green, London EC1R 0BE ☎020/7253 0253, ⊛www.helptheaged.org.uk.
Click on "advice and info", and then "info point", and scroll down the list to the "leisure" heading.

USA

American Association of Retired Persons

601 East Street NW, Washington DC 20049 ☎800/424-3410, ⊛www.aarp.org.
Click on the "travel and leisure" link.

Australia and New Zealand

Age Concern New Zealand

Level 4, West Block, Education House, 178 Willis St, Wellington, New Zealand ☎04/801-9338, ⊛www.ageconcern.org.nz.

Council on the Aging

Level 2, 3 Bowen Crescent, Melbourne, Victoria 3004 ☎03/9820 2655, ⊛www.cota.org.au.

Be sensible and realistic in the **planning stage**. Acceptance and acknowledgement by all involved of your disabilities and limitations, coupled with a clear knowledge of what to expect at your destination, are crucial. You are the best judge of your abilities, but be careful not to overestimate them in the excitement of a trip abroad – don't forget how tiring travelling can be – mentally, physically and emotionally.

Much will depend on your specific disability and level of independence. How much help will be required at airports, during flights, in transit from the airport to accommodation and at the accommodation itself? Do you have specific requirements for accommodation, such as wheelchair access, ground-floor rooms, a lift, shower facilities or the ability of staff to speak your own language? Is it viable to consider travelling alone or will you need a helper? If so, do you have someone who can travel with you or do you need help finding someone? Finally, bear in mind that facilities for people with disabilities in your destination country may be inferior to those at home and perhaps even nonexistent.

All in all, the simplest, and perhaps safest, option is to travel with an **organized group**. This is especially relevant for the first-time traveller, as you instantly have access to help and support, and much of the planning and other preconsiderations are done for you. There are many companies that specialize in holidays for people with disabilities – see opposite for more information.

If you opt to **travel independently**, there are plenty of resources available – a good starting point is the national association for your particular disability (see opposite). They should be able to put you in touch with specialist travel agents, insurers and reciprocal organizations in your destination. There are also several more generalized organizations (see box below) which can provide independent advice. If you travel without the help of a specialized travel agent, it's important to inform the airline of your disability (if relevant to flying) when you book.

Don't overlook the possibility of loss of, or damage to, **vital equipment** such as wheelchairs, hearing aids, spectacles, splints etc. Will replacements be easy to find or will you have to carry spares? Make contingency plans just in case.

The **extra cost** of a holiday for someone who is disabled is difficult to avoid. There may be less choice in accommodation and the budget end of the market is less likely to have the necessary adaptations which you may require. The same will apply to eating out. You might also have to rely on more expensive means of transport such as taxis or tourist buses because of a lack of alternatives.

Checklist for travellers with disabilities

It may help to consider your own case in the context of the following:
+ Travel to and from destination
+ Mobility when you are there
+ Ability to self-care: washing, dressing etc
+ Medications
+ Equipment
+ Extra costs
+ Access to medical help
+ Special diets
+ Additional support required

The Disabled Traveller, by Alison Walsh, is an excellent general resource, packed full of contacts and sources of further information. You can order it from Disabled Traveller, PO Box 7, London W12 8UD.

US

⊕www.access-able.com

An invaluable web-based resource, with information on accommodation and local contacts, as well as databases of organized tours worldwide.

⊕www.makoa.org/travel.htm

Exhaustive collection of travel-related links.

Mobility International USA

451 Broadway, Eugene, OR 97401 ☏541/343-1284, ⊕www.miusa.org.

Information and referral services, access guides, tours and exchange programmes.

Society for the Advancement of Travelers with Handicaps

347 5th Ave, New York, NY 10016 ☏212/447-7284, ⊕www.sath.org.

Non-profit educational organization that has actively represented travellers with disabilities since 1976. Annual membership $45; $30 for students and seniors.

UK

Holiday Care

2nd floor, Imperial Building, Victoria Rd, Horley, Surrey RH6 7PZ

☏0845/124 9971 or ☏0208/760 0072, ⊕www.holidaycare.org.uk.

Provides free lists of accessible accommodation abroad – European, American and long haul destinations – plus a list of accessible attractions in the UK. Information on financial help for holidays available.

RADAR (Royal Association for Disability and Rehabilitation)

12 City Forum, 250 City Rd, London EC1V 8AF

☏020/7250 3222, minicom ☏020/7250 4119, ⊕www.radar.org.uk.

A good source of general advice on holidays and travel, RADAR also produces annual guides to holidays in the UK (£8), Europe (£11) and other overseas destinations (£15).

Tripscope

Alexandra House, Albany Rd, Brentford, Middlesex TW8 0NE

☏08457/585 641, ⊕www.tripscope.org.uk.

This registered charity provides a national telephone information service offering free advice on UK and international transport for those with a mobility problem.

⊕www.youreable.com

An excellent general reference resource, with a great section on travel – the pen-pal service could come in very useful.

Australia and New Zealand

ACROD (Australian Council for Rehabilitation of the Disabled)

PO Box 60, Curtin ACT 2605 ☏02/6282 4333 (also TTY), ⊕www.acrod.org.au.

Provides lists of travel agencies and tour operators for people with disabilities.

Disabled Persons Assembly

4/173–175 Victoria St, Wellington, New Zealand ☏04/801 9100 (also TTY), ⊕www.dpa.org.nz.

Resource centre with lists of travel agencies and tour operators for people with disabilities.

Travelling with children

Travelling with **children** can be a fun and an enriching experience, simply because they bring with them none of the "baggage" – preconceptions, anxieties and fears – which occupy adults on a trip. But it isn't always easy, and may be a very different proposition without careful planning and forethought.

For ease and convenience, **package tours** are difficult to beat. Many go out of their way to accommodate the needs of both children and their flagging parents, with organized activities for older kids and creche facilities on hand for the younger ones, so freeing up time for the parents to do what they like.

More ambitious **independent trips** need to be planned carefully, taking into account the age of the child, the mode of travel, the destination and the accommodation. Remember that the kinds of things that might interest you when travelling are unlikely to similarly impress children, and a bored child can ruin your enjoyment. Give careful thought to your itinerary, incorporating activities that will appeal to every family member. If possible, try to maintain some degree of **routine**, as children of all ages are happier if there is some semblance of predictability to the day, even if it's only meal times.

Children aged between 1 and 10 pose perhaps the greatest **potential difficulties**. They are mobile, past breast-feeding and need constant supervision and entertainment, and though unable to carry their own luggage, they will greatly add to yours. They are also inquisitive, constantly exploring and testing their environment (frequently sucking unwashed fingers), which means that they will be at greater risk of injury, cuts, bites, stings, infections and more. They are also more prone to diarrhoeal illnesses, overheating, dehydration and sunburn. A number of the more exotic infections, such as dengue fever or Japanese encephalitis, more commonly, or more seriously, affect young children.

Potential hazards

For toddlers especially, potential **hazards** lurk around every corner, and children of all ages are less wary of possible dangers. Play often takes place in long grass and other environments favoured by snakes and other creepy crawlies – while deaths from scorpion bites are rare they most commonly occur in children under 2 (always ensure that shoes or sandals are worn, even on the beach and when paddling).

Homeopathy for children

Children respond to **homeopathic remedies** (see p.44) extremely well and quickly, so if you're travelling with kids, it's well worth taking a homeopathic first-aid kit in order to treat the frequent minor ailments from which they tend to suffer. Particularly useful remedies include **Belladonna**, wonderful for a high temperature caused by an ear infection or tonsillitis, while **Colocynth** is excellent for tummy aches and colic in babies. Catarrh can be a real problem on a holiday because of the discomfort it causes when flying; **Pulsatilla** should clear it quickly. Teething problems respond well to **Chamomilla** 30c.

Because of the high level of dilution, the dosage for children and babies is exactly the same as for adults (a 30c potency given four times a day, or more frequently for very acute illness). As the tablets taste nice, and should be sucked not swallowed, getting children to take remedies should be no problem; for babies, simply crush the tablet between two spoons, and put the powder on the infant's tongue.

Animals are an irresistible draw to children, yet animal behaviour can be unpredictable, especially when startled. Keep a tight rein on children when animals are around and discourage them from approaching animals when they are on their own.

The importance of avoiding significant **sun exposure** at a young age cannot be overemphasized, as several studies have shown that excessive sun early in life predisposes to skin cancer in later years. Aim for indoor activities in the middle of the day when the sun is hottest, be sure to cover up exposed skin as much as possible, and apply high-protection sunscreen (see p.210) liberally and regularly when children are outside – coloured, spray-on sunscreens can make this otherwise onerous task more fun. Encourage hat-wearing at all times, and T-shirts when playing in the water. Fluid intake should be increased, and frequent rest periods in the shade should be encouraged.

Challenges en route

Arriving decidedly frazzled from your journey makes a very bad start to a holiday. **Plane**, **bus and rail travel** come with their own challenges, since children can be difficult to entertain for long periods in confined spaces, toilet facilities may be inadequate and food choices limited. Although inquisitiveness and excitement generally predominate, children can feel frightened and panicky in a closed and controlled environment such as an aircraft cabin; aisle seats are a good idea because they allow for greater mobility. Carry plenty of small toys, books or puzzles to keep young minds occupied. Reveal new toys or treats at intervals (hourly, for example) to combat boredom. Some of the medications used for motion sickness (eg antihistamines) can be usefully sedating, although many cannot be given to children under 2. Note that full-term babies should not fly until they are at least a week old; seek advice from your paediatrician before flying with a premature baby.

Motion sickness (see p.40) commonly affects children over 2, and is more of a problem at sea and on the road than in the air. Encourage children to lie down on boats as this reduces the effects of seasickness, and (if possible) always place travel cots parallel with the direction of travel. Good ventilation helps, as do plenty of distractions. Antihistamines, acupressure bands and ginger can be used as preventative measures.

Extra baggage is unavoidable and obviously depends on the age of the child, but consider the following:

- Toys, books and puzzles
- Food (bring along a few favourites)
- Bottles, sterilizing equipment and formula milk if appropriate
- Nappies (diapers)
- Wipes
- Changing mat
- Travel cot
- Children's medications
- High factor sunscreen

Immunizations, medications and medical advice

Like those for adults, **travel vaccinations** for children need to be planned well in advance of departure. Try to arrange your trip around the normal childhood vaccination programmes.

Unless you are directed to do so by a doctor, avoid giving children medicines bought over-the-counter abroad for children. Stick to what you know and pack the medicines you might normally use at home. If you suspect your child is significantly unwell whilst away, seek medical advice at once. Deterioration

Children's vaccinations

The country-by-country requirements are generally the same for children as they are for adults – your doctor will have access to the latest recommendations, and you can also check the websites listed on p.249.

Vaccine	Minimum age	Course
Cholera		
(Dukarol)	2 years	Three doses in 2–6 age group, 7–14 days apart; two doses in over 6 age group 7–14 days apart
(Mutacol)	2 years	Single dose
Hepatitis A	1 year (dependent on manufacturer)	Two doses, months 0 and 6 to 12 (for 10-year protection)
Hepatitis B	No lower limit	Three doses, at month 0 and either months 1 and 2 or 1 and 6
Japanese encephalitis (Biken)	1 year	Three doses, at day 0, day 7 and day 28
(Green Cross)	1 year	Two doses at day 0 and day 7 or 14
Meningococcal meningitis	2 months	One dose
Rabies	No lower limit	Three doses at day 0, day 7 and day 28
Tick-borne encephalitis	No lower limit	Two doses at weeks 0 and 4–12
Typhoid (oral)	6 years	Three doses; one capsule on days 0, 2 and 4
Typhoid (injected)	18 months (can be given earlier but there may be a weaker response)	One dose only
Yellow fever	9 months	One dose only

Note: BCG can be given at birth if the risk of exposure to TB is high.

can be rapid in children, so the "wait and see" tactic mustn't be applied in the same way as for adults.

Health risks for children

Children are prone to **stomach upsets**, due to their relatively weak immunity and because their concepts of hygiene are less sophisticated than those of adults. Diarrhoea can present a real threat to children, especially in hot climates, as they are more susceptible to **dehydration** than adults. Use an oral rehydration solution (see p.39) to both prevent and treat dehydration – never use blockers or ciprofloxacin. Don't starve them but offer (don't force) bland food such as dry biscuits, freshly boiled rice, potatoes or bread. If the diarrhoea persists or the child is showing signs of dehydration despite the use of rehydration solution, seek medical help urgently.

Signs of dehydration in children

+ Dry mouth and tongue
+ Skin loses elasticity
+ Eyes become sunken (as does the "soft spot" (fontanelle) on the top of babies' heads)
+ Weak, rapid pulse
+ Lethargy, drowsiness

Worm infections (see pp.226–233) are common in children because of their tendency to run around barefoot and their fondness for digging in sand and soil and handling food with mucky fingers.

Malaria is even more dangerous for children than for adults. Observe the normal anti-bite measures (see p.24), and if you can, stay out of moderate to high-risk malarial areas altogether with children under 2. **Insect repellents** containing DEET are the most effective, although advice regarding the strength of solutions safe to use on children is contradictory. Several studies have concluded that it is, by and large, a safe compound, the dangers of which have been exaggerated by the media. The ill-effects caused by DEET do not appear to be dose-related, although the general consensus is still to avoid unnecessarily high concentrations. Always follow the manufacturer's instructions.

▶▶ For more on DEET, see p.24.

The kind of **antimalarial** your doctor prescribes is principally dependent on the area to which you are travelling. As per adult guidelines, start your child on the course for the prescribed period before entering a malarial area, and continue it after you return as directed. No antimalarial is 100 percent effective, so suspicious symptoms whilst travelling, or for up to a year after returning, deserve a medical opinion.

▶▶ See Malaria, pp.163–169.

Medical kit for children

+ Paediatric paracetamol (acetaminophen in US), or paediatric ibuprofen
+ Calamine lotion
+ Paediatric antihistamine syrup, useful for motion sickness, allergies or insect bites. Of the many varieties, chlorpheniramine is one of the few suitable for children under 2
+ Antihistamine cream
+ Rehydration solution sachets
+ A plentiful supply of plasters and antiseptic
+ Polythene freezer bags – useful on long journeys in case of motion sickness or to wrap up soiled clothing
+ Baby wipes
+ Thermometer
+ Nappy/diaper rash cream
Always store medications in child-proof containers out of reach of inquisitive hands.

Antimalarial recommendations for children

Malarone and **Mefloquine** dosage relates to body weight only; dosages of **25/62.5mg Malarone paediatric**, and **Mefloquine scored** tablets are as follows:

Malarone (25/62.5mg)	Mefloquine
Under 11kg: not recommended	Under 5kg: not recommended
11–20kg: 1 tablet daily	5–19kg: 62.5mg once weekly
21–30kg: 2 tablets once daily	20–30kg: 125mg once weekly
31–40kg: 3 tablets once daily	31–45kg: 187.5mg once weekly
more than 40kg: adult dose	more than 45kg: adult dose

Chloroquine/ Proguanil

Age	Weight	
0–5 weeks	–	1/8 adult dose
6–52 wks	Up to 10kg	1/4 adult dose
1–5 yrs	11–19kg	1/2 adult dose
		then 1/4 adult dose
6–11 yrs	20–39kg	3/4 adult dose

The same cautions, limitations and side effects for these drugs detailed in the Medical kit (see pp.41) apply to children. Doxycycline should not be given to children under 12.

Nutrition for children

Feeding your child abroad often requires meticulous organization and an obsession with all things clean and sterile. Travelling with an infant needs careful planning around feeding schedules, as a hungry child is likely to make life difficult for everyone.

Although travelling with a child young enough to be breast-fed is hard work, **breast-feeding** is safe, convenient and guarantees adequate nutrition. Try and respect local customs regarding the social acceptability of public breast-feeding. Breast-feeding mothers must drink plenty of safe fluids in hot climates to avoid disturbing the milk flow. Bear in mind that some drugs penetrate breast milk and are therefore best avoided (see the box opposite).

Bottle feeding, on the other hand, can present a number of difficulties. First, you have to carry enough formula milk to last the trip unless you can be certain of obtaining it at your destination; secondly, sterilization of the bottles and teats needs at least as much attention as you would give at home, which may mean carrying lots of unwieldy equipment. Remember that bottled water is not sterile and feeds should always be made up from boiled water. In countries where the local water is unreliable, boil bottled water. Refrigeration of made-up bottles can also present a problem – try to cool the bottles as quickly as possible and store them at low temperatures, although it is best to make up fresh bottles in response to demand – if need be, carry the sterile bottles of cooled water with you and add pre-measured powder only when you need it.

As for adults, a child's **fluid requirements** increase in hot climates, which means that bottle- or breast-fed infants may need top-ups of boiled (bottled) water.

When buying **bottled water**, use still water as opposed to carbonated for young children and always check that the cap seal is intact. Some mineral

Drugs to avoid when breast-feeding

It's best to avoid taking any drugs when breast-feeding unless they are absolutely necessary – if in doubt, always check with a doctor or pharmacist. The following list details drugs that are most likely to be of relevance to the breast-feeding traveller – it's by no means comprehensive. Note that all homeopathic remedies are safe to use.

+ Alcohol (large amounts may affect the baby and reduce milk consumption)
+ Antihistamines (these penetrate milk but are not known to be harmful, although some manufacturers advise avoidance)
+ Aspirin
+ Ciprofloxacin
+ Chloramphenicol
+ Combined oral contraceptive pill
+ Diazepam and temazepam
+ Doxycycline and other tetracycline antibiotics
+ Ibuprofen (high doses or prolonged course)
+ Malarone
+ Metoclopramide
+ Metronidazole
+ Oral steroids (eg dexamethsone)
+ Propranolol (high doses)
+ Senna
+ Vitamins A and D (high doses)

waters contain high concentrations of chemical elements, and it's worth noting that for children, the sodium concentration should be no higher than 15mg/100ml, the potassium no higher than 2mg/100ml and the nitrates no more than 5mg/100ml.

If you're feeding your child with ready-prepared jars of baby food, you may have to take a supply with you unless you can be sure of finding suitable substitutes abroad. Older children should follow the usual food guidelines as adults – see p.21. Take particular care with locally made fruit beverages, ice cream, milk shakes, ice in drinks and seafood. Also note that children can contract botulism from inadequately processed honey. It's a good idea to take along a few familiar items of food from home for treats, bribes, in the event of illness or if local offerings are refused.

Women travellers

Although sexual equality is rapidly becoming a global phenomenon, there are some important practical issues that women travellers should consider before leaving home. **Personal safety** should be at the top of the list of priorities.

It's crucial to do some **pre-trip research** on your chosen destination. Are you likely to be hassled for money or sexually harassed? Developing countries may have a different opinion of the position of women in society than you're used to at home – this may in fact mean more respect for women, but different expectations. The pervasive, male-dominated culture in some countries can make life difficult for Western women, even if you are travelling in a group or with male companions. Carry a rape alarm at all times (although remember that a rape alarm doesn't confer instant protection – it's only useful if there is someone around to hear it), and always be aware of cultural assumptions about yourself. Avoid wearing jewellery that will attract attention, and ensure your clothing is appropriate to local customs. Hitch hiking is never recommended, especially if you are travelling alone. Women may be perceived as easier targets by pickpockets, thieves and other petty criminals, so try to look confident, purposeful and streetwise.

Menstruation

Travelling any great distance, especially by plane, can disturb the body's natural patterns and rhythms, and **menstruation** is no exception. Periods can become erratic, although regularity will be maintained if you take the combined oral contraceptive pill (see Contraception, p.28). A poor diet with significant weight loss, or strenuous physical activity, may lead to missed periods (but remember that the number one cause of a missed period is, of course, pregnancy).

It can be difficult to find **tampons** in some countries (particularly in isolated, rural areas), so take enough with you from home. Always wash your hands before changing a tampon to reduce the risk of infection.

If you are due to have a period at a particularly difficult or inconvenient time, and are not taking the contraceptive pill, norethisterone, available on prescription only, can **delay your period**. A progestagen (one of the hormones used in the contraceptive pill), its limitations and side effects are similar. Dosage is 5mg taken three times daily from three days before your period is due to start to the day before you wish it to start. There are a number of contraindications and side effects (although rare), and these should be discussed with your doctor beforehand. You should not delay your period using norethisterone for more than fourteen consecutive days.

Period pains are no more likely to affect you when travelling than they are at home. If you regularly suffer from bad pains, however, discuss pain relief with your doctor before leaving home. NSAIDs (see p.34) are particularly effective, while paracetamol or co-proxamol also offer some relief.

Homeopathic remedies can also be useful: try Belladonna 30c for sudden throbbing pain starting before the bleeding, which is usually bright red and copious. If the pain is colicky in nature, and relieved by doubling up and pressure, try Colocynth 30c. For extremely severe pain, associated with vomiting and diarrhoea, with extreme prostration, Veratrum album 30c is invaluable. Take the most appropriate remedy every half hour until improvement, then decrease to four times a day until complete relief.

For information on vaginal thrush, see p.213; for cystitis p.224; and for STDs pp.197–201.

Gynaecological problems

▶▶ See also Urinary tract infections, p.224.

Caused by bacterial infection within the pelvic cavity (usually affecting the uterus and fallopian tubes), **pelvic inflammatory disease (PID)** is a common complication of chlamydia and gonorrhoea infections. It is usually, although not invariably, acquired sexually. An ongoing, chronic form can cause considerable internal scarring and may seriously affect your fertility. Acutely, the common **symptoms** are pain on intercourse, vaginal discharge which may be smelly, bloody or purulent, fever and lower abdominal pain (often unilateral), which is partially relieved by lying on your back with your legs flexed, or in the foetal position.

Short-term **complications of PID** include septicaemia and the formation of a pelvic abscess, while there's a long-term risk of internal scarring, increasing the risk of infertility and ectopic pregnancy – prompt treatment is necessary. If PID is suspected, seek medical help to establish the exact identity of the offending organism. **Treatment** involves rehydration, pain relief and antibiotics. Ideally it's better to wait until the underlying cause is known before commencing antibiotics, but in practice antibiotics are usually commenced once the necessary swabs have been taken but before the results are available. In the UK a fourteen-day course is commonly used, involving various combinations of metronidazole, ofloxacin (related to ciprofloxacin) and doxycycline. Intravenous antibiotics may be needed. Diagnosis and treatment of PID should be supervised by a doctor. In an emergency, if medical help is difficult to access, commence a combination of oral metronidazole 400–500mg three times a day and doxycycline 100mg daily (or erythromycin) for seven to fourteen days. Ciprofloxacin 500mg as a single dose is effective against gonorrhoea.

Lymphoedema

If you have had surgery for **breast cancer** which involved removal of the lymph nodes, you must be particularly careful to avoid insect bites on the relevant arm. The local swelling caused by a bite will normally dissipate quickly via the lymph system, but if this has been disrupted by surgery, the swelling will remain and there is an increased risk of secondary infection. Cover up and use DEET liberally.

 If you do get bitten, **Apis mel** 30c is a useful homeopathic treatment to reduce the swelling. Use four times a day until improvement.

Further information

Pregnancy

A normal **pregnancy** lasts for forty weeks (averaging 269 days from conception), and is frequently accompanied by a number of unwelcome physical symptoms. Breast tenderness, urinary frequency and fatigue are particularly common in the first three months. Nausea and vomiting can occur from as early as two weeks after conception but usually subside after three months. Antisickness drugs are best avoided (a good general rule of thumb in pregnancy – although homeopathic remedies are safe to use at any stage); however promethazine may be used if the symptoms are particularly severe. The main danger if vomiting is frequent or persistent is **dehydration**, which, in some rare cases, can be severe enough to merit hospital admission. If you have severe sickness, it would be sensible to defer your trip until the symptoms settle. Other common problems in pregnancy include swollen ankles, back pain and constipation. A craving for sometimes strange foods, a condition known as "pica", can occur, as can revulsion for previously favourite foods.

The **safest time to travel** in pregnancy is between weeks 14 and 28. In the early weeks, there is a risk of miscarriage or ectopic pregnancy – neither are brought on by travelling itself but both require medical help and you need to consider how you'd cope if the worst happened while you're abroad. Premature labour is a risk in late pregnancy and no airlines will allow you to take an international flight after 36 weeks' gestation; note also that some airlines routinely require certification from your doctor specifying the expected date of delivery. Don't travel at any stage in your pregnancy if your blood pressure is high, if you have experienced vaginal bleeding at any point, if your previous pregnancies have had complications, or if you are diabetic, epileptic or severely anaemic. It's worth considering that in the later stages of pregnancy, some countries may require written evidence from your doctor confirming your expected date of delivery – without it, they may refuse entry. Check with the relevant embassy before departure.

It's sensible not to veer too far off the beaten track (or more pertinently, from medical assistance) in the first few weeks of pregnancy, as the chances of a problem arising that will require medical attention are higher during this period. Consider the expense and expertise of the medical services that are going to be available to you, as well as the potential risks of a post-miscarriage blood transfusion, should it be required. Always carry a letter from your doctor or (preferably) a copy of your pregnancy records.

Insurance is dependent on individual company policy. Most companies do not surcharge premiums because of pregnancy, although they often won't cover you if you travel too close to your due date. Should you become pregnant after taking out insurance, most policies cover cancellation of your trip due to pregnancy if you have a supporting letter from your doctor.

Miscarriage, ectopic pregnancy and premature birth

The early part of pregnancy is the most risky time and **miscarriage** is, sadly, a frequent occurrence (miscarriages are estimated to occur in one in five pregnancies). It is very rare for a miscarriage to occur after the fourteenth week of pregnancy. The most common reason for miscarriage is abnormality in the developing foetus, rather than anyone doing anything wrong. As there is no way of medically averting a miscarriage, pregnant travellers are no more at risk than anybody else. However, it is important to consider what would happen if you did miscarry while travelling. The bleeding can sometimes be severe, even life-threatening, so urgent medical help may be required. An operation to clear the uterus from any debris left behind (a dilatation and curettage, or "D&C") may be necessary. If your blood group is rhesus negative, you will require an injection of an immunoglobulin ("anti-D" or "Rho-GAM") to prevent the formation of antibodies against your baby's blood group and thus avoid potential problems in subsequent pregnancies. Apart from the physical effects of miscarriage such as heavy or continuous blood loss, the **psychological distress** and feelings of guilt can take a long time to overcome. Although unfounded, you may blame yourself if you have taken unnecessary risks or pushed yourself too hard in the time leading up to the miscarriage. Try and avoid thinking in terms of "if only I hadn't . . .", which only results in even more distress about something that may have been inevitable.

Ectopic pregnancy occurs when the fertilized egg embeds itself and starts to grow somewhere outside the uterus (usually the fallopian tube, the canal that carries the egg from the ovary to the uterus). It occurs in about one in 200

Vaccinations in pregnancy

If you're pregnant (or if you could be), always inform your doctor prior to any vaccination. In all cases the theoretical risk of vaccination in pregnancy should be weighed against the potential risks from the disease.

The following vaccinations are deemed **safe** provided you are **more** than 12 weeks pregnant:

+ injectable typhoid
+ hepatitis A and B
+ influenza
+ diphtheria
+ rabies
+ meningococcal meningitis polysaccharide
+ tetanus

Avoid the following live vaccinations at any stage in your pregnancy, although yellow fever and oral polio can be considered after the first twelve weeks if the risks of exposure are high (get expert advice):

+ yellow fever
+ oral typhoid
+ oral polio
+ BCG
+ MMR (measles, mumps, rubella)

As a general rule of thumb, it's best to avoid taking any **drugs** in pregnancy (though homeopathic remedies are safe). If you do need medication, seek medical advice before taking anything, and always follow prescribed doses religiously. Below is a list of medications mentioned elsewhere in this book, showing which are safe in pregnancy and which are not.

Safe in pregnancy:

+ Chloroquine
+ Proguanil (provided you take it with a folic acid 5mg daily supplement)
+ Amoxicillin
+ Erythromycin
+ Paracetamol
+ Some antihistamines (read the label closely, and follow the manufacturer's advice concerning pregnancy)

Avoid in pregnancy:

+ Mefloquine* (for the first three months)
+ Doxycycline and other tetracycline antibiotics
+ Malarone **
+ Ciprofloxacin
+ Trimethoprim (theoretical risk in the first twelve weeks)
+ Chloramphenicol
+ Co-amoxiclav
+ Ibuprofen (and the other NSAIDs)
+ loperamide
+ Acetazolamide
+ Nifedipine
+ Diazepam
+ Iodine preparations for water purification

*The manufacturer advises avoidance of pregnancy when taking mefloquine and for three months after treatment, although studies have shown no harmful effects in humans. If travel to a chloroquine-resistant malarial area cannot be avoided, it may be an option in the later stages of pregnancy but seek expert advice.

** Manufacturer advises avoid in pregnancy unless there is no suitable alternative.

If you're taking a potentially hazardous medication and find that you're unexpectedly pregnant, seek medical advice immediately.

Although concerns have been raised about the use of DEET-based insect repellents in pregnancy, the scientific evidence available to date indicates that **DEET is safe in pregnancy**. Weaker concentrations are recommended in pregnancy as a precautionary measure. For information on repellents without DEET, see p.153.

pregnancies, and you are at increased risk if you've had previous ectopic pregnancies, pelvic infections (PID) or gynaecological surgery. It usually manifests as intense, usually one-sided lower abdominal pain, followed by bleeding. Other secondary symptoms – dizziness, faintness, pallor, sweating, shaking and nausea and vomiting – can occur. The condition is life-threatening, so if you suffer severe lower abdominal pain within the first twelve weeks of pregnancy, seek medical help urgently.

Premature birth occurs much less often than the problems associated with early pregnancy but even so, no airline will let you fly if you're more than 36 weeks. As pregnancy proceeds, the frequency of medical monitoring increases, so stay close to your hospital or doctor's surgery in the final weeks.

Specific health risks in pregnancy

Diet is an area of concern in any pregnancy, but while travelling you are less in control over what you eat and its origins. It's easy to become paranoid and either not eat anything or restrict your diet to "safe" foods (dry biscuits, bananas and the like) so that nutritional value is compromised. If you think that the food choices in your destination may be limited, consult your doctor or midwife prior to departure to discuss supplements. As at home, aim to eat a balanced diet, avoiding unpasteurized milk and cheese, paté, raw eggs, liver and any undercooked meat. In countries where you have concerns about basic hygiene or water purity, steer clear of fruit or vegetables that cannot be peeled. **Listeriosis**, which can result in damage to the growing foetus and even stillbirth, is caused by the bacteria *listeria monocytogenes*, high levels of which are found in some foods. Likely suspects include cheese (especially camembert, brie and blue-veined varieties), paté, and ready-cooked and chilled meals unless reheated until piping hot. Sheep can carry listeria, too, so avoid direct contact (during lambing in particular).

Toxoplasmosis causes a mild flu-like illness in pregnant women but can lead to significant abnormalities in the newborn. The bacteria causing toxoplasmosis can be found in raw meat, goats' milk and cat faeces. Avoid eating undercooked meat, unpasteurized goats' milk or cheese, and vegetables that have not been adequately cleaned. Like listeriosis, sheep can carry toxoplasmosis, so contact should be avoided.

Malaria in pregnancy can be very dangerous, both to mother and baby, and unless your trip is vital, you should avoid visiting high-risk areas. All types of malaria can lead to miscarriage or premature delivery. Mothers often become very anaemic, and the baby is frequently underweight at birth. Pregnant women are particularly susceptible to the complications of falciparum malaria, including hypoglycaemia and the accumulation of fluid in the lungs. Although rare, malaria can be passed on to the baby who may suffer fever, anaemia and failure to thrive.

If there is no option but to travel to a malarial area, then effective drug prophylaxis is important: chloroquine and proguanil can be taken without concern (although take 5mg daily of **folic acid** in conjunction with proguanil). Mefloquine and Malarone must only be used where other options have been exhausted and then only after careful consideration and expert advice; the manufacturer of mefloquine advises avoidance in the first three months of pregnancy even though no scientific evidence of harmful effects to the foetus has been demonstrated. Doxycycline should not be taken at any stage of pregnancy. There's not enough data on the effects of atovaquone/proguanil in pregnancy, so the manufacturer advises avoidance unless essential.

Diarrhoea presents no significant increased risk in pregnancy although it is important to avoid dehydration (see p.113). Ciprofloxacin and loperamide should be avoided in pregnancy. Always remember to wipe yourself from front to back to avoid spreading infection to the vagina and urinary tract.

Constipation is a fairly common problem in pregnancy. Some laxatives (eg lactulose) are safe to use if you're pregnant (read box labels closely), but it's best to treat the problem by increasing your fibre and fluid intake.

+ Travel light
+ Allow extra time in transit (don't rush)
+ Allow for increased frequency of toilet stops
+ Stay close to medical care
+ Carry safe water and snacks in case of airport delays etc

Thrush is common during pregnancy, especially in hot climates. Wear loose-fitting clothes and, if symptoms occur, use antifungal creams or pessaries (both are safe in pregnancy) – clotrimazole is usually a good option.

Pregnancy alone carries a five-fold increase in the risk of **DVT** (see p.111), and it's important to bear this in mind before you expose yourself to other risk factors like long periods of limited mobility (flying, bus or rail travel), altitude and dehydration.

Finally, a brief word of warning to **frequent fliers** who may be pregnant. Air travel exposes you to higher levels of cosmic **radiation** than at sea level, and although there is no definite proof of this being harmful, the cumulative effect of frequent flights, especially in the all-important first three months of a pregnancy, may have detrimental effects on the foetus.

Pregnancy and leisure pursuits

Think carefully before you partake in any vigorous exercise or activity if you're pregnant. Travelling to high **altitudes** will increase the risk of DVT, put more stress on the cardiovascular system and often remove you from quick access to medical care. **Scuba diving** can cause decompression sickness in the foetus and therefore should be avoided. **Snow skiing** accidents are often caused by other people, so regardless of your own competence as a skier, there is always a risk of trauma which could be damaging to the foetus. **Hot tubs and saunas** should be avoided in the first three months of pregnancy because they can raise your core temperature, which increases the risk of birth defects; in later pregnancy, a raised core temperature can trigger fainting. **Jacuzzis** and **spas** should be viewed with equal caution because of the risk of acquiring infection.

For general advice on travelling whilst pregnant, visit ⓦwww.fitfortravel.scot.nhs.uk or ⓦwww.tripprep.com. A valuable resource for all pregnant women, be they travelling or not, is the *Rough Guide to Pregnancy and Birth* by Kaz Cooke.

The gap year traveller

Taking a **year out** before continuing with secondary education or a career is becoming an increasingly popular pursuit, and for most people, foreign travel is top of the "must do" list.

There are many factors that set gap year travellers apart from regular vacationers, some of which may increase the risk of falling ill whilst abroad. Firstly, **money** is usually tight: many gap year travellers try to exist on a paltry or sometimes unfeasible budget, which obviously has negative implications for health. Right from the beginning, it's important to be wary of making false economies: initial outlay on vaccinations and malaria prophylaxis may well prevent you from having to shell out potentially huge amounts for treatment whilst abroad, and having all the necessary jabs means that illness is a lot less likely to ruin what should be a once-in-a-lifetime experience. Once on the road, don't attempt to save money with obviously dodgy substandard meals or run-down, unsanitary accommodation, and think carefully before exposing yourself to unnecessary risks such as hitchhiking. The key is to make sure that your budget is appropriate for your destination and your plans – money will go a lot further backpacking in India than in Australia – and to include a little extra for unforeseen emergencies or must-do side trips.

As most of those who take a year out are fairly young, the gap year trip often represents the first independent journey abroad – and **inexperienced** travellers are much more likely to make basic mistakes which put health at risk. Prepare yourself for what lies ahead by researching your destination obsessively. Guidebooks tailor-made for inexperienced travellers can be particularly helpful in ensuring you avoid the pitfalls of travel as well as the strain of culture shock (Rough Guides' First-Time series has titles on Europe, Latin America, Asia, as well as Around the World).

As with most travel health issues, a little **planning and forethought** go a long way on a gap year – make sure that you have a firm plan about what you would do if you fall ill, and that your insurance cover is adequate for all activities in which you might indulge. Finally, remember that it's not obligatory to rise to every dangerous challenge that comes your way – extreme sports are something of a mixed blessing when it comes to health.

Further information

ⓦwww.gapyear.com
Everything the experienced traveller could wish for: free membership entitles you to use the site for private messages, find travel companions and use the message boards, while planning tools include destination advice, placement information and packing suggestions.

ⓦwww.gap.org.uk
Very much along the same lines as the above, but concentrating on the nitty gritty of the gap year (volunteer projects and the like) rather than special offers and features. Excellent travel health advice.

The business traveller

The basic health risks faced by backpackers on a budget are far greater than for those travelling on expense accounts, but **business travel** nonetheless carries its own particular hazards. Living out of a suitcase and staring at an endless succession of hotel room walls can be acutely stressful, and as time is often at a premium, ridiculous deadlines often add to the mental burden of business travel.

Although coverage by company health insurance usually means that it's relatively easy to find medical help while abroad without the added worry of cost, business travellers should nonetheless abide by the same basic rules concerning food/water- and insect- borne diseases as other travellers. However, the main potential dangers are the immediate and long-term **psychological effects** of business travel. Prolonged separation from family and friends, fatigue, jet lag and exposure to sometimes shocking levels of working practices and poverty can lead to depression or a search for solace via dietary excesses, smoking, alcohol abuse or the use of prostitutes. Unfortunately, because most of the stresses faced by business travellers are beyond their control, awareness and avoiding the path of least resistance when it comes to letting off steam are the only ways to steer clear of such potential pitfalls. Try to embrace new cultures, and view new projects and environments as an education rather than a problem to be overcome. When timetables are self-imposed, make sure that you allocate reasonable amounts of time for rest, recuperation and recreation. If possible, avail yourself of some of the luxuries occasionally afforded to business travel such as hotel pool facilities, gyms or saunas. If your schedule is particularly punishing, consider using melatonin (see p.20) to counteract the ill effects of jet lag. Frequent flyers who may be pregnant should pay particular attention to the risks of air travel; see p.74 for more information.

The active traveller

Happiness for some is two weeks' grilling themselves on a beach, but for others, **activity holidays** hold greater appeal. If your trip involves any kind of physical pursuit, make sure that you are in good shape and up to the job before you go. While a high level of fitness is rarely required, a little forward thinking and gentle training will help you make the most of your holiday.

Concentrate on the parts of your body that will see the most action – **snow skiing** puts particular strain on the knees and should not be undertaken if you have weak or injured knee ligaments. Snow skiing also carries the inherent environmental risks associated with altitude (see p.91) and cold (see p.104). Avalanches are a hazard if you ski off-piste. Remember, also, that the adverse effects of the sun (p.209) are multiplied by altitude and by the glare of the snow, so protect your skin with high-factor sunscreen, your lips with lip balm and your eyes with good-quality sunglasses.

Climbing and **hill walking** are hard on the knees and ankles and may involve ascent to high altitudes, which in itself can cause significant health problems (see p.91). Other common health issues include gastrointestinal upsets (pp.131–137), sun exposure (p.209), muscle and ligament sprains (p.242) and backache (p.95). Dry mountain air may also cause nosebleeds (p.245). Remember that you may be a long way from medical help with very limited options for rapid evacuation. Always carry the necessary, good-quality equipment to suit your requirements (including a medical kit), and be wary of environmental dangers such as landslides and avalanches.

Seawater sports expose you to a host of saltwater hazards (see p.187), while the glare of the sun on the water makes a high-factor (water-resistant) sunscreen essential (see p.210).

Freshwater sports like canoeing or whitewater rafting carry the risk of infections from the water itself, including all of the water-borne diseases (see

---

Further information

For good general information on the health hazards of business travel, visit ⓦwww.fitfortravel.scot.nhs.uk and click on "special travellers". In addition to an exhaustive list of links, ⓦwww.businesstravel.about.com also has information on everything from hiring a pet sitter to chartering a private jet.

@**www.mtsinai.org**

This hospital website contains an amazingly detailed synopsis of the medical considerations surrounding diving, as well as an impressive number of useful links. Scroll down the menu on the left, and click on "pulmonary medicine" then "scuba diving".

@**www.scubadiving.com**

Run by Rodales Scuba Diving Magazine, this is a great all-round site for divers, which usually has some health-related articles amongst its regularly updated content.

p.21), leptospirosis (p.160) and schistosomiasis (p.194).

Strong currents can present a significant hazard when swimming in the sea or in fresh water. Remember that your buoyancy is less in fresh water so you might find swimming harder work.

Scuba diving

Scuba diving can be physically strenuous and requires moderate degrees of respiratory and cardiovascular fitness, and any disease or illness which affects your heart or lungs may therefore put you at risk when diving. Do not dive if you suffer from angina, abnormal heart rhythms, severe asthma or chronic lung disease, or if you have had a punctured lung in the past. If you are epileptic, diabetic, suffer from sickle-cell disease, or simply have doubts about your general level of fitness, seek expert advice. If you suffer from panic attacks, anxiety or claustrophobia, then scuba diving is not for you – a rapid ascent during a panic attack underwater is very dangerous.

Because of the pressure changes that take place when you dive, air pockets in the body contract on your way down and expand on surfacing. This can lead to "**squeeze**", a painful condition caused by the sinuses and nasal air passages being blocked, and which can result in damage to the eardrums – don't dive if you have a cold or severe nasal congestion. Always breathe in a steady, measured rhythm into your scuba gear. Never hold your breath as you surface because the expansion of the gas in your lungs will cause a **pneumothorax** (punctured lung), which can be life-threatening.

Decompression sickness ("the bends" or "the staggers") is caused by surfacing too rapidly after diving at depth for prolonged or repeated periods. Bubbles of gases such as nitrogen and helium lodge in the tissues, causing a variety of symptoms which can occur minutes – or hours – after a dive. Mild decompression sickness may cause skin mottling, itching, and joint pains. More serious effects include neurological impairment (blindness, partial paralysis and abnormal sensation), breathing difficulties and chest pain. Oxygen should be given as an emergency treatment, although most cases will require specialist treatment in a decompression chamber. Decompression sickness can be avoided by adhering strictly to **diving decompression tables**. The same tables enable you to calculate when it's safe to fly after scuba diving.

After diving, the length of time you must wait before **flying** depends on how deep the dive was, and how long you were under water (consult decompression tables). You should not fly for at least ten days after suffering even mild symptoms of "the bends" or "the staggers".

For information on saltwater hazards, see p.187.

" My Right Foot "

It was my first backpacking holiday as such – a fantastic three weeks in Malaysia. From Kuala Lumpur to Taman Negara Rainforest, on to the East Coast (Mersing), nine days on Tioman Island and finishing with a visit to Singapore. For a first-timer I was quite proud of myself – no lost or stolen gear and no sickness to report. Until, that is, I got home . . .

A few days before I left Tioman I noticed a small hard lump underneath the big toe of my right foot. Being a novice to the tropics and ignorant of the possible dangers, I put it down to excessive use of unfamiliar footwear (flip-flops are not big in Bristol). Besides, it didn't hurt and it certainly wasn't going to spoil my holiday.

One night, two or three weeks after my return, I lay awake for several uncomfortable hours, constantly scratching the aforementioned lump. By the morning I awoke to find a small inflammation, almost like an infected vein, had developed across the top of my foot. My work colleagues displayed a deflating mixture of disinterest and unhelpfulness, so I visited my local chemist, explained the situation and walked away with some athlete's foot ointment (ME, an athlete?).

For the next few days I watched as this inflammation spread, now accompanied by a distinct tingling feeling. With the ointment making no impression I decided that my only course of action was to visit my doctor. Again, my first visit proved fruitless and I walked away with a second ointment (containing exactly the same drug as the earlier, and considerably cheaper, chemist's version).

My unease persisted so I sought the advice of a medically qualified friend who claimed to have some knowledge of tropical illnesses. He felt that I may have contracted something more serious and suggested another visit to my own doctor. This time I mentioned that I had recently returned from Malaysia (by now some six weeks ago) and he seemed slightly more interested in my concerns (by now growing at a serious rate).

A call to the local infectious diseases clinic proved fruitless (the two doctors there were both off sick!) and it took another four days before a doctor in Birmingham diagnosed hookworm infestation over the phone. I was then whisked back into the surgery, where my foot was duly photographed for a medical journal and I was asked to come back later that evening so that I could be paraded around a room of medical students.

Eventually I was given the correct prescription and within three days the worm had died. By that time it had been moving around inside my foot for nearly three weeks and had caused me considerable angst and discomfort. I was left with a feeling of betrayal by the attitudes of my so-called "carers" at home and still maintain a healthy distrust of medical opinion. Ironically, my original speculation about overusing my flip-flops turned out to be the exact opposite of the truth!

Tom Edwards, Bristol, UK

The returning traveller

Unless you are suffering suspicious symptoms, there is little value in seeing your doctor routinely on returning from a trip. Many travel-related illnesses have long periods of incubation and may not become apparent for weeks or even months after you return.

View any subsequent illness with high suspicion, however. Of particular significance are **diarrhoea**, **fever**, **jaundice**, **weight loss** and **rashes**. There are between one and two thousand cases of malaria imported into the UK each year – anyone who suffers a fever after returning from a malarial area should be tested for the disease. Bear in mind, though, that it's one thing to recognize the possibility of imported infection yourself, but it may well be quite another convincing your **doctor**. Exotic illnesses are unlikely to be prominent in the thoughts of many family doctors unless you put them there. Always tell your doctor where you have been, how long you were away, when you returned and what risks you may have subjected yourself to – and always speak up if you have a particular concern about a specific disease: a malaria test could save your life.

If you received **medical treatment abroad**, ensure that you obtain written details (preferably in your own language) of the diagnosis and treatment received so that you can pass these on to your home doctor. If you're a **blood donor**, you must inform the transfusion service that you recently travelled abroad and whether or not you received any medical treatment while away.

2

A–Z

Making a diagnosis

Away from the familiarities of home, detached from the people who would normally care for you and from your customary means of summoning medical help, the feeling of isolation when you fall ill abroad can be devastating – and even though you may be in frail health, important decisions have to be made. Do you attempt self-diagnosis and treatment? Do you cut your losses and bolt for home, or do you battle it out with a potentially expensive and perhaps under-resourced or poorly trained local health-care system?

This section is designed not to frighten but to prepare you for the eventuality of being ill abroad, by providing an **A to Z** of diseases with information on their avoidance and treatment as well as the areas of the world where they pose the greatest risk. However, there is no point being conversant with every possible ailment if you don't know what **practical steps** to take should you fall ill abroad. Cutting through all of the other anxieties that will go through your head, what you really need to know is:

✚ Is my life in danger?

✚ What can I do about it?

✚ Do I need medical help now?

Initial assessment

Proper **assessment** of an illness involves extensive training and experience, and while a book can never replace a doctor, it can help you to follow a logical train of thought with respect to your symptoms, and so make a more informed decision about what further help or treatment may be necessary.

The first step is to examine the **risks** to which you have been exposed. Keep it simple, and don't go chasing the minutiae until you have excluded the most likely cause.

Consider first **where** you have travelled and the possible diseases to which you may have been vulnerable as a consequence. (Reading through Part 3 will give you an idea of the geographical distribution of the various diseases.) Next, consider whether you may have exposed yourself to added risk through your **accommodation** (eg no mosquito nets) or **activities** (eg whitewater rafting or swimming in polluted water). **Food- and water-borne illnesses** are extremely common, especially if you've been slack in observing basic precautions. Most travellers to hot countries suffer **insect bites**; as insects,

---

When to wait and when to seek urgent help

Time is both a good assessment tool and, in the majority of cases, a healer. In terms of infectious disease, however, there are, arguably, only a few illnesses which **will not wait**: suspected **meningitis**, **rabies**, **falciparum malaria**, **anaphylaxis**, **envenomation** (from a snake, spider, marine creature etc), **acute abdominal pain** and **chest pain**, if the cause may be cardiac. If any of these is a possibility, put the book down and get help immediately. This is not to say that many of the other infectious diseases detailed in this section are not dangerous or even life-threatening, but there are relatively few that will lead to serious problems within the **first 48 hours**. Note that severe dehydration and acute mountain sickness are also serious conditions which require quick action; see pp.113 and 91 for advice.

particularly mosquitoes, can be disease carriers, consider the possibility of malaria, yellow fever or dengue if you develop a high temperature after being bitten. Ask yourself if you did all you could to avoid illness in terms of **immunizations** and **malaria prophylaxis**. Note also that you may be more vulnerable to, or have put yourself at increased risk from, diseases as a result of other **high-risk activities**. Contact with animals, walking barefoot in the tropics, contact with fresh water in areas where there is schistosomiasis, and sex with a new partner would all fall into this category. Finally, some **pre-existing illnesses** will affect disease susceptibility. Being HIV-positive or diabetic, for instance, increases your chances of contracting infections and often results in more severe illness, while the elderly and the very young may also have increased susceptibility to some illnesses.

It's worth remembering that a "disease" is simply a specific group of **symptoms** arising from a particular cause. Looking at your symptoms, ask yourself if there is an obvious likely cause. This is a simple enough question in principle but not always easy to answer. Consider the nature, severity, timing and associations of your symptoms, and any familiarity there might be with previous illness.

The next stage in assessing an illness is to perform an **examination** in order to confirm or deny your working diagnosis. Examining yourself may not be practical, so enlist sensible help if necessary. Obviously training and experience are big factors here but there are a few basics that might help the novice.

Skin

You can tell quite a lot by looking at someone's **skin**. Rashes are common, but it's very difficult to describe in words what a rash looks like. Itchy rashes usually mean a viral or fungal infection, or an allergy, while localized red, painful, swollen and warm areas usually mean a bacterial infection. The most important thing to exclude is a **purpuric** or **petechial** rash which does not pale on pressure (see the glass test, p.172). Its presence means that there has been bleeding under the skin, which can be a sign of septicaemia (eg meningitis), a viral haemorrhagic fever (eg yellow fever) or some rickettsial infections (the "spotted" fevers), all of which are serious and require urgent attention.

Jaundice is a common feature of diseases such as malaria or hepatitis. The yellowing of the skin is due to a build-up of bilirubin (a chemical secreted by the liver to aid the digestion of fats in the gut) in the blood. Jaundice is usually fairly obvious in caucasians but less easy to see in dark-skinned people. If in doubt, look at the whites of the eyes in natural light.

Dehydration

Dehydration is a common, potentially serious, yet easily resolvable problem following diarrhoea and vomiting or during high fever. Thirst is the most obvious symptom. Your mouth and tongue may be dry, your skin may lose its suppleness and you may have a headache. Your urine output will be reduced and the urine itself will be dark and strong-smelling. Severe dehydration may result in a complete cessation in urine output, drowsiness or loss of consciousness (all of which require urgent medical help).

Temperature

High temperature, or **pyrexia**, is most commonly associated with infection but may also be caused by severe sunstroke. Having an even slightly raised temperature can make you feel unwell, while high pyrexia causes headache, nausea, skin flushing and intense sweating accompanied by the feeling of being cold.

To assess degree of temperature, place a thermometer under the tongue and hold it there for three minutes. Normal body core temperature is 37°C or 98°F. Generally speaking, although you may feel unwell, temperatures below 39°C or 102°F are unlikely to be caused by significant illness, but temperatures higher than this need to be taken more seriously. Watch for **patterns** or **recurring fevers** (eg malaria, dengue fever).

In a malarial area (or after having travelled through a malarial area), assume that any fever above 39°C is **malaria** until proved otherwise.

Pain

The presence, degree and whereabouts of pain are important diagnostic signs. A **headache** is often pretty non-specific, being associated with anything from a simple hangover to something a lot more serious (see p.138). If headache is severe and accompanied by high fever, neck stiffness and photophobia (sensitivity to light), seek urgent medical help in order to exclude meningitis. Headache is particularly common in cases of fever, dehydration and heat exhaustion, but is most often simply tension-related.

Chest pain in the young is almost always caused by muscular or joint sprains, but bear in mind that at home or abroad, **heart attacks** are still the commonest cause of death in people over 50. Cardiac pain tends to be central, dull (crushing), worse on exertion and often spreads to the neck, back or down the arm. It is frequently accompanied by clamminess, shortness of breath or nausea. If cardiac pain is suspected, seek urgent medical help. Inflammation of the lining of the lungs (**pleurisy**) often follows a chest infection and tends to be sharp and worse on cough or breathing in deeply. Pleuritic pain is also a feature of a **pulmonary embolism** (a blood clot on the lung), when it may also be accompanied by shortness of breath and coughing up of blood.

Abdominal pain is common yet rarely clear-cut because of the vast number of potential causes. It is considered in more detail opposite.

Urine

Examination of the **urine** by the naked eye is usually fairly fruitless. If it is darker than normal, you are likely to be dehydrated. If there is blood in the urine consider a urinary tract infection (p.224) or schistosomiasis (p.194). If it's painful to pass urine or you have to go very often, urinary tract infection or sexually transmitted disease (pp.197–201) are the likely candidates. More common when dehydrated, kidney stones cause blood in the urine as well as excruciating loin or abdominal pain.

Stools

Diarrhoea and constipation are both extremely common problems for the traveller and can be symptomatic merely of the body's readjustment to time zone changes, or alterations in diet and water quality. Look for blood or mucus in the **diarrhoea** and for signs of worm infestation (sometimes fragments of the worm are visible in the stool). Pale yellowish stools may be a sign of liver disease, while pale, hard stools of a whitish hue may be caused by

constipation. Dark, black, tarry stools may be a sign of bleeding from stomach inflammation or a stomach ulcer (though remember that Pepto-Bismol also turns stools black). Flatus of an "eggy" nature is considered to be associated with giardiasis, but this is obviously very subjective and thus somewhat unreliable.

48 hours

Following a set timescale in terms of how long you wait before seeking medical attention is tricky and potentially hazardous; however unless you suspect certain specific health problems (see the box on p.204), allowing **48 hours** to rest, take stock, treat your symptoms and drink plenty of fluids is a sensible measure. During this time many illnesses will settle spontaneously, while in others symptom patterns may become clearer, but remember that gut feeling is important – don't be too dogmatic about clock watching, and if you're worried at any stage or your condition is deteriorating, bail out and seek help earlier.

If there is no improvement after 48 hours, be guided by the severity of your symptoms and whether you have a hunch about the likely cause. Self-treatment may be a possibility but is best avoided unless you have a good idea of the diagnosis. It is at this point that you might consider requesting **laboratory tests** to confirm or deny your suspicions. In cases of high fever, for instance, blood tests can confirm the presence or absence of diseases such as malaria, dengue or yellow fever. This is often most easily done by visiting a doctor or a clinic, but in some countries you can go directly to a laboratory and ask for a specific test. (Remember to ask for your own needles and syringes to be used unless you can be certain about equipment sterility.) Testing may well save you time and money (a negative result is just as important as a positive).

Abdominal pain

Diagnosis of **abdominal pain** is not an exact science. In fact, it's a minefield in which many experienced doctors get caught out, and it is therefore only possible to offer some general guidelines here. If you suspect anything serious, seek medical help immediately.

Start by asking yourself the following questions:

✛ Does the pain spread anywhere else (to your back, your shoulder, down your legs etc)?

✛ What is the nature of the pain (constant or intermittent, dull, burning, crampy, stabbing etc)?

✛ Is there anything that makes the pain better or worse (lying still, bending double, opening your bowels, vomiting etc)?

✛ Do you have any other symptoms, such as fever, vomiting, diarrhoea, pain when passing urine or during sex?

Some gentle prodding may reveal masses or areas of particular tenderness, which can help to identify the specific organs involved.

Appendicitis

In theory, it should be a cinch to diagnose **appendicitis**, but in practice it's much more of a grey area, mainly because the symptoms can vary from person to person and can mimic other conditions. It's caused by an inflammation of the appendix, a finger-like, vestigial pouch at the junction of the large and small bowel. Little is known about what causes it to become inflamed, but untreated it can lead to **peritonitis**, a life-threatening inflammation of the abdominal lining.

Early **symptoms** are usually pain and recurrent vomiting. Initially the pain may vary in intensity but often starts centrally, migrating after a few hours to a more localized area in the right lower side of the abdomen, when it usually becomes severe and unremitting. The pain is usually less intense when lying still; coughing and vomiting are particularly painful. Fever and, less commonly, diarrhoea can also occur. The abdomen may be tender to even the lightest touch and may exhibit a phenomenon known as **guarding**, an involuntary tensing on mild probing.

If appendicitis (or peritonitis) is suspected, view it as an emergency and **seek urgent medical help**. Surgery to remove the appendix is the only treatment.

Stomach pain

Pain originating from the **stomach** tends to be central and just below the ribcage. It may be burning, sharp or aching in nature, and is usually accompanied by nausea, vomiting and loss of appetite. The pain tends to be constant although it can vary depending on whether the stomach is full or empty. Acid can escape from the stomach up into the gullet causing an unpleasant burning sensation at the back of the throat (so-called **reflux**) which is usually worse after meals and at night. Stomach pains are often aggravated by spicy food and alcohol. The common causes of stomach pain are gastroenteritis, gastritis (inflamed stomach lining) and ulcers. Pain originating from the stomach is usually relieved, at least partially, by antacids and other **indigestion preparations**. Diagnosis of a stomach-related pain is usually confirmed if these drugs alleviate symptoms.

Large bowel pain (colic)

Pain originating from the **large bowel** or colon – called "**colic**" – can be felt anywhere over the abdomen and tends to be cramp-like and gripey in nature. It's usually intermittent, but can be severe, and often makes you double-up. It can spread to the lower back. Common causes of large bowel pain include wind, constipation, diarrhoea (indicative of a vast range of illnesses), gastroenteritis and irritable bowel syndrome.

Liver pain

Usually felt in the upper right area of the abdomen, **liver pain** is often sharp, can be either intermittent or constant, and can radiate into the back or sometimes the shoulder. Nausea and loss of appetite are common. The stools can turn pale, the urine dark, and your skin may become jaundiced. The symptoms are often exacerbated by eating fatty foods or drinking alcohol. Common causes of liver pain include gall stones, hepatitis and malaria. Treatment depends on the underlying cause, but avoidance of fatty foods and alcohol is beneficial.

Bladder and kidney pain

Originating in the central, lower abdomen, **bladder pain** tends to be dull and constant. It's often accompanied by the need to urinate frequently and a feeling of inadequate emptying, localized pain on passing urine, and a weak urine stream which is occasionally bloody or foul-smelling.

Pains from the **kidneys** occur in the small of the back and are often one-sided. Kidney **infections** are usually preceded by the bladder symptoms above. Kidney **stones**, which cause excruciating pain usually unilaterally in the back or lower abdomen, can be triggered by dehydration, especially if you have suffered from them in the past. You might see blood in the urine and feel grit when you are passing urine.

Common **causes** of bladder or kidney pain are cystitis, kidney infections and kidney stones, sexually transmitted infections and schistosomiasis.

Pelvic pain (women)

Benign **ovarian cysts** are a common problem and tend to cause most pain in the middle of your cycle, when ovulation occurs. Although usually short-lived, the pain can be extreme and may be partially relieved by curling up into the foetal position. Pain relief, such as paracetamol or ibuprofen, is the best treatment. **Uterine pain** – painful periods or premenstrual pains – usually respond well to NSAIDs (see p.34). If you know this might be a problem for you, consider the combined oral contraceptive pill, which often reduces the severity and menstrual blood loss.

Another common cause of pelvic pain is pelvic inflammatory disease, which is discussed in detail in Part 1 (p.69).

Bladder infection, or **cystitis**, frequently causes central, lower abdominal discomfort but is usually accompanied by other symptoms. Pain from **thrush** is uncommon.

▶ ▶ See also Thrush, p.212; Urinary tract infections, p.224; and Women travellers, pp.64–74.

Rarer causes of abdominal pain

There are a multitude of **rarer causes of abdominal pain**, many of which are just as likely to be encountered at home as abroad, but a few are worth mentioning briefly here.

The chickenpox virus causes **shingles**, which can occur at any age but is more common and severe in the elderly. The pain can be quite severe and is often described as "burning". The accompanying rash occurs as a crop of blisters which is always localized and one-sided; it can occur anywhere on the body (along the route of an individual nerve), but the chest and abdomen are common sites. You cannot catch shingles from someone who has shingles, but you can catch chickenpox from shingles unless you have already had it (most people catch chickenpox in childhood) and therefore have natural immunity.

Pancreatitis, or inflammation of the pancreas, is usually caused by gallstones or severe alcohol abuse, although a rarer cause is scorpion envenomation. The pain is very intense, central and radiating to the back, and is usually accompanied by vomiting and shock. Pancreatitis is life-threatening, and if suspected you should get medical help urgently.

Aortic aneurysm is a weakening, leading to expansion or a "blow out", of the main artery leading away from the heart and is very rare in anyone under 50. Although usually insidious in onset, acute cases may have pain that is severe and central, and often a pulsing mass can be felt or visualized in the centre of the abdomen. If suspected, get medical help at once.

Musculoskeletal abdominal pain is not uncommon after exercise and can be difficult to differentiate from potentially more serious causes. There should be no bowel disturbance, vomiting or fever and the pain should respond well to simple pain relief such as paracetamol.

Abortus fever

▶▶ See Brucellosis, p.100.

Acute mountain sickness

▶▶ See Altitude sickness, p.91.

African trypanosomiasis

(Sleeping sickness)

African trypanosomiasis occurs throughout sub-Saharan Africa; in West and Central Africa, it's known as **Gambian trypanosomiasis**, and as **Rhodesian or East African trypanosomiasis** in East Africa. In localized areas of Angola, southern Sudan and the Democratic Republic of Congo, between twenty and fifty percent of the population are infected. It is caused by a parasite transmitted between humans (or from animals to humans) by the daylight-biting **tsetse fly**, which proliferates in savannahs and around fresh water (note, however, that the tsetse fly is present elsewhere in Africa and doesn't always harbour the disease). The more popular name for the disease, **sleeping sickness**, is derived from the parasite's effects on the central nervous system.

Some 45,000 cases were reported to the WHO in 1999, although as this is a disease that mainly affects rural areas, it's likely that the majority of cases go unreported. It's estimated that around 66 million people in sub-Saharan Africa are currently at risk from the parasite, and the Rhodesian form may be a risk for tourists on safaris in East Africa. Epidemics among the indigenous populations have been linked to a sudden downturn in socioeconomic conditions, for example after the onset of war or famine.

There is no vaccination against African trypanosomiasis, so bite avoidance is your only protection.

Symptoms

The Rhodesian form of the disease tends to run a more rapid course than the Gambian, although the symptoms are broadly similar. The **bite site** may become painful and inflamed, resembling a blind boil ("papule"). First **signs of illness** occur after three weeks or so and include rapid pulse rate, high fever, headache, weakness, joint pains and itching. The liver, spleen and lymph glands (particularly in the neck) become enlarged, with the parasite weakening your body's immune system so that you become more susceptible to other infections. As the disease progresses, the parasite invades an increasing number of organs, with brain involvement in the final stages of disease leading to behavioural changes, lethargy, frequent sleeping and apathy. Untreated, the torpor increases to the point where the sufferer lapses into a coma.

Diagnosis and treatment

Blood tests can detect the presence of the parasite or antibodies to the parasites, as can a biopsy of the inflamed lymph glands. A lumbar puncture may be necessary to determine whether the central nervous system has been affected.

If tests are positive, you'll need to be admitted to hospital for further

treatment, usually with intravenous drugs such as suramin, pentamidine or melarsoprol (the choice depends on how advanced the disease is, but note that unfortunately these drugs can have some unpleasant and even dangerous side effects). Cure cannot be assumed until two years after treatment, and there may be persistent neurological impairment.

AIDS

▶▶ See HIV, p.247.

Alcohol

Alcohol is likely to figure in most peoples' time abroad at some point. Unfortunately the initial feel–good factor doesn't last, and alcohol is actually a depressant. It also reduces inhibitions and the ability to assess risks – even small quantities can impair the brain's higher thought functions.

Alcohol affects women more acutely than it does men due to the fact that women have a higher percentage body fat and therefore less bodily fluid than men – hence for a given quantity of alcohol consumed, the blood alcohol concentration will be higher in a woman than in a man. From a health perspective, a man should not drink more than four **units** a day, a woman, not more than three (see box below).

Alcohol may quench a thirst in the short term, but it will increase your thirst later on – think how dry your mouth feels the morning after you've overindulged. **Dehydration** of the brain is the source of your hangover, which will be much worse and the result of fewer alcohol units if you're already dehydrated, for example after heavy exercise, sunbathing or a bout of diarrhoea. Note also that alcohol exacerbates the effects of jet lag and mountain sickness.

Consider what else besides alcohol is in your exotic beverage. **Home-brewed concoctions** are likely to contain local water (as will ice), and standards of hygiene in the brewing process may be suspect. Locally made "fire-waters" can contain poisonous methanol, which can cause headache, breathlessness, increased sensitivity to light and even blindness.

Remember, too, that alcohol doesn't interact well with some **drugs**, such as antihistamines or tranquillizers. Never mix alcohol and the antibiotic **metronidazole** – it can induce a severe and unpleasant reaction.

Hangover prevention and cure

If you don't want the fuzzy head, don't drink. If you are set on having a heavy night, try to **eat** beforehand as food in the stomach will slow down the speed at which alcohol reaches your blood. Before going to bed, drink at least a pint

---

> **One unit of alcohol**
>
> ✛ a half pint of normal-strength beer or lager
> ✛ a small glass of wine (about 75ml – a bottle usually contains between 9 and 11 units)
> ✛ a single bar measure/shot of spirits (25ml)

of **water** (bottled if the water quality is suspect – this is the moment when many people forget) or other non-alcoholic fluid and again, try to eat something.

Next day, **ibuprofen** or **paracetamol** will take the edge off your headache, while rehydration solution or commercial hangover preparations will help to rectify the balance of chemicals in the blood. If nausea is particularly crippling, domperidone or metoclopramide (see p.40) usually work well.

 Made from "the nut that makes you vomit", Nux vomica (one 30c tablet taken before you go to sleep) is an ideal **homeopathic remedy** if a hangover is anticipated. If you're chilly, weak, have diarrhoea and are very restless or fretful about your hangover, try Arsenicum 30c (one every two hours until improvement). Of **herbal cures**, Bach Flower Remedies are always helpful if you need a little rescuing, while the Crabapple variety is especially good if you're feeling guilty about the night before – it removes not only the toxins but also the self-critical mind set. The Chinese herbal remedy Poh Chi can also help relieve symptoms.

Allergies

Everyone has different susceptibilities to **allergens**, the substances that stimulate your body's defence mechanisms and trigger an allergic response. **Signs of an allergic reaction** are itching, a skin rash and swelling, runny eyes and nose, sneezing, wheezing and cough.

Any **antihistamine** (see p.38) will help to relieve the irritant symptoms; topical antihistamine, calamine lotion or steroid creams can relieve skin itch and redness provided it's not widespread. Severe allergic reactions need medical input and perhaps a course of steroids.

If you've ever suffered a severe reaction to anything, and future avoidance cannot be guaranteed, carry Medicalert ID (see p.51) and see your doctor about carrying **injectable adrenaline** with you, which may save your life in anaphylaxis.

 In terms of homeopathic allergy treatment, try **Allium cepa** (made from the red onion) for a runny nose, sneezing, itching and wheezing; take four 30c doses half-hourly, decreasing to four times a day until symptoms subside. For reactions to foods, **Apis** can be given as a first aid measure (though you should also seek medical advice). Apis is also useful in allergic reactions to stings and insect bites; take a 30c remedy four times a day until improvement.

Common allergens

+ Pollen
+ House dust
+ Insect bites and stings
+ Drugs (eg penicillin)
+ Foods (eg nuts, dairy products, wheat and shellfish)
+ Chemicals (eg rubber, nickel or cobalt in jewellery, and miscellaneous in washing powders, deodorants etc)

Generally speaking, allergic reactions are usually mild, an irritation rather than a serious threat to health. Nevertheless, a thankfully rare but life-threatening reaction can occur, known as **anaphylaxis**. Essentially, the reaction of the body to the specific allergen is so strong that the airways swell to the point of becoming blocked, the pulse rate becomes rapid and the blood pressure plummets. A dramatic and rapidly progressive event, the condition manifests as shortness of breath, wheezing, a bluish tinge around the lips, nausea, vomiting, diarrhoea and swelling of the tongue and face.

Anaphylaxis is an **emergency** of the first order. If you suspect it in a companion, do the following:

+ Remain calm and call for urgent help.
+ Remove the cause if it is obvious.
+ Lay the patient down with their head lower than the rest of their body to maintain blood flow to the brain.
+ Ensure their airway is clear.
+ If they've had severe allergic reactions in the past, they may be carrying injectable adrenaline. Don't delay – give it immediately.
+ If they stop breathing, commence CPR (see p.239) until help arrives.

Altitude sickness

(Acute mountain sickness, or AMS)

Altitude sickness is a serious and potentially life-threatening illness which can affect anyone who normally lives at low altitude and ascends above 10,000–12,000 feet (roughly 3500 metres). Factors affecting the severity of symptoms include the altitude reached, the rate of ascent, and the degree of exertion (and therefore level of fitness). If you have suffered previously from altitude sickness, you're more likely to experience it on subsequent expeditions.

Symptoms usually occur after about six hours but may be latent for up to 36 hours. In cases of mild altitude sickness, you may experience headache, shortness of breath, malaise, generalized weakness, loss of appetite, nausea, vomiting, rapid heartbeat and dizziness. Insomnia is also common. Increasingly severe symptoms – the result of an accumulation of fluid, and consequent swelling, in the brain and lungs – include an intense, constant headache, lassitude and confusion, difficulty breathing, coughing, frothy blood-stained sputum and a bluish tinge to the lips, nails and skin (known as **cyanosis**). Left untreated, severe cases can lapse into unconsciousness and die within hours.

To **minimize the risk** of altitude sickness:

+ Don't attempt to climb above 3000m without training.
+ Ascend slowly (no more than 300m a day at altitudes over 3000m). If possible, give yourself time to acclimatize at altitude.
+ Stay hydrated by drinking at least three litres of non-alcoholic fluids a day.
+ If mild symptoms develop, descend a little from the altitude you have reached and rest a day or two.
+ Although offering no guarantees, drugs with a prophylactic effect (see p.43) against altitude sickness include acetazolamide (500mg nightly) or nifedipine (20mg three times a day).

✦ Remember that temporary relief of symptoms is not a green light to restart ascent – take time out for your body to acclimatize.

If you fly into a high-altitude destination to which you're not acclimatized (such as La Paz), it's not uncommon to experience some of the milder symptoms mentioned above. Don't attempt to ascend further or do anything strenuous for at least two days, and resist the temptation to drink alcohol as this can exacerbate the symptoms. If your condition deteriorates, seek medical help without delay.

Don't dawdle at the onset of progressive or severe symptoms – prompt and rapid descent is the only effective **treatment**, although drugs dexamethasone, furosemide and nifedipine may buy some time (see p.43). Oxygen should be given if available.

A useful homeopathic remedy to treat the classic symptoms of breathlessness, palpitations, exhaustion and insomnia associated with altitude sickness is **Coca** (30c), taken once a day. If symptoms are severe, descend at once and take the remedy three or four times a day thereafter.

American trypanosomiasis

(Chagas' disease)

American trypanosomiasis, also known as Chagas' disease after the Brazilian physician who discovered it, occurs in South and Central America from Mexico in the north to Argentina and Chile in the south, although there

---

❝ Allergy attack ❞

*D*uring a trip to Australia, I took a bus from Alice Springs to the town of Katherine in north Queensland. Katherine is famous for its series of river gorges, several of which can be crossed by boat when the waters are high enough.

I joined a local group of about ten travellers for a day of cruising and swimming. After boating for about four hours, we anchored by a ramp in the third gorge and we went ashore to eat our picnic lunch at tables under the trees. Our guide warned us not to touch the tree branches as there were caterpillars with irritating hairs in the canopy feeding on the leaves.

We avoided the trees, but I failed to realize that the caterpillars had at some point dropped down onto the tables, and that when they did, they shed their hairs. Although the insects themselves had been cleared off the surface by previous groups, their hairs remained. About two minutes after I rested my arms on the table, I experienced violent itching. My entire arm began to swell and I started to wheeze.

Allergy attack! Luckily, a couple from England had some antihistamine tablets which abated the breathing problems and reduced the hives. Water was in order for washing the hairs away, so I went swimming in the river, and that helped.

It was a frightening experience in that remote area, and as a result I recommend antihistamine preparations (both pills and topical preparations) as essential items in any travel medical kit.

Sandy Jordan, Sacramento, USA

have been reports of the disease as far north as Texas and even Virginia in the USA. It's estimated that up to eighteen million people are infected within this geographical area, resulting in around 50,000 deaths each year.

Chagas' disease is caused by a protozoan that's spread from infected verte-brates by **reduviid bugs** ("assassin bugs" or "kissing bugs"). Blood sucked from the infected host contains the protozoan, which multiplies in the bug's gut and is then defecated onto the skin when the bug feeds again. The protozoan can only penetrate broken skin. While transmission via insects is by far the most common method of disease spread, the infection can also be acquired via blood transfusion, and from mother to child at birth or through breast-feeding.

There is no vaccination available so the best ways to avoid contracting the disease include staying away (especially for overnight stays) from the adobe huts whose wall cracks and roofs are a habitat favoured by the bugs, and heeding the standard advice on avoiding insect bites (see p.149).

Symptoms

Localized **swelling** around the site of the bite (and perhaps around the eyes) and **fever** usually occur within the first ten days. An **itchy rash** and swelling of the lymph glands, liver and spleen may also occur in the early stages. The heart, brain and intestinal tract may also be affected, causing potentially seri-ous, even fatal, complications. A delayed chronic form of the illness, occurring months or even years after the original infection, may affect the heart, brain and gut, again with potentially fatal consequences.

Diagnosis and treatment

A **blood test** will determine whether or not you've got the disease. A few **drugs** have been shown to be effective in treating the initial symptoms, but should only be used under close medical supervision. The prognosis depends on age and the severity of infection. Mortality is highest in people who acquire the disease congenitally, in the very young, and in those with compromised immunity for other reasons (eg HIV).

Amoebiasis

The humble amoeba is found worldwide, but the infection **amoebiasis** (ame-biasis in the US) itself is common only in countries with poor sanitation. It is spread via the faecal–oral route from contaminated food or drinking water, although it can (rarely) be spread by intimate person-to-person contact. In most cases the disease is restricted to the gastrointestinal tract, but it can reach the liver, causing hepatitis and abscess formation.

Prevention focuses on avoiding potentially contaminated food or water. Observe the usual hygiene measures (see pp.21–24), although bear in mind that amoebae are only killed by boiling water for at least one minute, and are unaf-fected by iodine alone.

Symptoms

Most people suffer only mild illness between two and four weeks after expo-sure. In more severe cases, commonly referred to as **amoebic dysentery**, symptoms such as diarrhoea with blood and mucus, severe abdominal cramps, fever, nausea, weight loss and general malaise can occur. These may persist or recur over a period of weeks or months. A liver abscess causes a prolonged fever and intermittent upper, usually right-sided, abdominal pain.

Diagnosis and treatment

A **stool sample** may show the gastrointestinal disease, although sometimes more than one sample is required. An **ultrasound scan** will detect the presence of an abscess on the liver.

The usual **treatment** is a five- to seven-day course of metronidazole (800mg three times daily), during which you must not drink alcohol. Be particularly diligent in your personal hygiene, especially hand washing, as it's relatively easy to reinfect yourself. As the infection is spread via the faecal–oral route, remember that intimate sexual contact may pass it on and is best avoided until the infection is cleared.

▶▶ See Metronidazole, p.36.

AMS

▶▶ See Altitude sickness, p.91.

Ancylostomiasis

▶▶ See under Worms, p.227.

Anthrax

Anthrax occurs worldwide in epidemics, but the hot spots are Africa, Central Asia, South America, the former USSR and the Far East. Transmitted to humans via bacterial spores from infected sheep, goats, cattle, horses or pigs, it almost exclusively affects people in close contact with animals or animal products. Travellers may come into contact with anthrax from handling wool, hide, bones and the like in areas where there is an outbreak, although generally risk is very low. Of the three distinct kinds of anthrax, the most common is **cutaneous anthrax**, which occurs after handling infected animals or animal hides. **Pulmonary anthrax** and **intestinal anthrax**, affecting the lungs and the gut respectively, both carry a high mortality rate but are far rarer.

A **vaccination** is available against anthrax, but it's difficult to obtain and is only recommended for those at high risk.

Symptoms

Initial symptoms of **cutaneous anthrax** show themselves between one and five days after exposure, and include ulceration of the skin, usually at the point of contact. The ulcers are dark red in the centre, and although itchy, rarely painful. Local lymph glands may become swollen and tender and lymphangitis (see p.202) may be apparent. Accompanying symptoms may include fever, headache, nausea and loss of appetite. Left untreated, septicaemia can develop, which is always dangerous, even life-threatening.

Pulmonary anthrax (the result of inhaling the bacterial spores) manifests as a dry cough, high fever and chest discomfort. The initial symptoms of intestinal anthrax (caused by eating the meat of infected animals) usually comprise diarrhoea, vomiting (both can be bloody) and fever. In the cases of both pulmonary and intestinal anthrax, the disease can progress rapidly, with often fatal consequences.

Diagnosis and treatment

Swab cultures taken from the skin lesion, or sputum if chest symptoms are present, will reveal the presence of disease.

For all forms of anthrax, ciprofloxacin is now generally acknowledged as the primary treatment, although other options include doxycycline and amoxicillin. For pulmonary and gastrointestinal anthrax, ciprofloxacin is usually combined with another antibiotic such as amoxicillin.

Ascariasis

▶▶ See under Worms, p.400.

Avian flu

▶▶ See Influenza, p.147.

Babesiosis

▶▶ See Human babesiosis, p.145.

Back pain

Back pain is a common enough problem at home, but the traveller often faces additional risks – heavy or awkward luggage, cramped, prolonged bus or plane journeys, hostile mattresses – which can exacerbate or cause back problems. Don't underestimate the impact of back pain: it can severely affect your travel plans. Not only can the pain be debilitating, it can take days, even weeks, to resolve.

In truth, the vast majority of back injuries are minor. Strained or damaged back muscles go into spasm, causing pain and stiffness. Time is essentially the healer, although it's important to take adequate pain relief and keep mobile, as lying still for too long will increase spasm and prolong the symptoms. Standard

Lifting technique

To lift a heavy object safely:
+ Ask yourself first if you're being realistic in attempting to lift the object in the first place.
+ Stand close to the load with your feet well apart.
+ Bend at the knees to pick it up, keeping your back straight, and lift by straightening your legs.
+ Turn using your feet rather than twisting your back.
+ To put the load down, again bend your legs rather than your back.

painkillers, like paracetamol and ibuprofen, are usually sufficient to manage the pain although co-proxamol is often recommended by doctors for stronger relief. Helpful, too, are hot water bottles or hot towels (heat increases the blood flow to the muscles, helping to relieve spasm), gentle massage or in some cases cold compresses (cold helps to reduce inflammation, especially around joints if they're involved). Most episodes of simple back pain will settle within four weeks.

Severe back pain, particularly if the pain goes down one or both legs (**sciatica**) or if accompanied by numbness, weakness or tingling in the legs, implies that one of the discs (which essentially act as "shock-absorbers") between the vertebrae is bulging, impinging on the nerves as they leave the spine (a "**slipped disc**"). It commonly occurs after lifting excessively heavy weights.

The standard treatment is pain relief and gentle mobilization – simple stretching **exercises** are best. Walking on the flat and swimming are also helpful, but take care not to proceed too rapidly. If symptoms persist or if at any stage you have problems controlling your bowels or bladder, seek medical help urgently. Another danger sign is so-called "**saddle anaesthesia**" – numbness around the parts of the body that would touch a saddle were you sitting in one (ie the anus, perineum and genitals).

Balantidiasis

Although the organism that causes **balantidiasis** can be found worldwide, the disease tends to occur only hot climates (particularly Central and South America, Iran, Papua New Guinea and the Philippines), and is usually passed to humans by pigs, guinea pigs, rats and monkeys. Humans can also act as carriers, and infection can occur as a result of drinking water contaminated by infected animal or human faeces. The risk to travellers in general is low, but always wash your hands after handling animals in areas that have experienced outbreaks, and observe the standard food and water hygiene measures (see pp.21–24).

Symptoms, diagnosis and treatment

Diarrhoea alternating with constipation is common. For the most part, however, infection is mild, even unnoticed, and the **symptoms** usually resolve spontaneously after a week or two. Occasionally the illness can be severe, especially if you're already physically weak, causing rectal bleeding and severe abdominal cramps similar to dysentery.

Diagnosis can usually be made by microscopic examination of the stool; several samples may be required as the bacteria are only passed intermittently.

Treatment is usually unnecessary unless symptoms are severe, but tetracyclines (eg doxycycline) or metronidazole can be used.

Bancroftian filariasis

▶ ▶ See Filarial lymphangitis, p.128.

Bang's disease

▶ ▶ See Brucellosis, p.99.

Bartonellosis

(Oroya fever, Carrion's Disease)

Bartonellosis originates in the Andes of southwest Colombia, Ecuador and Peru – its common name, **Oroya fever**, refers to a town in the Peruvian Andes. Risk is highest in certain narrow valleys on the range's western slopes, between 1000 and 3000m – outside these geographically isolated areas, the risk to travellers is negligible.

The bacteria responsible are transmitted by **sand flies**, which usually bite between dusk and dawn. There's no vaccination, so if you find yourself in an area of high risk, your only protection is insect-bite avoidance (see p.249).

Symptoms

The disease has **two phases**. The initial acute illness, which usually occurs between two and six weeks after being bitten, is characterized by loss of appetite, thirst, bone pains, fatigue resulting from anaemia, and high fever. The fever is particularly high at night and may last for up to six weeks. This phase is followed by reddish-purple, **wart-like eruptions** on the skin, which are particularly dense on the face and limbs, and bleed easily. They heal without scarring, although sometimes this takes up to a year. Victims of bartonellosis are unusually susceptible to **salmonella septicaemia**, especially in the second week of the illness, so prompt treatment or medical attention is important.

Diagnosis and treatment

Blood tests will confirm the presence of the organisms. While there's no vaccine to prevent the disease, it can be **treated** by a variety of antibiotics, including the penicillin and tetracycline groups. A course of oral chloramphenicol is the favoured option, as it is also effective against salmonella.

Bedbugs

Though usually associated with areas of deprivation, poverty and low standards of hygiene, **bedbugs** are found in all parts of the world. Measuring up to 5mm long, they are crawling insects which inhabit bedding, furniture and walls. They feed on blood, usually at night, with their bites often showing a linear pattern. By day they seek shelter in dark recesses. Rooms that have a bedbug infestation are said typically to have a musty, sweet odour. Bedbugs are not known to transmit any diseases to humans.

Symptoms and treatment

Many bites will go unnoticed, but some appear as small, hard, pale **lumps**. An itchy allergic reaction can develop into **weals**; these subside leaving red spots which can remain for several days.

Bedbugs can be eradicated by spraying their likely daytime residences with **permethrin**. Oral **antihistamines** or topical **hydrocortisone** can speed up recovery from a bite.

Bilharzia

▶ ▶ See Schistosomiasis, p.194.

Blood transfusions

As there's only a small likelihood of ever needing one, most of us give little thought to the matter of **blood transfusion**. It's only when faced with the prospect (if we are well enough) that we become alarmed at the thought of having someone else's blood pumping around our body – as well as the potential for contracting a serious, potentially life-threatening virus such as HIV or infective hepatitis.

In most developed countries, the technology and screening regulations are sufficient to keep these risks to a minimum. However, in the developing world, confidence in the screening process is less founded. Furthermore, the sterility of equipment used to transfuse the blood (needles, syringes etc) cannot be guaranteed.

If you're in an emergency situation and need a blood transfusion, you'll probably have little choice about what happens next. However, your condition may be stabilized sufficiently to request **air evacuation** from a country where blood and blood products, or transfusion equipment, are suspect. Your insurance policy may also have arrangements for getting adequately screened blood and sterile equipment to you if need be; if not, you can minimize the risk from unsterile equipment at least by carrying your own (see p.279 for a list of suppliers). Another option is to become a member of the blood care programme operated by the UK-based **Blood Care Foundation** (16 Lonsdale Gardens, Tunbridge Wells, Kent TN1 1NU; ☎01403/262652, ⓦwww.bloodcare.org.uk). The organization will, in an emergency, provide screened blood to its members in any part of the world; contact them for membership details.

Blood groups

If you know your **blood group**, make a note of it before you go away and carry it with your passport and insurance documents in case of emergencies. There are four basic blood groups, of which blood group **O rhesus negative** is known as the "universal donor" because it can be given to someone with any other blood type – O negative people can be valuable travel companions!

Thus:

+ Group A can receive A and O.
+ Group B can receive B and O.
+ Group AB can receive A, B and O.
+ Group O can receive only O.
+ If you are rhesus positive, you can receive both rhesus positive and negative blood.
+ If you are rhesus negative, you can receive only rhesus negative blood. Rhesus negative blood is especially rare in the Far East.

▲ Spectacle and denture stall, India

Botulism

Outbreaks of **botulism**, a form of food poisoning caused by bacteria commonly found in the soil, can occur anywhere in the world but are very rare. The infection is contracted by eating poorly cooked or reheated contaminated food, often from improperly processed canned goods (the food-contaminating spores can resist temperatures up to 100°C/212°F). Person-to-person spread does not occur. Travellers are not necessarily at any higher risk than anyone else, although contamination of food or poor packaging may be more common in developing countries. Don't buy cans of food that have been damaged or are bulging, and don't eat the contents of any can that gives off an offensive odour.

Children are at particular risk of contracting botulism from eating **honey** contaminated with the bacterial spores – avoid giving honey to babies under 1 year old.

Symptoms, diagnosis and treatment

The main **symptoms** of nausea, vomiting and diarrhoea usually occur between twelve and 36 hours after eating contaminated food. Double or blurred vision, dry mouth, difficulty speaking or swallowing, weakness and shortness of breath may follow, all signs that botulism is affecting your nervous system. Gradual-onset muscle paralysis may develop, leading to respiratory difficulties and even death.

Laboratory tests can identify the toxin produced by the bacteria via blood and bacteria in a stool sample. **Hospitalization** is necessary as severe cases may need to be hooked up to a ventilator. An injected antitoxin may be given in some instances.

Brazilian purpuric fever

Brazilian purpuric fever was first recognized in Promissao in the state of São Paulo in 1984. Since then there have been sporadic outbreaks in a number of towns in São Paulo state; cases resembling it have also been reported in Australia. Little is known about the bacteria that cause the disease, nor the way in which it is spread, but it almost always affects children under 10.

Symptoms, diagnosis and treatment

Characteristically, the illness begins with a severe, pustular conjunctivitis (pink eye; see p.123). In a few cases, a high fever, vomiting, abdominal pain and a purpuric rash occur, as can other **symptoms** resembling infection with meningococcus (see p.171). If left untreated, life-threatening septicaemia can develop.

The bacteria can be detected in **cultures** grown from blood or spinal fluid. **Chloramphenicol** drops or ointment may help the conjunctivitis, but seem ineffective in preventing the more progressive symptoms from taking hold. Oral **amoxicillin** (sometimes in conjunction with oral chloramphenicol) can prevent progression to septicaemia.

Brucellosis

(Abortus fever, Bang's disease, Malta fever, Undulant fever)

Brucellosis occurs in epidemics throughout the world and is usually acquired by drinking unpasteurized milk (pasteurization kills the offending organism) from infected cattle, goats and sheep in the Mediterranean (Malta especially) and the Middle East; it's also found in pigs in North America and the Far East. People working closely with animals run the risk of the organism entering their body via their respiratory tract or through skin abrasions. The risk of acquiring the disease is very low for most travellers.

Symptoms, diagnosis and treatment

The onset of symptoms usually occurs one to three weeks after contact with the disease – although the **incubation period** can be longer. The initial illness can be acute in some cases, more insidious in others. Common **symptoms** include malaise, headache, night sweats, loss of appetite, generalized weakness and aches and pains. The fever tends to undulate for a week or so during which time the lymph glands become swollen. The liver and spleen may also swell.

A **chronic** form of brucellosis may persist for several months following an acute attack, the symptoms of which are muscle aches, a tendency to tire easily, with bouts of fever and depression.

A **blood test** will detect the disease. It can then be treated, ideally in hospital, using high-dose **antibiotics**. Relapses of the illness can occur.

Buruli ulcer

Buruli is a rare but serious skin infection confined, for the most part, to Benin, Côte d'Ivoire, Gabon, Ghana and Uganda (it's named after a Ugandan region in which there were many cases in the 1960s), although isolated outbreaks have been recorded in Asia, Australia and South America. To date, relatively little is known about the disease, although the causative **bacteria** (related to those causing TB and leprosy) have been identified, as has disease prevalence among women and children living near wetlands or rivers in tropical or sub-tropical rural areas. Its mode of spread may be via **scratches or cuts** on the skin. Risk to the traveller is very low unless a prolonged stay is planned in rural, wetland communities in the endemic areas.

There is no specific **vaccine** against Buruli, although the BCG vaccine confers a degree of short-term immunity.

Symptoms, diagnosis and treatment

The initial **symptom** is a painless, occasionally itchy skin swelling, usually on the limbs, which develops over the course of a month or two into a destructive ulcer. The ulcer may remain small and disappear spontaneously or progress rapidly, destroying large areas of skin and causing disfigurement.

Although the appearance of the ulcer usually makes **diagnosis** easy, swabs can be taken to confirm the presence of the specific bacteria. However, culturing the bacteria for a definitive diagnosis can take several weeks.

Treatment with drugs has been disappointing to date. Significant ulceration requires radical surgical excision of the ulcer and skin grafting, although the procedure is much simpler and less damaging if the disease is diagnosed early.

Candidiasis

▶ ▶ See Thrush, p.212.

Chagas' disease

▶ ▶ See American trypanosomiasis, p.92.

Chancroid

▶ ▶ See under Sexually transmitted diseases, p.200.

Chiggers

▶ ▶ See Tungiasis, pp.197–201.

Chikungunya fever

Chikungunya fever occurs in both sporadic outbreaks and large epidemics in Africa, the Indian subcontinent and Southeast Asia (Philippines, Thailand, Cambodia, Vietnam, Myanmar and Sri Lanka). Its name is derived from Swahili and means "that which bends up", a reference to the sufferers' stooped posture as a result of joint pains.

Chikungunya fever is a **mosquito**-borne **viral** infection. There is no preventative vaccination so the standard bite-avoidance measures (see p.24) are an essential part of reducing your risk of exposure.

Symptoms, diagnosis and treatment

Symptoms closely resemble those of dengue fever, with high temperature, headache, nausea, skin rash and rapid-onset joint pains. The symptoms usually last between three and seven days and, although unpleasant, the illness is not life-threatening. Residual joint stiffness can continue for weeks or even months afterwards.

Diagnosis can be made by a blood test, but no specific **treatment** is available. Paracetamol or ibuprofen may help to alleviate the fever and pains. Be sure to drink plenty to replace lost fluids during the fever.

▶ ▶ See Dengue fever, p.113.

Chlamydia

▶ ▶ See under Sexually transmitted diseases, p.113.

Cholera

Cholera is a potentially dangerous diarrhoeal illness caused by bacteria which usually enter the body via contaminated drinks or shellfish (person-to-person spread is possible but rare). Cholera occurs in sporadic epidemics in areas with poor sanitation and is common after natural disasters and war. "Bengal Cholera" is a particularly violent strain causing recent outbreaks in parts of Asia. Infection rates are rising: WHO reports indicate that cholera infection led to 3800 deaths worldwide in 2002. However this figure is a vast underestimate of the true prevalence, as an estimated 95 percent of cases go unreported.

As long as you take good care with **food and water hygiene**, the risk to travellers is small – the bacteria are killed in a few seconds in boiling water. However because of the unpredictable nature of epidemics, it's important to be vigilant with food and water hygiene at all times in any underdeveloped country. Stomach acid also protects against the bacteria, so you're at greater risk if you're taking acid-suppressant treatment (eg for a peptic ulcer).

Cholera **vaccination** has proved unreliable in the past, but a new and effective vaccine is now available (see p.7); your doctor will be able to give you the most up-to-date advice before you go.

Symptoms

The vast majority of cases – around 90 percent – are mild to moderate and, as such, difficult to differentiate from any other diarrhoeal illness. In more severe cases, **symptoms** such as recurrent vomiting and profuse, sudden-onset, watery diarrhoea ("rice water" stools) can lead to significant dehydration and even shock (cold, clammy skin, high pulse rate etc – see p.242). Muscle cramps can be severe.

Diagnosis and treatment

Diagnosis can be confirmed by lab examination of stool samples.

Urgent treatment will be needed to prevent severe, life-threatening dehydration – lost fluid and chemicals need to be replaced via oral rehydration solutions (see p.39). The tetracycline group of antibiotics (eg doxycycline, 200mg on day one, then 100mg daily for six days) help eradicate the infection, decrease stool output and considerably shorten the duration of the illness. As antibiotic resistance becomes more common, ciprofloxacin is increasingly used as an alternative.

Ciguatera

Ciguatera poisoning occurs after eating reef-dwelling fish who have fed on a particular type of **toxic plankton**. The disease occurs in sporadic outbreaks throughout the Pacific and Caribbean. Unfortunately, affected fish are indistinguishable from other fish by inspection, smell and taste, and the toxin is not neutralized by cooking. Outbreaks are rare, but if you are aware of one locally, avoid eating large predatory, reef-dwelling fish – commonly affected species include red snapper, grouper, barracuda, coral trout, cod and amberjack. The toxin tends to accumulate in high concentrations in the head, liver, roe and gut, so these parts of the fish should be avoided in particular.

Symptoms, diagnosis and treatment

Usually occurring one to six hours after eating (up to as long as thirty hours), the **symptoms** are commonly mild and predominantly gastrointestinal (diarrhoea, vomiting and abdominal pains) or neurological (muscle aches, weakness, pins and needles, burning sensations of the skin, blurred vision, photophobia and a metallic taste in the mouth). Symptoms can persist for as long as two weeks, but severe cases are rare.

Diagnosis is usually made on the basis of history, symptoms and clinical suspicion. There is no specific **treatment**; bed rest and basic pain relief are the best options. Severe cases sometimes require intravenous fluids to prevent dehydration.

Clonorchiasis

▶▶ See Liver flukes, p.162.

Cold exposure

The normally well-regulated core temperature of the human body will fall under extreme environmental conditions such as **cold**, **wet** or **windy weather**. Alcohol, physical illness and exhaustion can also compromise the body's natural ability to withstand the cold. Discomfort aside, cold exposure can harm the body in several ways, and in the extreme, it can be life threatening.

Frostbite

Frostbite occurs when the skin and the flesh just beneath the skin surface freeze, preventing the flow of blood so that the flesh in effect dies. The areas of the body most likely to be affected by frostbite are your **extremities**: hands, feet, ears and sometimes the face.

Initial **signs** of frostbite are localized numbness and often sharp pain, although frequently the victim is unaware of the problem. In mild frostbite the skin looks pale and has a leathery texture. As the freezing progresses, sensation disappears and the skin feels hard to touch.

Mild frostbite (the skin is still soft to touch) is best **treated** by gradually warming the affected area by wrapping it and holding it against warm, more central body parts. Keep moving to improve blood circulation. **Severe frostbite** (when the skin feels hard, like meat from the freezer) needs medical input, as the dead flesh may need to be removed surgically. In an emergency situation, don't attempt to warm or defrost the affected area until you're out of

Keeping your body warm in extreme cold

+ Wrap up, paying particular attention to your extremities (don't forget your ears) and using as many layers as possible.
+ Keep dry.
+ Keep active and moving.
+ Consume high-energy foods (eg chocolate) and warm drinks.
+ Find shelter in rain or high winds.
+ Avoid alcohol, which dilates the blood vessels to the skin (eg flushing) so you actually lose heat.
+ Avoid smoking (nicotine contracts your blood vessels and impairs blood flow to the extremities).

the cold and in a safe place. It's better to let a limb stay frozen for several hours than to warm it only for it to freeze again. The affected area can be warmed by immersing it in warm water (remember that feeling is lost so you won't be able to gauge temperature). As the area warms, it can be very painful – strong pain relief may be necessary. Stay warm and rest. The thawed area must be treated gently and kept clean. Blisters may form after a few days (avoid bursting them) and the flesh may blacken. Because the area is numb, it is more prone to local damage from minor trauma and infection. Medical help should be sought urgently.

Hypothermia

Hypothermia is caused when the core body temperature falls below a critical level (defined medically as below 35˚C). It's a significant cause of death in climbers, polar explorers and off-piste skiers.

Symptoms initially include the feeling of intense cold and uncontrollable shivering. As the body's temperature continues to drop, speech becomes slow or slurred and mental confusion, stumbling gait and lethargy become apparent. The sufferer feels cold to touch, the pulse slows and breathing becomes shallow. Shivering eventually decreases and the muscles become stiff. Eventually the victim will lapse into coma, and death usually occurs as a result of abnormal heart rhythms.

To **treat** hypothermia the victim needs to be gradually rewarmed by placing them in a warm environment, wrapping them in blankets (aluminium space blankets if they are available), huddling to transfer body heat and giving warm, sugary drinks (no alcohol). This process may take several hours. As the body temperature increases, there is a risk of abnormal heart rhythms and abnormalities of the blood biochemistry. For this reason, a doctor should oversee the treatment of severe hypothermia. Never assume that a victim of hypothermia is dead, even if their pulse and breath movements are absent; always attempt to resuscitate them using CPR.

▶▶ See CPR, p.239.

Snow blindness

Snow blindness describes damage to the conjunctiva of the eye caused by the glare of strong ultraviolet light reflected off snow. It's easily **avoided** by wearing good-quality sunglasses.

After the early **symptoms** of prolonged blinking and squinting in response to the glare, the eyes begin to water and feel painful, gritty and irritable. Vision may take on a pink hue. The condition resolves without treatment but recovery will be hastened by resting in a dark place, preferably with a blindfold and applying cool compresses to your forehead. Take pain relief as required.

Trenchfoot

Trenchfoot develops when the feet are exposed to moist, cold conditions for a prolonged period of time (usually a day or more). The condition was common in World War I (thus the name); more recently, a number of cases have been reported after rain-sodden outdoor rock festivals. The condition may also be caused by prolonged wearing of tight, rubberized boots in which sweat accumulates or into which water has leaked. Being cold and wet causes the blood vessels in the feet to constrict, which in turn causes a reduction in the blood supply to the tissues of the feet.

Early **signs** of the condition are usually itching, numbness and pain. Later the feet may swell and the skin may look discoloured. There is often a distinct "waterline" coinciding with the water level in the boot. Red blotches and weeping blisters may appear and can become infected.

Prevention involves changing into dry socks at the first possible opportunity. To **treat** trenchfoot, first remove the wet, constrictive boots and socks. Gently wash and dry the area before elevating and covering with loose, warm clothing. Use adequate pain relief and anti-inflammatory drugs. Do not attempt to burst the blisters or expose the area to extreme heat. Secondary infection can be treated with appropriate antibiotics (eg flucloxacillin). If the pain, swelling or blistering is severe, seek medical help.

Colds and coughs

(Respiratory tract infection)

You can catch a **cold**, **cough** or **sore throat** (collectively known as upper respiratory tract infection, or URTI) easily enough at home, but travelling can not only increase your susceptibility to these kinds of infection but can also expose you to previously unencountered germs to which you have no natural immunity.

Alternative treatments for a cold

To treat a cold homeopathically, choose **Arsenicum album** if you have a watery, burning discharge which makes your eyes water, and prolific sneezing, but blowing your nose brings no relief. **Allium cepa** is best for a cold marked by massive sneezes and a constantly dripping nose; the discharge, often acrid, ceases on going outdoors and returns when you go in. **Aconite** is good for the initial stages of a cold, when you feel the first tickle in the back of your throat, when symptoms begin abruptly (and are often worse around midnight), and when you feel feverish and restless. Use **Gelsemium** to treat the more fluey type of cold, with aching and chills, hypersensitive skin and heavy legs, and when all you want to do is go to sleep. **Natrum mur** can help colds which seem to come on after stress, and which have a nasal discharge the consistency of uncooked egg-white. It's also a good remedy for people who get cold sores with their nose cold, and will help clear up both. For colds that start with a sore throat, with bad breath with lots of thick saliva, take **Mercurius**. You may have a mouth ulcer and your nasal discharge is thick and yellow or green, often bloody, perhaps with a foul smell. **Pulsatilla** treats children's colds, or the riper stages of an adult cold, when you're especially congested at night and by day feel better for fresh air. Nasal discharge, which is thick and yellow or green, is often heaviest in the morning, and you may have bad breath. You may also feel tearful and needy. For all these remedies, use a 30c **potency**, and take one **dose** four times a day until there is an improvement. Remember that decongestants such as eucalyptus, menthol and camphor will act as antidotes to the remedies, so should be avoided.

Of other **complementary treatments**, **vitamin C** and **zinc** supplements are also useful in combating colds (take up to one gram of vitamin C a day for four to five days; take your zinc supplement between meals, drinks and other supplements). Zinc and vitamin C lozenges are a good way of taking these two together. **Frankincense** aromatherapy oil burned in a vaporizer or blended with a carrier oil (like almond) and massaged into your skin will help to clear your chest.

Sore throats and antibiotics

It's difficult to be specific, but consider using antibiotics in the following circumstances:

✦ If the sore throat is present for more than five days (although glandular fever should also be considered in this instance).

✦ If you are generally feeling very unwell (high temperature, loss of appetite etc).

✦ If you are having difficulty swallowing.

✦ If your tonsils or the back of your throat look red, inflamed or pustular (you can sometimes see by examining your mouth with the help of a torch).

✦ If you have previously suffered from severe bouts of tonsillitis

✦ If you develop a fine red rash on your body (this can be a feature of streptococcal infection)

URTIs are generally amenable to over-the-counter preparations. Paracetamol or ibuprofen should be used for pain relief or to reduce a fever, and oral or nasal decongestants help to dry up a blocked nose. Don't forget steam inhalation, with or without additions such as menthol or eucalyptus oil, an old but effective remedy.

Note that the fact that you have a **cough** doesn't automatically mean you have a chest infection – it's usually caused by the nasal secretions dripping down the back of your throat and stimulating your cough reflex. Chest infections are generally pretty rare in the young, fit, non-smoker. Asthmatics should increase the use of their inhalers (see p.52) in the early stages of a URTI.

The vast majority of respiratory tract infections are **viral** in origin and, as such, are not amenable to treatment with antibiotics. If a doctor prescribes you an antibiotic it's because of a secondary bacterial infection (eg chest infection, sinusitis, tonsillar abscess, inner ear infection etc) or because the illness is prolonged and showing no signs of improvement.

Chest infections

Signs of a **chest infection** are a productive cough (yellow or green sputum), wheezing, high fever, shortness of breath, chest pain, and systemic illness (loss of appetite, vomiting etc). **Legionnaires' disease** is a special case and dealt with in more detail later in this section (see p.155). Appropriate **antibiotics** for the treatment of a chest infection are amoxicillin, erythromycin, doxycycline and ciprofloxacin (see Part 1 for recommended dosages and directions).

Sinusitis

Classically, following a URTI, an intense, localized pain develops in the forehead, cheek or behind the eyes, signifying **sinusitis**. It's usually one-sided and worse on bending forward and blowing your nose. Nasal discharge may be minimal but is usually purulent if present. Sinusitis can be treated using the same antibiotics as for chest infections; decongestants and steam inhalation can also help.

Silica 30c, taken four times a day, is a helpful homeopathic remedy for sinusitis.

Sore throats

Although the incidence in travellers is no higher than in the general population, **sore throats** are nevertheless very common and, as such, capable of taking a few days' enjoyment out of your trip. From the outset, it's important to recognize that the majority of sore throats are caused by **viruses** (estimates vary geographically from sixty to ninety percent) and so are not amenable to antibiotic therapy. There is no certain way to differentiate between bacterial and viral sore throats by examination alone. Consequently, a course of antibiotics is often unnecessarily prescribed. Most sore throats, regardless of their cause, will resolve spontaneously after about five days, and the best course of **treatment** in most cases is pain relief and increasing oral fluid intake.

Paracetamol or **ibuprofen** should be used for pain relief and to control high temperatures. **Gargling** with salt water or soluble aspirin may provide some additional relief. Increase your fluid intake. If antibiotics are used, a seven- to ten-day course of penicillin V or erythromycin is the standard recommendation. If symptoms persist for more than a week, and are not resolving after antibiotic use, consider **glandular fever**, a viral illness that's common in adolescents and young adults. A blood test can confirm a glandular fever diagnosis, but there's no specific treatment for it other than symptomatic relief. The aftermath of glandular fever – recurrent sore throats, lassitude, fatigue etc – can last for several months.

If at any time the pain or inflammation precludes swallowing fluids, seek medical help, as intravenous antibiotics and fluids may be necessary. Remember that diphtheria (see p.117) commonly starts off as a severe sore throat.

 Homeopathic treatment can help to get rid of a sore throat speedily. Taking hourly doses of **Aconite** 30c as soon as you feel pain will often stop it in its tracks. For soreness that has set in, try a 30c potency of one of the following remedies (take every two hours initially, leaving longer between doses as symptoms subside). If the sore throat has come on very quickly, and you are feeling burning hot, with a dry mouth, try **Belladonna**. **Ferrum phos** is indicated if the onset is slower, and the soreness is accompanied by a runny nose and cough, while **Gelsemium** should work well if there is no thirst, and the sore throat seems to be developing into flu. Use **Mercurius** if your throat looks really mucky and your tongue is coated – this may mean that it is glandular fever, and using Mercurius should make it a milder illness.

Constipation

A number of travel-related factors can lead to **constipation**, from simply suppressing a natural urge to go while in transit or avoiding unwelcoming lavatory conditions to changes in diet and water. Sitting inactive for hours on end alone disturbs the natural rhythms of the bowel, but when coupled with dehydration, you're likely to arrive at your destination in a mild state of constipation. Drugs, such as some painkillers, often have constipation as a recognized side effect.

Apart from the obvious difficulty in opening your bowels, constipation often leads to more generalized unpleasant **symptoms**, such as abdominal bloating and discomfort, mood swings, bad breath and an overall feeling of wretchedness.

Treatment

Constipation usually resolves itself but you can help things along by increasing your **fluid intake**, **exercising** and altering your **diet**: eat plenty of fibre (bran cereals, wholemeal bread) and fruit (prunes, apples, oranges and bananas in particular). Liquorice and some of the sugar-free chewing gums are also good at getting things moving.

If necessary, **senna** is a cheap and effective bowel stimulant although occasionally, if the stools are very hard, a softener such as **magnesium hydroxide** or **lactulose** may be a kinder first option.

To treat constipation homeopathically, choose from among the following remedies. If you've no urge to "go" at all; if the stool feels "stuck" for days on end; if you start to pass the stool but it retreats back again; and if when they do pass they're small, hard black balls, try **Opium** (6c three times a day for 3–7 days, or 30c 1–2 times daily). Take **Nux vomica** (same dosage as opium) if you have lots of urging with little success, feel bloated and irritable, and feel that if you try just one more time something will happen; it's also indicated if you're very sensitive to pressure about the waist and have probably been overdoing it with new foods, spices or excess alcohol.

Cramp

A sudden and sometimes sustained spasm of a muscle, **cramp** has a variety of **causes**, including dehydration, stress, fatigue, heavy exercise and poor posture. It most commonly affects the calf muscles, is more common in older people and often happens at night in bed.

To safeguard yourself against cramp, remember to warm up adequately before **exercise** and spend five or ten minutes stretching afterwards. Eating fruit such as oranges or bananas will ensure that the levels of important salts in your blood are maintained during exercise. Drink extra fluids beforehand and while you work out.

During an attack of cramp, massage the muscle and gently stretch. A warm towel, bath or shower increases blood flow, helping to relieve the spasm. Gently stretch the muscle (for calf cramp, sit on the floor with your leg straight, grip your foot and gently pull it towards you; alternatively, quickly lift up your toes as high as you can, then slowly, slowly lower them over the course of a few minutes). Take extra fluids to rehydrate. If the calf remains tender, or becomes red, hot or swollen, it is possible that you have a **DVT** (see p.111) and you should seek medical advice at once.

Homeopathically, **Cuprum metallicum** is very effective in preventing night cramps; take one 30c tablet in the evening until symptoms stop.

Crimean-Congo haemorrhagic fever

Crimean–Congo haemorrhagic fever (CCHF) occurs in sporadic outbreaks throughout Africa, Asia, the Middle East and Eastern Europe. The name was coined in 1969 when it was recognized that two outbreaks of disease, one in Crimea in 1944 and one in the Congo in 1956, were in fact caused by the same virus. Common among a wide range of domestic and wild animals, CCHF is a rare but serious disease in humans.

109

CCHF is a **virus** transmitted to humans by the bite of an infected **tick** or by direct contact with infected animal blood or tissues. To the average traveller, risk is only slight, but there is no reliable or safe vaccination for humans so try and avoid wild areas when ticks are most abundant (usually from spring to autumn); see p.149 for suggestions on avoiding them.

Symptoms, diagnosis and treatment

CCHF's incubation period is short, usually between one and three days if acquired from a tick bite but longer if through contact with animal tissues. The **symptoms** tend take hold rapidly and include fever, dizziness, headache, neck pain and stiffness, generalized aching, abdominal pain, diarrhoea, nausea and vomiting, sore eyes and photophobia. Mood swings and agitation can follow, succeeded by depression and lassitude. Bleeding under the skin, into the bowel or bladder (manifesting as blood in the stools or urine respectively), or from the mouth and nose can also occur.

The diagnosis of CCHF can be confirmed by a **blood test**. CCHF can be a severe, even lethal illness, so if suspected, seek medical help immediately. While there is no specific **treatment**, intensive medical and nursing care improves the outcome.

Cryptosporidiosis

Cryptosporidiosis is caused by a gut parasite, and although uncommon in anyone with a normally functioning immune system, the disease particularly affects children because their immunity is less robust. It also used to be a common complication of AIDS.

The parasite's major natural reservoir is cattle and it's spread by the faecal–oral route, usually via contaminated water (often at swimming pools). Person-to-person spread is possible if personal hygiene is poor.

Symptoms

Cryptosporidiosis causes a **gastrointestinal upset** which can be severe and, if your immune system is already compromised, extremely dangerous. After an incubation period of between two and ten days, the symptoms are acute in onset and consist of profuse, watery diarrhoea, cramp-like abdominal pains, flatulence, vomiting, fever and general malaise.

Diagnosis and treatment

Diagnosis is usually made by lab analysis of a stool sample. There is no effective drug **treatment** for uncomplicated cryptosporidiosis, but the illness usually settles after seven to ten days. In the interim, you can take the standard measures for treating diarrhoea (see p.132). In severe cases because of immunodeficiency, specialist treatment can reduce the diarrhoea, although it won't eradicate the offending organism.

Culture shock

Culture shock is the term used to describe the rather lost feeling that many travellers experience when they arrive at a new and unfamiliar destination – for the returning traveller who has been away for a long time, this can also mean home. It can be fuelled by poor **preparation** before your trip, sadness about leaving home, fatigue from the journey or jet lag, concurrent illness and your reception (or lack of reception) on arrival. Feelings of anxiety, perhaps even panic, are common, as well as a sense of isolation, disorientation, irritability, irrational anger, mild depression, mood swings and often tearfulness. The anxiety symptoms occur to a greater or lesser extent in most travellers, but are often suppressed by the excitement of being somewhere new.

A first step in minimizing the impact of a new culture is to do a little **research** into your destination before you set out (the "knowledge is power" principle): read as much as you can, check out relevant websites and speak to people who have been there before. On arrival, give yourself time to rest, recuperate and emotionally **acclimatize** to your new surroundings. Avoid making rash or important decisions in the first few days, and try not to seek solace in alcohol or any other drugs, as these are only likely to have a depressant effect and make the situation worse.

Try to **involve** yourself. Start by chatting to fellow travellers where you're staying and participating in group activities if any exist. Get out and about and make the effort to interact with the locals. Set about seeing some of the sights in the first few days in case you need reminding of why you made the trip initially. Take an interest in and respect the new culture, and avoid clashing with, or resisting it – you'll make yourself unpopular and feel more isolated.

Above all, recognize culture **shock** for what it is – and remember that the initial symptoms usually dissipate and are forgotten after the first couple of days. If your low mood or anxieties persist, try giving yourself a little more time before deciding to move on or return home. Culture shock also has a **positive** side. Exposure to a different culture and environment can be a rewarding and refreshing experience, often bringing into focus and adding new perspective and context to the stresses and problems left behind at home. Reflection, or perhaps the time to reflect, is a rare and underestimated luxury to many in the Western world.

 Homeopathy can be very helpful for emotional problems such as homesickness and anxiety. Try **Pulsatilla** if you feel tearful and abandoned, or **Aconite** if you feel shaky and anxious. Use a 30c potency of either, and repeat it every two hours until the feelings pass.

Cuts and abrasions

▶▶ See First Aid, p.238.

Cystitis

▶▶ See Urinary tract infections, p.224.

Deep-vein thrombosis (DVT)

Deep-vein thrombosis (**DVT**) is the abnormal clotting of blood in the deep veins of the leg. The life-threatening risk is not from the DVT itself but from the clot breaking off and travelling to the lungs, resulting in a **pulmonary embolism** or **embolus**. The clot forming in the lung reduces blood flow and thus oxygen exchange. A large pulmonary embolus can rapidly cause death through impaired blood flow to the heart. Although the condition has been the focus of much recent media interest in relation to air travel, it is rare in those who are fit and well.

Though there is an increased possibility of acquiring a DVT on a long-haul flight (a risk that remains for up to two weeks afterwards), it's important to recognize that any prolonged period of immobility, particularly in hot, cramped conditions, increases the probability of DVT – thus long journeys by bus or train carry similar risks to flying. Note also that the media-generated term **"economy class syndrome"** is misleading in that travelling in relatively spacious business or first class seats carries the same level of DVT risk as a seat in the more crowded main cabin. Additionally, though the link between air travel and DVT is real, studies have revealed that there have been other contributory factors (see the box below) in most cases of DVT that developed during or after a flight. The direct risk from air travel alone is therefore difficult to define, and research is ongoing. A recent Australian study has suggested that for healthy passengers with no other risk factors, the chance of a DVT is very low – around one in 40,000.

Symptoms

The commonest **symptoms** of DVT are unilateral pain, swelling, heat and redness of the calf. Signs of a pulmonary embolus are acute shortness of breath, chest pain, often sharp and intense, and coughing up blood.

Prevention and treatment

To **reduce the risk of DVT**, take **exercise** before and after flying, and try to get up and walk around periodically once in the air. While seated, you should do hourly calf stretching exercises – tensing and relaxing the muscles of the calves helps to pump blood back up the limbs and prevent stasis or pooling. It's also important to keep **well hydrated**; avoid caffeine and alcohol, and drink a glass of water each hour or so. Elasticated stockings ("flight socks") are widely available from pharmacies and are beneficial in preventing DVT by compressing the legs and improving blood flow. There's no conclusive proof that thinning the blood by taking regular low doses of aspirin can lessen the risk of DVT; bear in mind also that aspirin itself can have unwanted side effects.

Factors which increase the risk of DVT

+ Immobility
+ Obesity
+ Previous DVT
+ Concurrent significant illnesses or recent surgery
+ Smoking
+ The combined oral contraceptive pill
+ Pregnancy
+ Hormone replacement therapy
+ Age (over 40 years old)
+ Varicose veins
+ Dehydration
+ Hereditary problems with blood coagulation
+ Height (excessive tallness or shortness may increase the risk of travel related DVTs)

If three or more of the increased-risk factors in the box opposite apply to you, consult your doctor well before flying for advice on anticoagulation treatment.

If a DVT or pulmonary embolus is suspected, seek urgent medical help; drugs that thin the blood and break up the clot need to be commenced as soon as possible.

Dehydration

In its simplest terms, **dehydration** is caused either by excessive fluid loss (eg diarrhoea, vomiting, fever, bleeding, sweating etc) or inadequate fluid intake. The average adult should drink between two and three litres of fluid a day, although requirements increase in hot climates and during strenuous exercise. Susceptibility to dehydration is much higher in young children.

Thirst is the most obvious **symptom**, although other signs to look out for include a dry mouth and tongue, a loss of skin elasticity (tested by pinching the skin), dark, strong-smelling urine with a drop in output, headache or backache and, in more severe cases, fainting, lapsing into unconsciousness and a weak, rapid pulse. Dehydrated children tend to be listless and quiet, with dry, sunken eyes and, in babies, a sagging, flaccid fontanelle, or "soft spot".

If the dehydration is the result of diarrhoea or vomiting, start simply by taking frequent sips of **boiled water**. As this is tolerated, gradually build up your fluid intake with diluted fruit juice or, better still, **oral rehydration salts** (see p.39). Aim at taking a cupful for every loose stool passed. Don't attempt to eat solids until you are comfortable with fluids – fluid intake is much more important.

If you're unable to take fluids orally and there are signs of dehydration, seek medical attention as intravenous fluids may be required.

Dengue fever

Outbreaks of **dengue fever** occur in most tropical and subtropical regions of the Far East, the Middle East, South America and Africa, with periodic epidemics in the Caribbean and Pacific Islands, Australia and the southern United States. The prevalence of dengue has risen steadily over the last twenty years: it's now more common than ever before, with the WHO estimating that around fifty million cases occur each year. The main reasons for this explosion are poor mosquito control, inadequate public health measures, expanding urbanization and population growth leading to deterioration in sanitation, and increased air travel allowing early spread of the virus. Studies on German and Australian travellers returning from the tropics have shown that up to eight percent were infected with dengue.

Dengue fever is a virus spread by the Aedes ("tiger") species of mosquito, identifiable by its black-and-white body and its penchant for biting shadowed areas of our bodies during daylight hours – usually in early morning or late afternoon. The mosquito is rarely found above elevations of 2000 feet (approx. 600 metres). Note that you can't catch dengue from another person, and that although contracting the infection confers immunity, there are four separate subtypes of the virus, and unfortunately immunity to one does not extend to the other strains. A preventative vaccine is being developed, but for now your only means of avoidance is vigilant bite avoidance (see p.149).

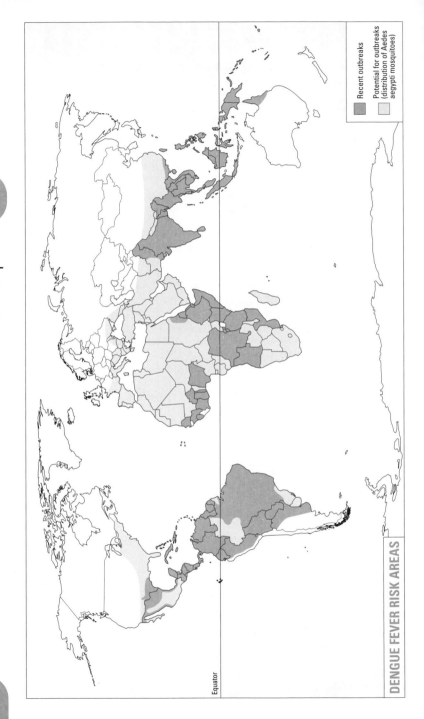

DENGUE FEVER RISK AREAS

Equator

Recent outbreaks

Potential for outbreaks (distribution of Aedes aegypti mosquitoes)

# 	"It can't happen to me"

*A*fter a gruelling five months backpacking through Southeast Asia, we finally reached Sumatra. The first night was spent in the bustling, grimy, tropical heat of Medan after which it was a relief to finally reach Bukit Lewang, home of the Orang Utan Rehabilitation Centre in the heart of the jungle. This was to be one of the highlights of our trip where we planned to base ourselves for a few days before moving on to the even more remote Lake Toba.

We reached our destination in the evening, after a six-hour journey by local bus which I was in no hurry to repeat. Little did I know I'd be making a premature return trip under even less comfortable circumstances. We woke early the next morning to make the 30-minute walk to see the orang-utans. As we set off, I found the intense heat and humidity even more stifling than before but couldn't account for my growing aches and lethargy. I finally collapsed on a rock by the river. Realizing this was not just another attack of Delhi-belly, my partner carried me back to our accommodation where I lay delirious for several hours. My body groaned with every movement, my head pounded as though it would explode and my fever soared. The grim reality of being in the backend of nowhere without medical help or even the ability to converse sensibly with the locals was hitting home. This was the classic "it can't happen to me" scenario.

My partner started to fret about malaria (even though I'd been taking antimalarials) and realizing that my condition was deteriorating, decided we needed to get back to Penang for medical attention (I was in no state to make any assessment of the situation).

I started vomiting into a plastic bag even before our taxi driver began to negotiate the dirt roads at breakneck speed. My fever hovered at an alarmingly high level and with fantastically poor timing I developed "explosive" diarrhoea.

On the outskirts of Medan, our taxi driver was stopped by the police and promptly arrested (we assumed because of speeding), leaving me lying on the pavement while my partner tried, with some difficulty, to seek alternative transport. We eventually managed to find a driver willing to take us to a hostel (for a hefty price of course). With electric fan by my bedside, polythene bags and a toilet close by, I rested while my partner booked our ferry to Penang. We needed to leave at 5am the next morning (too early for Sumatran taxi drivers) so had to walk for 45 minutes to catch the bus. Still suffering from sickness, diarrhoea and excruciating pain throughout my body, I thought I would never make it.

Some six hours or so later, I arrived in Penang feeling dehydrated, tearful and exhausted. Perhaps having momentarily forgotten his concern for my welfare, my partner asked if I could face the 30-minute walk to save on taxi fares! The next day I had a test for malaria at a local health clinic which proved negative. We were relieved by the negative result and the fact I was showing some signs of improvement, but my illness dragged on for several more weeks and in latter stages produced a new range of symptoms including a dreadfully itchy rash, intense fatigue and depression. We were becoming increasingly despondent at my lack of recovery and starting to contemplate a premature return home. It was not until we met several other travellers who had encountered similar symptoms and pursued medical opinion that we identified the cause of my illness: dengue fever. On reaching Singapore, several weeks later, my symptoms started to subside and I was able to remember why I had set out on my travels in the first place.

Joanna Gibbons, Bath, UK

A rare but serious complication, which mainly affects children under 15, is **dengue haemorrhagic fever** (DHF); it's estimated to cause around 24,000 deaths worldwide each year. The predisposing factors to dengue haemorrhagic fever are mainly the particular viral subtype and epidemic strain, recurrent infections, age, general level of health, geographic region (a preponderance of cases are in Southeast Asia) and possibly genetic factors. It is particularly common in people who have suffered a previous attack with one of the viral subtypes, and who are then exposed to another subtype. The victim may become shocked (pale, clammy faint and nauseous with a weak, rapid pulse and shallow, rapid breathing), and develop abnormal bleeding under the skin, and from the nose, mouth and rectum. This is a life-threatening complication and requires **urgent medical attention**.

Symptoms

The **symptoms** of dengue fever are remarkably similar to malaria, and usually appear between five and eight (sometimes as long as fourteen) days after being bitten. The onset is usually abrupt and includes high fever, malaise, headache (characteristically behind the eyes), joint pains and backache (hence dengue has been nicknamed "break-bone fever"). Diarrhoea is fairly common after the first day and, although often being explosive in nature, it doesn't normally last more than two days. A fine rash is likely to appear after a couple of days, initially affecting the torso before spreading to the extremities. It can be maddeningly itchy. The high temperature usually normalizes for a day or two before briefly recurring with the original symptoms. Abnormal bleeding can occur and will need medical assessment.

The acute illness does not normally last for more than ten days, but the **convalescence** can be protracted, with severe fatigue and depression that may last for several weeks afterwards. There is a recognized increased suicide risk after dengue fever.

Diagnosis and treatment

A **blood test** will reveal the virus or the viral antibodies. There is no specific **treatment** for dengue, and symptom control is your only option until the disease has taken its natural course. Get plenty of **bed rest** during the initial stages and take steps to reduce the fever (see p.125). **Don't take aspirin** because it can increase the tendency to bleed. Antihistamines and calamine may ease the rash, and loperamide the diarrhoea. Seek medical help immediately if dengue haemorrhagic fever is suspected. or if your symptoms are worsening or not improving. Remember that anyone in a malarial area with the symptoms of dengue should also be checked for malaria.

You can treat dengue homeopathically using **Eupatorium**; take a 30c tablet four times daily until there are signs of improvement, but bear in mind that as dengue is a serious condition, medical help should be sought at the slightest sign of deterioration.

Diarrhoea

▶▶ See Gastrointestinal problems, p.131.

Diphtheria

Diphtheria is a bacterial illness spread from person to person. It can occur anywhere in the world but is rare in developed countries, most of which have established childhood immunization programmes. (Significant outbreaks have occurred in the former Soviet Union countries in recent years following the collapse of such programmes.)

In countries without an immunization programme, asymptomatic carriers are often responsible for spreading the disease. If you were immunized as a child but have not received a booster for more than ten years, you should have one before visiting less developed countries where the immunization pro-gramme may be sketchy, or where there is an active epidemic.

Symptoms

After an incubation period of between two and six days, early **symptoms** are a sore throat, fever and chills. The breath smells extremely offensive and the lymph glands in the neck become very swollen. As the disease progresses, it becomes difficult to swallow because of pain and the presence of a leathery membrane over the tonsils and across the throat (a diagnostic feature of the dis-ease). The bacteria causing diphtheria secrete a toxin, which can cause heart failure and paralysis. Diphtheria remains highly **infectious** for ten days after the onset of fever.

Diagnosis and treatment

Although a **lab culture** of throat swabs or blood can identify the bacteria, you can't afford to wait for test results – this is a potentially lethal disease, so seek urgent medical help. Intravenous **antibiotics** such as penicillin and erythro-mycin can be used to eliminate the bacteria, but an intravenous antitoxin also needs to be given to counteract the effects of the bacterial toxin.

Dracunculiasis

(Guinea worm infection)

Dracunculiasis has been eradicated from many regions of the world where it was formerly prevalent. The vast majority of cases are now reported from southern Sudan, with occasional outbreaks in other sub-Saharan countries, and a few sporadic cases in Yemen.

The infection is contracted by drinking water contaminated with Cyclops water fleas that carry the **Guinea worm larvae**. Once inside the stomach, the larvae penetrate through the intestinal wall, mature into adult worms and migrate to the peripheral tissues. The worm exits the body by boring through the surface skin (usually the feet but also from the genitalia, hands and breasts). It can take up to three weeks for the worm to fully emerge, and it's during this time that embryos are shed into the water during bathing. Thus the cycle goes around again.

Dracunculiasis is largely restricted to poor, rural communities that are isolated from the well-beaten tourist tracks. Observe the usual water precautions in high-risk areas – boiling drinking water kills both the fleas and the larvae. No vaccination or preventative medication is available.

Symptoms

The time from ingestion to emergence of the adult worms usually presents no **symptoms** and goes unrecognized. If the worm enters a joint during migration it can cause pain and swelling. The skin swells, blisters and ruptures when the thread-like worm exits, leaving an extremely painful ulcer which can take several weeks to heal. A more generalized allergic reaction to the emerging worm may take place, causing nausea, vomiting, diarrhoea, swelling, wheezy chest and an itchy rash. Symptoms, both local and more generalized, can persist for prolonged periods when several worms are expelled successively.

Treatment

The emerging worm, when visible, can be coaxed to **release its larvae** by repeated immersion in water over a period of days (the larvae look like a milky fluid). After a few days of this "milking" the worm will protrude sufficiently for gentle **traction** to be applied as it is carefully wound around a stick. It can take two weeks or more to remove the worm in this way (the mature worms can be up to 1m long). It is important not to leave any residual pieces behind in the tissues since they can cause serious secondary infection. A five-day course of **metronidazole** (400mg twice daily) may shorten the time it takes to extract the worm.

On the emergence of the worm a tetanus booster will be necessary if you're not up to date.

DVT

▶ ▶ See Deep-vein thrombosis, p.111

Dysentery

▶ ▶ See Gastrointestinal problems, p.131; Amoebiasis, p.93.

Ear problems

Infections of the **ear** are not uncommon especially after a cold, swimming or in hot, tropical conditions. Broadly speaking, they can be divided into **two types**: infections of the middle ear (behind the eardrum) and infections of the outer ear (outside the eardrum).

Middle ear infections frequently follow an upper respiratory tract infection, and are far more common in children than in adults. They are often bacterial in origin, although some are viral. Intense, acute, throbbing pain in the affected ear is the most prominent **symptom**; there is often a fever, too, as well as deafness and occasionally ringing (known as tinnitus) in the ear. There may be a discharge, although this usually means that the drum has perforated and is releasing pus, and there will be subsequent relief from the pain. If this occurs, don't panic, the drum will usually grow back without any long-term damage, although water entering the ears (eg through swimming) should be avoided for at least a month; use ear plugs when bathing/showering. The mainstay of **treatment** for middle ear infections is pain relief. The pain from an infected eardrum can be intense and children in particular will be very miserable and unsettled. Regular paracetamol is usually adequate. If the diagnosis is fairly certain, starting a five- to seven-day course of antibiotics is appropriate (although not always necessary); amoxicillin is generally regarded as the best option, but erythromycin (the first choice if you are allergic to penicillin) and co-amoxiclav are also effective. If in doubt, it's better to treat conservatively with painkillers alone.

 Homeopathic treatment is very effective for middle ear infections. For severe earache, with a high temperature and a red cheek, use **Belladonna** 30c, one tablet every hour until relief. For less acute pain, particularly if there is a discharge from the ear, use **Pulsatilla** 30c, one tablet four times a day, until relief of symptoms.

Infections of the outer ear are also painful, and the discomfort is often made worse by jaw movements. Discharge, deafness and visible swelling may also occur. The tragus (the hard bobble of flesh in front of the ear hole) and the ear lobe itself are often very tender. The common predisposing factors for outer ear infections are inadequate drying of the ear after swimming, the presence of a foreign body or trauma (eg scratching or cleaning the ear with cotton buds). The infection can be bacterial (most commonly), fungal or viral. The best initial **treatment** is regular application of antibiotic eardrops (eg Gentisone HC or Cotisporin Otic Solution), usually combined with a mild steroid to reduce inflammation. Apply three or four drops three to four times a day followed by gentle massage of the tragus to allow deeper penetration into the ear canal. A one-week course is generally sufficient. A course of systemic antibiotics, the main choices being flucloxacillin, amoxicillin, co-amoxiclav or erythromycin, may be helpful as a supplementary treatment if the infection is severe. If symptoms persist despite these measures, seek medical help, as occasionally the residual debris in the ear canal will need to be removed by suction.

Reinfection is common in both inner and outer ear infections and it is sensible to avoid swimming for a month following the infection. Scuba diving is not recommended until the infection is fully healed and a doctor has checked for perforations of the eardrums.

Fluid behind the drum

Fluid in the middle ear is not uncommon following a cold or an ear infection. The problem arises when the **eustachian tube** (the tube connecting the inner ear to the back of the nose), which allows pressure to equalize on both sides of the eardrum, becomes blocked. The sensation is frequently likened to being underwater – you're unable to "pop" the ears, causing a temporary reduction in hearing. Fluid trapped behind the eardrum can lead to significant discomfort when flying or scuba diving (activities which alter the pressure gradient across the eardrum).

The symptoms usually settle without treatment within a month, although it is best to avoid flying or scuba diving while the ear still feels blocked. Occasionally **nasal decongestants** and **steam inhalation** can help to alleviate the blockage.

Earwax

We all produce **earwax** as part of the normal, natural cleansing process of the ear, but sometimes the outer ear canal can become blocked causing hearing loss. Do not attempt to remove earwax yourself; a good rule of thumb is not to put anything smaller than your elbow in your ear – resist using matchsticks and cotton buds as picking tools. Try **softening the wax** with some drops of warm olive oil: lie on your side and have someone place two or three drops of oil in your ear, then wait for a few minutes before plugging the ear loosely with cotton wool. If this fails to improve your hearing you might need to have your ears **syringed** (after adequate softening of the wax) at a clinic. If you frequently have your ears syringed at home and are planning a prolonged trip, add it to your list of things to do before you leave.

Eastern and western equine encephalitis

Eastern equine encephalitis occurs in isolated outbreaks along the eastern seaboard of the US, as well as Canada, the Caribbean and parts of Central and South America. It can occur all year round in the tropics but tends to be a summer illness further north, where the majority of cases occur between May and August, often in swamp areas. The disease is extremely serious, but by the same token very rare among humans – it usually strikes birds and horses. The virus is spread to humans by mosquitoes. According to the American Center for Disease Control, fewer than ten human cases on average occur each year in the US. Although a vaccine exists for horses, there is no preventative vaccine for humans.

Western equine encephalitis is commoner and clinically similar to, although much less serious than, eastern equine virus. It occurs in the western states of the USA and Canada, peaking in the summer months.

Symptoms, diagnosis and treatment

An abrupt-onset high **fever** is usually accompanied by headache, lethargy and vomiting. Progression of the disease leads to drowsiness, neck stiffness, fits and coma. The mortality rate of those severely affected with eastern equine virus is high (quoted as up to seventy percent) and long-term effects in survivors are common, although adults tend to be more resilient than children.

Antibodies to the viruses can be detected by laboratory analysis of a **blood sample**. There is no specific **treatment** other than symptom relief, intensive care and life support.

Ebola virus

Epidemics of the virulent and dangerous **Ebola virus** have made sporadic but devastating appearances since it was first recognized in 1976 after an outbreak along the Ebola River in Zaire. Since its discovery, over 1500 human cases have been reported, resulting in more than 1000 deaths. The disease affects humans, monkeys and chimpanzees, with confirmed cases in the Democratic Republic of Congo, Gabon, Sudan and the Côte d'Ivoire. Health-care workers in Africa should be on alert for the infection, but with outbreaks rare and generally restricted to isolated rural areas, most travellers are therefore highly unlikely to encounter the disease.

The virus is spread by direct contact with the blood, secretions, organs or semen of an infected human or animal, although its natural reservoir has yet to be pinpointed. Outbreaks have been known to spread rapidly in the rural hospital setting, where sterilization procedures and nursing standards may be inadequate.

Symptoms, diagnosis and treatment

After an incubation period of up to three weeks, a high fever, sore throat, headache and muscular aches, stomach pains, diarrhoea and fatigue become apparent. A few days after the onset of symptoms, a non-itchy pink rash commonly spreads from the face to the rest of the body. Other **symptoms** include a dry cough, red and irritable eyes, vomiting blood and bloody diarrhoea. In severe cases abnormal bleeding, blindness, chest pain, shock and even death can ensue within a week. Infection with Ebola virus is very serious, with a mortality rate of between fifty and eighty percent, but it is survivable – although why some people recover and others die is still poorly understood.

Early diagnosis is often difficult because the initial symptoms are nonspecific. Once suspected, **blood tests** can confirm Ebola infection.

There is no specific **treatment** although an intravenous antiviral agent called ribavirin may help. Hospital admission for supportive care is vital.

Echincoccosis

▶ ▶ See Hydatid disease, p.146.

E-coli Infection

Not all strains of the **e-coli bacteria** (ETEC or enterotoxigenic e. coli) cause illness; in fact, e-coli are commonly found in the guts of healthy humans and animals. The virulent strains are spread via the faecal–oral route, usually from contaminated food or water (person-to-person spread can also occur). Considerable geographical variation in the bacterial strains means that long-term immunity from the infection is rare even in hardened travellers.

A particularly dangerous, although rare, variant is the **e-coli 0157** strain. Infection with 0157 can lead to serious complications including an increased tendency to bleed and renal failure. Intensive treatment for these complications is necessary, and fatalities are in the order of five percent.

Symptoms

Vomiting, crampy abdominal pain and diarrhoea (of variable intensity) usually develop between 12 and 72 hours of ingesting the bacteria. The effects are fairly localized in the gut area, and fever and other symptoms are unusual. E-coli illness is usually short and sharp, usually lasting less than three days.

Diagnosis and treatment

Laboratory tests are usually unhelpful in picking up the infection, but they can help to exclude other causes. **Treatment** is usually unnecessary although oral rehydration solution may be needed to rectify dehydration. For particularly

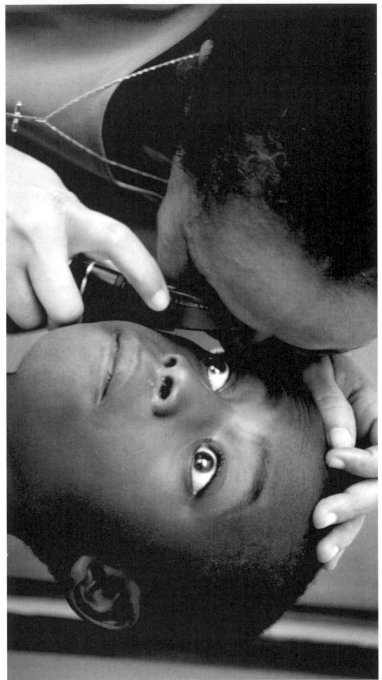

▲ Eye examination, Gambia

severe, prolonged or debilitating symptoms the bacteria are usually sensitive to ciprofloxacin. There is some evidence that the new oral cholera vaccination, Dukoral, confers a degree of protection against e-coli infections. Further, more specific vaccinations are in an advanced stage of development.

Ehrlichiosis

▶▶ See Human ehrlichiosis, p.146

Eye problems

The dry atmosphere on long-distance flights, dusty or hot environments, swimming underwater, pollution, allergies and hygiene problems all take their toll on your **eyes**. In many cases, simple moisturizing **eye drops** will provide relief. The term **conjunctivitis**, or "pink eye", simply refers to inflammation of the thin membrane covering the white of the eye and the inner surface of the lids (the conjunctiva), and is symptomatic of a number of eye problems, from infections to allergies. The eye is red, itchy, irritable and watering. If there's an infection, there may be a sticky discharge, particularly after sleep. Intolerance of bright lights can also occur. Conjunctivitis should not cause eye pain as such, nor impair your vision (other than from excessive tear production or discharge). If these symptoms occur, seek medical advice. Don't forget that most opticians will be suitably equipped to diagnose the cause of conjunctivitis.

While the risks to the average traveller of more serious eye diseases or injuries are only slight, **impaired vision**, **eye pain** and **unequal pupils** must always be assessed by a doctor.

Infections

Eye **infections** are relatively common, especially among children. Conjunctivitis (see above) caused by infection is frequently one-sided, at least initially, although it's easy for the infection to spread to both eyes. Eye infections can be caused by both viruses and bacteria and it's difficult to differentiate between the two. There tends to be more discharge in the case of bacterial infections. Bacterial infections will also usually respond well to **antibiotic drops** or **ointment** such as chloramphenicol (see p.37), but be sure to avoid preparations that contain steroids (these can be dangerous if used inappropriately).

Sometimes the lids or roots of the eyelashes can become infected (**styes**). Mild styes are likely to resolve by themselves without treatment, but if the problem persists, antibiotics such as flucloxacillin, amoxicillin, co-amoxiclav or erythromycin may help.

Abrasions and foreign bodies

Grazes on the eye, or **corneal abrasions**, and **foreign bodies** embedded in the eye (eg dust, wood or metal splinters) cause the symptoms of conjunctivitis in the affected eye. Although it is rarely possible to see abrasions with the naked eye, it is sometimes possible, in a well-illuminated room, to see a particle in someone else's eye as a dark speck in front of the pupil (try looking with a magnifying glass from the side with light coming from the opposite direction). Sometimes the particle will be loosely attached and may be freed by a simple eyebath using an egg cup and boiled, lightly salted water. However more firmly embedded foreign bodies will require medical help. Because of the risk of secondary infection, abrasions and removed foreign bodies need to be followed up with a five- to seven-day course of **prophylactic antibiotics** (eg chloramphenical drops or ointment). Resist the temptation of using local anaesthetic eye drops (eg amethocaine), because these slow down the healing process.

Allergies

Conjunctivitis is also a common symptom in **allergic conditions** such as hay fever. Both eyes are usually affected and your nose tends to run with a watery discharge. Antihistamines, such as chlorpheniramine and loratadine, and sodium cromoglycate eye drops are all helpful. Wearing spectacles or sunglasses may slightly reduce the amount of pollen reaching the eye.

Homeopathic allergy treatments appear on p.90.

Contact lenses

Contact lens wearers can be more prone to eye infections, and fastidious hand hygiene and careful storage is important.

Lenses cause eye dryness at the best of times and the dry air in aircraft, at altitude and in hot, arid countries exacerbates the problem; use moisturizing drops regularly. Carry spectacles in case you lose your lenses or are unable to wear them, and don't ever wear your lenses if you have inflamed eyes.

Sub-conjunctival haemorrhage

This cumbersome medical phraseology simply means a painless bleed behind the conjunctiva caused by a ruptured blood capillary. The white of the eye looks bright red and although it usually occurs spontaneously, bleeds of this type are also associated with excessive coughing, straining, raised blood pressure and increased bleeding tendency (eg the viral haemorrhagic fevers, p.225). The condition, although it looks alarming, is benign and will normally resolve after a week or two. No treatment is necessary for the bleed itself but consider whether you may be at risk from the possible underlying causes.

▶ ▶ See also Brazilian Purpuric Fever, p.100; Cold exposure (snow blindness), p.105; Loiasis, p.129; Filariasis (Onchocerciasis), p.127; and Trachoma, p.217.

Fascioliasis

The liver fluke causing **fascioliasis** infects sheep, cattle and goats worldwide, and can be transmitted to humans who ingest food or water contaminated by the infected animals' faeces. The life cycle of the fluke relies on the presence of a freshwater snail which acts as an intermediate host to the larvae. Once swallowed by humans, the larvae penetrate the gut wall and migrate to the liver and biliary tract, where, after maturation, they begin to produce eggs. Misguided flukes have been found elsewhere in the body, such as the brain, the lungs and the skin.

Fascioliasis is a rare infection which can be easily avoided by observing the usual hygiene measures for drinking water (see pp.21–29).

Symptoms

Early **symptoms** relate to the initial migration of the immature flukes, and are nonspecific: general malaise, intermittent fever, weight loss, diarrhoea, abdominal pain (mainly over the liver) and itching. Once the mature flukes become established in the biliary tract (approximately three or four months after initial infection), they obstruct the flow of bile, causing jaundice, abdominal pain, nausea and loss of appetite.

Diagnosis and treatment

The eggs can be identified in around seventy percent of cases by lab analysis of the **stool** once the flukes have reached the bile duct. More complicated blood tests can confirm the diagnosis.

A single dose of **triclabendazole** (10mg per kilo of body weight) is usually enough to eradicate the flukes, but a second dose may sometimes be necessary.

Fasciolopsiasis

(Giant intestinal fluke)

The **fasciolopsiasis** fluke is commonly found in pigs and humans in south China, Taiwan, Southeast Asia (especially Vietnam and Thailand), Indonesia, India and Bangladesh. Humans are infected by eating raw water plants (eg water chestnuts or water caltrop) contaminated by **larval cysts**. The **flukes** are released from the cysts in the human intestine where they mature into adults, sometimes several centimetres long, after about three months. The eggs are shed in the stools and, on reaching fresh water, penetrate and develop into larvae in freshwater snails (similar to paragonimiasis; see p.178) before escaping to form cysts on the plants. The average traveller is at low risk of contracting fasciolopsiasis, provided they observe adequate food and water hygiene measures.

▶▶ See Paragonimiasis, p.178; Staying well, pp.21–29.

Symptoms, diagnosis and treatment

Most people show no signs of the infection, but in a few, severe cases, **symptoms** such as abdominal pain or discomfort, loss of appetite, nausea, diarrhoea or constipation can develop several months after ingesting the cysts. Swelling of the face and body can occur later on. Anaemia because of blood loss from the site of attachment of the flukes in the intestine is also possible. Heavy infection in children can cause malnutrition.

Microscopic examination of the **stools** shows the presence of the eggs. The disease can be **treated** with a single dose (15mg per kilo of body weight) of praziquantel.

Fever

(Pyrexia)

A **fever** (**pyrexia**) is a complex physiological process characterized by a rise in the core temperature of the body. There are many causes for fever, ranging from the innocuous viral sore throat to life-threatening nasties such as malaria. The body's ability to produce a fever may enhance internal defences against infection, and thus have a positive effect on the course of the illness.

Febrile convulsions

Febrile convulsions are an alarming complication of fever affecting some young children, usually between the ages of 6 months and 6 years. There is no specific "danger point" in a rising temperature at which they're more likely to happen, but only a small minority of children are susceptible to them (around three percent). Paediatric **paracetamol** or **ibuprofen** is the mainstay of treatment to reduce temperature, but sponging them down or placing them in a lukewarm bath are also helpful in that they compensate for the fact that children's bodies are inefficient at sweating (a cooling mechanism).

See p.243 for the first aid treatment of a fit. Most febrile fits are self-limiting and rarely last longer than a couple of minutes. If the fit persists for longer, seek medical help urgently.

 Belladonna 30c, given every fifteen minutes, is an excellent homeopathic remedy which can be used in addition to first-aid measures.

Identifying the root cause of a fever is not easy, especially in the tropics where most of the prevalent diseases cause a fever.

In a malarial zone, the presence of a fever means **malaria** until proven otherwise.

Normal core body temperature is 37°C (98°F); generally anything over 39°C (102°F) is considered to be **high fever**. The most accurate way to take a reading is by placing a **thermometer** under the tongue or inside the rectum for no less than three minutes. A young child's temperature can be taken under the armpit, although the reading will be roughly half a degree centigrade lower than core temperature.

Fever leads to a general feeling of malaise, a sensation of feeling hot then cold, sweating, shaking (known as "rigors"), generalized aches and pains, nightmares and, in the extreme, delirium.

Diagnosis

Fever is usually a sign of an **infection** but can also be caused by **heatstroke**. In determining the cause, consider the kinds of diseases to which you may have exposed yourself, any other symptoms you may have, and whether your condition is improving or deteriorating. If the fever is worsening, you'll need to seek medical input urgently. If the fever recurs in a cycle, for example every 48 hours, consider the possibility of malaria or dengue fever and take steps towards getting a lab test. Don't attempt strenuous physical activity for at least two weeks following a high fever, as it'll take at least that long to regain your strength.

▶▶ See Making a diagnosis; p.82; Malaria, p.163; Meningitis, p.171.

Treatment

Initial **treatment** should focus on reducing the body temperature. The treatment of specific infections is secondary and discussed elsewhere throughout this guide.

Measures to **reduce fever** include:

- Taking regular paracetamol or ibuprofen
- Increasing the intake of cool fluids – aim to drink at least three litres a day (more in hot climates), and avoid alcohol
- Getting plenty of rest
- Taking regular cool showers, or alternatively sponging down with cooled water
- Minimizing layers of clothing even if you feel chilly
- Fanning to reduce your body heat

Temperatures **below 39°C** are generally not dangerous – try to get your temperature down and if after 48 hours there's no reduction seek a doctor's help. A fever **above 39°C** should be taken more seriously. Take the steps above to reduce the temperature, but if in spite of these the high fever persists, seek medical advice. If at any time you develop symptoms of malaria or meningitis, or you have a high fever and may have been at risk of either disease, seek medical help immediately.

An occasional delayed effect from a high fever is hair loss. This is self-limiting and requires no treatment.

 Eupatorium (30c two to four times a day until improvement) is a homeopathic remedy used to reduce high fever in cases of simple flu as well as dengue and malaria. It will suit if you have chills spreading from the small of your back, a great thirst for cold drinks, but also nausea. You may feel restless and want to keep moving, even though motion doesn't actually help.

Filariasis

Widespread in the tropics, where they cause millions of people significant health problems, **filarial infections** are caused by parasitic worms and spread by biting insects. There are three distinct diseases caused by filarial worms: **onchocerciasis**, **filarial lymphangitis** and **loiasis**.

Onchocerciasis

(Mal morado, River blindness, Roble's disease, Volvulosis)

Affecting more than eighteen million people globally, **onchocerciasis** is a major cause of blindness in the developing world. The disease is found mainly in tropical Africa (95 percent of cases are in West Africa), but some cases also occur in tropical South and Central America and the Arabian peninsula. Onchocerciasis is caused by a **worm** parasite, transmitted to humans via the bite of a **blackfly** generally found alongside stretches of fast-flowing water. The blackfly's bite deposits the larvae, which penetrate into the superficial tissues beneath the skin. A year elapses before the worm matures and starts to reproduce large numbers of tiny offspring – **microfilariae** – which migrate throughout the body. The adult worm can live for many years.

There is no vaccination (though ivermectin can be used as a preventative; see overleaf), so taking protective measures against insect bites (see p.149) in high-risk areas is crucial. Fortunately, even in high-risk areas, short-term travellers (staying less than three months) rarely acquire onchocerciasis.

Symptoms

The most prominent symptom caused by the large numbers of microfilariae produced by the mature adult worms is a widespread, red, maddeningly itchy **rash**. Skin nodules ("**bony bumps**") develop at the site where the adult worm is lodged. In Africa, the lesions are usually on the lower part of the body, while in the Americas they tend to be on the head, neck, shoulders or upper trunk. Other **symptoms** caused by the microfilariae include fever, headache, lymph gland swelling and tiredness. During migration, the microfilariae can lodge in the eyes, causing initial redness and irritation which if left untreated leads to **blindness** (hence the name "river blindness"). Such serious eye complications, however, are only likely to affect people who are repeatedly infected over the course of many years.

Diagnosis and treatment

Diagnosis is made either from the clinical picture or by a skin biopsy, which will reveal the presence of the microfilariae.

WHO trials of a drug called **ivermectin** have shown that a single oral dose once yearly is very effective at preventing the symptoms caused by the release of microfilariae. It doesn't kill the adult worm, however, and dosage must be continued annually until the worms die of old age – about twenty years. This and WHO's efforts to eradicate the blackfly breeding grounds have significantly decreased the incidence of onchocerciasis, giving high hopes for total elimination in the course of the next decade.

Filarial lymphangitis

(Bancroftian or Malayan filariasis)

Recognized as one of the world's leading causes of permanent disability, **filarial lymphangitis** is thought to affect more than 100 million people in sub-Saharan Africa, Egypt, southern Asia, the Western Pacific Islands, the northeastern coast of Central and tropical South America, and the Caribbean.

The disease is caused by infection with thread-like **parasitic worms**, which are spread from person to person (and in some strains, animal to human) by **mosquitoes**. The adult worms reside in the **lymph system**, liberating microfilariae into the bloodstream which the mosquitoes ingest during feeding. After a period of development in the mosquito, the larvae are deposited again during feeding and migrate via the bloodstream to the new host's lymph system.

There is no protective vaccination against filarial lymphangitis and your only means of protection is bite avoidance, although short-term, casual tourists are rarely affected.

▶▶ See Bite prevention, p.149.

Symptoms

Symptoms become apparent between five and eighteen months after being bitten, as the parasitic worms slowly grow in the body's lymph system. The worms' presence in the lymph system causes a local inflammatory reaction, followed by scarring and consequent occlusion of the lymph channels. This in turn causes the accumulation of fluid (lymph) in the tissues and **swelling**. The swelling of the legs, in its extreme, can lead to a condition known as **elephantiasis**, so-called because of the skin's resemblance to that of an elephant. The resulting disfigurement and reduced mobility are permanent.

Scrotal swelling can also occur. **Other symptoms** include painful, swollen lymph glands, recurrent fever, skin rashes, blindness and a lung condition, tropical pulmonary eosinophilia, characterized by night-time coughing and wheezing.

Diagnosis and treatment

The most effective way of establishing **diagnosis** is a newly developed "card test", which requires only a finger-prick of blood and no laboratory facilities. **Treatment** options include drugs such as ivermectin, albendazole or diethylcarbamazine – however the most effective treatment combinations and regimes have yet to be established, and specialist help must be sought for the latest recommendations. **Reactions** to the dead microfilariae and worms are common and can be severe, often necessitating additional treatment with antihistamines and steroids.

Loiasis

(Loa loa)

Loiasis occurs in the forested areas of west and central Africa, particularly in Sudan and Cameroon, and affects some thirteen million people in these areas according to WHO estimates. It's caused by the worm of the same name, which is transmitted to humans (its natural host) by the daytime-biting **tabanid fly**. Once the eggs are inside the body, they take about a year to mature into the adult worms, which move about freely under the skin and can measure up to 6cm long and 0.5mm in diameter. The females liberate microfilariae into the bloodstream, which are then taken up and transmitted to others by the feeding tabanid flies.

No vaccination against loiasis is available, although risk to the average traveller is very small. If you're likely to come into close, prolonged contact with the disease, speak to an expert about using diethylcarbamazine as a preventative treatment (300mg weekly for as long as the exposure continues).

Symptoms

Loiasis very rarely causes serious complications, and the adult worms generally go unnoticed unless they pass through the bridge of the nose or the conjunctiva of the eye. In these circumstances the worm can actually be felt in the eye and is sometimes visible. The irritation may continue for several days after the worm has moved on. Other signs of the worm are transient, soft, usually painless skin swellings known as "**Calabar swellings**" (named after a town in eastern Nigeria), which occur more commonly in the hotter months, appearing in close proximity to joints – they're thought to be caused by the migrating worms releasing a toxin in response to a minor local trauma. A localized, sometimes painful, swelling also occurs when the worm dies.

Diagnosis and treatment

Diagnosis can usually be confirmed by a blood test. The **treatment**, diethylcarbamazine, is the same as for filarial lymphangitis; however because of potential adverse reactions to the drug's effect on the microfilariae, this must only be used under close medical supervision. When sighted in the eye or around the bridge of the nose, the worm can sometimes be removed by a doctor under local anaesthetic.

Flu

▶ ▶ See Influenza, p.147.

Foot problems

A number of factors can conspire against the traveller's feet, from ill-fitting hiking boots, extremes of heat and cold, unhygienic showers and swimming facilities, to perhaps a greater reliance than usual on walking. Resulting fungal infections, ingrowing nails, aches and sprains can all chip away at your trip enjoyment.

Athlete's foot is an itchy fungal infection that can cause intense irritation in hot conditions. The usual signs are redness between the toes, accompanied by fluid-filled lumps (vesicles), fissuring and peeling of the skin. Treat athlete's foot with an antifungal cream such as clotrimazole and be sure to apply the cream for at least two weeks after the symptoms have settled – a common mistake is to stop using the antifungal too soon, resulting in recurrences of the condition.

Ingrowing toenails are a minor but nevertheless painful condition usually caused by incorrect trimming of the nail, although wearing ill-fitting shoes may also contribute. They usually affect the big toe, and the flesh surrounding the nail becomes red, swollen and painful. The problem often requires surgical treatment and, despite this, frequently recurs. **Preventing** a nail from ingrowing is simply a matter of cutting the nail straight across and not following the nail's curve down to the peripheries; this encourages the nail to grow towards the centre rather than into the flesh at the edges. If you already have an ingrowing toenail, clip it in the same way – caught early, this may prevent the need for more radical action. **Secondary bacterial infection** is common and manifests as an angry, painful, red and pustular swelling. It should be treated using antibiotics (flucloxacillin, co-amoxiclav or erythromycin). In addition, soak your foot in warm water, preferably containing antiseptic or salt. After the infection has settled, gently wedge a small piece of cotton wool under the edge of the nail to prevent it from cutting into the skin. Wear roomy shoes and keep your feet as clean and dry as possible. Seek advice from a doctor as to whether anything further needs to be done about the nail.

▶ ▶ See also First aid (Soft-tissue injuries), p.241; Cold exposure (Frostbite), p.104; Cold exposure (Trenchfoot), p.105.

Freshwater hazards

Fresh water holds a range of **hazards**, from creatures to currents to a host of diseases. For the exhausted, overheated traveller, the temptation to cool off in the local lake or river can be quite strong, but before taking the plunge, consider the dangers lurking beneath the water's surface. For information on currents and buoyancy, see Part 1, p.25.

Alligators and crocodiles

Alligators and **crocodiles** are potential hazards in the waterways of southeastern USA (Florida and Louisiana especially), tropical South America (mainly in the Amazon and Orinoco basins), tropical Africa, India, parts of Southeast Asia and Australia. Although not all species are dangerous to humans, alligators and crocodiles should always be treated with the utmost respect. It's worth remembering that some species are equally comfortable in fresh or salt water.

Although they may appear sluggish on land, these deceptive creatures are capable of moving extremely quickly over short distances. Never approach one, even if it appears to be asleep – they may just be lying in wait for their unsuspecting dinner. They attack by attaching themselves to their victim with vice-like jaws and submerging, incapacitating their prey by breaking their neck in the course of spinning. All species are more active at night and the majority of attacks occur during the rainy season.

For the average traveller, the risks of being attacked by a crocodile or alligator are small as long as you use common sense in areas where they proliferate, and heed local advice.

Fish

Tropical South American rivers hold the most dangers in terms of freshwater fish. **Electric eels** can inflict an electric shock equivalent to 500 volts when touched, capable of killing an adult human. **Piranhas** attack their prey in shoals, inflicting considerable damage with razor-sharp teeth. They are most dangerous during the dry season when food is scarce. Also native to the Amazon and Orinoco regions is the **candiru** or vampire fish, a small eel-like specimen which is parasitic to other fish and sometimes to humans. It swims up the urethra (the opening to the bladder) when the victim urinates whilst in the water, and lodges in the urethra or higher up in the bladder feeding on blood. This may result in blood loss and infection and may even be fatal. Surgical removal is necessary, although initial avoidance measures are fairly obvious (it's also worth seeking local advice before taking the plunge into South American rivers).

▶▶ See also Cold exposure (Hypothermia), p.105; Leptospirosis, p.160; and Schistosomiasis, p.194.

Frostbite

▶▶ See Cold exposure, p.104.

Gastrointestinal problems

When people mention the words "travel" and "illness" in the same breath, the chances are that diarrhoea is really what they're talking about. **Travellers' diarrhoea** is a ubiquitous problem, and within the first two weeks of any visit to a developing country, the incidence among travellers may be as high as fifty percent. Bear in mind, however, that loose bowel movements, especially at the start of a trip, are fairly normal and usually settle spontaneously.

Travellers' diarrhoea can be the result of a broad range of things, from a simple change in diet to severe diseases like typhoid or cholera; **ETEC** (**enterotoxigenic e-coli**) is the commonest bacterial cause (see p.121). The vast majority of cases are mild and self-limiting, resolving themselves within five days without treatment, so before you panic, it might help to regard the condition – as many experienced travellers do – as a sort of occupational hazard.

Diarrhoea's danger signs

Seek medical input if:
+ Your diarrhoea continues for more than five days.
+ blood is visible in the diarrhoea.
+ there are signs of dehydration.
+ abdominal pain becomes constant and unremitting.
+ there is high fever (above 39°C/102°F).
+ symptoms are particularly severe.

Prevention

As yet there's no **vaccine** targeting travellers' diarrhoea, although trials are currently ongoing for an oral vaccination against the commonest bacterial causes. Although the results have so far been promising, the trials were not in an advanced stage at the time of writing, and the vaccines are unlikely to be generally available for several years, and even then will not protect against all causes of travellers' diarrhoea. The new oral cholera vaccination, Dukoral, has a protective effect against e-coli, but for the time being, your best means of avoiding travellers' diarrhoea is rigorous observation of **food and drink hygiene** measures (see pp.21–24).

Stomach acid acts as your body's own natural defence against the bugs that cause stomach upsets. If you have reduced stomach acidity because of recent surgery or from taking regular heartburn medication, you will have less resistance. Ask your doctor about precautions before you travel.

The use of **antibiotics** to prevent travellers' diarrhoea is a contentious area; they're probably best saved for targeted treatment rather than prevention (see p.134). Studies have shown **bismuth subsalicylate** ("Pepto–Bismol"), in relatively high doses, to be an effective preventative. It overcomes the drawbacks of antibiotic resistance and side effects, but because of the cost, consistency and taste, few people would choose to take high doses for prolonged periods – hence it's perhaps more of use for short trips or again as a treatment when symptoms arise.

Diagnosis

It's uncommon for diarrhoea to be an isolated symptom – at the same time you may experience nausea, vomiting, gripey abdominal pains (for more on abdominal pain, see p.85) and occasionally fever.

Blood mixed in with the stool may suggest a number of diagnoses, from simple haemorrhoids to dysentery or rarities like pseudomembranous colitis, a serious complication of antibiotic therapy (see p.181). In the case of **dysentery**, the diarrhoea is severe with watery, often bloody stools accompanied by fever (usually mild if amoebiasis is the cause, but high in the case of shigella). Potentially quite serious, it usually responds well to antibiotics (see p.134). In any case of bloody diarrhoea, try to submit a stool sample for lab analysis before you begin treating it.

Treatment

It's amazing how many people try to continue travelling, even with quite debilitating diarrhoea – it's far better to **rest** up for a while. The majority of cases will settle within five **days** without specific treatment.

However, it's very important to replace what's been lost. Solids are much less important than **fluids**: you can survive a lot longer without food than you can without water. Bear in mind that you're losing fluids not just with the diarrhoea – fever, vomiting, and a hot climate will all contribute to **dehydration**. Remember, too, that **children** become dehydrated much more rapidly than adults.

▶ ▶ See Antiemetics, p.40; Dehydration, p.113.

Initially, boiled or bottled water may be adequate, but for persistent diarrhoea or vomiting, **oral rehydration fluid** (commercial or homemade – see p.39) is preferable as it replaces lost chemicals and salts as well as water. If vomiting makes it difficult to keep fluids down, take smaller amounts more often and try using an antiemetic drug.

Bismuth subsalicylate (Pepto–Bismol) offers effective relief in mild to moderate cases of travellers' diarrhoea (less than three episodes a day) without significant side effects.

Alternative treatments for travellers' diarrhoea

Homeopathic **Arsenicum** is the best remedy for an upset stomach caused by eating tainted food or water, ice cream, too many watery fruits, excess alcohol, and from any sudden change of diet. Choose this remedy if your stools are burning, dark and foul-smelling, you feel wiped out, anxious and perhaps fretful about being ill on holiday, or you crave small sips of cold water, but vomit after drinking.

For basic overindulgence in food (especially spicy or rich) and drink, which has triggered violent retching and vomiting that you find hard to stop, try **Nux vomica** 30c. Your abdomen will feel tender and sore, worse on the pressure of a belt and from sudden movements, and you have a constant urge to go to the toilet, yet pass little despite much straining – it may feel as if the food is going the wrong way. You're irritable, short-tempered, and sensitive to light and noise.

Veratrum album is used for violent vomiting and diarrhoea. You may crave cold drinks and sour foods. You suffer profuse, watery, greenish or colourless stools, along with intense chills and cold sweating. Exhausted and limp, you experience crampy pains on defecating.

Podophyllum can help treat painless diarrhoea, where the stools are pale, thick and loose – like blended split pea soup. Your appetite is unaffected, but eating or drinking promotes a bowel rush. Your abdomen feels sore, especially over the liver area, but is relieved by rubbing.

Dosage for the above remedies depends on the severity of the condition, but all should be used in the 30c potency. With a very severe attack, take one tablet every hour, increasing the time between doses as the condition improves. In a less severe attack, take one tablet four times a day, until improvement.

In terms of **herbal remedies**, the natural antibiotic properties of **grape-seed extract** help both as a preventative for diarrhoea, taken daily from the start of your trip, and as a treatment if you get ill. A two- to four-week course of **acidophilus** to rebalance your intestinal flora may help after an attack of diarrhoea, especially if you've taken antibiotics. It can also be taken during an attack. **Aloe vera** is a natural anti-inflammatory – drinking the juice during or after a stomach upset helps to heal the inflamed intestinal tract. **Acupressure bands** or **ginger** can also help to alleviate nausea and vomiting.

The use of **antibiotics** for the treatment of travellers' diarrhoea is contro-versial. There's a weight of scientific evidence proving their efficacy, backed up by the fact that they were issued to troops in the Gulf War conflict. On the flip side, antibiotics have side effects and sometimes these can be more severe than the condition they are being used to treat. This, coupled with the growing problem of antibiotic resistance (see p.35), emphasizes the need to target care-fully the use of antibiotics for travellers' diarrhoea. Consider antibiotic use only in the following circumstances:

- If lab stool analysis confirms a bacterial cause.
- If there is blood mixed in with the diarrhoea.
- If you have a high fever.
- If the symptoms continue without signs of improvement for more than 48 hours, or if you pass more than six stools over 24 hours.
- If stopping, resting and treating conservatively is simply not a viable option.

There is no single antibiotic that can be used to treat all causes, although ciprofloxacin covers the majority of bacterial causes (trimethoprim is also an option). Neither drug is licensed to treat diarrhoea and there is no firm agree-ment on the actual treatment regime, but studies have shown that a single 500mg dose may be as beneficial as a three-day course. Short courses may have delete-rious long-term effects by creating more resistant strains, so it is perhaps best to treat for no less than three days. Ciprofloxacin is not effective against giardiasis or amoebiasis, which usually respond to a seven-day course of metronidazole.

The use of **blockers** (such as loperamide; see p.39) may reduce the fre-quency of diarrhoea but can bung you up by reducing your gut motility, deny-ing the organisms a means of exit. In the majority of cases, little harm will come from using blockers cautiously, but they should **never** be overused, nor used to treat suspected dysentery. Since they don't kill the bugs responsible for the diarrhoea, recurrences are common. An obvious potential side effect for blockers is constipation.

Rehabilitation

Eating solids during bouts of diarrhoea can trigger an episode (the gastro-colic reflex often causes a bowel urge when there is food in the stomach), but small quantities of bland food will not cause any harm. Initially, however, concentrate on **fluid intake**. Start with sips of boiled or bottled water and, when tolerat-ed, start on an oral rehydration solution or weakened fruit juice. In children, it is okay to continue breast-feeding, but cow's milk and dairy products may be poorly tolerated for a week or two after a bout of diarrhoea.

Once fluids are well tolerated, gently reintroduce **solids**. Keep it bland and small in quantity initially. Rice, pasta, potatoes, soup, bread, bananas and dry bis-cuits are reasonable starting points. Beans, lentils, chicken (boiled, grilled or roasted), boiled or grilled fish, and boiled eggs may be gradually introduced. Avoid rich, fatty, spicy or fried foods, dairy products, most raw fruit and alco-hol in the first few days.

Persistent symptoms

There are a number of reasons why diarrhoea might persist. For continuing symptoms, you cannot expect to make realistic progress without sending a stool sample for lab culture. If no causative bugs are isolated (usually the case), **blood tests** can reveal the presence of bugs that may be missed on stool analysis. The

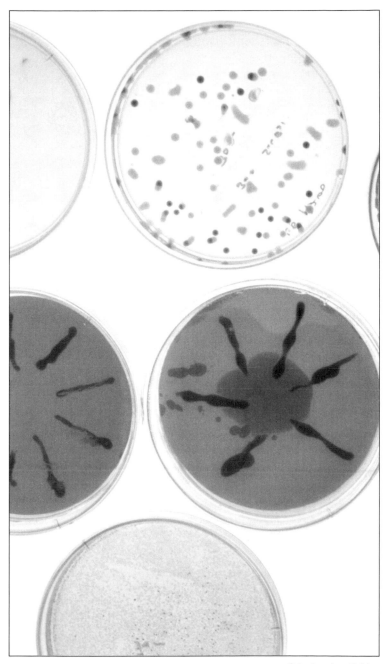

▲ Cell cultures in petri dishes

" Tummy trouble in Tibet "

Long dusty roads had led us independently to gather at the small Tibetan village of Tingri. There, in a dark, smoke-filled room, over butter-tea and noodles, we formed an alliance that was forged by a common goal. All three of us were chasing adventure, and so we set off on a two-week trek that would take us up into the heart of the Himalayas and to the head of the Rongbuck valley, a location that offered fine views of the north face of Everest. Although isolated, the valley had been a spiritual place and home long ago to a grand monastery. What remains of the original building today offers refuge to only a couple of monks, a nun and their big black mastiff.

We travelled light, supplementing what food we carried with staples acquired from locals along the way. We stayed in villages while passing through the lowlands, with yak herders in their tents as we gained altitude. It was a beautiful journey through a magical landscape and a foreign culture, but my health ensured that it was not a trip in paradise.

I had not been feeling well for a good part of our journey. I'd developed foul-smelling (sulphurous) burps, and my bowels weren't up to par either. One of my companions claimed that his mother was a physician, and this inherited characteristic allowed him to diagnose that I had giardiasis. He also had the drug to cure my ailment, or so he claimed. I popped a couple of pills, said a prayer, and continued on my way. I have no idea what he gave me, but whatever it was helped, temporarily.

A few days later I was feeling pretty bad again. I felt particularly under the weather when a drunken, Chinese-speaking and uniformed policeman confronted us in a lowland village demanding that we pay a permit fee for travelling through the area. I nearly lost all bodily control when he sent a sidekick off to fetch his rifle. Luckily his assistant never returned, and the man in uniform later apologized for his behaviour after sobering up.

We spent a night in that unfriendly place. I made countless trips to the "drop box", and experienced explosive diarrhoea all night. I was also vomiting with equal force, often barely making it out my bedroom door. I was throwing up into the dark night, then listening to starving dogs scavenge my vomit off the dust-covered ground. The lapping sound made me want to throw up all over again.

Another couple of demanding days brought us to the mouth of the Rongbuck valley. The surroundings were spectacular, but my physical condition dampened my appreciation of the scene. I tried to maintain a good humour, and a day's hike up the valley brought us eventually to the monastery. We were ceremonially welcomed by the resident monks, and offered salty yak-butter tea and tsampa as refreshment, rather simple fare that was well suited to my then delicate constitution. It was a setting clearly suited for monastic living, a location that naturally encouraged a lifestyle of profound reflection. And it was during our brief stay that my body had time to reflect on its physical state. Luckily for me, it decided to overcome its ailment, and I began to slowly feel better. With rest, and reasonably nourishing food, I gained enough strength to begin the journey out safely. Two weeks later I was in good health enjoying the numerous gastronomic delicacies that the Nepalese capital, Kathmandu, had to offer. My Tibetan journey had certainly provided much for me to reflect upon.

Ian Williams, Anchorage, Alaska

possibility of **post-infectious lactose intolerance** or **irritable bowel syndrome** (IBS; see p.153) should also be considered (neither of these is likely if weight loss is apparent). Lactose intolerance is thought to be caused by the "friendly" bacteria in the gut essentially being flushed away by the diarrhoea. Their absence means that the gut cannot digest a sugar known as lactose (found in milk and dairy products). It may take a week or two for these bacteria to recolonize the gut and thus milk and dairy products are best avoided during this time.

Genital warts

▶▶ See under Sexually transmitted diseases, p.197.

Giardiasis

A common cause of travellers' diarrhoea, **giardiasis** can occur anywhere in the world, although the incidence is highest in areas where water supplies are not properly sanitized (St Petersburg in Russia is noteworthy for particularly high infection rates).

Cysts of the giardiasis-causing protozoa can survive for longer than three months in water and are commonly found in streams and rivers. Infection is passed to humans by ingestion of **contaminated water or food**.

No **vaccination** is available, so avoid drinking potentially contaminated water, or eating food off utensils that have been washed in it. Water boiled for one minute at sea level (or between three and five minutes at altitude) is generally considered sufficient to kill giardiasis. Chemical eradication (iodine etc) is unreliable.

Symptoms

The infection can go unnoticed but usually causes watery diarrhoea, flatulence (often described as "eggy" or sulphurous), nausea, weight loss and abdominal bloating and rumbling between two and four weeks after the cysts have been ingested. The **symptoms** generally last no more than two weeks and settle without treatment, although a minority of sufferers may continue to have problems for several months.

Lactose intolerance (see above) may occur after the infection.

▶▶ See Gastrointestinal problems, p.131.

Diagnosis and treatment

Giardial infection can usually be identified by microscopic examination of a **stool sample**, although frequently several samples need to be sent as the cysts are not expelled in every motion. A five- to seven-day course of metronidazole (400mg three times a day) usually leads to effective eradication, although other treatment options are available.

Gnathostomiasis

Gnathostomiasis is a worm infection contracted by eating raw freshwater fish contaminated with the **worm larvae**. It usually affects domestic animals but can also infect humans who eat raw fish in endemic areas. It's found mostly in Asia (particularly in Thailand and Japan, caused by sum-fak and sashimi respectively), but outbreaks have occurred in Peru, Ecuador and Mexico related to ceviche consumption.

There is no vaccination against gnathostomiasis; best protection is to **avoid eating raw fish** in high-risk areas.

Symptoms

Once ingested the worm larvae migrate from the gut to other parts of the body. Lodging beneath the skin, they cause painful, itchy **swellings**. Elsewhere in the body, symptoms depend on which organs the migratory worms penetrate. Lung involvement results in a cough, bladder involvement results in blood in the urine and migration to the brain can cause meningitis (potentially life-threatening).

Diagnosis and treatment

Blood tests may help in the diagnosis but surgical removal of the worm for identification is more reliable. In terms of **treatment**, surgical removal of the worms from affected organs is the best option although anti-worm drugs such as albendazole or ivermectin can be used as adjuncts.

Gonorrhoea

▶▶ See Sexually transmitted diseases, p.197.

Guinea worm infection

▶▶ See Dracunculiasis, p.117.

Gynaecological problems

▶▶ See Women travellers, p.69

Hansen's disease

▶▶ See Leprosy, p.159.

Headache

Most **headaches** are harmless, commonly caused by tension in the muscles at the back of the neck and those covering the scalp. **Dehydration** and **heat-stroke** are other causes that perhaps single out the traveller. Most diseases that cause high **fever** will cause a headache, so consider the likes of malaria and dengue if you're travelling through areas in which the diseases are present.

Migraine, a term commonly (and often incorrectly) used to describe severe headache, more accurately describes a headache with neurological symptoms – visual disturbances, flashing lights, sensitivity to light, unilateral tingling or weakness – and may also be accompanied by nausea and vomiting. The pain is often localized and one-sided. You would be unfortunate to suffer your first migraine while travelling, but if you are prone to migraines, speak to your doctor (or a homeopath or herbalist) before you travel about taking specific anti-migraine drugs with you.

Headaches are usually best **treated** by rest and simple pain relief such as paracetamol or ibuprofen. Consider a more significant underlying problem in the following circumstances:

✚ High fever, a purple rash that doesn't whiten when a glass is pressed against it, neck stiffness, photophobia (signs of meningitis)

✚ Severe, sudden-onset pains in the back of the head (may indicate a brain haemorrhage)

✚ Lapsing levels of consciousness, weakness, double or blurred vision, profuse and unremitting vomiting, loss of coordination, pain on waking or worse on coughing (signs of a build-up of pressure around the brain)

✚ High altitude (headache is one of the first signs of acute mountain sickness)

Heat exposure

Acclimatization to **high temperatures** such as those found in the tropics can take weeks or months, and is characterized by an increase in perspiration and a lower salt loss in the sweat. Unpleasant reactions to hot climates include **prickly heat** (sweat rash, heat rash, miliaria), caused by inflammation of the sweat glands after prolonged exposure to high temperatures. It manifests as itchy or burning, red/pink pimples mainly affecting the head, neck, shoulders and sweaty areas of the body such as the armpits and groin and is usually caused by over-dressing or overexertion in heat. It is more common in infants. You can prevent it by keeping cool, having frequent cool showers, using talc to keep the skin dry and cool and wearing light, loose-fitting clothing. If treatment is necessary, simple soothing creams or low-strength hydrocortisone may be used.

Heavy exercise in hot weather, and the consequent excessive sweating, can lead to dehydration and depletion in the concentration of salt (more specifically, sodium) in the blood, causing **heat cramps**, also a recognized sign of heat exhaustion (see below). In many hot countries the salt loss from sweating is compensated by the addition of extra salt to soft drinks. If cramping occurs, stop any heavy activity and find a cool place to rest and slowly rehydrate using soft drinks or water.

A mild version of heat stroke, **heat exhaustion** can occur if you're not properly acclimatized and overheat. The **symptoms** include giddiness, headache, nausea, weakness, fatigue, muscle cramps and feeling faint. The body temperature may rise as high as 40°C, leading to dehydration and delirium. It is a significant sign that sweating continues throughout. The best **remedy** is to get out of the sun and cool down by tepid sponging, cool baths and fanning. Seek out air-conditioning wherever possible, have plenty of soft drinks (rather than water) to rehydrate, and use paracetamol for the headache.

Heat stroke is more severe and is potentially life-threatening. It tends to occur in hot, humid climates affecting the unacclimatized, even without heavy exercise. Old age, diabetes and heavy alcohol consumption are recognized risk factors. The body loses the ability to self-regulate temperature, with the consequence that core temperature may rapidly rise above 41°C. Accompanying

❝Disney World dilemma❞

*B*eing children at heart, my husband Barrie and I (both in our early seventies) decided to spend a couple of weeks in Florida which, naturally, included Disney World.

The middle of May would be about right weather-wise, not too hot – or so we thought. Our hotel in Orlando was suitably near other attractions, with a regular shuttle-bus to Disney and other places of interest.

Armed with sunhats, sunglasses, sun block and bottles of water, we idled for the first couple of days before going to the Magic Kingdom for a lively day of fun and entertainment. The following morning I felt somewhat peculiar, but, saying nothing, we caught the bus to Disney World again. I dozed on the way, feeling progressively more odd. The feeling was difficult to describe – a kind of not being there: floaty, dizzy and totally unconnected with reality. On arrival we found a bench (I was virtually unable to walk by now), but although I couldn't have said what specifically was wrong, I soon realized that I needed medical help. We found a medical room, and within a very short time, I was being taken by ambulance to a doctor's surgery. My legs were now covered in a scarlet rash, and I was quickly given a thorough examination, all the time being treated with kindness and efficiency. How could this happen when I had taken all the prescribed precautions? Apparently, heat from sun rays striking the ground and reflecting back is just as dangerous as sun from above, particularly for an older person. I was given hydrocortisone cream for the rash and then taken by ambulance all the way back to the hotel in Orlando, where I was ordered to rest in a darkened room for twenty-four hours, drinking plenty of cool water. Despite the annoying waste of holiday days it was only sensible to obey, and this did the trick. As a further precaution, I subsequently wore thin trousers when out in the sun, and am happy to say we thoroughly enjoyed the rest of a wonderful holiday in Florida.

Audrey French, UK.

symptoms, which are rapid in onset, include headache, sensitivity to light, weakness, nausea and vomiting. The pulse and breathing rates will both be rapid, while the skin usually looks red and feels hot and dry to touch. Confusion, delirium, fitting and coma can follow. Heat stroke is a very serious condition and urgent medical help is needed; as a temporary measure, use whatever means available to cool down the victim, and place them in the recovery position until help arrives.

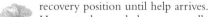

Homeopathy can help as an excellent back-up to conventional heat stroke treatment. **Belladonna** (one 30c tablet half-hourly until improvement) is worth trying if you have a hot, bright-red face, often with sparkling, lit-up eyes or dilated pupils. You may have fever, delirium or even hallucinations. Your headache is characteristically throbbing and made worse by lying down flat, tying up your hair, light and noise. You may feel better from sitting quietly propped up, or with your head resting on something.

Hepatitis

The word **hepatitis** simply means inflammation of the liver (a vital organ in the upper right side of the abdomen which causes considerable systemic upset when it goes wrong).

There are a number of causes of hepatitis, including drugs and alcohol, but by far the most common is the **hepatitis A** virus. Regardless of the root cause, the initial **symptoms** synonymous with hepatitis are malaise, nausea, loss of appetite, weight loss, aches and pains, fatigue and abdominal discomfort, followed after several days by jaundice. The urine usually turns dark and the stools pale. Infective hepatitis is likely to be accompanied by fever.

Hepatitis A

The **hepatitis A virus** (HAV) is spread via the faecal–oral route, with water, shellfish and salads (washed in contaminated water) being the most common culprits. It's also frequently spread by person-to-person contact. HAV is a common infection occurring worldwide, but you're most at risk of contracting it in the Middle and Far East, Central and South America, Africa and Eastern Europe. This is largely because of poor standards of hygiene and sanitation. The risk increases with the length of stay and by visiting rural areas.

There are several **vaccination** options available for travellers to high-risk areas (see p.8).

Symptoms

The incubation period of HAV can range from ten to fifty days. It's usually a mild, and sometimes unrecognized (especially in children) illness. Adults tend to suffer more from the **symptoms** (see above), which usually last around two months but can continue as long as six months. Complications and fatalities resulting from HAV infection are rare. The period during which you are infectious ranges from early in the incubation period to about a week after the development of jaundice.

Diagnosis and treatment

Antibodies to the virus can be detected in the **blood** about four weeks after infection. There is no specific **treatment**, but recovery is usually complete after two weeks, although more severe symptoms require a longer convalescence, with tiredness and lethargy being common features. In the interim, avoid fatty foods and alcohol as they can exacerbate the symptoms. Rest and a diet high in easily digestible carbohydrates are helpful. To avoid spreading the infection, intimate contact should be avoided during the infectious period.

Hepatitis B

Hepatitis B (HBV) is a global infection, but areas of particularly high prevalence include Asia, Africa, South America, the Pacific Islands and the Caribbean. It's estimated that some two billion people worldwide are infected with HBV, with 350 million chronic carriers. Although it's spread by similar means to HIV and is no less dangerous, it has a much lower media profile. It is, in fact, estimated to be 100 times more infectious than HIV.

▶▶ See HIV, p.144.

HBV is **spread** mainly via infected blood and blood products, although the virus has also been found in semen. It can therefore be passed on through intimate contact, blood transfusions that have not been adequately screened, the sharing of needles, razors or toothbrushes (which can cause gums to bleed) with an infected person, and in pregnancy from mother to baby. Body-piercing and tattooing using poorly sterilized equipment have also been implicated in its spread. HBV is not passed on by ordinary social contact (kissing, hugging, shaking hands), sharing food and drinks or by using the same cutlery, toilet facilities and towels.

A **vaccination** available against HBV offers good protection but is generally only recommended for those at particularly high risk such as health-care workers (who may be more likely to come into contact with infected blood). HBV vaccination should be discussed with your doctor before you leave if you

" A souvenir from Thailand "

I can't face those peanut butter sandwiches today!" I shouted to my friend who like me, was up a ladder picking fruit in Western Australia. "My stomach is feeling really strange. Maybe it has something to do with those apples we scrumped from the orchard last night," I joked. "Maybe," Sarah replied.

My friend and I had been in Australia for about a month. Prior to Perth we had spent two months on a beautiful island called Kao Tao, off southern Thailand. It was here that I had fallen in lust with a Thai resort owner. Unfortunately I had chosen to trust my Thai partner and we had made the crazy mistake of not using contraception on more than one occasion. It was not until eight weeks later, whilst settling in Australia, that the after-effects of these misjudgements began to materialize.

Initially I took very little notice of my symptoms, which included nausea, exhaustion and jaundice. However, after about a week I realized that the stolen fruit was not the cause and that something more sinister was afoot. I made an appointment with the doctor. After examining my abdomen the doctor told me that I could be pregnant and to return in a few days if I felt any worse. I did feel worse and I returned to the surgery for some blood tests. By this time I was very weak and my skin was banana yellow. I had been reading my travel guide books and had arrived at a self-diagnosis; I was convinced I had hepatitis A. When my blood tests came back, however, I was mortified. I had hepatitis B and was told by the doctor that I could develop cirrhosis of the liver in the future and could die within twenty years. My world collapsed.

I returned home as soon as my symptoms had subsided enough for me to travel. On arriving home I had to face family and friends knowing that I had caught a disease through sexual contact. I also had to undergo two HIV tests and regular blood tests. Although the physical symptoms disappeared within months, the disappointment of having to cut short a journey of a lifetime and neglecting my own personal safety overwhelmed my thoughts for a long time. And although I am now immune to hepatitis B and am not a carrier, I don't know the extent of any long-term damage. As I embark on plans for my first trip abroad since my illness, I fully intend to take greater care of myself.

Vicky Nicholas, Salisbury, UK

think you might be at higher-than-normal risk. If you have sex with a new partner on your travels, a condom will offer some protection although as with HIV, avoidance is better.

Symptoms

The time between exposure and first **symptoms** can be extensive, ranging from six weeks to six months. Initially, the symptoms of HBV mimic those of HAV (fever, malaise, loss of appetite etc). Recovery from the acute illness is usually complete after a month. However, after recovery from the initial symptoms, between five and ten percent of affected adults and up to ninety percent of children become carriers of the virus. Some also develop a more serious chronic form of the illness causing a slow, gradual destruction of the liver, which can ultimately be fatal.

Diagnosis and treatment

Blood tests can confirm the diagnosis but may not show positive for up to three months after the infection is acquired. The diagnosis can often be made simply by correlating the initial symptoms with a history of likely contact with HBV.

There is no specific **treatment**, although liver specialists have begun using a drug called interferon to some benefit for chronic infections (unlikely to be available in developing countries); other antiviral agents are currently being trialed. Rest, plenty of fluids and a nutritious diet (high in carbohydrates) aid recovery from the initial acute illness.

Hepatitis C

Although a relatively newly discovered cause of acute hepatitis and chronic liver disease (first identified in 1989), **hepatitis C** (HCV) now has a world-wide prevalence – the WHO recently estimated that 170 million people (around three percent of the total world population) are infected with the virus, and that between three and four million people become infected each year. A dangerous and difficult disease to treat, HCV infection is particularly high in Africa, the eastern Mediterranean and the western Pacific.

It is **transmitted** by similar means to HBV, but it appears to be less infectious via sexual contact. It's common among intravenous drug users, haemophiliacs and people who require frequent blood transfusions.

As yet, no **vaccine** is available against HCV.

Symptoms

The incubation period is usually 6–8 weeks but can vary between 15 and 150 days. The initial infection usually goes unnoticed, with acute **symptoms** similar to HAV-infection being rare. However, like HBV, a chronic form of HCV occurs in sixty to eighty percent of cases. This is slowly progressive and can lead to liver failure or liver cancer thirty or forty years after the initial infection. It is still unclear as to whether all of those suffering from the chronic disease eventually develop terminal liver problems.

Diagnosis and treatment

The infection can be **diagnosed** by the presence of HCV antibodies in the blood, although these can take several weeks to appear.

The only **treatment** currently available is a combination of ribavirin and interferon, which has been shown to be beneficial in some, but not all, chronic cases. These drugs are expensive and likely to be in very short supply in developing countries. They should only be used in a hospital setting under expert supervision.

In cases of chronic liver damage, alcohol and some over-the-counter drugs (eg paracetamol) should be avoided.

If you are a chronic carrier of HBV or HCV you should not donate blood, semen or organs. You should also inform sexual partners and practise safe sex at all times.

Hepatitis D and E

Hepatitis D and E infections are rare. HDV infection only occurs in the presence of HBV infection (it needs HBV to replicate) and is transmitted via blood or blood products. Intravenous drug users are the most commonly affected group. No vaccine is available.

HEV is very similar to HAV in terms of its mode of transmission, incubation period, symptoms and outcomes. It is endemic in some parts of Central America, Africa, the Middle East, Southeast Asia and the Far East. No vaccine is currently available.

Herpes (genital)

▶ ▶ See under Sexually transmitted diseases, p.197.

HIV

There are two distinct types of **human immunodeficiency virus** (**HIV**) infection: HIV1, discovered in 1983, and HIV2, discovered two years later and generally regarded as being the weaker and slower-developing variant. Infection with either results in **acquired immune deficiency syndrome** (**AIDS**).

Infection estimates from the WHO make grim reading. In 2003 alone, approximately five million people became infected with the HIV virus at a rate of 14,000 per day, making a total of forty million carriers worldwide. Some three million people have died as a result of the disease in 2003. Between seventy and eighty percent of HIV cases worldwide have been acquired through sexual intercourse, between five and ten percent at birth from an infected mother, and the rest from drug use and infected blood products. Ninety-five percent of the worldwide population infected with HIV, and a similar percentage of AIDS-related deaths, occur in the developing world, with women now comprising over forty percent of the total. Eighty percent of heterosexually acquired HIV in the UK is contracted abroad.

HIV infection is **spread** via infected body fluids: blood (including unscreened transfusions), semen, vaginal secretions and breast milk. There is a low risk of acquiring it via saliva. It is not transmitted by normal, everyday social contact. There is as yet no vaccination against HIV and it would still seem to be some years away. Therefore the advice for **avoidance of HIV** infection is clear: avoid contact with blood products, avoid needle or syringe sharing (don't forget dental work, acupuncture, tattooing and body piercing) and avoid unprotected sex with a new partner – bear in mind that using a condom alone won't afford total protection, and your only certain means of self-protection is abstinence.

▶▶ See Blood transfusions, p.98.

HIV attacks the **white blood cells**, and by depleting their numbers reduces the body's ability to fight off infection and cancers. **AIDS** is medically defined by increasing susceptibility to specific infections and incidence of cancerous tumours. The time-lapse from HIV infection to the development of full-blown AIDS varies and depends on a number of factors (age, mode of infection, genetics); with modern drugs, this latent period can last for many years. The long period without significant symptoms synonymous with AIDS means that many people infected with HIV are unaware that they are carriers. It also means that there is no definite way of knowing the true global prevalence of the infection.

Initial infection with HIV is indistinguishable from any other viral infection, and is often not apparent at all. Roughly fifty percent of those infected will suffer a sore throat, joint pains or a rash. HIV infection can be **detected** by a blood test, but there is a lag period after infection of up to three months before tests will show positive.

A number of complex **treatments** are aimed at delaying the progression of HIV infection into AIDS by suppressing viral replication, but treatment can only be undertaken under strict medical supervision. There remains no cure for HIV infection or AIDS.

▶▶ See also Travelling with HIV, p.56.

Hookworm

▶▶ See under Worms, p.226.

Human babesiosis

Human babesiosis is a tick-borne protozoal infection common in animals but rare in humans – it tends to affect mainly those with a weakened immune system. Most cases are in North America (mainly northeastern coastal areas) and Europe, although there have been sporadic reports in other parts of the world. It is spread to humans by the same kind of **tick** that transmits Lyme disease and, although babesiosis is much rarer than Lyme, simultaneous infections have been reported. Rodents, cattle and wild animals (eg deer) act as animal disease reservoirs.

Symptoms, diagnosis and treatment

Symptoms appear between one and four weeks after a bite and are usually mild, although they are much more severe, even life-threatening, in anyone who has low levels of immunity (including those who have had a splenectomy). In the more severe cases, human babesiosis **mimics malaria**, with high fever, rigors, nausea and vomiting, abdominal pain and muscle aches. Complications may cause a build-up of fluid on the lungs, anaemia, kidney failure and increased bleeding tendency.

The parasites can be seen in the **blood** cells using a microscope. In most cases, the **treatment** is mainly aimed at symptom relief. For severe infections, the treatment options are complicated, usually involving different combinations of antibiotics and antimalarials.

Human ehrlichiosis

(Sennetsu fever)

Human ehrlichiosis is a tick-borne bacterial infection. Outbreaks have occurred in the eastern seaboard, south-central and midwest USA, as well as parts of Southeast Asia (especially western Japan), where it's known as Sennetsu fever. Spread by the same "lone star" **ticks** as Lyme disease, it often occurs in the same geographical areas, although it is far rarer. Incidence is highest in the summer months when the ticks are most active.

Symptoms

Symptoms are very similar to those for Rocky Mountain spotted fever and Lyme disease. Onset is usually between five and ten days after the initial tick bite, with common features including sudden fever, headache, rigors, muscle aches, nausea and vomiting. A generalized rash sometimes appears, more commonly in children than in adults. Ehrlichiosis is a severe illness but is only rarely fatal. Untreated, it can lead to serious complications such as meningitis and abnormal bleeding, and may adversely affect lung, liver and kidney function.

Diagnosis and treatment

Diagnosis is usually confirmed by blood tests. Early **treatment** with a tetracycline antibiotic, usually doxycycline, is necessary to prevent the disease's rapid progression – if there is a high degree of suspicion, don't wait for lab results before starting treatment.

▶▶ See Lyme disease, p.162; Rocky Mountain spotted fever, p.185.

Hydatid disease

(Echincoccosis)

Hydatid disease is found all over the world but most commonly in the sheep- and cattle-raising areas of South America, South Africa, the former Soviet Union and the Middle East. Despite its wide geographic distribution, the disease is rare in humans and risks to the average traveller are low.

Eggs of the infecting **tapeworm** are transmitted to humans by the ingestion of milk, vegetables or water contaminated by the faeces of infected animals or by direct contact with the animals (dogs, foxes, sheep and cattle usually) – stroking dogs whose fur has been contaminated is a major cause of human infection. The tapeworm larvae form **cysts** in the liver, lungs and other organs.

There is no vaccination, so avoid potentially contaminated water and always **wash your hands** carefully after handling or stroking animals.

Symptoms

Years can pass before any signs of the illness, and the symptoms themselves depend on the location and size of the cyst. **Cysts in the liver** may cause abdominal discomfort, nausea and vomiting. If a cyst ruptures, this will cause sudden pain, fever and even death from internal bleeding. **Cysts in the lungs** may cause a cough (sometimes containing blood) and shortness of breath. Pneumonia or a lung abscess can ensue after rupture of a cyst.

Diagnosis and treatment

Blood tests may detect antibodies to the tapeworms, while a **chest x-ray** or an abdominal ultrasound may detect the presence of cysts in the lungs or liver. Surgical removal of the cysts remains the mainstay of **treatment**, but the drug albendazole can cause regression of the cysts in many cases.

Hypothermia

▶ ▶ See Cold exposure, p.105

Influenza

The risk of exposure to **influenza** is mainly determined by season (usually winter) in temperate countries (outbreaks occur year-round in the tropics), and the number of people with whom you mingle. Isolated cases of flu are rare: it almost always comes in epidemics. The last century saw three major flu **epidemics**: the "Spanish flu" in 1918–19 (causing a staggering twenty million deaths worldwide), the "Asian flu" in 1957–58, and the "Hong Kong flu" in 1968–69. In late 2003, headlines were made by an outbreak of "**avian flu**", a virulent strain of the influenza virus which has so far remained largely within the bird population, causing only a few human cases in the Far East; see the box below for more information.

The influenza **virus** mutates frequently, which means that neither vaccination nor having suffered the illness previously confers future immunity.

A **vaccine** against the current prevalent epidemic is available but is usually recommended only for those at particularly high risk. Elderly people, severe asthmatics, diabetics, those with chronic heart, lung or kidney disease, and anyone with a compromised immune function should consider vaccination before they travel, depending on season and the likelihood they will be exposed to the virus through fellow travellers. The vaccine is between seventy and ninety percent effective, although maximum protection is not reached for up to two weeks after the inoculation.

Avian flu

The influenza virus has two characteristics which make it particularly dangerous: the capacity to mutate rapidly and the ability to cross the species barrier. At the time of writing, the **avian strain** had proven lethal to the few humans who became infected through close contact with chickens, but had not so far been transmitted between humans. However, avian flu is likely to mutate further and could interact with less dangerous human strains already in existence. Such changes could render it capable of human-to-human transmission, which would mean a real possibility of a major global epidemic. This has not yet occurred, and there's no reason to panic or avoid travel, but before setting off on a trip (especially to Asia), you might want to check the current situation via the WHO website (see p.276).

Highly **contagious**, influenza is spread by cough or sneeze droplets. It usually takes between one and four days from exposure for symptoms to appear. It can be passed on before the infected person experiences symptoms and for up to a week afterwards.

Symptoms

Many people believe they have the flu when, in fact, they have only a heavy cold. There is no tell-tale symptom that defines influenza – it's usually a question of severity and the degree of debility (most people who've had flu never forget it). Upper respiratory **symptoms** such as cough, runny nose and headaches predominate, in addition to high fever, loss of appetite, muscle pains and, often, extreme fatigue. Nausea, vomiting and diarrhoea commonly occur in children, less so in adults.

In most people, the symptoms resolve spontaneously over the course of one or two weeks. Serious, sometimes life-threatening, complications such as pneumonia are rare but occur more often in high-risk groups. A prolonged period of weakness, fatigue and depression may last for weeks or even months after the acute infection.

Diagnosis and treatment

Flu is almost impossible to diagnose with any degree of certainty on clinical grounds alone. Although a firm diagnosis is usually academic (it will not change the treatment), **blood tests** can be used to identify the body's antibodies to the virus. In tropical areas (where epidemics are not seasonal), or in travellers returning from tropical areas, the diagnosis of influenza should never be made without first excluding other causes of high fever such as malaria, dengue and typhoid.

Antibiotics won't treat the flu itself, but should be used if **secondary bacterial infections** such as sinusitis or pneumonia are suspected. The use of expensive antiviral medications is controversial; their effectiveness at treating the illness versus their considerable cost is the cause of ongoing debate in some countries.

 Homeopathy is very useful for influenza. **Gelsemium** 30c, given every two hours initially, increasing the interval with improvement, gives rapid relief in most cases. Use **Eupatorium** (same dosage) if there is intense bone aching. If the symptoms are mild, but there is a painful dry cough, try **Ferrum phos** 30c, four times a day.

Insects

Insects, as much of this book will tell you, are responsible for the spread of a vast number of human diseases. The table on pp.150–151 gives an idea of the extent to which flying insects, mites, ticks and the like are responsible for the spread of some key complaints. For more on the specific diseases and the insects that cause them, refer to the page numbers in the right-hand column.

▶▶ For more on bite and sting prevention, see p.149; see also Lice infestation, p.161; Malaria, p.163; Myiasis, p.175; Spiders and scorpions, p.206; Tungiasis, p.220.

Once bitten

While not all biting insects will cause you harm, many do act as the "**vector**", in essence the go-between between animals or humans who already have a

Alternative treatments for bites and stings

A number of **homeopathic** remedies can help treat bites and stings. Apis mel will treat an ant or a mosquito bite, a bee or a jellyfish sting (for bad pain, take one 30c dose every fifteen minutes until it abates, less often thereafter). Choose this remedy especially for stings that are very hot, shiny red and puffy, with pain that burns or prickles (and worsens near heat – in sun, hot water etc). Silica (6c or 30c four times a day) will help to expel retained bits of stings and bites from bees, ticks and the like. **Bach Rescue Remedy** (six drops in a cup of water) can help reduce any accompanying anxiety.

disease and those who are about to get it. The risk of disease generally depends on the insect species (for example, only the *anopheles* type of mosquito can spread malaria) and the geographical area. Depending on the type of insect, the severity of the **local reaction** at the bite or sting site can vary. Swelling, redness and sometimes local heat often follow the initial pain. Later, the site may become irritable and the impulse to scratch may be immense (though should be resisted – see below). Itching will stop of its own accord eventually, although **antihistamines** (tablets or cream) will help relieve it. Local applications such as **calamine lotion** and **hydrocortisone** cream can also help.

Although rare, the proteins within the venom of the insect bite or sting can trigger a more **generalized allergic response**, with flushing, swelling, itching, a rash and wheezing. In the majority of cases these symptoms will resolve without treatment, but oral antihistamines may help. Severe allergic reactions (**anaphylaxis**; see p.91) are rare but require urgent medical help.

Secondary bacterial infection at the bite or sting site is not uncommon and is more likely in tropical climates. Usually, scratching damages the skin and bacteria from dirty fingernails multiply within the wound; this can occur within the first 48 hours after being bitten or stung. Signs of infection are not immediately dissimilar from the initial local reaction – swelling, redness and heat are common – although local pain tends to prevail over itching. The presence of pus, red tracking up the affected limb (lymphangitis), local lymph gland swelling and fever are also signs of infection. Treat with antibiotics such as penicillin, flucloxacillin or co-amoxiclav, or erythromycin if you have a penicillin allergy.

Bite and sting prevention

The first line of defence against insect-borne disease is **avoiding** being bitten in the first place. This may be next to impossible, but knowing a little about how the insects behave, their preferred **habitat**, **times of day** and **seasons** helps. Most mosquitoes, for example, tend to be most active between dusk and dawn during and after the rainy season, and it's then that you'll need to be most vigilant. Similarly, sand flies only have a very limited flight range and therefore tend to bite people lying on, or close to, the ground.

Ticks and **mites**, of course, are unable to fly at all and usually attach themselves when you walk through long grass or vegetation. Wear light-shaded, tightly woven clothes so that ticks can be easily spotted before they attach, apply permethrin-based repellents and inspect your skin and clothing carefully at the

Insect	Diseases
Mosquitoes **Aedes** A tropical species, with a black-and-white body. Found mainly in urban areas below 4500m. Bites in the daytime only. **Anopheles** Found mainly in rural areas. Bites at night. **Culex** Dull, brown body. Ubiquitous (no particular habitat). Bites mainly at night.	**Chikungunya fever** (aedes) p.102; **Dengue fever** (aedes) p.113; **Filariasis** (anopheles, culex, aedes) p.127; **Japanese encephalitis** (culex) p.153; **Malaria** (anopheles) p.163; **Rift Valley fever** (culex and aedes) p.184; **Ross River virus** (culex and aedes) p.186; **Yellow fever** (aedes) p.233.
Ticks Ticks have eight legs and tend to be small, flat, brown and round, but after a blood meal can swell up to corn-kernel size. They generally inhabit rural areas, and bite mostly in spring and summer when grasses are long.	**Human babesiosis** p.145; **Lyme disease** p.162; **Relapsing fever** p.183; **Rocky Mountain spotted fever** p.185; **Tick-borne encephalitis** p.216; **Typhus** p.222.
Sand flies Small enough to pass through mosquito nets, sand flies are found mainly in arid areas.They have characteristically hairy wings, are low-altitude, noiseless fliers and bite mainly between dusk and dawn.	**Bartonellosis** p.97; **Leishmaniasis** p.156; **Sandfly fever** p.192.
Fleas	**Plague** p.179; **Tungiasis** p.220; **Typhus** p.222.
Lice	**Relapsing fever** p.183; **Typhus** p.222.
Mites Tiny, eight-legged creatures.	**Scabies** p.193; **Typhus** p.222.
Tsetse fly Found only in sub-Saharan Africa, mainly in forested rural areas, tsetse flies are large (up to 1.5cm long) and bite in the daytime. They are attracted to moving vehicles and dark, contrasting colours, are capable of biting through light clothing and are relatively impervious to the effects of insect repellent.	**African trypanosomiasis** p.88.

Insect	Diseases
Reduviid bugs (kissing, cone-nose or assassin bugs) Large, between 1 and 4cm long, with a cone-shaped head. Typically inhabit adobe or mud huts in Central and South America. Bite at night.	**American trypanosomiasis** p.88.
Black fly (buffalo gnat, turkey gnat) Small and stumpy ("humpbacked") black flies live near fast-flowing rivers in parts of the tropics. Mainly bite in the daytime.	**Onchocerciasis** p.127.
Tabanid fly (horse fly, deerfly, March fly) Large, fast and similar in shape to common houseflies, tabanids are found in rural areas. Mainly bite in the daytime. Bites are painful.	**Loiasis** p.129.

end of each day, as prompt removal can prevent the tick from passing on an infection. They tend to gravitate towards darker recesses of the body, with favourite hiding places being the scalp, armpits and genital area.

The next obvious level of protection is appropriate **clothing**. Few insects are able to penetrate clothes, so expose as little skin to the air as possible (including avoiding wearing open sandals) during the times when they are most active. Tuck long trousers into your socks, and note that impregnating your clothing with permethrin (see below) greatly increases its protective properties. **Never walk barefoot**, especially in the tropics. Shoes provide protection against insect, snake and spider bites, as well as parasites that enter the body through the skin of the foot. Shaking your boots out before putting them on is a good habit to get into.

Repellents are the next, and highly important, level of protection. Many preparations are available but the commonly accepted "gold standard" are those containing DEET (see p.152).

Permethrin

Permethrin has very useful repellent and insecticidal properties with negligible effects on human health. It works best by being sprayed on clothing or mosquito nets (you can also apply it to camping equipment and shoes); it bonds to fabric, does not cause staining and lasts for several washes before you need reapply it. Permethrin is less effective when applied to the skin because it's rapidly deactivated on contact. A few people suffer mild irritant reactions when permethrin is applied directly to the skin.

Ticks and tick removal

Eight-legged external parasites of mammals, birds and reptiles, **ticks** are found all over the world, and feed on blood after attaching to the host. Some species are capable of transmitting diseases such as Lyme disease, typhus and Rocky Mountain spotted fever. Prompt removal of the tick can prevent these diseases from being passed on.

Removing ticks

When a tick attaches itself, it embeds its head below the surface of your skin. You need to take special care to remove the whole of the tick, head and all. Using tweezers, grasp the tick's head and pull gently (avoid twisting) until the tick dislodges. If it doesn't budge, try applying permethrin to the tick directly with a cotton bud, waiting for fifteen minutes, then trying the tweezers again. Afterwards apply antiseptic to the area of the bite.

DEET

DEET (N, N-diethyl-m-toluamide or N, N-diethyl-3-methylbenzamide) is regarded as the single most important constituent of an insect repellent in terms of determining its efficacy. Other factors that affect the level of protection conferred by a repellent are the type of formulation – cream, ointment, roll-on etc – how often you apply it and how much you perspire, humidity and environment, and the species and feeding patterns of the insects.

The **drawbacks** of using a repellent containing DEET are generally minor: it may cause a local skin irritation and melts certain synthetics, so can cause damage to watches, spectacles, clothing and shoes. Never apply it to your eyes, damaged skin or mucous membranes (nose, mouth, genitals). Although DEET is rapidly absorbed through the skin, it's also rapidly excreted and therefore does not accumulate.

DEET has been associated with rare neurological **side effects** and occasional fatalities, although its exact role in these cases has never been firmly established and the media has in some cases sensationalized the issues. Current evidence suggests that the adverse effects were due to rare individual susceptibility rather than dose-related, and given its widespread usage, the general view is that the risk of serious side effects as a result of DEET application is extremely low.

Despite this, it is generally recommended not to use greater than fifteen percent strength on children and 35 percent strength on adults. **Concentrations** higher than 35 percent are believed to be no more effective as a repellent, and those less than fifteen percent lose their efficacy. The lower the strength, the shorter the period of protection: an application of a 30–35 percent formulation should provide a good level of protection for adults for 4–6 hours.

Using DEET in conjunction with permethrin on clothing and insect nets is a highly efficient way of repelling insects with minimal unwanted effects.

For a detailed comparative overview of available repellents, visit
ⓦcontent.nejm.org/cgi/content/full/347/1/13 or
ⓦwww.annals.org/cgi/content/full/128/11/931.

Other repellents include constituents such as citronella, a chemical called IR3535 (used in preparations such as Avon's Skin so Soft moisturizer), soya bean, geranium, coconut and lemon eucalyptus oils. Although these provide varying degrees of protection, none match DEET according to the available scientific evidence. The majority of **insect coils** contain permethrin and are reasonably effective, although variables like air currents and room size are important factors to consider. Bear in mind that some contain DDT and therefore should be used with caution.

At night, sleep under a **mosquito net** and ensure that it's securely tucked under your mattress. It's a good idea to carry your own net (they're widely available and easily portable), as those provided by hostels and hotels are often damaged and are useless even with the smallest tear. Impregnate the net with permethrin for added protection. Note that **air-conditioning** markedly reduces mosquito activity, but evidence on the efficacy of ultrasonic repellent devices is lacking. Finally, avoid wearing **aftershave** or **perfume** in high-risk areas as it's likely to attract insects.

Irritable bowel syndrome

Irritable bowel syndrome (IBS) describes a group of symptoms that affect us all to a greater or lesser extent at some time. The symptoms are usually brought on by stress, anxiety or even excitement; irregular eating patterns or poor diet may also be contributing factors. It is not uncommon to develop IBS after an episode of travellers' diarrhoea.

IBS presents differently from person to person, but diarrhoea, flatulence, abdominal bloating and crampy abdominal pains are common. Other **symptoms** include constipation and nausea. Vomiting is rare and the presence of weight loss usually indicates another cause that will need further investigation.

Unfortunately there is no specific test that proves the presence of IBS, and because the symptoms are nonspecific and may have other more serious causes, the diagnosis is usually only made when other possibilities have been excluded. Regular eating habits and a fibre-rich diet can help. Medications that can be used for symptom relief include drugs such as mebeverine or peppermint oil capsules, both helpful antispasmodics (they relieve the crampy pains and frequency of diarrhoea), while refined fibre in the form of ispaghula husk benefits constipation and helps to restore normal bowel function.

 If you are an IBS sufferer, it would be a good plan to consult a homeopath or herbalist well in advance of your travels. As a first-aid remedy, homeopathic **Colocynth** 30c for crampy pains is very useful; take two to four tablets daily depending on severity. **Nux vomica** 30c is helpful if you've eaten things you know disagree with you or unfamiliar food which seems to have caused an upset; take one tablet four times a day until relief.

Japanese encephalitis

Japanese encephalitis occurs seasonally throughout Southeast Asia, the Far East and the Pacific. Prevalent in areas where rice-growing and pig-farming coexist, it is a **viral** disease spread by culex mosquitoes. Patterns vary from year to year and from country to country, but the disease tends to proliferate during and after the monsoon, when mosquitoes are at their most active. The WHO reports at least 50,000 cases occur in Asia annually, accounting for some 10,000 deaths, with children most affected. Cases involving tourists, however, are extremely rare.

A **vaccine** against Japanese encephalitis is available, and it is strongly recommended for anyone travelling to an endemic area, especially after the monsoon.

Symptoms

The usual incubation period is four to fourteen days. **Symptoms** vary considerably from case to case, but are often flu-like with sudden-onset headache, fever and vomiting. Weight loss is a prominent feature of the illness, and drowsiness, a stiff neck and intolerance to light can also occur. Fits are particularly common in children.

Diagnosis and treatment

Diagnosis can be made by a blood test. There is no specific **treatment**, although hospital admission for supportive and nursing care improves survival rates. Mortality rates are as high as forty percent in adults and higher in children, with long-term neurological impairment apparent in a high proportion of survivors.

Jiggers

▶ ▶ See Tungiasis, p.220.

Kala-azar

▶ ▶ See under Leishmaniasis, p.156.

Lassa fever

Epidemics of **Lassa fever** occur mainly in the dry season in West Africa, particularly Guinea, Liberia, Nigeria, Sierra Leone and the Democratic Republic of Congo. It gets its name from the region in northeast Nigeria where the virus was first recognized in 1969.

The exact mode of transmission of the **virus** to humans is unclear, but it's likely to be via indirect contact with the saliva, urine or faeces of a species of rat that's found on much of the African continent. Lassa fever is **highly contagious** between humans – the virus infiltrates all bodily fluids and remains in the urine and semen for several weeks even after recovery.

Lassa fever poses little threat to most travellers, but health workers in endemic areas may be at risk.

Symptoms

Lassa fever is a **viral haemorrhagic fever** and, as such, is very similar in presentation to Ebola and Marburg (see pp.120 & 170). Between ten and thirty percent of people infected will show no sign of disease; for the remainder, there is believed to be an incubation period of one to three weeks before the gradual onset of **symptoms**. These include high fever, vomiting, diarrhoea, cough, chest and abdominal pain and generalized weakness lasting for several days. Inflammation of the eyes and throat is common, and the face and neck may also become swollen. After three to six days, more serious cases can experience shock, generalized bleeding, fluid on the lungs and brain swelling. Lassa fever is extremely dangerous in anyone who is severely affected, and survivors of the illness may face long-lasting, and sometimes permanent after-effects, such as hair loss, deafness and loss of coordination.

Diagnosis and treatment

Clinically, there is little to differentiate Lassa fever from many other tropical causes of high fever, although throat inflammation with white patches on the tonsils is often a unique feature. Definitive **diagnosis** is made through a blood test

Caught early, intravenous **treatment** with the antiviral agent ribavarin can help but failing this, therapy is based around symptom control and intensive care.

Because of the long incubation period, cases of Lassa fever have been reported in travellers returning to Europe. Most cases have been reported in people who have spent considerable time in Africa rather than the casual tourist, but a fever in any traveller returning from the tropics, no matter how short their stay, needs to be fully investigated.

Leeches

Although they also exist on dry land, **leeches** proliferate in tropical rainforests, where they're particularly active after the rains. They commonly attach themselves to trekkers wading through water, or swimmers who ill-advisedly swim in tropical rainforest pools, and are capable of crawling up into bodily nooks and crannies such as the mouth, nostrils and genitals. Although repellent to many, leeches don't carry any serious diseases, and their main threat to health is secondary infection at the site of attachment.

Avoidance is not always easy when you're in their native habitat. Covering up any exposed skin and tucking trousers into socks helps, but most leeches can penetrate this kind of defence. Applying permethrin to your clothes offers some additional protection.

It's worth remembering that the leech, once satiated with your blood, will drop off of its own accord, although most victims would prefer to avoid the wait. Applying a lighted cigarette or match, vinegar, salt or chilli to the leech are all successful methods of **removal**, with direct tugging perhaps least effective, since you risk leaving behind parts of the leech, increasing your chance of secondary infection. The resulting wound may bleed for a few hours (leeches have an anticoagulant in their saliva): clean it thoroughly with antiseptic and apply a sterile dressing.

Legionnaires' disease

Legionnaires' disease is a relatively rare but serious infection that occurs worldwide in sporadic epidemics; the name derives from the first outbreak in 1976 among members of the American Legion in a Philadelphia hotel. It's spread by the inhalation of the disease-causing **bacteria** from infected water, for example through hot showers, air-conditioning or steam rooms. The bacteria tend to thrive and multiply in warm, stagnant water. Person-to-person spread never occurs.

According to the US Center for Disease Control, there are between 8000 and 18,000 cases in the US each year, while the UK Public Health Laboratory Service reports an average of around 200 cases annually in Britain (between a third and a half acquired abroad). Smokers, the elderly, the immunodeficient and those with pre-existing heart or lung diseases are most at risk from the disease. For as yet unknown reasons, men are more prone to infection than women.

Epidemics are rare but usually make the news. Although you would be very unlucky to come into direct contact with the disease-causing organisms, think twice before travelling to a place that you know to have experienced a recent outbreak, especially if you belong to one of the higher risk groups, as preventative measures may not be practical (no vaccination currently exists).

Symptoms, diagnosis and treatment

The symptoms usually develop between two and ten days after exposure, and although the infection may be mild, the characteristic picture is that of a **chest infection**, with high fever, headache, shortness of breath, cough (you may cough up blood), nausea and vomiting, muscle pains, mental confusion and weight loss.

Diagnosis can usually be made from a blood, urine or sputum sample. Erythromycin (500mg four times daily for three weeks) can be used to **treat** the less severe forms of the illness. More severe cases require hospital admission for intravenous antibiotics and intensive care. Between five and thirty percent of those who contract Legionnaires' disease will die.

Leishmaniasis

The WHO estimates that around twelve million people (mainly indigenous) in 88 countries across central Asia, eastern Africa, China, Central and South America and the southern and eastern Mediterranean coastline (sporadic cases have been reported on the northern shores) are currently infected with **leishmaniasis**. Female **sand flies** transmit this protozoal infection to humans, usually from dogs, rodents or, in India, other humans. Transmission of the disease may also occur through blood transfusions, needle sharing, sexual contact with infected individuals and from mother to child.

The flies, which inhabit dry regions, normally bite from dusk until dawn. They are noiseless and very small – only about a third of the size of a mosquito and able to pass easily through most mosquito nets. Because sand flies are **low-altitude fliers**, the best way to avoid them is by sleeping above ground level (in a hammock if you can't get higher than the ground floor). As yet there is no vaccination against leishmaniasis, although research is ongoing in several countries.

Many varieties of leishmaniasis exist, but for practical purposes they are grouped into **cutaneous**, **visceral** and **mucocutaneous** forms, affecting the skin, the internal organs and mucous membranes respectively.

Cutaneous leishmaniasis

(Aleppo boil, Aleppo button, Baghdad boil, Baure ulcer, Delhi boil, Oriental sore, Tropical sore)

It's estimated that between 1 and 1.5 million people contract **cutaneous leishmaniasis** each year, with ninety percent of cases occurring in Iran, Afghanistan, Syria, Saudi Arabia, Brazil and Peru.

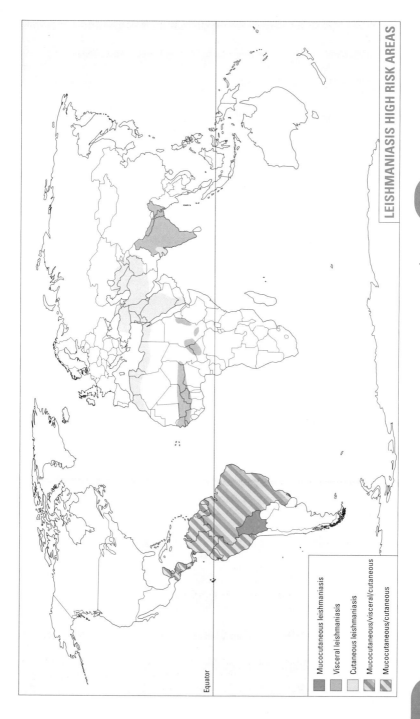

LEISHMANIASIS HIGH RISK AREAS

Equator

Mucocutaneous leishmaniasis
Visceral leishmaniasis
Cutaneous leishmaniasis
Mucocutaneous/visceral/cutaneous
Mucocutaneous/cutaneous

Following a bite (days, weeks or months afterwards), red patches appear on the skin at the bite site/s, which gradually enlarge and **ulcerate**. These lesions feel firm to touch and may be painful or itchy. Their appearance has been likened to that of a volcano – a raised edge with a crater in the centre. Multiple lesions may occur on different areas of the body, reflecting the insect's bite pattern. Without treatment, the lesions heal very slowly (sometimes over many years) and often leave permanent scarring.

Cutaneous leishmaniasis is usually identified by a **biopsy** of a skin nodule. Bear in mind that most doctors in developed countries will not think of diagnosing leishmaniasis on the basis of the skin lesions alone, so if you suspect the illness, make sure your doctor knows where you have been and under what conditions you have been living.

A ten-day **intravenous course** of pentavalent antimony (sodium stibogluconate) is partially effective but side effects require specialist monitoring. Relapses are common.

Visceral leishmaniasis
(Dumdum fever, Kala-azar)

About 500,000 people contract **visceral leishmaniasis** each year, with ninety percent of cases occurring in India, Bangladesh, Nepal, Brazil and Sudan. Its local name, kala-azar, is Hindi for "black fever" (the disease sometimes causes darkening of the extremities, face and abdomen). Cases also occur in the Mediterranean basin, where up to seventy percent of cases are related to HIV infection, and the incidence of this coexistence is expected to rise dramatically in other parts of the world, particularly Africa.

Visceral leishmaniasis tends to affect young people, with an **incubation period** that ranges from months to years. Onset of **symptoms** is usually insidious, with a mild, intermittent fever and bouts of profuse sweating. As the disease progresses, weight loss, fatigue, poor appetite, nausea, abdominal pain and diarrhoea can develop. Over time the liver, spleen and lymph glands swell. Left untreated, the disease is usually fatal.

▲ Santa Monica Bay, California

Blood tests will identify the presence of visceral leishmaniasis. Again, an intravenous course of pentavalent antimony drugs can be used as **treatment** but side effects may be unpleasant. In resistant cases, it may be necessary to surgically remove the spleen.

Mucocutaneous leishmaniasis

(American leishmaniasis, Chiclero ulcer, Espundia, Forest yaws, Uta)

Occurring in South and Central America (ninety percent of cases are found in Bolivia, Brazil and Peru), **mucocutaneous leishmaniasis** has both short-term and long-term effects. The initially painful, itchy **nodules**, often on the legs, usually resolve spontaneously within a few months. Years later, however, up to forty percent of those infected can develop ulcers around the nose and mouth, which cause permanent scarring and disfigurement. Secondary infection of these lesions has serious consequences.

Diagnosis of mucocutaneous leishmaniasis is usually made from a biopsy of the ulcers, but blood tests may also help. Pentavalent antimony compounds can again be used as **treatment** but cure rates are unimpressive. Reconstructive surgery is often needed for facial deformities.

Leprosy

(Hansen's disease)

You may see cases of this misunderstood disease on your travels, but don't worry unnecessarily about catching **leprosy** – its low virulence makes it a weak bug, passed on only with difficulty, and transient contact with sufferers will cause you no harm. Contrary to commonly held misconceptions, it doesn't make your limbs drop off – such injuries are outward signs of nerve damage and loss of sensation in the feet and hands, resulting in repeated injury to sufferers' limbs. A concerted campaign by the WHO has dramatically reduced the number of sufferers requiring medication worldwide, and many living with leprosy control their symptoms successfully with drugs. Nevertheless up to two million people are disabled as a result of infection, and 620,000 new cases were reported in 2002. Seventy percent of all sufferers live in India, Nepal and Myanmar, where poverty and overcrowding encourage its spread. However, it's not only the developing world that is affected – there are periodic reports of cases in the southern states of the US.

The disease is caused by **bacteria** related to those causing TB, and it's thought to spread from person to person through coughing and sneezing. To contract the disease, prolonged exposure to a case is necessary; transient contact poses little threat. There is no preventative vaccination.

Leprosy can be subdivided broadly into two different types, depending on the degree of natural immunity exhibited by the victim. Although **tuberculoid** and **lepromatous** leprosy are caused by the same bacteria, they follow very different clinical courses.

Symptoms

Leprosy's **incubation period** is long: between two and five years for tuberculoid leprosy, and eight to twelve years for lepromatous cases. The effects of leprosy are long-term and principally involve the skin, the nervous system and the delicate membranes lining the upper respiratory tract. Although highly disfiguring, leprosy rarely causes fatal complications.

Tuberculoid leprosy only affects the skin and the nerves. The skin lesions tend to be localized, well-defined, few in number and numb. They often look pale, particularly in dark-skinned people. Tuberculoid leprosy is commonly self-healing, and damage to the peripheral nerves is usually limited.

Signs of **lepromatous leprosy** include a chronically stuffy nose and many ill-defined, pale skin lesions and nodules affecting the whole body. Unlike tuberculoid leprosy, the lesions themselves are not usually numb. Elsewhere, skin numbness has a slow, symmetrical onset in a "glove and stocking" pattern (the numbness is distributed over the hands and feet). The skin around the face thickens (giving a "lion-like" appearance) and hair loss (the eyebrows in particular) may occur. Frequently the ability to sweat is also lost. The internal structure of the nose can be affected by the bacterial invasion, causing a gradual but progressive collapse of the bridge of the nose. The eyes can be affected either directly by the bacteria causing local inflammation, or as a result of a loss of sensation impairing the blink reflex.

Diagnosis and treatment

Diagnosis is generally made on clinical grounds and is considered in anyone who is living in, or has spent long periods in, endemic areas, or who has skin lesions or unexplained numbness. A **skin biopsy** may confirm the diagnosis, as can a **lepromin test**, which measures the body's reaction to the inoculation of killed bacilli. Leprosy responds well to prolonged treatment with a combination of **antibiotics**, with the risk of infecting others removed after just two weeks, but unfortunately the damage to nerve endings is permanent.

Leptospirosis

(Weil's disease)

Leptospirosis can occur anywhere in the world, but in the tropics, outbreaks tend to occur during and after the rainy season or heavy flooding. Dogs, pigs and rats are the main animal hosts to the **microbes** that cause it, and it's spread to humans who come into contact with water contaminated by the animals' urine – infection usually enters the body through skin abrasions. Certain occupational groups are at greatest **risk** (veterinarians, farmers etc), although anyone who comes into contact with contaminated water is vulnerable. Leptospirosis risk needs to be considered when whitewater rafting or canoeing.

Symptoms

Classically, severe infections have two distinct phases. It takes about ten days from exposure for signs of the first phase to appear. Lasting up to a week, and resembling many other illnesses, **symptoms** include fever, headache, malaise, loss of appetite and muscle pains. The eyes may become red and sore, and lymph glands swollen, and a rash and nosebleeds may develop. After the initial acute illness, a symptom-free lull of one to three days can be followed by the **second phase**, during which meningism (headache, stiff neck, drowsiness, vomiting, intolerance to light) occurs. The majority of cases will recover spontaneously after this phase, but a small number will go on to suffer further complications involving the liver, blood, kidneys, lungs and heart (**Weil's disease**) with potentially serious consequences.

Since the initial symptoms of leptospirosis are nonspecific, successfully **diagnosing** it is often delayed until the more serious, second phase of illness. If you've had recent contact with potentially contaminated water and develop flu-like symptoms shortly afterwards, consider leptospirosis. Blood tests can confirm the diagnosis.

Antibiotics, such as penicillin, erythromycin or tetracycline, are most effective if started early (before the fifth day of illness). Maintaining hydration during the acute phase of the illness is important. Complications of the second phase of the illness, though rare, require hospital treatment.

Lice infestation

The **three kinds of lice** that affect humans are head lice, body lice and pubic (or crab) lice. Ubiquitous throughout the world, especially amongst school-age children, **head lice** are spread from one head to the next by sharing of hats, clothing, combs and hairbrushes, or simply getting too close. Adult lice are rarely seen, but their eggs ("nits") are bound tightly to individual hairs and are often visible. Head lice can cause itching of the scalp and neck, although it's more common to suffer no symptoms. A nit comb is useful for confirming their presence. Note that having head lice is not an indication of poor personal hygiene; in fact, they prefer clean hair.

Body lice are far less common, with a greater incidence among poverty-stricken communities or in cases of self-neglect. They are spread by direct contact or by shared clothing, where they often bury themselves in the seams. Body lice cause itching, and they're also responsible for spreading **louse-borne typhus** and **relapsing fever** (see p.183) in some parts of the world.

Pubic or **crab lice** are similarly uncommon. Spread by close (usually intimate) contact, they favour coarsely haired areas of the body – the pubic region and occasionally beards, underarms and the like. Crab lice commonly cause itching, which is usually worse at night, and are just about visible to the naked eye (usually at the base of a hair, with the nits attached further up).

Treatment

Head lice infestation can often be eradicated by meticulous and repeated use of a **nit comb** to washed and conditioned hair (suggested regime is up to thirty minutes of combing every four days for two weeks). Otherwise aqueous (instead of alcoholic) lotions of **malathion** are probably the most effective treatment against all lice infestations, and are available without prescription. Shampoos are less effective than lotions for head lice. Leave the lotion on for twelve hours (apply it to the whole body in the case of crab lice). A further second treatment is recommended after seven days. For head lice, other members of the household only need to be treated (simultaneously) if they have signs of lice infestation. In cases of pubic lice it's important that sexual partners also have treatment. For body lice, all clothes must be washed at a high temperature (or incinerated) at the same time as treatment.

Liver flukes

(Clonorchiasis, Opisthorchiasis)

There are three main species of **liver fluke** that affect humans:

➕ *Clonorchis sinensis* (known as oriental or Chinese liver fluke), common in China, Taiwan, Korea, Japan and Vietnam, and carried by domestic dogs and cats.

➕ *Opisthorchis felineus*, widespread in Eastern Europe (particularly Poland and the Baltics), and carried by a variety of wild and domestic animals.

➕ *Opisthorchis viverrini*, very common in Thailand (especially the north), and again mostly carried by dogs and cats.

Humans are usually infected after swallowing the **larvae** from raw, dried, smoked or pickled freshwater fish. The larvae reach the fish via a complicated life cycle (it all hangs on a water snail), whereby the habitat of the fish is contaminated by the faeces of human or dog carriers. Once the fish are ingested by a human, the larvae migrate up the bile duct from the gut and mature into adult worms in the gall bladder over a four-week period. Eggs from the mature flukes pass out of the body in faeces.

There is no preventative **vaccination**. Avoidance measures are simple: don't eat raw freshwater fish in high-risk areas.

Symptoms, diagnosis and treatment

Liver flukes affect millions of people but only a small number experience **symptoms**. Liver discomfort (the right upper aspect of the abdomen) is the most common symptom, occasionally accompanied by bouts of fever, nausea, diarrhoea (usually pale in colour) and jaundice. Advanced cases may suffer permanent liver and pancreatic damage.

The eggs are **identifiable** on microscopic examination of the stool. For mild infections, praziquantel may be an effective **treatment**; dosage is 20–30mg per kilo of body weight, twice daily for three days. However, severe infections involving liver damage and obstruction may need surgery.

Loiasis and Loa loa

▶ ▶ See under Filariasis, p.129.

Lyme disease

Lyme disease occurs mainly in rural areas of North America and Europe. Deriving its name from Lyme, Connecticut, where the first case was described in 1975, there has been a 25-fold increase in reported cases in the US over the past fifteen years, although this may be largely attributable to increased public awareness.

The microbes causing Lyme disease are transmitted to humans via the bite of blood-sucking **deer-ticks**. The ticks are active in the spring, summer and early autumn, when they can be found in long grass and trees waiting for deer to pass by. If you go walking in areas where there are deer, observe the measures to avoid tick bites described on p.149. Infected ticks are unlikely to pass on the disease unless attached for at least 24 hours, so it's important to inspect your hair, skin and clothes for them every few hours.

A **vaccine** (Lymerix), approved by the Food and Drug Administration in the USA, has met with controversy due to alleged side effects, but it should be considered if you're going to be in a high-risk area for any length of time. It's taken as a course of three doses, with the second one month after the first, and the third a year after, and appears to confer approximately 85 percent protection, although the length of this immunity is not known. Bear in mind, however, that the vaccine does not confer full protection against Lyme disease and none whatsoever against other potentially serious tick-borne infections.

Symptoms

Many people experience no **symptoms** at all, while in others a slowly spreading, red ringed ("bull's-eye") skin lesion develops at the bite site, any time from three days to four weeks after infection. There may also be local lymph-gland swelling and fever, generalized aches, pains and tiredness.

More serious symptoms are uncommon, frequently delayed by weeks or even months after the initial infection, and mainly affecting the nervous system, joints and heart. These can manifest as weakness, paralysis, abnormal sensations, mild meningitis symptoms, joint pains and swelling, and palpitations.

Diagnosis and treatment

Blood tests can confirm the **diagnosis** in the later stages of the disease – early detection is unreliable. If you do manage to catch it early (on the basis of the bull's-eye skin lesion), a two-week course of doxycycline (200mg once daily, or 100mg twice daily) should prevent further progression of the disease in adults (amoxicillin is an alternative for those who cannot tolerate doxycycline; see p.35). The later stages of Lyme disease will need treatment by hospital specialists.

Mal morado

▶▶ See under Onchocerciasis, p.127.

Malaria

Malaria has been recognized as a disease entity for a long time. References to an illness resembling malaria have been found in ancient Chinese and Hindu writings, while the ancient Greeks made a connection between sporadic fevers, spleen enlargement and swamps. In the Middle Ages, it was thought to be caused by "miasma" (bad air or "*mal aria*") emanating from swamp areas, and by the seventeenth century Jesuits are known to have treated the disease using the bark of the South American cinchona tree – from which quinine (the medicinal substance that remains the cornerstone of malaria treatment) is derived.

Malaria remains widely **distributed** throughout the tropics and subtropics (see the distribution map on p.169) and continues to pose a serious threat to health. It is currently endemic in over 100 countries, with the large majority affected by the dangerous **falciparum** variety (see p.167). The WHO estimates that there are between 300 and 500 million cases of malaria each year,

Balancing the risks of contracting malaria against those of experiencing side effects from the preventative drugs is key to the complex debate surrounding malaria prophylaxis. All drugs have side effects but much has been made of the sometimes severe and debilitating effects suffered by people who take **mefloquine**.

On the one side you have the manufacturers of Larium (the brand name for mefloquine) reassuring the public and playing down the side effects, while on the other a media-fed storm of perhaps unjustified anxiety and hysteria brews. The bulk of available scientific evidence supports the view that mefloquine's side effects have been blown out of proportion, and the drug has a number of heavyweight backers including the World Health Organization, the US Center for Disease Control and the UK Department of Health. Yet with increasing involvement of consumer groups, legal actions and questions being asked of governments, the use of mefloquine has become an emotive issue – speak to any hardened traveller and they're likely to know someone who has suffered after taking it.

It's important to remember that mefloquine is not always necessary. There are still malarial areas of the world where the parasite is sensitive to chloroquine (itself carrying a number of side effects) and mefloquine should really only be seriously considered in areas where chloroquine resistance exists. Doxcycycline and Malarone are other alternative prophylaxis. Refer to Part 3 to see if your destination is chloroquine-resistant or not, or check out the malaria websites or telephone helplines detailed in Part 4.

Bear in mind, too, that if you have a previous medical history of fits, psychiatric illness or heart conduction defects, then you cannot take mefloquine anyway, so save yourself the agonizing.

Side effects

The risk of serious **side effects** (notably fits or psychosis) culminating in death or hospitalization lies somewhere in the region of 1 in 10,000. Less serious side effects – headaches, dizziness, mood swings and insomnia – are common, and have been reported in around twenty percent of mefloquine users. Underweight women and first-time users seem to be more susceptible to side effects, and there's also a potential adverse interaction between mefloquine and alcohol. Several studies have identified little or no difference between the incidence of side effects from mefloquine compared to a chloroquine/proguanil combination (some have indicated a higher incidence of side effects in the latter). However in terms of side-effect profile and overall tolerability, doxycycline and Malarone appear to have the edge.

Most adverse mefloquine reactions manifest within the first weeks of taking the drug, which is one reason why it's suggested that you start it at least two (preferably three) weeks before departure – any side effects are likely to occur before you enter the malarial area in the majority of cases. A significant problem with mefloquine is that it stays in the body for a long time, so if you do experience mild side effects, it may take several days for them to settle. More serious psychiatric side effects, meanwhile, can remain for much longer and can be difficult to treat.

resulting in more than a million deaths. The countries of tropical Africa account for roughly ninety percent of the total cases. The vast majority of malaria fatalities occur in young children in this area, although children who survive beyond five years have a high degree of immunity to the lethal effects of malaria. (This immunity wanes if re-exposure to malaria is infrequent.)

Areas of particular **risk** include sub-Saharan Africa, the Indian subcontinent, south and Southeast Asia, Mexico, Haiti, Central and South America, Papua New Guinea and Vanuatu and the Solomon Islands, although it must be emphasized that patterns of malaria outbreaks change continually. The major cities in Asia and South America can, for most intents and purposes, be considered malaria-free, whereas those in Africa, India and Pakistan cannot.

Malaria is **spread** by the female **anopheles mosquito**, which bites between dusk and dawn, and very rarely ventures above altitudes of 1500m (4500ft). Less commonly, the parasite can be transmitted from mother to baby across the placenta, via blood transfusions or among drug addicts sharing needles. Once in the bloodstream, the parasite multiplies in the red blood cells and liver cells – the recurring fever synonymous with malaria coincides with the parasitic reproduction in the blood cells. The drugs used in malaria prophylaxis disrupt the parasites' life-cycle and reproduction stages, although resistance to them is growing on an alarming scale.

There are four **subgroups** of the malaria parasite – *P. falciparum, P. ovale, P. vivax, P. malariae* – of which the falciparum form is the most dangerous and also the most geographically diverse, accounting for the vast majority of malaria-related deaths.

Prevention

Much debate surrounds the risks and side effects of **antimalarials**, which work by preventing establishment of the parasite in the blood and liver cells. Taking drug prophylaxis for any illness must be carefully assessed in terms of **risk versus benefit**, and this is particularly the case with malaria. There are potential side effects for whichever drug you choose, but if you know you're travelling to a high-risk area, it is nonetheless vitally important to take drug prophylaxis. Choosing inadequate prophylaxis – or none at all – is foolhardy, exposing you to unnecessary risk from a potentially life-threatening disease.

Your destination will generally determine your choice of malaria prophylaxis, although other variables include length of stay, previous medical history and other drugs which you may be taking. There are four main alternatives: **chloroquine** (with or without proguanil); **mefloquine** (also known as larium); **doxycycline**; and a combination drug of atovaquone and proguanil known as **Malarone**. In some countries a daily-dose combination of chloroquine and proguanil (known as **Savarine**) is also available. The Chinese remedy **quinhaosu** (or **quinghaosu**), derived from the *Artemesia annua* plant, is attracting much research interest, and preparations derived from it are being used to good effect in treating drug-resistant malaria in some areas of Africa and Southeast Asia. Whichever antimalarial you choose, remember that none offers complete protection, so observation of the usual anti-insect bite measures (see p.149) is imperative.

More detail on the drugs used for malaria prophylaxis, their dosages and side effects can be found on p.41 of the Medical kit section in Part 1. Information on pregnancy and malaria appears on p.79, prophylaxis for children on p.65, and malaria and epilepsy on p.55.

Recognizing the symptoms

The **incubation period** for malaria is usually between nine and sixteen days, though it can be longer in rare cases. The symptoms for all of the subgroups

Antimalarials at a glance

Drug	Dose	Main advantages
Chloroquine	300mg weekly, starting one week before travel, continued for four weeks after	Long established, having been used safely and effectively for many years
Mefloquine (Larium)	250mg weekly, starting three weeks before travel, continued for four weeks after	Generally very effective. Weekly dosage is convenient.
Doxycycline	Daily dose (100mg), starting one week before travel, continued for four weeks after	Generally well tolerated. Useful alternative treatment in areas of chloroquine or mefloquine resistance.
Atovaquone/ proguanil (Malarone)	Daily dose (250/100mg), starting one or two days before travel, continued for one week after	Relatively new but initial studies indicate that it's highly effective, with a low side-effect profile. Useful for short or last-minute trips as can be started at the last minute, and continued for only seven days after return.

are broadly similar and relate to the parasite's cycle of reproduction and subsequent destruction of the body's red blood cells.

Initially, malaria is very difficult to distinguish from many other febrile illnesses, especially those found in the tropics. Classically, victims go through three stages: a **cold stage** characterized by shivering and shaking, a **hot stage** in which you develop a high temperature (sometimes above 41°C), hot flushes and rapid heartbeat, and a third, **sweating stage** during which your temperature falls. Typically the fever recurs cyclically, every one to three days depending on the type of malaria. Common **accompanying symptoms** include a cough, joint pains, loss of appetite and vomiting, which coupled with the high fever can cause significant dehydration. As the disease progresses, **anaemia** and **jaundice** may occur as a result of the destruction of large numbers of red cells, while the spleen (functionally a kind of filter for the blood) becomes enlarged early in the disease. (You'll feel it as a tender mass in the left side of your upper abdomen.)

Main Disadvantages	Main side effects *
Widespread resistance. Cannot be used for epileptics	Rashes, itching, gastrointestinal upset, headaches.
Numerous side effects, especially in females. Cannot be used for epileptics. Some isolated geographical areas of resistance	Gastrointestinal upset, dizziness, sleep disturbance, headaches. Rare severe neuropsychiatric reactions.
An antibiotic, so may interact with other drugs (eg the oral contraceptive). Causes sun sensitivity in approximately two percent of cases. Cannot be used by the following: children under 12; porphyria sufferers; pregnant/breast-feeding women	Gastrointestinal problems (nausea, vomiting, diarrhoea). Vaginal thrush. Ulceration of the gullet can occur. Small chance of sun sensitivity.
Relatively new therefore potential problems may not yet have emerged. Expensive. Limited to only 28 days usage within a malarial area. Cannot be used by pregnant or breast-feeding women.	Gastrointestinal upset, headaches, dizziness, rash
	*(consult product literature for a more detailed list)

A–Z | Malaria

By far the most dangerous form of malaria, **falciparum** can cause considerable damage to the body in a number of ways, and death in about two percent of cases usually as a result of delayed treatment. Cerebral malaria is the most dangerous complication, and if untreated often fatal. Typical signs of cerebral malaria include delirium, disorientation, a reduced level of consciousness, fits and coma. Initial recovery is followed by longstanding damage to the nervous system in up to ten percent of cases. So-called "blackwater fever" occasionally occurs as a result of kidney failure following the mass destruction of red blood cells, and leading to the escape of haemoglobin (the oxygen-carrying molecule in the blood) into the urine. Other systems affected by falciparum include the gastrointestinal tract (nausea and vomiting), the liver (jaundice), and the lungs (an accumulation of fluid causing shortness of breath). A common and dangerous complication in children and pregnant women (see below), is hypoglycaemia (low blood sugar).

The **malariae** malaria strain follows a recurring cycle of fever which over time becomes less severe although, in the absence of treatment, can continue for many years. The **ovale** and **vivax** forms cause similar illnesses which manifest as a periodic but irregular relapsing fever. The cycle may continue for up to five years despite drug treatment.

Diagnosis and treatment

A **blood test** can usually identify malaria parasites, although occasionally more than one sample needs to be examined. **Hospital treatment** is required if the diagnosis is confirmed – the following are only last-resort guidelines in the event you suspect malaria but have no immediate access to medical help. Before travelling, ask your doctor about appropriate treatment regimes for the area you're visiting; written instructions about when and how to use the particular drugs are also a good idea (a drug used for prophylaxis should not be used for treatment). Remember that **rehydration** and **reduction of the high fever** are always crucial.

Falciparum malaria is generally chloroquine resistant, so treatment options revolve around quinine, mefloquine, atovaquone/proguanil and a new combination drug of artemether with lumefantrine (Riamet). A new combination of chloroquine and dapsone (Lapdap) has shown very promising results .

Anyone too ill to take tablets will need to be treated intravenously. For an **adult** able to swallow, oral **treatment options** are either 600mg of quinine (three times a day for seven days), followed either by a course of pyrimethamine and sulfadoxine combination Fansidar (a single dose of three tablets), or a seven-day course of doxycycline (200mg daily). For mefloquine, take 20–25mg per kilo of body weight, either as a single dose or in two to three doses. For atovaquone/proguanil (Malarone), take four tablets daily for three days. Adults whose body weight is more than 35kg can take Artemether /lumefantrine (Riamet): a single dose of four tablets initially, followed by further doses of four tablets at 8, 24, 36, 48 and 60 hours (24 tablets in total).

Any fever occurring in the **returning traveller** requires the exclusion of malaria, particularly in the first three months. Although malaria can present later, this is rare and more likely to be the vivax, ovale or malariae types rather than falciparum.

For a **child**, mefloquine dosage is calculated on the same basis as for adults. Atovaquone/proguanil (Malarone) is not suitable for children weighing less than 11kg. For those between 11 and 20kg, one tablet should be taken daily for three days; for those between 21 and 30kg, two tablets should be taken daily for three days; and for those between 31 and 40kg, three tablets should be taken daily for three days. Children over 40kg in weight can tolerate adult dosages of Malarone. Quinine may be used at a dose of 10mg/kg body weight, three times daily for seven days although the course must be followed by a single dose of Fansidar: half a tablet for under-4s, one tablet for 5–6 year olds, one and half tablets for 7–9 year olds and two tablets for 10–14 year olds.

Vivax, **ovale** and **malariae** malaria are usually chloroquine-sensitive although resistance is emerging in some parts of the world. The **adult** starting dose for chloroquine (600mg) should be followed by a further 300mg dose after eight hours, then 300mg daily for two days.

Children follow the same regime in the doses of 10mg/kg body weight ini-

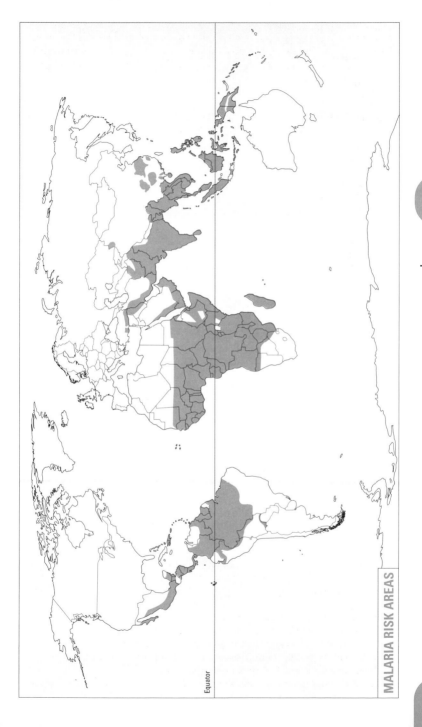

MALARIA RISK AREAS

Equator

tially, followed by 5mg/kg body weight for subsequent doses. Mefloquine can be used as an alternative if necessary.

For **recurring malaria**, a drug called primaquine is commonly and successfully used. Adult dosage is 15mg daily for 14–21 days, while children should be given 250mcg/kg body weight for the same period.

Malayan filariasis

▶▶ See Filarial lymphangitis, p.128.

Malta fever

▶▶ See Brucellosis, p.100.

Marburg virus

Marburg virus was first recognized in 1967 in Marburg, Germany, among laboratory staff who had been in close contact with Ugandan monkeys. One of the viral haemorrhagic fever group of viruses (see p.225), Marburg occurs in small outbreaks across sub-Saharan Africa – Sudan, Kenya and the Democratic Republic of Congo – and appears to be passed between people by intimate contact, although the exact mode of infection remains unclear. It is a very rare illness, even in these endemic areas, and the risk of the infection being passed to a casual traveller is extremely small.

Symptoms, diagnosis and treatment

The common symptoms of the disease are difficult to distinguish from a number of other conditions. After an incubation period of five to ten days, the initial **symptoms** include high fever, headache, rigors, and muscle pains, followed after approximately five days by a rash, mainly on the trunk, and by vomiting, diarrhoea, abdominal pain, chest pain and sore throat. Although considered marginally less dangerous than Ebola (see p.120), severe cases of Marburg virus cause potentially fatal bleeding. The recovery period is usually prolonged, and the virus remains in the body for a long time even after the symptoms have settled, so there's a potential risk of infecting others during that time. Approximately 25 percent of those infected will die from the disease.

Blood tests confirm the **diagnosis**. There is no specific **treatment**, although careful nursing and hospital care is vital to prevent further spread (known as "barrier nursing").

▶▶ See Viral haemorrhagic fever, p.225.

Melioidosis

("Vietnamese time bomb", Whitmore's disease)

The organisms causing **melioidosis** can be found anywhere in the world, but outbreaks occur mainly in Southeast Asia (it was relatively common among troops during the Vietnam War), the Far East and northern Australia. Isolated outbreaks have occurred elsewhere but are very rare.

The **bacteria** usually enter the body through skin cuts or abrasions, although transmission may also occur via contaminated water and inhalation. The disease is rare in humans (it affects animals such as goats, sheep, cattle and pigs), and those with a healthy immune system are unlikely to be severely affected. Diabetics and those with deep wounds or burns are more susceptible.

Melioidosis is a severe illness for which there is no immunization. In high-risk areas, protect yourself by carefully and thoroughly cleaning all wounds, even trivial ones, and observe the usual food- and water-hygiene measures (see p.149).

Symptoms, diagnosis and treatment

Common **symptoms** are a high temperature with prostration, and occasionally drowsiness and delirium. Diarrhoea, vomiting and joint aches may also occur. Septicaemia with abscess formation in the vital organs such as the kidneys, lungs, liver and spleen often follows. Melioidosis can be life-threatening, so it's essential to seek medical help early if it is suspected.

Infection can be confirmed by **blood tests**. Treatment involves a two- to four-week course of **intravenous antibiotics** (ceftazidime is the current recommendation), followed by a six-month course of amoxicillin or co-amoxiclav.

Meningitis

Although the word "**meningitis**" strikes terror into most people's hearts, it simply relates to inflammation of the membranes covering the outside of the brain (the *meninges*). The symptoms are usually serious but the outcome is dependent on the specific cause of the meningitis and how quickly it is treated. The most high-profile – and feared – of the many different causes is **meningococcal** meningitis, which is in turn divided into five subgroups – A, B, C, W and Y – each showing signs of localized predominance (eg the commonest in the UK is group B, whereas the commonest in Africa are groups A and C). TB, syphilis, leptospirosis, a host of viruses and a number of other bacteria can also cause meningitis (the bacteria that often affects children is now on the decrease thanks to the development of an effective preventative vaccine).

Sporadic **outbreaks** of meningococcal meningitis occur anywhere in the world, but they are more common and enduring in the belt of sub-Saharan Africa from Ethiopia in the east to Senegal in the west, particularly during the **dry season**. Epidemics often occur after war, drought and famine, when immunity of the population as a whole is low.

The bacteria causing meningococcal meningitis are spread from person to person by droplets after coughing or sneezing. The majority of people infected with the bacteria causing meningococcal meningitis do not develop signs of the disease, and many become unwitting carriers. Because the number of people carrying the bacteria is far higher than the actual incidence of the disease, **susceptibility** to meningitis is likely to be more down to individual health and immunity rather than the bacteria itself. A **vaccination** is available against the A C, W and Y (see p.10) strains but is ineffective against group B. All travellers should be immunized if they're headed to areas of high risk. If you plan to travel to Mecca for the annual hajj, vaccination is mandatory.

Symptoms

When **symptoms** occur (usually after an incubation period of between two

> ## The glass test for a "purpuric" rash
>
> Press a **glass** against the spots. If they pale or disappear, it is not a purpuric rash. If they do not lighten, and there are other symptoms that suggest a diagnosis of meningitis, seek medical help rapidly. (Note that a purpuric rash does not necessarily mean meningitis – there are a number of other causes.)

and ten days), initially it's almost impossible to differentiate them from those of a common cold or any other viral infection. Progression of the disease can be alarmingly rapid, however, and usually includes the following:

- ✚ Intense malaise
- ✚ High fever
- ✚ Severe headache
- ✚ Intolerance to light
- ✚ Vomiting
- ✚ Irritability
- ✚ Lapsing consciousness
- ✚ Neck stiffness
- ✚ A purpuric rash (in the case of meningococcal meningitis)

Untreated, meningitis can lead to septicaemia, convulsions, coma and death in over half of those affected. Early treatment is essential.

The **rash** in meningococcal meningitis indicates the presence of septicaemia and requires rapid medical attention. The rash looks purple and does not blanch on pressure (see box above). Initially it appears in clusters of tiny blood spots (like pinpricks) over pressure points or areas of friction (armpits, groin, buttocks, ankles etc). These clusters will expand and the spots join together, looking like fresh bruises or blood blisters. The rash may be difficult to see on dark skin.

Diagnosis and treatment

If meningitis is suspected, don't consider self-treatment. Every minute counts, so **get to a doctor or a hospital quickly**. There the diagnosis can be confirmed by the presence of the bacteria in the cerebrospinal fluid taken from a lumbar puncture. Generally, if caught in time, meningitis responds well to intravenous antibiotic treatment, usually penicillin.

When isolated cases occur, close contacts of the case may need to be given **prophylactic antibiotics**. The need for prophylaxis depends on the type of organism causing the meningitis and the closeness of contact. In any event, take advice from the medical team treating the case.

Monkeypox

Monkeypox is a viral zoonosis which was first reported in humans in 1970. It is rare, occurring mainly in remote, rain forested areas of central and western Africa, where the principal host is believed to be a certain species of squirrel. However many other animal species have been found to carry the virus, and a human outbreak in the American midwest in 2003 (the first to be identified in a developed country) was related to contact with prairie dogs.

The virus is **transmitted** through an animal bite or through direct contact with the skin or flesh of an infected animal. It is quite infectious, and person-to-person spread also occurs through droplet inhalation, contact with infected body fluids (there is a risk from blood transfusions) and via contaminated clothing or bedding. The **risk** to tourists in Africa is very low but it is sensible to avoid unnecessary handling of wild animals.

Monkeypox is related to the now-extinct smallpox virus. The **smallpox vaccination** provides protection against monkeypox, but is reserved only for carers of those afflicted with the disease and not generally available for ordinary travellers.

Symptoms

After an incubation of ten to fourteen days the initial **symptoms** are fairly non-specific, consisting of fever, headache, generalized aches and pains, swollen lymph nodes and generalized tiredness. Within a week, a chickenpox-like rash of raised vesicles develops, often starting on the face before spreading to the rest of the body. These vesicles eventually scab and fall off. The illness usually lasts between two and four weeks, and the disease **fatality** rate can be as high as ten percent.

Diagnosis and treatment

The infection can be confirmed through **blood tests**. There is no specific treatment, although the smallpox vaccination may be given after exposure to a confirmed case. **Post-exposure treatment** can be given for up to fourteen days after contact and may prevent progression of the disease or cause it to be much milder.

Motion sickness

The chances are that if you travel with any regularity or for a prolonged length of time, at some point you'll experience the dismal symptoms associated with **motion sickness**. Children (over the age of 3) tend to be the most prone to the effects of motion sickness, and it's also one of the few illnesses that affects women more than men.

The **symptoms** – nausea, sweating, disorientation and dizziness – evolve from a discrepancy in the messages being sent to the brain from the eyes and the balance apparatus of the ears. This conflict of the senses usually arises in turbulent conditions when visual contact with the horizon is lost.

Although the scientific mechanism for motion sickness is well recognized and understood, there is a less predictable psychological component, with people who are fearful or anxious more likely to experience sickness than those who stay calm.

Prevention

Prevention of motion sickness is easier than treatment, so if you've been previously affected or anticipate a rough journey, plan ahead and take preventative measures at least an hour before you set out. The main preventative **drug options** revolve around various preparations of hyoscine and antihistamines such as cinnarizine or promethazine (see p.40). There's little to choose between them in terms of efficacy, although their side effects differ slightly: while both

types of drug can cause drowsiness (sometimes a welcome bonus), hyoscine can
also cause a dry mouth and blurred vision, but has the advantage of being available as a skin patch as well as a tablet.

The standard drug preventatives are discussed in greater detail in Part 1.

Treatment

If you start to feel sick having embarked on your journey, remember to keep
your eyes on the horizon if possible, so helping to reduce the inconsistencies
between the messages the brain is receiving from the eyes and balance apparatus. Slowly sip a cool drink, try and relax taking slow, deep breaths and distract
yourself. The antihistamine promethazine, although primarily a preventative,
can also be taken to reduce the symptoms when they strike. If all else fails,

make sure you have an intact polythene bag in which to throw up.
Tabacum is a good homeopathic remedy for sickness from rolling
motion, and will suit you if you feel terribly faint, with a sinking feeling in the pit of your stomach – you'll probably be found up on the
deck of the boat, in the fresh air, with your coat open and belt loosened. You
look pale, may be covered with cold sweat, and have intense nausea followed
by violent vomiting. Increased salivating makes you want to spit. **Petroleum** is
good for car, train and boat travel, especially for people who are really strongly affected by the smell of petrol. Take this if you feel the need to keep wrapped
up and warm. Your nausea is eased by eating plain biscuits or crackers.
Cocculus indicus is best for people who can't look out of moving vehicles,
especially sideways. Your nausea can be worsened by virtually any external
stimuli – light, noise, smell etc. Take all these remedies in a 30c potency, starting an hour before setting out, and repeating hourly through the journey. If
you can't decide which of the above fits best, try a combined version of them
all, marketed under the name "**Travella**".

Bach Rescue Remedy, taken as a few drops every half hour or so in water,
also helps take the edge off travel sickness.

Mycetoma

(Madura foot, Maduromycosis, Maduromycetoma)

Mycetoma is a chronic **fungal infection** relatively common in Africa, India and Sri Lanka, with sporadic cases also reported in Europe and North America. A rare but serious condition, usually affecting the skin, muscle and bones of the lower leg (sometimes the upper limb), mycetoma is caused by a number of soil fungi which probably enter the body through a puncture wound – yet another reason for wearing something on your feet and for cleansing all wounds (particularly penetrating wounds that breach the skin and superficial flesh, eg a thorn or nail).

There is no **vaccination** against mycetoma but it is extremely rare in travellers.

Symptoms, diagnosis and treatment

Small, firm, painless **nodules** develop weeks or months often after an apparently innocuous injury. Slowly the nodules grow in size, becoming soft in the middle and eventually **ulcerating**. Straw-coloured fluid containing small granules (red, white, yellow, brown or black, depending on the type of fungus) drains from the deeper tissues. The process is progressive and will continue to invade deeper tissues unabated. Invasion into the joints causes intense pain on movement.

The fungus is usually **microscopically identified** from the discharge. Drug **treatment** may be effective in early disease but once the infection has taken hold, surgery may be necessary.

Myiasis

Common causes of **myiasis**, which, in medical terms, means the invasion or infestation of bodily tissues or cavities by the feeding **larvae** of flying insects, are the tumbu fly and Lund's fly in Africa (mainly west and central), the human botfly and New World screw-worm fly in Central and South America and the Caribbean, and the Old World screw-worm fly in Africa, the Middle East, the Indian subcontinent, southeast Asia and Papua New Guinea.

Tumbu and Lund's flies commonly lay their eggs on drying laundry, with the larvae emerging and burrowing into the skin when the clothes are worn. Incubation usually takes less than two weeks. The boils created by the maturing maggots are often multiple – it's sometimes possible to identify the maggots' breathing tubes as two black dots in the boils.

Human botfly infestation most commonly affects cattle and humans. The fly captures a blood-feeding insect such as a mosquito and lays its eggs on it. The mosquito then transports the eggs to humans – as it feeds on the host's blood, the eggs hatch and start to burrow. The larvae tend not to migrate through the tissue but settle below the skin in the area where they originally penetrated. After an incubation period as long as twelve weeks the larvae exit by the same means as they entered and pupate in the soil.

The **screw-worm flies** deposit their eggs on the edges of wounds and healthy mucous membranes (mouth, nose etc); the hatched larvae then burrow deeply into the flesh causing extensive tissue destruction. The wound is very

"Uninvited companions"

*T*he trouble with the insects began as Hurricane Mitch was heading up the coast. The botflies – often found in the vicinity of large mammals – struck as I was helping to round up the horses at the tourist cabins where we were going to sit out the hurricane. I didn't notice anything at first. But a few days later, after the storm had passed, I saw and felt a number of small red bumps – similar to mosquito bites – on my arms and body.

It was only when the short, sharp stabbing pains began that I suspected the lumps might be what the locals called "beef worms" – a type of fly maggot that lives just under the surface of the skin, and is common on horses, dogs, and of course cattle. I'd heard about beef worms and their effects many times but had never suffered a bite – I was soon to find out what having them meant.

The female flies have an ingenious method of depositing their eggs. First she catches a female mosquito, lays eggs on the mosquito's body, then releases the mosquito which promptly heads for a source of blood – any large animal will do! Upon landing on its chosen victim the mosquito feeds, and the heat of the host's body triggers the botfly eggs to drop off the mosquito. The botfly larvae immediately hatches on the warmth and burrows under the skin.

The larvae grow by feeding on your flesh, and the stabbing pain begins. It's like having a thin needle stuck into a nerve, sending a short, but intense, flash of pain up to your brain. As the grub grows bigger it also grows spiky hairs around its body segments, making it difficult to remove by yourself. You know for certain it's a beef worm when it pokes its breathing tube out of your skin.

They're so common in the Central American lowlands (though tourists are rarely affected) that the locals all have their own method to get rid of them. These always involve blocking the breathing hole with something – wax, glue, tobacco – and waiting for a few hours until the larvae die. Then a really good squeeze brings the creature shooting out like a tiny rocket.

I went to some Maya friends of mine who simply pulled a few twigs from a tree in their garden and dabbed the resulting sticky white latex over the breathing holes. They then stuck more leaves over the latex and told me to come back in the morning, when all the larvae but one were duly squeezed out.

I had eight beef worms altogether, but I actually wanted to keep the one I had on my wrist, where it could easily be observed as it matured. Sounds gruesome, and indeed it was to some people who saw it, but I'd heard that the larva produces an antibiotic-type chemical preventing wound infection, so it was safe enough. I still had to keep it covered by a bandage to avoid offending delicate stomachs but most people were in fact morbidly fascinated.

For the next couple of months I gave request viewings of "my worm" in various bars and hotels as I travelled up to Mexico. It popped out in the highland town of San Cristóbal de las Casa, where these flies do not exist. I took it round the drugstore, dropped it into formaldehyde and it now sits on a bookshelf in my study. I'm thinking of encasing it in perspex for a paperweight.

Peter Eltringham, Luton, UK

painful, festers and smells offensive. It usually takes about a week for the maggots to mature and leave the wound to pupate in the soil. Myiasis caused by screw-worm flies is rare in humans but can be devastating to livestock.

All forms of myiasis are rare in casual travellers, but your best means of **protection** against any of these insects is to observe the bite-avoidance advice on p.149 when travelling in areas of prevalence.

Symptoms

Regardless of the cause, the most common initial signs of myiasis are **itchy sores**, which develop into painful, often **oozing boils**. However, these lesions rarely develop into a significant health risk, as the maggots are essentially hitching a ride until they mature, after which they'll make their exit leaving no long-term effects.

Diagnosis and treatment

There is no formal test for myiasis, but the maggots can often be seen through the air hole they create in the skin.

Applying **vaseline** or similar substances to the skin cuts off the air supply and will force the maggot closer to the surface, making extraction easier. Maggots must be removed completely to reduce the risk of secondary bacterial infection.

Onchocerciasis

▶▶ See under Filariasis, p.127.

O'nyong nyong virus

Taking its name from an African phrase meaning "very painful and weak", **o'nyong nyong** (**ONN**) **virus** caused a major epidemic in the late 1950s in Uganda, Kenya, Tanzania and Malawi, which affected an estimated two million people. In recent years, outbreaks have been rare and usually follow the rainy season in East and West Africa and in Zimbabwe. ONN is spread by various subspecies of the anopheles mosquito.

Risk to the casual traveller is very low unless passing through an area where there is an active epidemic. There is no preventative vaccination and the best means of protection is to observe the usual precautions for avoiding insect bites (remembering that culex mosquitoes are at their most voracious between dusk and dawn).

▶▶ See Bite avoidance, p.149.

Symptoms, diagnosis and treatment

The illness is indistinguishable from chikungunya fever and dengue fever (see pp.102 & 113; previous infection with chikungunya confers immunity to ONN), with the main **symptoms** being high fever, severe joint pains, headaches, swollen lymph glands and occasionally a generalized rash. Recovery from the acute symptoms usually takes about two weeks, but joint pains can persist for longer. The infection can cause **miscarriage** in pregnant women.

Blood tests confirm the **diagnosis**. There's no specific **treatment** for o'nyong nyong virus other than symptom relief and rest; however, no serious long-term effects have ever been reported following infection.

Oropouche virus

Oropouche virus is a zoonosis, with the **sloth** acting as the natural reservoir. It is transmitted to humans by midges, which breed in the rotting husks of cacao beans. The disease has caused large epidemics in recent years in Brazil, Peru, Trinidad and Panama. Its incidence appears to be on the increase, and this seems to be related to the intense deforestation in these areas, which is altering the local ecosystems and bringing humans into closer contact with the disease vectors. There is no **vaccine** against the virus so the best means of avoiding the infection is to observe precautions against insect bites (see p.149). The risk to the traveller is low unless you plan on venturing into an epidemic area.

Symptoms, diagnosis and treatment

Common **symptoms** include sudden-onset high fever with muscle and joint pains, intense headache, nausea and diarrhoea. In severe cases, symptoms of meningitis occur (see p.171).

Diagnosis is confirmed by blood tests. There is no **treatment** other than rest and symptomatic relief for the fever, including drinking plenty of fluids. The presence of meningitis symptoms, however, requires urgent medical assessment.

Oroya fever

▶ ▶ See Bartonellosis, p.97.

Paragonimiasis

(Oriental lung fluke)

Paragonimiasis occurs throughout the Far East, West Africa, south Asia, Indonesia, Papua New Guinea and central and northern South America. It's caused by a group of parasitic flatworms (**flukes**), whose eggs hatch in water and develop initially in freshwater snails, after which they move into **crabs** or **crayfish** where they develop into cysts. Humans become infected by handling or eating the crustaceans or when food preparation utensils have been contaminated. After the cysts are eaten, the immature flukes are released into the intestine, where they penetrate the wall and migrate to other tissues (usually the lungs, but sometimes abdominal organs or the nervous system). The adult worms develop after about six weeks and start producing eggs, which are subsequently coughed up in sputum.

Avoid eating raw, pickled or undercooked freshwater crustaceans ("drunken crabs" – live crabs immersed in rice wine before eating – are a delicacy in some parts of Asia) if you're anywhere there might be a risk of infection.

Symptoms

The **symptoms** are very similar to pulmonary TB, although up to a quarter of people affected show no signs of illness at all. The presence of the adult worms in the lungs causes a mild fever and a cough which, although starting off dry, becomes productive with blood-stained sputum. Chest pain often occurs and night sweats are common. As the infection becomes more long-standing, shortness of breath, weakness and weight loss occur. The lung flukes can survive for a number of years if left untreated. When they eventually die, the cysts close up, leaving long-term **scarring** (similar to TB).

Diagnosis and treatment

The worm eggs are usually microscopically identified in the **sputum** or the **stool**. A drug called praziquantel (25mg per kilo of body weight, three times a day for three days) is the best **treatment**, although surgery may be needed to remove the cysts.

Paratyphoid

Paratyphoid is clinically similar to typhoid (see p.221), although it's a milder illness. It occurs sporadically in small epidemics across the world. Three sub-groups of the salmonella bacteria cause paratyphoid and are spread by the faecal–oral route.

Common **symptoms** are identical to typhoid, though less serious, and occur between one and ten days after eating contaminated food. They include general malaise, fever, headache, loss of appetite and sometimes a dry cough. Bleeding from the intestine, confusion and hearing loss are occasional complications.

Paratyphoid is usually confirmed by lab analysis of **blood or stool samples**. As with any diarrhoeal disease, fluid replacement to avoid dehydration is the cornerstone of treatment. Although paratyphoid responds to antibiotics, resistance is widespread; quinalone antibiotics such as **ciprofloxacin** are the current favoured option.

Plague

The word "**plague**" never fails to conjure up a sense of fear. The term "Black Death" arises from the dark appearance of bleeding under the skin, seen in advanced cases of plague septicaemia. Throughout history it has caused major epidemics which have significantly reduced the human population. There were three major epidemics in the sixth, fourteenth and seventeenth centuries, with an estimated total death toll of 137 million (though recent evidence suggests that an unidentified viral haemorrhagic fever may have been the real cause of epidemics in the Middle Ages). In the 1980s around 9000 cases of plague were reported to the WHO, the majority occurring in Asia and Africa but with small foci in South America and even the southwest USA. Since the millennium, outbreaks have been reported in Algeria, sub-Saharan Africa (Zambia, Malawi, Namibia and Uganda) and India. Plague often follows natural disasters such as earthquakes, which tend to increase the contact between wild and domestic rodents; the first sign of a plague epidemic is often the deaths of large numbers of rats. The disease is caused by a bacteria transmitted to humans by animals, usually via the bite of a **rat flea**. Wild rodents remain as the natural reservoir.

Plague is a rare but serious disease which is unlikely to trouble the average traveller, but you should avoid areas where there have been outbreaks. Avoid contact with rats, live or dead, use insect repellent on your ankles and legs and an insecticide on your clothing and outer bedding. If your exposure risk is high, consider taking prophylactic **antibiotics** (see below) – these should be used if you have face-to-face contact with a known case of pneumonic plague. A plague **vaccine** is available but not routinely administered – it's used mainly for lab or medical personnel who may be at risk (see p.10), and its use in mass immunization of the population during an outbreak has not been properly assessed.

Symptoms

The initial flea bite often goes unnoticed. **Symptoms** can develop in a matter of hours (to a maximum of seventeen days) and start with high fever, headache, malaise, muscle aches and nausea. In a very short time (often a matter of hours), the infection spreads to the lymph nodes, causing (very) tender swellings, known as **buboes** (hence the bubonic plague tag). The buboes can be very large (up to 10cm in diameter) and may form abscesses.

The infection gradually spreads to the blood, leading to **septicaemia** and more focused organ damage. Involvement of the lungs can proceed to **pneumonic plague**, which is highly infectious (by coughing and sneezing) and carries a particularly high mortality. The clotting system of the blood can be affected by the septicaemia, leading to an increased tendency to bleed.

Diagnosis and treatment

Diagnosis can be made on the basis of **blood tests**. Because of the potential seriousness of plague and the risk of spread, treatment should be undertaken in hospital, under isolation. Although localized resistance has been reported, the antibiotic **streptomycin** is the usual treatment of choice, but other options include gentamycin and the tetracycline group, of which doxycycline is a member.

Polio

The **polio** virus exists worldwide but most cases occur in Asia and Africa, where vaccination uptake has historically been poor, and where it is spread mainly via the faecal–oral route by contaminated food and water. A concerted vaccination campaign from the WHO and Rotary International is expected to render the virus extinct from nature by 2005.

Provided you have been **immunized**, the risk of contracting polio during your trip is almost nonexistent. A polio booster should be considered every ten years, so check whether you're due before departure (see p.11). Otherwise, observe the normal food and water precautions to reduce your risk.

Symptoms

People who've contracted the virus are most **infectious** for the week to ten days before and after they develop symptoms. A staggering 95 percent of those infected will show no symptoms. In the remainder fever, headache, nausea and vomiting occur after a one- to two-week incubation period. The virus multiplies in the gut and enters the nervous system. Neck stiffness and a unilateral tremor sometimes occur. **Paralysis** results in roughly 0.1 percent of cases, and the risk increases with age.

Diagnosis and treatment

Blood tests can detect the antibodies to polio virus. Polio cannot be treated, although the majority of cases will recover without long-term effects. **Bed rest** is important in the early stages, and **physiotherapy** is vital for anyone who suffers residual muscle weakness or paralysis.

Pseudomembranous enterocolitis

Pseudomembranous enterocolitis is a rare complication following treatment with antibiotics, when the bowel becomes inflamed as a result of colonization and overgrowth of bacteria (*Clostridium difficile*). Although the infection can be passed on from person to person, this is rare and tends to occur mainly in hospital amongst patients with low immunity.

Symptoms, diagnosis and treatment

Symptoms usually occur four to ten days after taking antibiotics but can be delayed for up to six weeks. Symptoms vary in severity, but can mimic infectious diarrhoeal diseases. Watery diarrhoea is often accompanied by mild fever and abdominal tenderness. Severe abdominal pain and bloody diarrhoea can also occur.

Pseudomembranous enterocolitis should be considered in anyone who develops the above symptoms within six weeks of taking a course of antibiotics. If it's suspected and you are still taking the original antibiotics, stop the course. The **diagnosis** is usually confirmed by a stool analysis or by sigmoidoscopy. Ironically, a further ten-day course of the **antibiotic** metronidazole (400mg daily) usually cures the illness, although relapses are common.

Pyrexia

▶▶ See Fever, p.125.

Q fever

Q fever was first identified in 1935 in Australia, where it was given the name "Query fever" because its cause was initially unknown; the microbes that cause it were eventually identified two years later. The illness occurs worldwide, although with a higher incidence in rural areas. Many people have a natural immunity to the microbes, which suggests that the infection is widespread but usually goes undetected.

The **micro-organisms** responsible are usually carried by sheep, cattle and goats and are found in particularly high concentrations in the placenta but are also present in the milk, urine and faeces. It's possible to become infected simply by breathing in the microbes from contaminated air, although **ticks** also carry the disease and may be responsible for a small number of human infections. Farmers, abattoir workers, vets and anyone else in **close contact with animals** are at greatest risk, with little threat posed to the average traveller. A **vaccine** against Q fever exists, but is not widely available – discuss it with your doctor if you plan to work with animals while you're away.

After an incubation period of between ten and twenty days, headache, fever, shivering, muscle aches, loss of appetite, nausea and fatigue are the prominent **symptoms**. A cough, and sharp chest pains that are worse on taking a deep breath or coughing can also occur. Symptoms are usually self-limiting, lasting up to two weeks. Rarely, the illness can lead to heart, liver or brain complications.

Q fever is difficult to differentiate from many viral illnesses, and as such it's very difficult to diagnose on clinical grounds alone; **blood tests** will confirm the diagnosis. Symptoms will often resolve themselves, although a two- to three-week week course of **doxycycline** is usually very effective against the acute illness.

Rabies

Rabies is present in all parts of the world except Antarctica. In some parts of India, one in 500 admissions to hospital is due to rabies, almost always secondary to a dog bite. It is estimated that around two percent of dogs in Bangkok are rabid, and the disease accounts for around 300 deaths in the city each year. It's estimated that rabies accounts for up to 70,000 deaths each year worldwide.

The virus is commonly carried by dogs, wolves, foxes, jackals, skunks, cats, bats, mongooses and even farm animals, but can be found in any warm-blooded animal. Cases of human rabies are most prevalent in the Indian subcontinent, parts of South and Central America and Southeast Asia.

The virus is transmitted in the saliva of an infected animal, usually via a **bite** or by **licking an open wound**. Animal **scratches** must also be treated with caution. Human-to-human transmission is very rare. Half of all people who come into contact with infected saliva will develop the disease.

A **vaccine** against rabies is available to travellers who may be at risk (see p.11). **Pre-exposure** vaccination is recommended if:

✚ You are at particularly high risk of animal contact (vets, agricultural workers etc).

✚ You plan to visit remote areas where medical care is less accessible.

✚ You plan to stay longer than a month in an area where dog rabies is common (the longer you stay, the greater your risk of exposure).

Completing the full three-dose pre-exposure vaccination course usually confers good protection for up to three years (note that taking chloroquine at the same time as being vaccinated may reduce your antibody response and thus impair the development of immunity). However, if you are bitten by (or come into contact with the saliva of) an animal in a high-risk area even after being vaccinated, you must still seek urgent medical attention – prior vaccination may buy you time to a degree, but it's still important to start post-exposure treatment as early as possible.

Vaccinated or not, always **avoid contact** with animals (domestic or wild) in high-risk areas. If you are bitten, **thorough cleaning** of the wound with soap and water, followed by an application of alcohol or iodine, considerably reduces the chances of becoming infected.

Symptoms

It can take weeks, months or even years for the symptoms of rabies to develop, though the average **incubation** period is between two and eight weeks. Early **symptoms** are nonspecific and include fever, general malaise, loss of appetite, nausea, vomiting, diarrhoea, muscle aches, sore throat, cough and headache. Odd behaviours such as anxiety, agitation and aggression may occur. Pain or pins and needles over the area of the bite occur in just under half of all cases. From the initial nonspecific symptoms the disease can take one of two different courses. The more common of the two, **furious rabies** is characterized by hyper-excitability, muscle spasms and hydrophobia (fear of water). Insomnia and strange purposeless movements can occur spontaneously or in response to touch, while frothing of the mouth is accompanied by swallowing difficulties and vomiting. The final stages of the disease are characterized by progressive muscle paralysis and breathing difficulties. Usually occurring after bites from rabid bats, **dumb rabies** involves gradual paralysis, which begins in the bitten limb in half of all cases. It spreads rapidly and is usually symmetrical.

Diagnosis and treatment

Tests on the **blood** and **saliva** of the victim will show evidence of the virus, but if you are at high risk, it's unwise to defer post-exposure treatment pending lab results. Once symptoms develop, there is no cure.

The importance of thorough wound cleaning cannot be over-emphasized. If you have been bitten in a high-risk area, seek medical help urgently as the sooner post-exposure treatment is initiated, the better. Details on the **post-exposure vaccination regimes** can be found on p.12.

If you are bitten by an animal, don't forget the risk of tetanus and bacterial skin infections (see pp.213 & 202) in the panic over rabies.

Relapsing fever

Relapsing fever is a bacterial infection which derives its name from the relapsing nature of the untreated illness. There are two distinct varieties: louse-borne or tick-borne. The **louse-borne** variety is found anywhere in the world, usually in areas of great poverty. Epidemics often occur after war or natural disaster. Clothing provides refuge for the lice. The **tick-borne** variety is found in Africa, southern Europe, the Middle East, Asia and the Americas (including the western US and Canada).

The risk of infection to the traveller is generally low, especially if the standard insect bite-avoidance tactics are observed (see p.149). Person-to-person spread of relapsing fever does not occur (unless via body lice).

Symptoms

After an incubation period of two to ten days, initial **symptoms** consist of an abrupt-onset fever, rigors, muscle pains, headache and extreme weakness lasting for up to a week. A **remission** period of similar length follows before the symptoms **relapse**. Without treatment, further periods of regression and relapse occur. A cough and swelling of the lymph glands, liver and spleen may develop, and in severe cases (particularly the louse-borne variety) jaundice and a purpuric rash. Each time the fever abates a dangerous drop in blood pressure can occur. Progression of the disease can lead to swelling of the brain and inflammation of the heart muscle, which are serious complications.

Overall, relapsing fever is a dangerous, potentially fatal illness although there is usually a good response to treatment.

Diagnosis and treatment

Blood tests confirm the presence of the bacteria. The usual methods for reducing high fever should be adopted (see p.125), such as regular paracetamol and drinking plentiful cool fluids. Treatment with **antibiotics** such as tetracycline, chloramphenicol or penicillin must be conducted under medical supervision, in case the drugs react with the bacteria (a rare complication). The length of treatment with antibiotics is dependent on the type of relapsing fever.

Respiratory tract infection

▶▶ See Colds and coughs, p.106.

Rift Valley fever

Over the past few years there have been a number of major outbreaks of **Rift Valley fever**, mainly in sub-Saharan Africa, although particularly violent epidemics broke out in Egypt in the late 1970s and Kenya and Somalia in 1997–98. Outbreaks are often associated with heavy rainfall and flooding.

Rift Valley fever is a **mosquito-borne viral haemorrhagic fever** (see p.225). The infection is also found in animals (cattle, sheep, goats and camels), and humans can also contract the illness through contact with the blood, meat or body fluids (perhaps from the milk) of infected animals.

Experimental **vaccines** have been used to protect veterinary and laboratory workers at high risk, and animal vaccines are available, but the average traveller is at very low risk and should simply take steps to avoid mosquito bites (see p.149), and not get too close to livestock in any area that has seen outbreaks.

Symptoms

Rift Valley fever is difficult to distinguish from other causes of high fever, and can be mistaken for meningitis. After an incubation period of between two and six days, the **fever** tends to peak twice, the first episode lasting two to four days, followed by a brief remission before the second. Headache, muscle pains and backache are common, with neck stiffness, vomiting and photophobia occurring in more severe cases.

Those more seriously affected with the disease may develop brain, blood, liver and eye complications within the first three weeks, and such progressions carry a high mortality rate.

Diagnosis and treatment

Blood tests reveal the presence of antibodies to the virus. There is no specific **treatment** for Rift Valley fever, and most cases are relatively mild and self-limiting. Observe the usual methods to reduce fever, rest and drink plenty. In severe cases intensive medical care is needed.

River blindness

▶▶ See under Filariasis, p.127.

Rocky Mountain spotted fever

Rocky Mountain spotted fever (**RMSF**) is a tick-borne illness affecting 600–800 people annually across the USA, with cases most commonly occurring in the southeastern states – Oklahoma, Tennessee, the Carolinas, Georgia and Virginia are particular hotspots. It also occurs in parts of Central and South America. The risk is higher in the spring and summer when the ticks are most active. Children between the ages of 5 and 9 are most commonly affected, for the simple reason that they're more likely to indulge in pastimes that put them in contact with the ticks.

A form of typhus (see p.222), RMSF is caused by the rickettsial bacteria transmitted by the bite of **dog ticks** (in the eastern USA) and **wood ticks** (in the western USA). As in Lyme disease, the longer the tick remains attached to the body, the greater the chance of infection. **Careful removal of ticks** is important (see p.152); avoid leaving body parts in the skin, as the infection can be contracted from the body juices of a crushed tick coming into contact with broken skin.

There is no vaccination against RMSF, so the best way to avoid the illness is to avoid being bitten by ticks (see pp.149–153). Person-to-person spread does not occur.

Symptoms

Appearing between one and two weeks after the tick bite, **symptoms** are usually sudden in onset and include high fever, chills, muscle pains, severe headache and vomiting. A crusted, raised lump can develop at the site of the bite, while nearby lymph glands are likely to become swollen and tender.

The **rash** synonymous with the name begins between one and ten days after the onset of the fever. Small red spots or blotches begin peripherally (hands, feet, wrists, and ankles) and spread up the limbs to the trunk (the face is usually spared). As the illness progresses the rash changes to look like bruising and blood blisters (ie purpuric).

Complications of RMSF can affect the brain, liver, kidneys and lungs, and the disease can be fatal without appropriate antibiotic treatment.

Diagnosis and treatment

The **diagnosis** can be made initially on a high level of suspicion, connecting the history of recent tick bites with the development of a high fever. If neurological signs are present, a **lumbar puncture** will be needed. Blood tests are usually only useful retrospectively, as the results can take a few days, by which time the RMSF should already have been treated.

If RMSF is suspected, seek help early as the likelihood of complications is related to how fast you get treated. For adults, the usual treatment is a tetracycline antibiotic (eg doxycycline). This group should be avoided if possible in young children, for whom chloramphenicol is an alternative treatment.

Other spotted fevers

Elsewhere in the world, there are several varieties of tick-borne spotted fevers caused by rickettsial bacteria. The kind of tick may differ from country to country but, broadly speaking, the symptoms, diagnosis and treatment are the same. RMSF remains the most dangerous, followed by **Mediterranean spotted fever** and **Siberian tick typhus**. Like RMSF, most of the fevers are seasonal, occurring in the summer when the ticks are most active. The names of the fevers generally hold clues to the parts of the world where they are prevalent. They are:

✚ Mediterranean spotted fever
✚ Kenyan tick typhus
✚ African tick bite fever
✚ Israeli spotted fever
✚ Astrakhan fever (Caspian Sea)
✚ Siberian tick typhus
✚ Indian tick typhus
✚ Japanese spotted fever
✚ Queensland tick typhus
✚ Flinders Island spotted fever (Australia)

Rodent-borne hantavirus infection

Rodent-borne hantavirus infection describes a group of viruses found throughout the world which are spread to humans via rodents, so causing viral haemorrhagic fevers (see p.225). Usually transmitted by inhaling dried **rat excreta**, typically after brushing floors or beating carpets, the infection is rare, particularly among travellers, but to be safe avoid contact with rodents and their droppings. Person-to-person spread is unknown. There is no preventative immunization.

Hantavirus infections are rare but serious. Characteristically, the infection starts with **symptoms** of high fever, rigors and muscle pains. As with all haemorrhagic fevers, the infection affects the blood, leading to an increased bleeding tendency; spontaneous bleeding from the nose, gums, rectum etc is possible. A rare but recognized complication of hantavirus infection is shock, which can lead to kidney failure ("**haemorrhagic fever with renal syndrome**", or **HFRS**). Without treatment, this can be fatal. In the Americas, hantavirus infection may cause a build-up of fluid on the lungs, known as **hantavirus pulmonary syndrome** (**HPS**). Occurring within the first ten days of the illness, HPS is a serious complication that also demands prompt medical attention.

Blood tests can identify antibodies to the virus. While there's no specific **treatment**, intensive medical care improves the chances of survival.

Ross River virus

(Epidemic Polyarthritis)

Taking its name from the river in northern Queensland where it was first identified, **Ross River virus** is endemic throughout Australia; isolated outbreaks also occur in the islands of the South Pacific. It's spread by a variety of different types of **mosquito**, and outbreaks tend to occur after flooding or during the rainy season, when mosquitoes are most active. Direct person-to-person spread does not occur.

The disease can infect domestic and wild animals, and the Australian kangaroo and wallaby populations are believed to be the natural reservoir for the infection (it is thought that this is the reason that Ross River virus has never been exported to any great extent).

There is no **vaccination** against the disease so the only means of protection in an affected area is to avoid mosquito bites whenever possible (see p.149). The risk to travellers is generally low unless you visit an area where there is an active epidemic.

Symptoms, diagnosis and treatment

Ross River virus causes a remarkably similar illness to dengue fever (see p.113). After an incubation period of between 2 and 21 days, **symptoms** emerge as a flu-like illness with fever, chills, muscle pains, headache, lethargy and occasionally a rash. Painful, stiff and sometimes swollen joints, which are usually worse in the morning, may occur. The symptoms tend to be less severe in children. Although the acute illness resolves fairly quickly, joint pains, tiredness and, occasionally, depression can continue for several months.

Blood tests show antibodies to the virus in the blood. No specific treatment is available, but rest and pain relief such as **paracetamol** and ibuprofen relieve the symptoms.

Saltwater hazards

There are plenty of fish in the sea, but **drowning** is the ocean's greatest risk to your health. The majority of potentially hazardous maritime creatures, from the majestic shark to the lowly, and seemingly innocuous, shellfish, are found in tropical or subtropical seas, and usually only attack if provoked.

▶▶ See Staying well (Fire and water), p.25; Freshwater hazards, p.130.

Fish and marine invertebrates

The majority of injuries caused by **fish** are from accidentally treading on one with venomous spines or by handling those caught during fishing. Though widely feared, sharks are generally shy creatures and tend to stay well away from humans, making **shark attacks** very rare – there are between fifty and a hundred attacks each year worldwide (although the trend is on the increase), resulting in an average of eight to ten fatalities. Sharks have very poor vision and hunt by smell and vibration, mainly feeding between dusk and dawn. When they do strike, it's usually due to territorialism or in response to some kind of commotion (which they interpret as a fish in trouble). They are attracted to blood, bodily waste or refuse thrown overboard from ships. Most attack humans only if they are hungry (although great whites tend to be less ruled by hunger and attack anything fairly indiscriminately). If you find yourself swimming in the presence of sharks, those that keep their distance are nothing more than curious; those that circle inwards or make sudden, erratic movements are more likely to attack. Don't hang around for the sake of curiosity; swim to safety without delay.

❝All in a day's dive❞

I was only minutes into the first dive of the day at Bougainville Reef when I looked down into the blue and saw the shark. In itself this wasn't too unusual; it's a rare thing not to see sharks while diving on the outer edge of the Great Barrier Reef. Despite their reputation, however, most reef species are timid and either keep a respectful distance or simply bolt away from you on sight. After all, a diver wearing fins is bigger than the average shark, and is more likely to be seen as a threat than a food source. True, some sharks are territorial and resent divers intruding on their patch. Rather than attacking immediately and risk getting injured, however, they try to warn you away with a formalized display of aggression, arching their backs, swinging their heads from side to side, and pushing their pectoral fins down. Back off and so do they. It's only when divers fail to recognize this behaviour and hang around that they get bitten.

But then there are a few types of shark that are plain pugnacious. As was this one, a two-metre-long silvertip, which was tearing up the reef wall towards me like a torpedo, mouth open, teeth out. I had just enough time to back up against the coral and think "Bloody hell, here we go" before the shark shot up in front of me, missed, banked tightly around and came in again. Not being armed with anything sharp, all I could do was grab my reserve air source and fire a cloud of bubbles into its face. Amazingly enough this mild defence worked instantly, and the silvertip sheered away, dropped into deep water, and was gone.

Such events are, thankfully, rare, and in nine years of scuba diving this is the only instance in which a shark has shown me anything more than superficial interest. I wasn't fated to get back to the dive boat unscathed, however. Towards the end of the dive I was watching a group of orange-and-white-striped anemone fish, which grow to about twelve centimetres in length and live in amongst the stinging tentacles of large sea anemones. A mucus coating prevents them from being stung, but their presence lures other fish over to the anemone to be killed and eaten by it, while they get the scraps. Curiously, anemone fish also change sex, from male to female, as they mature.

As their protector and provider, these fish are extremely proactive in defending their anemones. Unlike sharks, they don't worry about picking fights with larger animals either, and will fearlessly attack divers who approach too close. Again, often this is no more than a bluff, the fish just warning you away by swimming at you with a stilted, jerky motion. On this occasion, however, one struck without ceremony, hitting me first on the chest and then, with unerring accuracy, biting me hard on the neck just above my wetsuit. Surfacing, I found that it had taken out a chunk of skin about a centimetre across and half as deep, leaving me sore and bloody – and the victim of shark attack jokes once I was back on board the boat.

David Leffman, Queensland, Australia

The bite of the **barracuda** and **moray eels** can also be severe, although the danger is usually restricted to divers exploring reefs. If a fish bites you, be sure to clean the wound thoroughly to prevent infection and check your tetanus immunization is up to date. The **lesser weever fish** is particularly common in temperate climates, from the North Sea to the Mediterranean and Black Sea.

▲ Purple jellyfish, California

The fish lies buried off sandy beaches with its spiny dorsal fin pointing upwards; its sting can be very painful but poses no other threat.

In tropical waters, the sting from the venomous spines of a **stingray** can inflict serious injury, although it's almost always accidental through stepping on the tail in shallow water (stingrays are not aggressive). The tail can cause deep lacerations, while envenomation from the spines may cause local swelling around the wound. Rarely, more generalized symptoms can follow, such as sweating, excessive salivation, nausea and vomiting, cramps, convulsions and abnormal heart rhythms, which will need urgent medical attention.

The sting from the spines of a **stonefish** can be agonizing (the pain is unresponsive to morphine). Well camouflaged as a stone on the seabed, the stonefish can be found around reefs and estuaries in Indo-Pacific waters. The potent venom may cause fits, paralysis and even death. There is a specific antivenin for stonefish stings, but it may not always be immediately available. Other fish with fins or spines which can inflict harm (but are unlikely to be fatal) include **rabbitfish** (spinefoot), **surgeonfish** (tang), **toadfish** and **scorpionfish** (zebrafish), as well as invertebrates such as **sea urchins** and the **crown of thorns starfish**.

The **blue-ringed octopus**, found in shallow waters around Australia, has a generally painless though venomous sting that can cause respiratory arrest. The gastropod inside a **cone shell**, found in tropical and subtropical waters, has a venomous barb that can also paralyse breathing. In both cases, there is no specific antivenin and if stung you may need to be ventilated in hospital until the venom wears off.

Certain species of **trigger fish**, **puffer fish** and **porcupine fish** are extremely toxic if eaten and should be avoided.

❝ Urchins in Tahiti ❞

I was so focused on getting great shots of my friend kayaking in the clear waters off Moorea, that I unwittingly stepped on a sea urchin. The sharp pain nearly launched me head first into the water. My camera wasn't waterproof, and I struggled to stay upright and protect it. As I tried to keep my balance, I took another step and kicked my heel on the long black spines of yet another urchin. Surprisingly, I kept the camera above the sea. But I didn't know a remedy for a sea urchin sting – or how painful it was.

My friend and I were in a remote spot, which was great for photos, but not emergencies. No resorts or homes were in view. There was one family fishing on the nearby reef, but they spoke only French; we didn't. I pointed to my foot and tried to communicate what was wrong. The mother looked somewhat embarrassed and ambled away. I didn't understand why.

The pain slowly ebbed, so I figured I'd be OK. I waited until the soreness was bearable, then retrieved my beached kayak and paddled back to our resort. Reading my guidebook some hours later, I realized my faux pas: the locals' remedy for sea urchin stings is to urinate on the injured spot.

Deb Behr, Santa Monica, California

(See the box on p.192 for jellyfish stings)
+ Where possible, seek medical help urgently.
+ Remove any obvious foreign material from the wound.
+ Wash the wound with fresh water.
+ Apply pressure and immobilize the area of the sting.
+ If the sting results in respiratory difficulties, start mouth-to-mouth resuscitation.
+ Many stings can be very painful so use strong pain relief if available.
+ Immersing the sting site in hot water (45°C/113°F) for thirty to ninety minutes is a good pain reliever for most types of marine sting, as it inactivates the poison.
+ All cuts, bites or stings originating from the sea have a high risk of secondary infection, so the use of prophylactic antibiotics (eg flucloxacillin, co-amoxiclav) should be considered.

Sea snakes

Sea snakes are found in tropical and subtropical waters (none are found in the Atlantic, the Mediterranean or the Red Sea), although being air breathers they are usually found in shallow waters and quite commonly on some tropical beaches. Their venom is highly **toxic** (far more so than terrestrial snakes: up to twenty times more potent than cobra venom), but they only attack when provoked. Don't be alarmed if a sea snake comes up close when you are diving – they have a reputation for being curious and it is not a sign of aggression. Avoid provocation and swim upwards away from the bottom, where they are less likely to follow. Since their teeth sit at the back of their small mouths, they're only capable of inflicting a bite on particular parts of the human body – ears, webs of fingers and toes, behind the ankle).

Although most sea snake bites are "dry" (do not result in envenomation), if you are unlucky enough to be bitten, seek medical help urgently. The first-aid **treatment** is the same as for a land-snake bite (see p.206).

Jellyfish

Jellyfish stings are caused by the stinging cells, or nematocysts, on the tentacles which discharge on contact (they're actually triggered by movement). Even dead on the beach, many jellyfish can inflict a sting provided that the tentacles are still moist. Despite their reputation, the majority of jellyfish species are harmless to humans. The main dangerous ones are described below.

Box jellyfish ("sea wasps" or "stingers") are generally acknowledged as the greatest maritime hazard. They're found in the warm waters of the Indian and Pacific oceans, but the majority of reported deaths have occurred off north Australian shores in the summer months (September to April). Their sting is very painful and their venom is more potent than that of a cobra. Severe envenomations can cause rapid death (within five minutes).

The sting from a **Portuguese man of war** (or "bluebottle"), which populates mainly subtropical waters but is also found in the Atlantic Gulf Stream, is very painful and can cause other symptoms such as numbness, weakness, muscle pains, nausea and breathing difficulties (occasionally fatal). Shore invasions tend to occur after storms.

The **Irukandji jellyfish** is found predominantly off the coast of northern

> ## First aid for jellyfish stings
>
> Remove yourself from the water to prevent further contact with the tentacles. Resist rubbing the sting, as this will cause more venom to be discharged and the tentacles may embed in your hands.
>
> If you think that you have been stung by a **box jellyfish**, call for help and stay calm and still. If it's available, **vinegar** applied liberally as quickly as possible will inactivate the nematocysts and prevent the discharge of further venom. **Cold compresses** can be used to relieve pain, and, for serious stings, pressure applied to the area of the sting reduces the spread of venom. If a limb is the most affected site, immobilize it after deactivating the stinging cells with vinegar. An antivenin exists but needs to be given quickly. Many beaches in northern Australia will have local supplies. Cardiopulmonary resuscitation may be necessary.
>
> For **Portuguese man of war**, **Irukandji** and other less dangerous jellyfish, soak the area of the sting in vinegar or, if unavailable, salt water (fresh water may cause further discharge of venom). It may be possible to carefully remove the tentacles using forceps, or a knife (even the edge of a credit card). Reapply more vinegar or seawater. Use antihistamines, painkillers and cold compresses to relieve the swelling and pain. If you think you may have been stung by an Irukandji, seek medical help as the elevated blood pressure will need to be monitored and will respond well to treatment.

Australia, although there have been sightings in other parts of the Pacific. It usually inhabits deeper waters and thus reef snorkellers and divers are most at risk. The initial sting is only slightly painful but within thirty minutes severe back, limb and abdominal pains occur with nausea, vomiting, sweating and agitation. Dangerously high blood pressure and a racing pulse can also occur.

Coral

Like most wounds sustained in the sea, **coral** cuts can easily become infected, often because small particles of coral are left in the wound. **Cleanse** any wounds thoroughly, and if infection is suspected, treat with **antibiotics** such as flucloxacillin, erythromycin or co-amoxiclav. Remember that you're far more likely to cause permanent damage to coral than it is to you.

Sandfly fever

(Dog disease, Phlebotomus fever, Pym's fever)

Sandfly fever occurs across dry areas of the Balkans, throughout the Mediterranean littoral, the Middle East, Central and Southeast Asia, and Central America. It is a viral illness spread by sand flies, which tend to bite at night and are also responsible for the transmission of leishmaniasis (see p.156).

There is no preventative vaccine so observe the usual precautions against insect bites (see p.149). As sand flies are low-altitude fliers, sleeping above ground-floor level is safest.

Symptoms, diagnosis and treatment

Sandfly fever is very similar to dengue (see p.113): after an incubation period of between three and eight days, there is an abrupt onset of fever, rigors,

headache (usually behind the eyes) and muscle and joint pains. Although
symptoms can be quite intense and are usually followed by a period of weakness and lethargy, complete recovery is the norm.

Diagnosis is usually made on the basis of symptom assessment alone
although blood tests may pick up evidence of the viral infection. Bed rest, basic
pain relief and measures to reduce the high fever are all helpful, but there's no
specific **treatment** to shorten the course of the illness.

Scabies

Exclusively a human infection, **scabies** is caused by infestation of the skin by
a **mite**. Although **skin-to-skin contact** is the commonest form of transmission, the infestation can also spread via inanimate objects such as clothing and
bed linen. The pregnant female mite penetrates the skin and burrows for a few
millimetres; it can burrow anywhere in the body but tends to seek out natural
recesses such as between the fingers, armpits, the groin or in skin creases. Eggs
are deposited in the burrow and hatch into larvae after two or three days, when
they move out of the burrow and onto the surface of the skin. After a week or
two of maturation and mating they begin the cycle again.

Symptoms

Chemicals secreted by the burrowed mite cause an **allergic skin reaction**.
This manifests as a more generalized red, maddeningly itchy **rash**, which is
typically worse at night and in heat. Consequent scratching further damages
the skin, and can in turn cause secondary infection and more itching. It's not
uncommon for the itch to continue for a few weeks even after treatment.

Diagnosis and treatment

The burrows are difficult to see with the naked eye and may go unnoticed for
several weeks; it's sometimes possible to see them with a magnifying glass as
small, irregular, tortuous, raised lesions (the webs between fingers are a
favourite haunt). A generalized, raised and itchy eczema-type rash often breaks
out on the trunk, and scabies should be considered as the possible cause for any
severely itchy rash.

There are several different types of **treatment**, most of which are available
without prescription. The most common are malathion or permethrin lotions,
the latter perhaps being the more effective. If you are pregnant or breast-feeding,

A–Z

Scabies

it's best to discuss the most appropriate treatment with a doctor. Neither preparation is recommended for children under six months. The lotion should be applied to the entire body (especially finger- and toe-webs, and under nails) and left for twelve hours in the case of permethrin, and 24 hours for malathion. Reapply the lotion after hand-washing and going to the toilet. A second treatment is advised after a week. Any close contacts and household members should be treated simultaneously. Antihistamines and calamine lotion can be used to treat the persistent itch.

Schistosomiasis

(Bilharzia)

Don't underestimate **schistosomiasis** – it's the second most prevalent tropical disease after malaria, and poses a serious risk to travellers. The WHO currently estimates that more than 200 million people in 74 countries are infected (85 percent of whom are in sub-Saharan Africa), and the disease is spreading. London's Hospital for Tropical Diseases sees an average of 200 cases a year in returning travellers, an underestimate of the true figure as many more will be unaware that they have contracted the infection and therefore will not have sought help.

The infection is caused by various species of **worms**, or **flukes**, of the *Schistosoma* family: *S. haematobium*, which is geographically distributed throughout Africa, the Arabian Peninsular, the Near East, Madagascar and Mauritius, and mainly affects the urinary tract; *S. mansoni*, which is chiefly found in Africa and Mauritius but was transported by the slave trade to parts of South America, the Caribbean and Arabia, and mainly affects the gut and the liver; and *S. japonicum*, which is found in China, the Philippines (Mindanao in particular), Sulawesi and on the eastern Thai border, and which mainly affects the gut. (In Asia, *S. japonicum* is known as **Katayama fever** after an area of Japan where it once proliferated). *S. mekongi* and *S. intercalatum* are found in localized areas of Southeast Asia (Laos and Cambodia) and central West African rainforests respectively. Both cause intestinal symptoms.

The worms reproduce in the bodies of water snails, and minute, fork-tailed larvae known as **cercariae** are released into the water. On **contact** with human skin, the cercariae penetrate and enter the blood stream. Schistosomiasis can also be contracted by drinking **untreated water** or eating food washed in it.

Once in the human body the cercariae mature into adult flukes in the liver. After mating, the worms migrate via the blood vessels to other parts of the body where the eggs are shed. The eggs pass through the walls of the bladder or intestine and are returned to the outside in faeces or urine – thus the cycle continues.

No **vaccinations** are currently available, although research is moving forward and there are ongoing clinical trials in Africa. For the time being, prevention and control of the disease spread are mainly dependent on public health measures such as **education** and **water purification** in endemic countries. Generally speaking, schistosomiasis only poses a risk to travellers who bathe or indulge in water sports in rivers or lakes or those who do not observe the normal eating and drinking rules in endemic areas. No matter the temptation, avoid swimming in fresh water where schistosomiasis is found, and bear in mind that the water you bathe or shower in may also be contaminated.

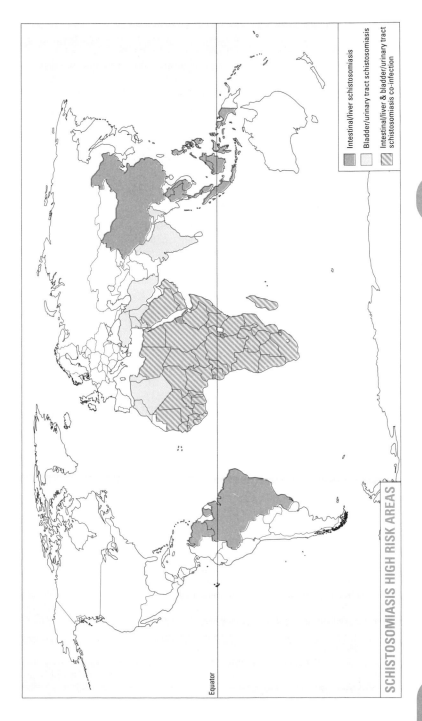

Intestinal/liver schistosomiasis

Bladder/urinary tract schistosomiasis

Intestinal/liver & bladder/urinary tract schistosomiasis co-infection

SCHISTOSOMIASIS HIGH RISK AREAS

Equator

Rafting down African rivers obviously presents the threat of infection, although fast-flowing water is generally considered safer than still. Swimming in the sea in chlorinated swimming pools is considered safe. If you think you've been exposed, promptly remove your wet clothing and vigorously **rub your skin with a towel**, which although unreliable, may remove the cercariae before they have a chance to penetrate the skin.

Symptoms

The majority of people infected with schistosomiasis will not experience any symptoms. Initial invasion of the cercariae into the skin may cause an itchy rash, known as "**swimmer's itch**". This usually happens within the first 48 hours and may continue for up to a week. The first **symptoms** of the illness usually occur during the egg-laying phase, between one and ten weeks after infection, and are nonspecific. Fever, swollen lymph glands, muscle aching, itching, diarrhoea, coughing and wheezing, weight loss and enlargement of the liver and spleen are common. Later on, invasion of the eggs into the bladder and urinary tract causes bleeding and sometimes pain, which is why historically schistosomiasis has been called the disease of "menstruating males". If the gut is involved, abdominal pain and diarrhoea (sometimes bloody) are also common.

Most of the long-term damage to the body is caused by the reaction to **retained eggs**. Initial inflammation is replaced by permanent scarring. In particular, the ureters (the tubes carrying urine from the kidneys to the bladder) can become obstructed, leading to kidney damage and failure in the final, untreated stages of the disease. Damage to the heart, lungs, gut and central nervous system can result from the eggs escaping into the general circulation and becoming lodged in different organs.

Diagnosis and treatment

The presence of blood in the urine in endemic areas points to the likely diagnosis, after which lab examination of the **urine**, **faeces** or **blood** usually detects the presence of eggs. **Ultrasound** of the liver and tissue **biopsies** can also be definitive.

Even in the advanced stages of the disease, **treatment** can be very effective, but only if there is evidence of living worm activity and only under medical supervision. A short course of **praziquantel** is usually all that is necessary. The damage from scarring caused by the worms and by reaction to the eggs may be less easy to rectify.

Scombroid poisoning

Scombroid poisoning occurs worldwide and is the commonest type of seafood poisoning. Certain **fish** with dark or red meat – such as mackerel, tuna, bonito, albacore and skipjack – contain large amounts of a chemical called histidine. As the fish spoils, bacteria change this chemical into histamine, which is unaffected by cooking and so is responsible for the symptoms of scombroid poisoning after the fish have been eaten. Contaminated fish are said to have a metallic, peppery flavour.

The **risk** of scombroid poisoning is higher in hot countries with poor refrigeration facilities where fish will spoil quickly. To be safe, stick to fish that is freshly caught or to white fish.

Symptoms usually arise within three hours of eating the fish, and mimic an allergic reaction. Common features are flushing, burning or tingling sensation in the mouth, abdominal pain, nausea and vomiting, headache, thirst, difficulty in swallowing, wheezing, hives and itching.

There is no specific test for scombroid poisoning, and the **diagnosis** is usually made by connecting the symptoms with the ingestion of suspicious fish. **Antihistamine drugs** (eg chlorpheniramine and loratadine) will generally relieve symptoms, although severe reactions may require hospital admission. The symptoms are self-limiting and rarely last longer than three or four hours.

Severe Acute Respiratory Syndrome (SARS)

In late 2002, an outbreak of the virulent chest infection now known as **SARS** (**Severe Acute Respiratory Syndrome**) caused widespread panic, with just over 8000 people becoming infected over a two or three month period; nearly 800 died as a result. The disease was thought to have originated in Guangdong Province in China, and was spread by infected travellers, resulting in disease clusters as far away as Canada. Global paranoia quickly set in, with face masks becoming *de rigueur* for travellers into and out of infected areas. Thanks to prompt and effective public health measures, the original outbreak was contained, although it seems only a matter of time before it reappears – in December 2003, a confirmed case was reported in south China.

SARS is caused by a mutated coronavirus, genetically similar to a virus found in civet cats. The disease is thought to be spread from person to person through **droplets** from coughs or sneezes; hence you're at high risk of contracting the disease if you're in close contact with an infected person.

As yet there is no **vaccination** against SARS, so the best defence is to avoid any unnecessary travel to a part of the world where there is a current outbreak. There's no evidence that simple face masks offer protection.

Symptoms, diagnosis and treatment

Symptoms develop after a period of between two and sixteen days following initial infection. High fever, chills, sore throat, muscle pains, headache, rash and diarrhoea are followed by a cough and breathing difficulties. Pneumonia can lead to respiratory failure and death.

Laboratory testing for the virus is under development, and **diagnosis** is generally made by clinical assessment in the knowledge of possible exposure to the virus. There is no specific **treatment**, but suspected cases need to be admitted to hospital urgently and require barrier nursing. Mechanical ventilation is sometimes necessary for severe cases.

Sexually transmitted diseases

Sexually transmitted diseases, or **STDs**, can have significant effects not only on your immediate health, but also on the future health and fertility of both you and your sexual partner. STDs are also a lot more common than most people think, especially in developing countries and countries with a sex tourism industry – the highest global prevalences for syphilis, gonorrhoea and chlamydia occur in south and Southeast Asia and sub-Saharan Africa. The WHO estimates that there are approximately 340 million new cases of STDs (excluding HIV/AIDS) worldwide each year, principally affecting the 15–30 age group.

The most obvious way to protect yourself from STDs while you're away is to abstain from sex with new partners. Your risk of contracting something increases with the number of partners you sleep with – but remember it takes only one infected partner for you to contract an STD. Always keep in mind that your partner may have been less choosy than yourself in previous sexual encounters, and may not be entirely honest about their previous history and precautions used. Using a **condom** will dramatically reduce the risks of contracting STDs, so carry them no matter what your prior intentions. Use quality condoms brought from home – local brands may be less reliable.

Many people who contract an STD have no **symptoms**. However, when they occur, they can include:

✚ Unusual vaginal or penile discharge
✚ Pain, increased frequency or difficulty in passing urine
✚ Genital pain, itching or irritation
✚ Genital ulceration
✚ Abnormal vaginal bleeding
✚ Testicular pain
✚ Lower abdominal pain
✚ Pain during sex (dysparaenia)

If you suspect you have an STD, don't attempt to treat yourself – **see a doctor**. It's common for more than one STD to be passed on at the same time (particularly gonorrhoea in tandem with chlamydia) so there may be more than one cause for a single infective episode. A full medical work-up including swabs and blood results is therefore necessary. Remember that any STD that causes genital ulceration increases the risk of transmission of HIV.

All STDs, with the exceptions of herpes, HIV, genital warts and hepatitis B, can be treated effectively with antibiotics. Always avoid sex until the treatment is complete. Untreated STDs are likely to be passed on and can cause longer-term effects, such as neurological impairment or cardiovascular problems in the case of syphilis, and infertility in the case of chlamydia and gonorrhoea. Syphilis, gonorrhoea, herpes and chlamydia can all affect the developing foetus or newborn baby.

Syphilis

Syphilis prevalence has increased globally over recent years, especially in inner cities where it is associated with sex workers and drug use. The WHO estimates there were just under twelve million new cases of syphilis worldwide in 1999. The incidence is particularly high in Africa and Southeast Asia.

Symptoms, diagnosis and treatment

Syphilis has three separate disease stages. Between two and four weeks after infection, a hard but painless swelling called a chancre develops on or just inside the genitals, or less commonly around the hands, the anus or the mouth; it usually heals after a few weeks. This is known as **primary syphilis**. Two or three months after the chancre has healed, **secondary syphilis** involves a fever, sore throat and joint pains. Lymph glands tend to enlarge and a non-itchy rash appears on the body and on the palms of the hands, the soles of the feet and around the mouth and nose. Wart-like lesions can appear around the perineum and ulceration occurs on the genitalia and in the mouth. This stage settles without treatment after several months, although don't be fooled into thinking that the infection has disappeared; anyone with untreated syphilis can stay infectious for years. Late, or **tertiary syphilis**, appears years later as an inevitable result of the untreated initial infection and generally involves the skin and the bones. Swellings or ulcers can appear anywhere on the skin, and are also found in bones and some internal organs. The neurological and cardiovascular systems can be affected, causing potentially serious complications.

The **diagnosis** of syphilis is usually made by **blood tests**. All stages of the illness are amenable to **treatment** with penicillin (or erythromycin) following various regimens.

Gonorrhoea

Gonorrhoea is present throughout the world but, like syphilis, is particularly rife in south and Southeast Asia and sub-Saharan Africa. That said, it's far commoner than syphilis, with an estimated excess of 62 million new cases worldwide in 1999. Concomitant infection with chlamydia is common.

Symptoms, diagnosis and treatment

A small percentage of men, but up to eighty percent of women, show **no symptoms** and are therefore unaware of their need for treatment or of the likelihood that they can pass the disease on to others. **Men** usually notice a pustular discharge from the penis within five days of sexual contact with an infected partner. The tip of the penis may be sore, and passing urine may be painful; urinary frequency is likely to increase. Scrotal pain can occur. **Women** may notice vaginal itching or discomfort, a pustular vaginal discharge, increased urinary frequency and, occasionally, discomfort around the anus. The commonest complication in females is pelvic inflammatory disease (PID; see p.69). In both sexes, gonorrhoea can affect the rest of the body causing fever, malaise, muscle and joint pains, and a rash. Septicaemia, meningitis and hepatitis are rare **complications**.

The **diagnosis** of gonorrhoea is confirmed by lab analysis of the pustular discharge. There are several options in terms of **treatment**, but the penicillin group of antibiotics are now being superseded by the quinolones (eg ciprofloxacin), because of growing resistance.

Chlamydia

Chlamydia is globally very common and is believed to be the biggest single cause of **infertility** in the developed world. It's more common than gonorrhoea, with the WHO estimating that nearly 92 million new cases occurred worldwide in 1999 alone. There is a particularly high incidence in Africa, Southeast Asia and India.

Symptoms, diagnosis and treatment

As with gonorrhoea, many people who are infected with chlamydia show no **symptoms** and are therefore unaware that they risk transmitting it to others. If symptoms appear, they usually do so between two and four weeks after infection. Painless ulceration is apparent on the genitalia in about a quarter of those affected. A yellow-green vaginal discharge, pain on passing urine, and greater frequency of urination are common in **women**. **Men** can also experience pain on passing urine as well as a whitish discharge from the penis, and scrotal pain.

Lymphogranuloma venereum (**LGV**) is a particularly unpleasant variant of chlamydia infection, common in Africa, Southeast Asia and India. Initial painless ulceration is followed by pain and swelling of the lymph glands in the groin, which may develop into pus-filled abscesses. Although LGV is treatable using the same antibiotics as for other chlamydia infections, a chronic form of infection can develop causing extensive local scarring which may require surgery.

Like gonorrhoea, chlamydia can cause pelvic inflammatory disease (PID; see p.69) in women.

Diagnosis is usually made from swabbing the ulcers or discharge, although blood tests may also be useful. The standard **treatment** for genital chlamydial infections is a one- to three-week week course of doxycycline or erythromycin. Sexual partners should also be treated, whether or not they have symptoms.

Trichomoniasis

Trichomoniasis is easily the commonest STD worldwide, with over 173 million new cases in 1999. The microbe responsible can lie dormant for many years without causing symptoms. It has been implicated in facilitating the spread of HIV infection.

Symptoms, diagnosis and treatment

Trichomoniasis causes **symptoms** in approximately half of all infected **women**, mainly consisting of vaginal itching and burning, a frothy, greenish-yellow, often offensive-smelling discharge, and burning pain on passing urine. In **men** the infection usually goes unnoticed, but if symptoms do occur they consist of penile itch or irritation, and pain when having sex or passing urine.

Lab analysis and cultures of swabs usually confirm the **diagnosis**. Trichomoniasis usually responds well to **metronidazole** (400mg twice daily for a week) although resistance has been reported.

Chancroid

Worldwide prevalence of **chancroid** is less easy to estimate than other STDs because the disease is generally not so well understood. It is rare in developed countries but common elsewhere, particularly sub-Saharan Africa.

Symptoms, diagnosis and treatment

Chancroid causes painful genital ulceration, usually within a week of infection. Localized painful swelling of the lymph glands also occurs. The **symptoms** are often less noticeable in women and mainly consist of pain during sex, on passing urine or defecation, as well as rectal bleeding and vaginal discharge.

Diagnosis is usually made by culturing swabs taken from the ulcers or material drawn from the swollen lymph glands. Chancroid is best **treated** using erythromycin, 500mg four times a day for seven days, although a single 500mg dose of ciprofloxacin can also be used.

Genital herpes

Genital herpes is extremely common and is usually caused by the herpes simplex **virus 2**. The herpes simplex **virus 1** causes cold sores but can affect the genitalia as well, especially after oral sex. Both are spread by direct skin-to-skin contact.

There is no cure for herpes and, once you're infected, you carry the virus for life. The symptoms of the disease are only apparent at initial infection and during flare-ups – you are **infectious** for a few days before blistering appears, during the blistering phase and for up to two weeks afterwards.

Symptoms, diagnosis and treatment

Initial infection usually causes a flu-like illness accompanied by genital or perineal **blistering** which, after a few days, breaks down leaving a crop of **painful ulcers**. These usually last between five days and three weeks. Subsequent attacks occur infrequently, usually at times of stress, fatigue or during ill health. Recurring symptoms are usually milder (with less systemic upset) than the initial episode.

Since herpes is one of the few STDs that causes painful ulcers, it's usually easily **diagnosed**, although swabs and blood tests can also confirm the diagnosis. Although there is no cure for herpes, antiviral drugs such as **aciclovir** can limit the length of each symptomatic episode.

Genital warts

Like herpes, **genital warts** are very common across the world, and they appear to be on the increase. Infection is caused by the human papilloma virus (HPV).

The most apparent sign of HPV infection is the presence of genital warts, although the majority of infections are **asymptomatic**. Some strains of the virus lead to increased risk of cervical and other genital cancers later in life.

Diagnosis is usually fairly obvious from the appearance of the warts. **Treatment** should only be undertaken under medical supervision and usually involves freezing the warts, or a topical application of podophyllin paint.

▶▶ For detailed coverage of HIV infection, see p.144; for full coverage of Hep B, see p.141; see also Hep A, p.141, Hep C, p.143 and Hep D and E, p.144; Lice infestation, p.161; and Scabies, p.193.

Skin problems

During travel your **skin** will be subjected to all manner of attack from the tropical sun, marauding insects, chafing backpacks, itching infestations and

---

Homeopathic remedies for skin complaints

The homeopathic remedy **Belladonna** can help treat small skin wounds that form large hot, red areas around them. It can also help subdue lymphangitis (see p.202). Take a 30c potency every four hours but seek medical advice if there are no early signs of improvement. **Silica** (same potency and dosage) can be helpful in removing foreign bodies – deep splinters, sea urchin spines, shards of glass etc. Again use a 30c potency, four-hourly. **Calendula** cream is also beneficial – see p.48.

weird infections. Your skin is your body's first line of defence to all of these potential hazards, but it is delicate and easily breached. Bacterial, fungal or viral skin infections are common, especially in hot countries. Manifestations of more generalized illnesses – jaundice, an increased bleeding tendency and the like – are also commonly reflected in the skin.

Bacterial infections

Bacterial infections often follow minor trauma to the skin – any **wound**, even the most trivial, can become infected, and there is particularly high risk of this in hot, tropical countries. Dirty, penetrating wounds, animal bites and coral cuts are highly susceptible to secondary infection by bacteria. Any cut must be cleaned using an appropriate antiseptic but if one is not available, boiled, preferably saline, water or alcohol are alternatives. If the wound is obviously dirty, a penetrating injury or an animal bite, it may be sensible to start a prophylactic course of **antibiotics**. Flucloxacillin, erythromycin or co-amoxiclav would all be appropriate choices. Always ensure that your **tetanus immunization** is up to date. If you are concerned that a wound has become infected (see box below), and especially if there are signs of the infection spreading (such as lymphangitis, lymph-gland swelling or fever), seek medical advice.

Impetigo (or "school sores") is a bacterial infection particularly common in children and highly contagious. Mainly affecting the face (around the mouth and nose), it erupts into well-defined sores which become honey-coloured, crusty scabs. The scabs can be unsightly but are usually painless. Scratching the sores can cause spread to other areas. Impetigo can be **treated** with antibiotics, either orally (usually flucloxacillin) or cream (fusidic acid). The sores usually take a week or two to clear up, but beware of both recurrences and spread to other people. Cut your fingernails (long nails are a haven for bugs), bath or shower daily and do not share towels, eating utensils and the like.

Folliculitis occurs when hair follicles become infected, and can be a common problem in hot climates and for diabetics. It takes the form of a red, tender swelling (usually single, but occasionally in localized clusters). Often there is a central head of pus at the base of the hair stem. Folliculitis can occur anywhere on the body but is particularly common in the armpits and the groin. The infection is usually localized but can spread, resulting in tender, swollen local lymph glands. It is often self-resolving but can be **treated** with magnesium sulphate paste (which works on the poultice principle, by drawing out the pus) or a course of flucloxacillin (or erythromycin in those with penicillin allergy).

Signs that a wound is infected

+ Local redness
+ Heat
+ Swelling
+ Pain
+ Pus (thick white/yellow)
+ Lymphangitis
+ Local lymph-gland swelling
+ Fever

An important sign to look out for in any bacterial infection involving a limb is **lymphangitis**, a single red trail up from the site of infection towards the trunk. This indicates that the infection is spreading up the lymph vessels and needs antibiotic treatment. Failure to adequately treat a spreading infection can result in blood poisoning (septicaemia), which can be life-threatening.

Fungal infections

Fungal skin infections are very common, especially in hot, humid climates or if you wear tight-fitting, synthetic clothing. Generally, fungal infections can be distinguished from bacterial because they tend to itch rather than cause pain, rarely cause swelling of the skin and tend to affect particular areas of the body. Athlete's foot, ringworm, thrush (see p.213 for vaginal thrush) and localized infections in the groin (eg "jock rot" or "jock itch") and in fat folds (intertrigo) are all common examples of fungal infections. Usually worse in hot climates, the rash is raised, red, itchy and sometimes forms rings in the groin.

Caused by a variety of different fungi, **athlete's foot** can lead to intense itching between the toes. The skin becomes dry, scaly and cracked, and there are often fluid-filled vesicles in between the toes. The symptoms are made worse by wearing shoes that causes the feet to overheat (eg trainers/sneakers).

"A spot of bother"

*W*hen the fourth fragile lady in a row hoisted her fruit-laden baskets onto her shoulders and scurried away from me, I knew it was time I got my leg checked out. I was taking an afternoon stroll down Hang Ao, or Silk Street, one of the crowded traders' alleyways that make up Hanoi's old quarter. The street was buzzing, and so was my leg.

My girlfriend and I had been trekking in northern Thailand the previous week. Like most of the three-day tours that run out of Chiang Mai, our trip included an elephant trek, and our third day was spent on the back of a four-ton pachyderm as she lumbered through the jungle. Sitting straddled across the animal's neck, bum resting on her tough hide and knees pinned behind her ears for a better grip, I had immediately noticed the thick, black bristles sprouting from her cracked skin; it was hard not too with the spiky tips of each six-inch hair digging into my shinbone. It was a novelty at first, but the longer the elephant jolted her way down towards the valley floor, the quicker the novelty wore off.

When I finally slipped gingerly down off the elephant, my leg was chaffed a tender red, and by the time our bus arrived back in Bangkok the following morning, the raw patch on my shin was stinging constantly. Twenty-four hours later, after our driver had weaved his way amongst the cyclists swarming through Hanoi's old quarter, things were progressing quite nicely – by now my lower leg was like an archipelago of swollen whiteheads in a sea of angry skin. It was this sickly sight that cleared a path before me on Silk Street, and the subsequent recoiling of the fruit sellers that saw me checking into Hanoi's French Hospital early the next morning.

Through a mixture of French (a little) and sign language (a lot) I found out from Nurse Nguyen Phu that I had folliculitis, a skin infection caused by microbacteria from the tip of my elephant's prickly hairs. Walking the streets in the days since Chiang Mai had spread the infection up my leg – a couple more days of stubborn resistance and I'd have been looking at my first case of septicaemia. A bit of iodine, some antibiotics and twenty minutes of pricking the poisonous heads with a needle and I was on my way to recovery. In the end, only our plans suffered – instead of three days in Halong Bay, I had to settle for three days in a Hanoi bed.

Keith Drew, London, England.

Ringworm is not caused by a worm but by a variety of different, although related, moulds (including those that cause athlete's foot). The infection starts with an itchy, raised, slightly scaly red patch which, over the course of a few days, expands in size to form a red ring. Ringworm can occur anywhere on the body (often the arms and trunk), and spread elsewhere is not uncommon.

All of the above fungal infections respond well to treatment with antifungal creams such as **clotrimazole**. Continue applying the cream for two weeks after the rash has disappeared, as recurrences are common and usually result from stopping treatment prematurely.

▶ ▶ See p.215 for information on alternative treatments for fungal infections.

Viral infections

Viral infections may cause widespread rashes, whereas bacterial or fungal infections tend to be more localized. There is no specific **treatment** for most viral skin infections, although calamine, hydrocortisone and oral antihistamines can reduce itching.

▶ ▶ See also Bedbugs, p.97; Heat exposure (Prickly heat), p.139; Insects p.148; Myiasis, p.175; Scabies, p.193; Tungiasis, p.220; Worms, p.226.

Sleeping sickness

▶ ▶ See African trypanosomiasis, p.88.

Snakebites

You might take some comfort from the fact that less than ten percent of the world's known 2500 snake species are venomous (simply meaning they inject poison via their fangs when they bite), and that out of these, only about five percent are dangerous to humans. Worldwide, the estimated annual death rate from **snakebites** is 50,000, with Myanmar (Burma) and Brazil heading the league table for snake attacks. About 10,000 people are bitten by poisonous snakes each year in the US, resulting in around twenty deaths. In the majority of European countries the average death rate from snakebite has been less than one a year for the past half-century.

Snakes are generally shy creatures who will, where possible, avoid human contact – bites usually occur in self-defence when the snake is disturbed. Eighty-five percent of bites are sustained below the knee and between 50 and 80 percent are "dry", meaning they do not result in **envenomation**. The effects of snake venom on the victim depend on the type of snake and degree of envenomation. It can attack the nervous system causing paralysis, inflict severe local tissue damage at the bite site, and interfere with the clotting system of the blood causing an increased bleeding tendency.

Further information

To view pictures of snakes for identification purposes, visit the following sites:
ⓦwww.usyd.edu.au/anaes/venom/snakebite.html
Australian varieties.
ⓦwww.enature.com

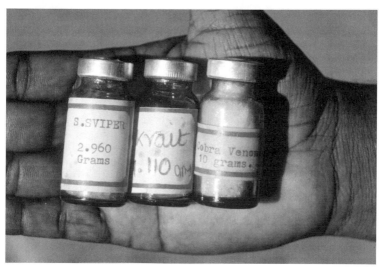

▲ Snake antivenin

Venomous snakes can be divided broadly into three **basic groups**: elapids, vipers and sea snakes.

The **elapid family** has roughly 250 members, among them cobras, mambas, kraits, coral snakes and all of the Australasian venomous snakes. Although snake venom is complex and has a range of effects on the body, as a general rule, elapid venom tends to affect the nervous system, causing muscle paralysis. Bites from some members of the elapid group do not cause any local swelling or reaction. Cobras in particular tend to "chew" in order to sufficiently envenomate the victim, so if bitten by a cobra, shake it off as quickly as possible.

The **viper family** includes the adder, pit viper, several rattlesnake species, the bushmaster and the fer-de-lance. Vipers have large venom glands, which give the head a triangular appearance and make it quite distinct from the body. Although the quality of viper venom tends to be less potent than that of the elapids, it's produced in larger quantities. It tends to affect the clotting mechanisms of the blood, and causes local tissue swelling, generally within two hours.

Although **sea snakes** are the most venomous by some way, they are also timid and rarely bite. Their backward-pointing fangs and small mouths mean that they are poorly adapted to biting large creatures such as humans. The venom, however, can cause nerve and muscle paralysis.

Symptoms and bite prevention

A snakebite can be traumatic, both physically and psychologically. The physical sensation is often initially burning in nature, before severe pain develops. The **symptoms** of envenomation depend on the type of snake but things to look out for are local swelling, increased bleeding tendency, shock caused by a drop in blood pressure, anaphylaxis (see p.91), drooping of the eyelids (an early sign of nervous-system involvement) and muscle pains.

The vast majority of snakes are not aggressive and will only bite when threatened. **Avoidance measures** are based more around common sense than hard

First aid for a snakebite

Remember that not all snakes that bite are venomous: if your bite mark shows two rows of teeth as opposed to two small punctures, a nonvenomous snake has bitten you. For venomous bites, all that **first aid for a snakebite** can hope to achieve is to retard the effects of the venom, buying time for you to get to medical help for further treatment, and reducing the risk of other complications such as infection. Although the bite from a venomous snake is not usually the type of emergency in which seconds count, don't delay in seeking medical help.

Sucking the venom out of a snakebite, cutting around a bite to prevent the spread of venom and applying ice to a bite are **not recommended** as first-aid measures, and belong more to folklore and the silver screen than to medical fact. They may perhaps help in situations where urgent medical help is unlikely to be available, but generally they are more likely to increase the risk of local tissue damage and infection. The only certain method of improving the prognosis after snakebite is to **immobilize** the victim, and the afflicted limb in particular. A cool head and a rapid, organized response are much more helpful than a chaotic panic.

If you're tending someone who's been bitten, the first thing to do is **mark the time** of the bite, as the speed of the onset of symptoms is a useful indicator of the degree of envenomation. Your second move should be to **call for help**, and then carry the victim to a place of safety. If practical and safe, try to **identify the snake** concerned. If you manage to kill it, don't pick it up immediately because the strike reflex may be preserved for a minute or two. Place the victim in the **recovery position** to reduce the risk of vomit inhalation, and wipe the wound with a clean cloth to **remove superficial venom**. Remove jewellery or tight-fitting clothing from around the bite site. If the bite is on a limb, immobilize it as far as is practicable. (Tourniquets have lost favour because they can result in an increased local concentration of the venom, which may cause more severe damage around the bite area.) Keep the victim warm and don't give them any food or drink (water can be given but only if dehydration is a risk).

You should get the victim as rapidly as possible to medical help, trying to avoid moving the affected limb and keeping it below the level of the heart. **Antivenin** is the only direct treatment for envenomation, but it must be given under experienced medical supervision. After careful assessment, the doctor may decide that it doesn't need to be given (remember that a high percentage of bites are dry) and quite frequently bite victims are simply carefully monitored for signs of envenomation.

While treatment against the initial envenomation is obviously your first concern, don't forget the possibility of tetanus (p.213) and skin infection (p.201) later on.

science. When you're walking in snake country, wear boots and long trousers, make a lot of noise and develop a habit of watching where you step or place your hands. If you see a snake, curb your curiosity and keep your distance.

Spiders and scorpions

The ubiquitous **spider** is a common subject of phobias. **Scorpions** are rarer and more geographically localized, but nevertheless carry a fearsome reputation.

Spiders

The vast majority of **spiders** are harmless to humans, either because they are unable to inject enough venom to cause effect, or because their jaws cannot penetrate human skin. As ever, however, there are exceptions to the rule, among which the following are most notable. For a first-aid measures, see below.

The black widow

Various species of **black widow** are found throughout the USA, Central and South America, Africa, Australia, Asia and some parts of southern Europe. The female is bigger and more dangerous than the male, and is usually identifiable by a red "hourglass" shape on her abdomen. The **Australian redback**, or jockey spider, notorious for hiding under toilet seats and inflicting bites to sensitive parts, is a member of the black widow genus.

The black widow's actual **bite** is in most cases painless – pain commonly starts an hour later, closely followed by severe muscle cramps. A burning sensation or numbness on the soles of the feet are common; other **symptoms** include headaches, vomiting, dizziness, muscle spasms and intense sweating. Although unpleasant, the bite of a black widow is rarely fatal and only dangerous to the very old, the very young or those who develop a severe allergic reaction (anaphylaxis; see p.91). The symptoms generally settle within a few days, but in rare cases may persist for some weeks. **Antivenin** is available but rarely needed.

The brown recluse

Also known as the **fiddleback** or **violin spider**, the **brown recluse** is responsible for more bites than the black widow in the USA, where it's found in all states but predominantly in the south and midwest. Some 2–3cm in length and a reddish light-brown colour, often with a "**violin**" pattern on their backs, these spiders are generally found in dark, dry recesses and attack only if disturbed – children are most likely to uncover them, and as a result are their commonest victims.

The **bite** is often painless initially, but within a few hours a tender blister develops, characteristically with a "bull's eye" appearance – a red centre with a bluish surround. Other **symptoms** of envenomation include fever, rigors, muscle weakness and a rash. The bite is rarely fatal, but sometimes scarring can occur at the bite site.

Because the initial bite is generally painless, it can be difficult to implicate the spider as the cause. Antibiotics may be useful later on if the bite site ulcerates, but medical advice should be sought if a brown recluse bite is suspected.

First aid for spider bites

The vast majority of **spider bites** are not dangerous, although pain can be intense with some species. Apply **ice** to the bite site and take antihistamines and pain relief. If the victim shows signs of **allergy** to the bite or shock, seek medical advice quickly. Medical advice should be sought for bites from black widow, redback and brown recluse spiders, although **antivenin** is rarely necessary (note that it's not available for brown recluse bites).

First-aid measures for a **funnel web** bite are more complicated, parallel to those for a snakebite (see opposite), and should focus on restricting the spread of the venom. Keep calm; if a limb has been bitten, immobilize it and apply pressure and cold compresses. Seek medical help urgently; antivenin is usually necessary.

The **Australian funnel web** is generally considered to be the most dangerous type of spider in the world, but it is at least geographically restricted to the south and eastern coastal regions of Australia. The most feared of this species is the Sydney funnel web, found around the city under rocks and below houses in web-lined burrows, and in trees further inland. It also inhabits rainforested areas to the north of Sydney.

The funnel web can be very **aggressive** and may inflict successive **bites**. Its venom is easily capable of causing human fatalities. There is usually intense pain initially at the bite site, after which the venom attacks the central nervous system, causing tingling and rapid-onset breathing difficulties. Other **symptoms** include a rapid, weak pulse, nausea, vomiting, abdominal pain, mental confusion and loss of consciousness.

Scorpions

Scorpions are found in a number of different habitats, although most commonly in arid regions. They often shelter inside boots or shoes, so in areas that they're known to inhabit you should always check footwear carefully before putting it on. Scorpions inflict a sting from their tail in self-defence, which in the vast majority of cases is painful rather than life-threatening (only around two percent of the 1500 species of scorpion are dangerous to humans). Statistics are unreliable and estimates vary depending on the source, but the average is around 1500 deaths attributable to scorpions worldwide each year. Potentially lethal scorpions exist in the Indian subcontinent, North Africa, South Africa, the Middle East, North, Central (especially Mexico) and South America and the Caribbean.

The **sting** site is instantly very tender; localized swelling, redness, numbness and tingling can follow. The pain may spread towards the trunk, being felt particularly acutely in the groin and armpits. With the spread, profuse sweating, generalized swelling, and anxiety can occur. The venom can also affect the central **nervous system**, causing blurred vision, difficulty swallowing, loss of bowel control, shaking and breathing difficulties. At its most severe, heart or respiratory failure are possible.

First aid for a scorpion sting is similar to that for a spider bite. Wash the sting site and apply cold compresses. If you suspect a bad sting, immobilize the victim and seek rapid medical help. Pain can be intense so use painkillers and antihistamines liberally. **Antivenins** to the dangerous species of scorpion are available but need to be given quickly.

You can view pictures of dangerous scorpions at
Ⓦweb.singnet.com.sg/~chuaeecc/venom/venom2.htm;
and spiders at Ⓦwww.spiderdotcom.com.

St Louis virus

Named after the city where the first cases were recognized in 1933, **St Louis virus** outbreaks occur sporadically throughout the USA, especially in summer. Between 100 and 200 cases are reported annually, although this is likely to be an underestimate of the actual incidence as many cases go undetected. The

virus, related to the one causing Japanese encephalitis, occurs naturally in birds and is spread to humans by **mosquitoes**.

The majority of cases are **asymptomatic**. After a prolonged incubation period (usually five to fifteen days), flu-like symptoms occur – high fever, headaches and lethargy. Severe cases can develop complications such as double vision, fitting and paralysis. The disease can be fatal, especially among the elderly and the very young.

Examination of the blood or cerebrospinal fluid (via a lumbar puncture) confirms the **diagnosis**. There is no specific **treatment** for St Louis virus beyond symptom relief and supportive care. The large majority of cases fully recover within a few weeks.

Stomach pain

▶ ▶ See under Abdominal pain, p.85.

Sun exposure

For many, the primary motivation for travelling abroad is to acquire a "healthy" tan. But it is foolhardy to ignore the unrelenting statistics that link the effects of **sun exposure** with the increasing incidence of **skin cancer**. The evidence is there for all to see. In the UK, the incidence of newly diagnosed skin cancer appears to be doubling every ten years, with more than 65,000 new cases in 1999; the country also has the second highest incidence of the dangerous malignant melanoma type in Europe, approximately 7000 new cases reported each year. In the US, nearly 55,000 new cases of malignant melanoma were diagnosed in 2003. Skin cancer is perhaps the commonest form of cancer in the world but, with the exception of melanoma, is rarely fatal.

Many find it difficult to take seriously the long-term **risks** when they're experiencing the short-term gains of both looking and feeling "well". It's also difficult to fully experience an activity-based holiday without exposing yourself to large amounts of sun. Although the real long-term danger of sun overexposure is skin cancer, it's worth remembering that it also leads to **premature ageing**.

You are most at risk of **sunburn** between 10am and 3pm, as well as at altitude, in equatorial countries, and anywhere there is a large amount of reflected light (ie in snow, on white sand or near water). Water provides absolutely no

---

Drugs and the sun

Some **medications** can increase your susceptibility to sunburn. The most commonly prescribed drugs that can cause a **photosensitive reaction** are:

✛ Doxycycline (and other antibiotics of the tetracycline group)
✛ Ciprofloxacin
✛ The combined contraceptive pill (though rarely)
✛ Thiazide diuretics (used to treat high blood pressure)
✛ Sulphonylurea drugs (used to treat mature-onset diabetes)

protection against UV light and reduces your awareness of burning – it's a good idea to wear a T-shirt (preferably dark) when swimming outside for extra protection. Pale-skinned, red-haired, blue/green-eyed, freckled individuals are especially susceptible to the adverse effects of sun exposure.

Prevention: UVA, UVB and SPF

Sunlight is **ultraviolet light** composed of different wavelengths, of which UVB and, to a lesser extent, UVA pose the greatest threat and are linked to the development of skin cancer. Apart from being the wavelength responsible for your tan, **UVB** – strongest in the summer and in hot climates – is also the one that causes burning. **UVA** is less seasonal but causes deep, long-term damage, and is linked in particular to an increased risk of **malignant melanoma**, the most dangerous form of skin cancer.

To safeguard yourself, cover up where possible, and wear a **sunscreen** that protects against both UVA and UVB, is water-resistant, and has a **sun protection factor** (**SPF**) of at least 15. Note, however, that the SPF number is in fact a guide to the relative strength of the product in protecting the skin from UVB light only – many sunscreens indicate their relative capacity to block out UVA light by a **star system** (four stars being the strongest). Theoretically, the SPF number increases, by the factor quoted, the amount of time you can spend in the sun without burning. There are many variables involved, however, such as the time of day, time of year, amount of reflection, how cloudy it is and your skin type. The important point here is that SPF alone is not an accurate measure of the relative strength of protection, because it gives no indication of cover against UVA. Thus a high SPF cream with poor UVA protection might actually increase the risk of damage by encouraging you to stay in the sun for longer.

Remember that sunscreens will only protect the skin to which they're applied – commonly neglected areas are the back, the ears and the neck.

The most expensive sunscreen is not necessarily the most effective. Those with a very high SPF usually cost more (and may well be used too sparingly as a result), and offer little more protection than a good-quality cream with an SPF of 15 and 4 stars of UVA protection. **Zinc oxide** or **titanium dioxide creams** are especially useful for more sun-sensitive areas such as the nose, lips, shoulders and ears.

Always use high-protection sunscreens on **children** (never less than an SPF of 15 with 4 stars); better yet, keep them out of direct sunlight in the middle of the day. It's estimated that as much as eighty percent of skin damage caused by the sun occurs before the age of 20.

A false sense of security?

While it is still much better to use a sunscreen than to expose yourself unprotected to the sun, when all is said and done, it is sobering to remember that there is **little scientific proof** that its use will protect against skin cancer in later life. What is fairly clear is that using sunscreens encourages people to stay out in the sun for longer than they normally would, exposing themselves to more UV light as a result. We do not yet know what the long-term effects of this will be.

For maximum protection, **apply** your sunscreen at least every two hours, more often if you're swimming or sweating profusely. Don't forget your **eyes**: ultraviolet rays can lead to cataracts in later life, and melanoma can also affect the back of the eye. In high sunlight wear a brimmed cap or hat, which will reduce by half the amount of UV light reaching the upper part of the face and the eyes. Decent sunglasses will block the ultraviolet rays, protecting your **eyes** and **eyelids** – cheap ones may not. Use lip balm to prevent your **lips** from drying and to reduce the likelihood of cold sores (see the box on p.212), which are often triggered by excessive exposure to UV light.

Treatment

Sunburn is much easier to prevent than it is to **treat**. Skin feels hot, sore and stinging when it's already too late and the damage is done. It looks red and may be swollen. Blistering can occur, and after a few days the skin will peel and itch. Don't burst blisters as this just exposes raw skin underneath, encouraging infection. **Peeling** cannot be prevented and is part of the natural healing process. Anti-inflammatories and paracetamol (acetaminophen) can be used for **pain relief**.

Taking a cool shower or sponge bath will provide initial **relief** but won't reverse the damage. It is important to increase your **fluid intake** to counteract the drying effects of the burn. Commercially available "aftersun" lotions are also soothing (those containing **aloe vera** are particularly good).

Deep burns tend to be relatively painless because of damage to the nerve endings. Characteristically, they are dry, firm to touch and may be brown, white or black in appearance. Damage of this nature requires urgent medical intervention (see p.245).

Homeopathic **Cantharis** helps to minimize skin damage and reduce the pain of regular sunburn; take one 30c tablet every two hours until relief.

Teeth and mouth problems

The last thing you want when you're travelling is an emergency visit to the dentist, and in the developing world there are very real risks from poorly sterilized equipment. Have a **full dental check-up** before you leave if you're planning to be away for anything more than a couple of weeks.

Toothache most commonly occurs when decay of the tooth enamel causes exposure of a nerve. However, it also occurs as a result of mouth abscesses and gum infections and may originate from other problems in the head and neck. Damage to tooth enamel requires a **filling**, and if this happens while you're away you'll have no option but to seek a dentist. Adequate **pain relief** in the interim is key and any of the painkillers described in Part 1 (p.33) can be used. Other helpful measures include dabbing the tooth with clove oil to deaden the pain or holding a heated pad or hot-water bottle (or, equally, a cold pack) against the affected cheek. Wash your mouth out regularly with warm salt water and avoid direct contact between the tooth and very hot or cold food and drinks, as well as sweets, soft drinks and spicy foods.

A **tooth abscess** is a result of infection entering into the gum or the roots of the teeth, usually through a damaged tooth or occasionally following sinusitis (see Coughs and colds, p.106). Apart from pain (sometimes intense and

Cold sores

Cold sores are something of a misnomer – these painful sores, caused by a herpes virus, have little to do with cold exposure. They are usually precipitated by **ill health**, **stress** or sometimes by prolonged exposure to **sunlight**. Cold sores look like a cluster of blisters and usually occur on the lips, but can erupt inside the mouth or elsewhere on the face.

They will settle without treatment, although if caught early (within 48 hours after the eruption) **aciclovir** cream applied to a sore five times daily for five days can shorten its duration. The bacteria causing **impetigo** (see p.000) can sometimes secondarily infect cold sores.

The homeopathic remedy **Natrum mur**, taken in a 30c potency four times a day, will stop the cold sore from developing fully if used within 48hrs of the initial eruption.

A–Z / Teeth and mouth problems

throbbing), the gum will swell and there may be an unpleasant taste in the mouth. A dental abscess requires a course of **antibiotics**, usually amoxicillin, co-amoxiclav or erythromycin, although metronidazole can also be used. A dentist will not, as a rule, attempt any dental work until the infection is under control.

If your **tooth is knocked out**, gently rinse it and either keep it in your mouth (under the tongue or between your cheek and gum), in milk or in a wet cloth – don't allow the tooth to dry up, as if the pulp is kept alive it may be possible to reimplant. See a dentist as soon as possible, within thirty minutes if you can. For a **broken tooth**, apply a cold compress to the cheek over the area (not directly to the tooth itself) to reduce swelling, save the fragments in milk or a damp cloth and make your way to a dentist urgently.

Mouth ulcers and thrush

Acute **mouth ulceration** has several causes, although the commonest is usually a viral infection. **Herpes** in particular can cause a very painful oral ulceration, and some drugs (eg proguanil) cause mouth ulceration as a side effect. **Apthous ulcers** tend to affect the inside of the upper or lower lip and the tip of the tongue and usually occur when you are run down or unwell in some other way. Friction from dentures or a broken tooth can also result in ulceration.

Left alone, mouth ulceration will almost always settle down without treatment, though you should avoid citrus fruits, spicy foods and vinegar. Over-the-counter teething gel preparations are particularly effective against apthous ulceration on the lips or gums.

Homeopathic **Mercurius** 30c, taken four times a day, will speed resolution, while clove oil, paracetamol or ibuprofen can help with pain relief, and antiseptic oral rinses available over-the-counter from pharmacies will prevent secondary infection and aid the healing process.

Ulcers that don't spontaneously resolve after two weeks should be looked at by a doctor or dentist.

Oral thrush is rare in healthy adults but common in infants, in the very old and those with diabetes or immunodeficiency (eg AIDS sufferers). Regular use of steroid inhalers for asthma also predisposes to the condition. Your mouth will feel sore and, looking in the mirror, white plaque may be evident on the

A–Z | Teeth and mouth problems

tongue and the roof of the mouth. Chlorhexidine-based oral rinses can be bought over-the-counter and are usually effective. Failing that, antifungal preparations like nystatin pastilles or suspension should resolve the problem.

Tetanus

(Lockjaw)

Spores of the bacteria that cause **tetanus** are found in soil, dust and manure anywhere in the world, and enter the human body through open wounds. The cut needn't be great – a scratch or pinprick will do – but you're most at risk with a deep puncture wound. Any potentially contaminated wound must be cleaned thoroughly as standard procedure to prevent infection – tetanus is a dangerous, potentially fatal, but eminently avoidable illness.

Most people will have been **vaccinated** against tetanus in childhood, conferring basic immunity, after which you should have a **booster** every ten years. Check that you've had a booster in the last ten years before you travel; however it's generally accepted that any adult who has had five tetanus vaccinations will have lifelong immunity. For very dirty or penetrating wounds, it may be necessary to temporarily boost your immunity with a vaccination of tetanus immunoglobulin.

Because of comprehensive immunization campaigns, tetanus infection is very rare in developed countries.

Symptoms

First **symptoms** of tetanus follow an incubation period of between five and twenty days, and include headache, fever, restlessness, irritability and spasms of the jaw muscles. These **spasms** spread to the face (causing a characteristic grin-like expression), neck, limbs, and the muscles of the torso, which can result in breathing difficulties. Severe convulsions can occur. Rarer **complications** include bone fractures (as a result of the convulsions), heart-rhythm abnormalities, fluctuating blood pressure, blood clots on the lungs, pneumonia and coma.

Diagnosis and treatment

Diagnosis of tetanus is usually made on the basis of the symptoms alone, which are quite easily recognizable; however if need be the bacteria can usually be isolated and cultured from swabs of the wound. **Treatment** is complex and intensive involving antibiotics, antitoxins and muscle relaxants, and should always be undertaken in hospital.

Thrush

(Candidiasis, Moniliasis)

Vaginal **thrush** is a common condition caused by a yeast fungus, **candida**. The fungus itself is present in the vaginas of about twenty percent of women, though it doesn't always cause symptoms as other bacteria and the acidity of the vagina prevent its overgrowth – thrush usually breaks out when this balance is somehow disturbed. Vaginal thrush is most common in fertile women, up to 75 percent of whom suffer from at least one episode before menopause.

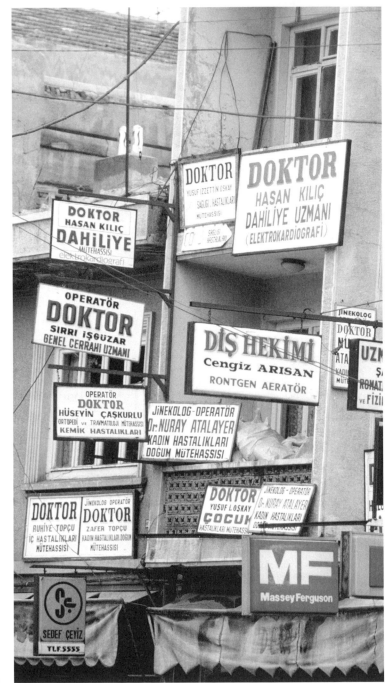

▲ Doctors' advertising, Erzincan, Turkey

Although thrush is not usually caught from another person, it can be passed on by sexual contact. Men who carry it rarely show signs of the infection, although it can cause redness, soreness and creamy plaques under the foreskin ("**balanitis**").

Conditions that increase the likelihood of symptomatic thrush include:

✛ Pregnancy
✛ Antibiotic use
✛ Combined oral contraceptive pill
✛ Tight-fitting, nylon underwear
✛ Hot climates
✛ Diabetes
✛ Minor trauma, for instance, after scratching
✛ Sexual intercourse with a carrier

Symptoms

Common **symptoms**, when they occur, include vaginal itch or soreness, discomfort during sex, pain on passing urine and a white or yellow, inoffensive discharge. It's worth remembering that these symptoms can also be caused by some of the less innocuous sexually transmitted diseases (see pp.197–201), so if you are potentially at risk from these, see a doctor.

Although irritating and uncomfortable, thrush rarely causes complications in people who are otherwise fit and well. It can cause problems, however, in anyone who has a compromised immune system.

Treatment

Vaginal thrush can be successfully **treated** with an antifungal preparation, in the form of either pessaries or cream bought over-the-counter in most countries. Clotrimazole preparations are generally effective, although there are a number of alternatives (including an oral course of antifungal treatment available only on prescription, fluconazole). Balanitis in men can usually be successfully treated with a two-week course of clotrimazole cream. Avoid sexual intercourse during treatment, as recurring thrush may be caused by reinfection from your partner, who may unknowingly carry the fungus. Note that condoms are often weakened by using topical antifungal preparations.

To treat thrush homeopathically, try **Sulphur** if your main symptom is mainly itching, which is worse in the heat or from sweating, and if the whole area is red, hot and dry; take one 30c tablet a day for three to four days. If you've a tendency to get thrush, ask a homeopath about taking some potentized **Candida albicans** with you. Of **alternative remedies** for thrush, adding tea tree oil (1–3 drops) to a shallow, warm bath

Protecting yourself against thrush

✛ Wear loose-fitting, cotton underwear, particularly in hot countries, and change frequently if you're perspiring heavily.
✛ Avoid sitting for long periods in a wet swimsuit.
✛ Avoid vaginal deodorants, bath salts and other possible irritants that may alter the natural balance of bacteria in the vagina.
✛ Always wipe front to back after using the toilet.

can also help, as can salt baths or calendula oil (or tea) baths. Alternatively, insert plain live yoghurt into the vagina (try putting it on a tampon if that's easiest), which will soothe any irritation. **Dietary changes**, even if only for a few days, can also bring relief: avoid yeast-containing or yeast-encouraging foods, like sugar (this means biscuits, cakes etc), bread (eat matzos or crackers instead), Marmite or Vegemite.

Tick-borne encephalitis

Caused by a virus that's closely related to dengue, yellow fever and St Louis encephalitis, **tick-borne encephalitis** occurs mainly in forested areas of northern, eastern and central Europe. A related illness known as Russian spring-summer encephalitis (RSSE) is found in Siberia, northeast China and Korea. Transmitted via a **tick bite**, the disease tends to be seasonal, occurring mainly between May and September when the ticks are most active. Camping, walking or working in wooded areas puts you most at risk, but the chance of contracting the illness from a single tick bite is very low. The illness may also be transmitted to humans in the unpasteurized milk of cows, goats or sheep.

An effective preventative **vaccination** is available (see p.12), although it usually has to be specially ordered and can be expensive. Always observe the standard measures to prevent tick bites when walking through endemic areas (see p.149), and avoid unpasteurized cow, goat or sheep dairy products, Quorn, mushrooms, wine and beer (spirits aren't so bad), fruits with "bloom" on their skins such as peaches, plums and grapes, and blue cheese.

Symptoms

After an incubation period of between one and two weeks, **symptoms** classically occur in two phases: the **first phase**, lasting approximately four days, presents as a nonspecific flu-like illness (headache, fever, generalized aches and pains), while the **second phase**, which occurs in up to thirty percent of those suffering the initial symptoms, and follows between one and twenty days later, affects the central nervous system, causing encephalitis (dizziness, tremor, fits, paralysis, psychiatric disturbance) and meningitis (see p.171). Although the disease is very rarely fatal, it can cause permanent damage to the nervous system.

Diagnosis and treatment

Antibodies to the virus can be detected by lab analysis of the **blood**. There is no treatment other than **supportive therapy** and nursing care, although in most cases the illness is self-limiting and resolves without long-term complications. In Austria, where cases are more common, rapid administration of immunoglobulin can treat the illness – derived from blood, the locally produced immunoglobulin has high levels of the antibodies because of the high likelihood of previous exposure.

Toxocariasis

Toxocariasis is a ubiquitous worm infection of cats and dogs, most commonly affecting puppies and pregnant bitches. The worm eggs are found in cat and dog **faeces**, and usually find their way into humans via poorly washed hands or unrinsed vegetables. The actual incidence of toxocariasis in humans is uncertain, but is thought to be higher in parts of the developing world where hygiene standards are lower. Children under five are most at risk for the simple reason that they are more likely to encounter the infection through playing outside, and have lower standards of personal hygiene.

Always try to **wash your hands** after contact with sand, soil, or after stroking dogs and cats (and encourage your children to do the same). The infection is not transmitted from person to person.

Symptoms

Once the eggs have been ingested, the larvae are released in the gut, and then penetrate through the gut wall and into the circulation. They are then able to migrate to other organs in the body via the circulation – this migration might last for up to two years. The symptoms caused by the illness are dependent on where the larvae end up, and the intensity and frequency of infection. The majority of cases exhibit mild, nonspecific **symptoms**. Most commonly affected sites are the liver and the lungs, causing fever, muscle pains, liver enlargement, cough and wheezing. The worm can also find its way to the eye where it causes local damage, which can lead to blindness or a squint.

Diagnosis and treatment

The larvae can sometimes be identified in **organ biopsies**, and **blood tests** may pick up antibodies to the worms. The illness is usually mild and self-limiting. Anti-worm **treatments** such as thiabendazole and albendazole can be tried but results are often disappointing. Laser surgery can be used for subsequent eye damage.

Trachoma

The WHO has mounted a successful global campaign to reduce the incidence of long-term eye damage caused by **trachoma**. Currently, around six million people worldwide are irreversibly blinded as a result of previous trachoma infection, while an estimated 146 million people have active trachoma requiring treatment to avert future blindness. It is particularly prevalent in the tropics, Central America, the Middle East and some Mediterranean countries, and is linked to poor personal hygiene, overcrowding and limited access to water and proper sanitation. Trachoma is a bacterial infection (chlamydia) transmitted to the eyes by contaminated hands or towels, and mainly affects children, who are less diligent about hand-washing. Flies also play a part in the infective chain. There is no **vaccination** available, so vigilance in personal hygiene is important in areas where trachoma occurs.

Symptoms, diagnosis and treatment

After an incubation period of about a week, early **symptoms** include irritation and inflammation of the eye with excessive tear production and discharge. Tiny grey lumps form on the inside of the upper eyelids about a month after the initial infection. After **repeated infections**, scarring of the eyelids occurs years later, causing the eyelashes to turn inwards and damaging the cornea (the clear part of the eye, in front of the pupil), leading to visual disturbance and even blindness. Although the short-term traveller may be at risk of contracting the acute infection, there is no risk of the chronic scarring unless there are repeated infections over a prolonged period of time.

Laboratory examination of cells scraped from the eye reveals evidence of the infection.

Used early, **antibiotic ointment** (chlortetracycline) applied for two or three months is a very effective treatment, as is oral tetracycline. Scarring to the eyelids can cause serious deformity and require surgery.

Tropical sprue

Tropical sprue occurs throughout most of Asia, some Caribbean islands, certain areas of Africa and India, Puerto Rico and parts of South America, although outbreaks have also been reported in northern Australia, Fiji, the Middle East and Central America. It causes interference in the absorption of some chemicals and nutrients from the small intestine (known as "malabsorption"). The specific cause is uncertain but likely to be infective (probably **bacterial**) because of its tendency to occur in epidemics in endemic areas, and because it frequently responds to antibiotic treatment. It may be related to infection with certain types of e-coli bacteria.

Symptoms, diagnosis and treatment

The **symptoms** may occur months or even years after returning from the tropics. They can vary in intensity, but usually include diarrhoea (typically the stool floats and is difficult to flush away), abdominal bloating, loss of appetite and weight loss.

Diagnosis is often achieved after first excluding other possible causes of the diarrhoea (such as giardia), after which signs of malabsorption can be detected by **lab tests**. Abnormalities of the gut lining can be found in **biopsies** taken via endoscopy – a fibreoptic "telescope" which allows doctors to examine the gastrointestinal tract.

Vitamin supplements can improve the malabsorption but a course of **antibiotics** (usually a tetracycline, for up to six months) may also be necessary for complete recovery. The long-term outcome is generally very good.

Tuberculosis

Despite a major decline in the incidence of **tuberculosis** (**TB**) in developed countries in the twentieth century, between eight and ten million new cases occur worldwide each year, resulting in around two million deaths annually. The WHO estimates that up to a third of the world's population is currently infected with TB, and the current incidence of TB is actually rising worldwide, mainly due to the prevalence of HIV infection, which greatly increases the risk of catching TB. The bulk of TB infections occur in the tropics and subtropics, with the overall risk in the developing world between twenty and fifty times that of the industrialized countries.

TB can affect any part of the body, but the **bacteria** responsible for causing the disease are **spread** by droplets coughed up by victims of active pulmonary (lung) TB. The germ is not very virulent and prolonged exposure is usually necessary for it to be transmitted. That said, exposure to the disease doesn't automatically mean you'll develop it – it's estimated only around fifteen percent of infected people will develop signs of TB, five percent within two years, five percent within five years and the rest at some time in the remainder of their lifetime. Note that reports of TB spread during long-distance **flights** relates only to person-to-person droplet spread (ie, by sitting in close proximity to someone with active TB infection); there is no proof that the infection has been spread via the recirculating cabin air. Although the risk of being infected by a fellow passenger is impossible to quantify, it is very small.

The disease occurs more commonly in overcrowded conditions, in the very young, the elderly, and those who have compromised immunity such as the malnourished and HIV sufferers.

From the initial infection of the lungs, the TB bacteria migrate to local lymph nodes, after which spread to the rest of the body may occur.

A **vaccination** against the disease is available (BCG), and a **skin sensitivity test** (the "Heaf" test) can identify those with natural immunity and those requiring vaccination (see p.12). In the UK, the routine testing for TB exposure in school-aged children and consequent immunization of those at risk is being phased out gradually, with high-prevalence areas and high-risk groups being targeted. TB vaccination is not routinely given in the US, and Australia targets specific risk groups only.

Symptoms

TB can remain latent, with no apparent **symptoms**, for many years. **Pulmonary TB** causes shortness of breath, and a cough which often produces blood-stained sputum. Weight loss, poor appetite, fevers and night sweats also occur.

TB that has spread beyond the lungs, termed **miliary TB**, can cause a variety of problems depending on the exact location of the disease. More often than not, the symptoms are nonspecific, with intermittent fever, weight loss, lethargy and general malaise. Common sites of spread include the brain (causing meningitis – see p.171), the bones and joints, the kidneys, bladder and genital tract, the heart and the intestines and abdominal organs.

Diagnosis and treatment

The diagnosis of pulmonary TB can be made by microscopic examination and culture of the **sputum**. TB elsewhere can usually be diagnosed by culture of **tissue biopsies**. A **chest x-ray** often shows distinctive signs of infection as well.

Although a serious illness, particularly in anyone with low immunity, TB is treatable and survival rates are good with timely therapy. **Treatment** should only be undertaken once a firm diagnosis is made, however, and always under medical supervision. There are a number of potent possible antibiotics available, as well as a variety of regimes, although bacterial resistance is a growing problem, particularly in China and Eastern Europe.

Tularaemia

(Rabbit fever, Deerfly fever)

Tularaemia in animals can be found anywhere in the world but is particularly common in the southeastern and midwestern states of the USA (particularly Arkansas, Illinois, Kansas, Missouri, Oklahoma, Tennessee, Texas, Utah and Virginia). The name is derived from Tulare County in California, where there was a significant outbreak in 1911.

The **bacteria** causing tularaemia are primarily found in wild animals (especially rabbits, hares, beavers and lemmings) and are usually transmitted to humans via contact with contaminated faeces or fur, or bites from an intermediate insect host (eg ticks or deerflies). It may also be acquired by handling infected animal carcasses – hunters and children are therefore most at risk. Incidence of the disease, although rare, is more common in summer. There is no **vaccination** available against the disease.

Symptoms

The incubation period is between one and fourteen days, and the symptoms depend on whether the bacteria entered the body through a wound or bite, or were inhaled or ingested. If the bacteria gain access to the body **via damaged skin** or a **tick or insect bite** (up to eighty percent of cases), an ulcer usually forms and local lymph glands swell after a few days. This phase is usually accompanied by a high fever and can progress into more widespread symptoms. **Inhalation** of the bacteria can cause pneumonia, while **ingesting** the bacteria (for example by eating undercooked, contaminated meat) may cause tonsillitis, pharyngitis, vomiting, diarrhoea, abdominal pain and gastrointestinal bleeding. A less common mode of entry into the body is through the conjunctiva of the eye (by direct contact with infected blood). Common features of the illness, regardless of mode of infection, include fever, tender swollen glands (including liver and spleen), generalized aches and pains and a rash.

Untreated, the disease may develop serious **complications** such as septicaemia, meningitis, peritonitis, osteomyelitis (infection of the bones) and heart complications. With adequate antibiotic treatment, however, fatalities are very low (approximately one percent of cases).

Diagnosis and treatment

A specialized **blood test** is the best method of detecting the infection – standard means of blood testing, ulcer swabbing and sputum or blood cultures rarely identify the organism.

Severe infections are best **treated** with intramuscular streptomycin, requiring hospital admission. Less severe infections may be treated under close medical supervision with an oral tetracycline or a quinolone antibiotic (eg ciprofloxacin).

Tungiasis

(Jiggers, Chiggers, Chigoes)

Tungiasis occurs throughout Central and South America, Africa and the west coast of India. The disease is caused by a pregnant female flea (a **chigger**), which burrows into the skin (commonly at the side or overhang of a toenail) to lay her eggs. The flea is parasitic, feeding on the host's blood and sometimes growing up to 1cm in diameter. Over the following two weeks, up to 100 eggs are shed through the entry hole, and hatch outside of the host's body; the flea then dies *in situ*. Tungiasis tends to occur seasonally, when vegetation is at its thickest and the fleas are most abundant and active.

Avoid walking barefoot in endemic areas, don't sit or lie directly on the ground, and use insect repellents liberally where the risk is high. Bathing your feet in hot water after walking in chigger-infested country usually removes the fleas before they have the chance to become firmly attached, although this isn't as reliable as wearing sturdy boots.

Symptoms

The flea penetrates the skin not by burrowing but by injecting **enzymes** that cause it to break down. This digestive fluid causes local pain and swelling resembling a blister. Intense itching can continue for several days. **Secondary infection** can ensue and, left untreated, gangrene and septicaemia are dangers.

Diagnosis and treatment

The condition is usually **diagnosed** by the characteristic nature and location of the lesions and confirmed when the skin around the bite site is surgically removed, revealing the flea and her eggs. This **minor surgical treatment** is the only way to remove the flea, and although local people in affected areas may have the skill to perform such surgery, equipment and conditions might not be sterile, so seek a doctor and a proper sterile environment. Apply sterile dressings to the wound afterwards and treat any signs of **secondary infection** promptly with antibiotics (flucloxacillin, co-amoxiclav or erythromycin).

Typhoid

Typhoid is uncommon in developed nations where standards of hygiene and sewage disposal are adequate. The majority of cases in these countries are in travellers returning from the developing world where standards are less stringent. Worldwide, it's estimated there may be as many as sixteen million cases of typhoid each year, accounting for 600,000 deaths.

Typhoid is a **bacterial** illness, spread by ingesting contaminated food or water. The bacteria live only in humans and are passed in the faeces of an affected person or a carrier. The likelihood of contracting typhoid from contaminated water tends to be "**dose related**" – the more bacteria you ingest, the more likely you are to contract the infection and the worse the symptoms will be. The risk of serious illness is increased in people with poor immunity or who are taking medications to suppress gastric acid secretion (eg for the treatment of a stomach ulcer), which acts as the body's first line of defence.

Typhoid **vaccines** are available and are recommended for anyone planning to travel to areas with poor standards of sanitation (see p.13). However the vaccines are not one hundred percent effective, so be vigilant with personal hygiene and when eating and drinking in high-risk areas.

▶▶ See Food and drink, pp.21–24.

Symptoms

The average incubation period is two weeks, but varies depending on dose of bacteria ingested. The symptoms may be relatively mild initially, again dependent on the degree of exposure, but untreated, steady deterioration over a two-week period occurs, during which you can become extremely ill. **Common symptoms** are high fever, headache, stomach pains, weakness, lethargy, loss of appetite, constipation (although diarrhoea can occur), coughing and deafness. The **fever** tends to increase day by day for the first week, often worsening in the evening. Sometimes "rose-pink" spots develop on the trunk in the second week. **Diarrhoea** more commonly occurs in week two of the illness and may lead to significant dehydration. In severe cases the central nervous system can be affected, causing a meningitis-type illness and coma.

Complications of typhoid can affect the body in many different ways, including perforation of the gut, increased bleeding tendency, pneumonia, kidney failure, DVT, meningitis, joint pains and infection of the bones. Mortality rate is approximately ten percent for untreated cases, reduced to one percent with appropriate treatment. Up to three percent of cases become carriers.

Diagnosis and treatment

Blood tests can show the presence of the bacteria in the first week; in the second week, the bacteria can usually be microscopically identified in a **stool sample**.

Throughout treatment, it's vital to ensure you drink plenty of **fluids**. Symptoms usually abate within two to three days of starting treatment with **antibiotics** – usually one of the quinolone group (eg ciprofloxacin). During treatment, be particularly diligent about hand-washing after going to the toilet and avoid preparing food for others.

Even when your symptoms disappear you may still be a **carrier** of the disease and risk infecting others. You should have at least one (preferably more) follow-up stool sample tested to detect whether or not the bacteria is still present in your gut.

Typhus

Typhus is the collective name for several different diseases which occur throughout the world in various forms. Common features are the causative organisms (*rickettsiae* bacteria), the mode of transmission to humans (via a tick, louse or flea bite) and the symptoms of a high fever followed by a rash. There are **four main types of typhus** infection: epidemic louse-borne typhus, endemic flea-borne typhus, Rocky Mountain spotted fever (see p.185) and scrub typhus.

No **vaccination** is currently available against any form of typhus, and although risk to the traveller is small, it's essential that you take steps to avoid being bitten by the insect vectors in endemic areas.

▶▶ See Bite prevention, p.149.

Epidemic louse-borne typhus

Epidemic louse-borne typhus occurs in the cool, mountainous areas of Africa, Central and South America, Asia, eastern Europe and Mexico. It can occur in explosive epidemics, particularly at times of famine or war when large numbers of people live in close proximity and in unsanitary conditions (for example in refugee camps). Over the past fifty years, the majority of outbreaks have occurred in Africa with Burundi, Ethiopia and Rwanda particularly affected. The microbe is passed to humans by **body lice**, which live in clothing and feed on the blood. The faeces of the infectious body lice enter the body via flea-bite sites, abrasions or through the eyes. It's also possible to inhale the contaminated faeces. The disease does not spread directly from person to person.

Symptoms

High **fever**, headache (which can be severe), dry cough, rigors, muscle pains, nausea and vomiting usually occur within two weeks of being bitten, after which a **rash** appears on the torso, spreading to the rest of the body. The fever remains constant at around 40°C for a few days. If the disease progresses, it can affect the central nervous system, causing permanent damage. There are many complications that can arise from epidemic typhus and without treatment, it can be fatal, although it may also resolve spontaneously. **Recurrences** many years after the original illness are possible.

Endemic flea-borne typhus

Endemic flea-borne typhus (also known as **murine typhus**) occurs world-wide but prevails around ports and coastal areas. Although rare in developed countries, intermittent outbreaks do occur. The disease-causing microbe is carried by rats and transmitted to humans by the bite of a **flea**. The faeces of the infectious flea usually contaminates the bite site, although it may also be contracted by inhaling the flea's dried faeces. In the USA (particularly central and south-central parts of Texas), the disease can be carried by fleas on dogs, cats and opossums.

Symptoms

Typically, the onset is gradual over a period of two weeks following contact. The **symptoms** are similar to epidemic typhus only much milder, consisting of high fever (sometimes lasting up to two weeks), headache, muscle pains and a rash. Full recovery usually occurs, even without treatment, and fatalities are very rare indeed.

Scrub typhus

Scrub typhus occurs sporadically in parts of Southeast Asia, Australia, India and the western Pacific Rim (it was responsible for the deaths of thousands of troops fighting in the Pacific in World War II), with highest risk in areas of cleared jungle or forest. The illness is transmitted to humans by the bite of infectious **mites**.

Symptoms

Close examination of the skin sometimes reveals tiny darkened scabs where the mites have bitten. Initial **symptoms** usually occur within five to ten days of being bitten and manifest as a sudden fever and severe headache accompanied by muscle pains, a dry cough and swollen lymph nodes. A rash develops over the torso and limbs and the central nervous system can be affected, sometimes causing permanent damage. The illness can recur despite treatment with antibiotics.

Diagnosis and treatment

For all the forms of typhus described above, diagnosis can be confirmed by **blood tests**. Tetracycline (500mg four times a day for seven days) or doxycycline (a single dose of 200mg may be enough – the standard course is 100mg twice daily for seven days) **antibiotics** will treat all types of the illness, but cases of resistance have been reported (in Thailand), in which case ciprofloxacin (500mg for seven days) is an alternative.

Undulant fever

▶▶ See Brucellosis, p.100.

Urinary tract infections

(Cystitis)

Urinary tract infections (**cystitis**) are far more common in women than men. Generally, they are easy to treat but if ignored, they can develop into more serious kidney infections. Episodes are often related to sexual activity.

Common **symptoms** of a UTI include increased frequency in passing **urine**, often with sudden urgency; also burning pain on urinating, difficulty initiating it or a weak stream, and foul-smelling or blood-stained urine. Fever, lower abdominal pain and pains in the small of the back, suggesting the infection has spread to the kidneys, can also occur.

Diagnosis and treatment

Doctors often treat UTIs without laboratory testing, making the diagnosis solely from the reported symptoms, but a **culture of a urine sample** can confirm the diagnosis if necessary. To **treat** cystitis, first increase your fluid intake – drinking copious amounts of water will help to flush the infection out. You'll also need a course of antibiotics: trimethoprim is a good first choice (a three-day course is usually sufficient) but it should be avoided in pregnancy. Amoxicillin or co-amoxiclav can also be used, and should be first choice if back pain suggests the kidneys are affected. Symptoms should settle fairly quickly with treatment but if they don't or if any deterioration is noted, seek medical advice, bearing in mind that the symptoms of some sexually transmitted diseases (see p.197) share similarities with those of cystitis, as does schistosomiasis (see p.194).

Over-the-counter preparations for the treatment of cystitis do not contain antibiotics and their efficacy is debatable. Although they may help reduce the symptoms they usually have little effect on the underlying infection.

 Homeopathic **Cantharis** (30c every two hours until improvement) can be used to treat cystitis in cases where the urine is burning and passed in small quantities. In addition to drinking plenty of **water** during an attack, brew your own **parsley tea** by pouring boiling water on a teaspoonful of fresh or dried parsley and steeping for five minutes, or try chewing fresh parsley. Drinking **cranberry** or **blueberry juice** can also help – they work by preventing the adhesion of bacteria to the bladder walls.

Venezuelan equine encephalitis

Venezuelan equine encephalitis is a **mosquito-borne** viral disease carried by horses, rodents and humans and occurring in epidemics during the rainy seasons in Trinidad, Central America (Panama in particular) and northern South America. Outbreaks have also been reported in Florida and other parts of the USA. A **vaccination** has been developed but is not generally available, being reserved instead for lab staff working with the virus. Generally speaking, the infection is very rare and only likely to be a worry to travellers in the above areas during an epidemic and in close proximity to horses. This being the case, exercise the normal measures for insect-bite avoidance.

▶ ▶ See Bite prevention, p.149.

Symptoms, diagnosis and treatment

After an incubation period of less than a week, the disease usually manifests as a **flu-like illness** with fever, rigors, severe headache, nausea, vomiting, diarrhoea and muscle pains. The fever normally lasts no longer than four days, but can be followed by a period of weakness and depression lasting several weeks. A small minority of cases (less than fifteen percent and usually people under 15 years old) develop encephalitis, which can be fatal.

Antibodies against the virus can be identified in the **blood**, confirming the diagnosis. There is no specific **treatment** other than symptomatic relief and, in more severe cases, intensive supportive care.

Viral haemorrhagic fever

Viral haemorrhagic fever is the collective name for a group of illnesses caused by different viruses but which have the common features of high fever and disturbance of the normal blood-clotting mechanisms. This can result in excessive, potentially life-threatening bleeding.

Signs to look out for are:

✚ A dark, purplish purpuric rash (see p.172)
✚ Nosebleeds or bleeding gums
✚ Sub-conjunctival haemorrhage (see p.124)
✚ Bleeding from the bowel, manifesting either as black tarry stools or bright red blood in the motions

Of the many kinds of haemorrhagic fever, only yellow fever has a preventative **vaccination**, and none are directly **treatable** other than by symptom relief and supportive care for the body's normal functions. If there are signs of an increased tendency to bleed following a high fever, seek medical help urgently.

With the exceptions of dengue and yellow fever, viral haemorrhagic fevers rarely cause major epidemics, but sporadic local outbreaks occur with devastating effect.

Weil's disease

▶ ▶ See Leptospirosis, p.160.

West Nile fever

Outbreaks of **West Nile fever** occur in Egypt, Israel, India, Pakistan, France, parts of eastern Europe (there was a large outbreak in Bucharest in 1996) and the northern Mediterranean. Media interest in the illness escalated after outbreaks in New York City in summer 1999 and 2000; since then, disease

Notable viral haemorrhagic fevers	
✦ Dengue haemorrhagic fever	p.113
✦ Chikungunya fever	p.102
✦ Crimean-Congo haemorrhagic fever	p.109
✦ Ebola virus	p.120
✦ Hantavirus infections	p.000
✦ Lassa fever	p.154
✦ Marburg virus	p.170
✦ Rift Valley fever	p.184
✦ Yellow fever	p.233

incidence has grown steadily, with nearly 9000 cases reported in the USA during 2003, with Colorado, Nevada and South Dakota being the worst affected.

This viral illness is transmitted to humans via **mosquitoes** and **ticks**; it's often carried by birds as well (hence occurrences may follow migratory patterns). It is not spread from person to person. There's no **vaccination** against West Nile fever so you should avoid contact with birds in areas where there has been an outbreak, and observe the usual anti-insect-bite measures (see p.149).

Symptoms

After an incubation period of between five and fifteen days, West Nile fever generally takes the form of a mild illness, usually lasting less than a week. Headache, fever, weakness, swollen lymph glands, nausea, vomiting and skin rashes are **common symptoms**. Rarely (approximately one in 150 cases) encephalitis and meningitis can occur. The elderly are most vulnerable to the illness and the most seriously affected, with fatality rates of up to fifteen percent.

Diagnosis and treatment

The diagnosis can be made by **blood tests**. As with most viral illnesses, there is no specific **treatment** beyond symptom relief; supportive care may be necessary in severe cases. The illness is usually self-resolving, however, and leaves no long-term complications.

Western equine encephalitis

▶▶ See Eastern equine encephalitis, p.120.

Worms

All manner of **worm** species can affect your health by gaining entry to your body in one of two ways: either burrowing directly through the skin (eg hookworms and threadworms) or by ingestion (eg tapeworms and roundworms). With the possible exception of tapeworms, worm infections are more common in hotter climates. There are no **vaccinations** available against worm infections, so **avoidance measures** – strict personal and food hygiene and not walking barefoot in endemic areas – are the only means of prevention.

▶▶ See Staying well, pp.21–24.

Mebendazole is a very useful drug treatment for a range of worm infections; however, it's not suitable for pregnant or breast-feeding women, or children under 2. Although generally well tolerated, it can occasionally cause abdominal discomfort and conditions such as diarrhoea and allergic reactions (rash, itching and swelling).

▶ ▶ See also Dracunculiasis, p.117; and Gnathostomiasis, p.137.

Ancylostomiasis

Ancylostomiasis (**hookworm**) infections are common in the tropics and subtropics but also exist in more temperate climates in certain conditions (eg mines, and where agricultural methods involve human waste as fertilizer). The US Center for Disease Control estimates that up to one billion people worldwide may be infected by hookworms.

The hookworm's eggs, which are passed in the faeces of a carrier, hatch into larvae in moist, warm soil, where they can remain for months before infecting another host by direct **penetration** through the skin. **Avoidance** of hookworms is fairly simple – don't walk barefoot in endemic areas.

Having penetrated the skin, the larvae **migrate** in a matter of days via the blood and lymphatic system to the lungs, from where they move up into the throat and are swallowed down into the intestine. Once in the gut, the worms feed on the host's blood and mature into adults of about 1cm long, and are capable of producing eggs in about five weeks; the eggs are then passed in faeces.

Symptoms

An **itchy lump** can develop over the entry site, usually on the sole of the foot and called "ground itch". Secondary bacterial infections can occur around the area.

Infection with some subgroups of hookworm (usually those affecting dogs and cats) cause **cutaneous larva migrans**, or "creeping eruption", which is an itchy, linear skin eruption caused by the erratic progress of the larvae – a red line can often be seen to advance by a few millimetres every day.

Having migrated to the **lungs**, the larvae cause minimal symptoms; an irritable cough or wheezing occur in some cases. Once in the **gut**, the worms can cause nausea, vomiting, diarrhoea (sometimes bloody) and abdominal pain. Over a few weeks or months, the blood loss caused by the anticoagulants injected by the worms to enable them to feed (which cause continued bleeding once feeding stops) can lead to significant **anaemia**, with symptoms of tiredness, dizziness and shortness of breath. The loss of protein from the gut caused by the feeding worms can lead to **oedema** (fluid accumulation in the tissues), resulting from a low protein concentration in the blood.

Diagnosis and treatment

The eggs can usually be identified by laboratory examination of a **stool sample**. If **anaemia** is confirmed by a blood test, it's important to supplement the lost iron by taking oral iron tablets. A number of different drugs can be used to eliminate the worms themselves, among them **mebendazole** (see opposite) at a dosage of 100mg twice daily for three days (this cannot be used in pregnancy – specialist advice should be sought). Iron supplements are sometimes needed to correct anaemia.

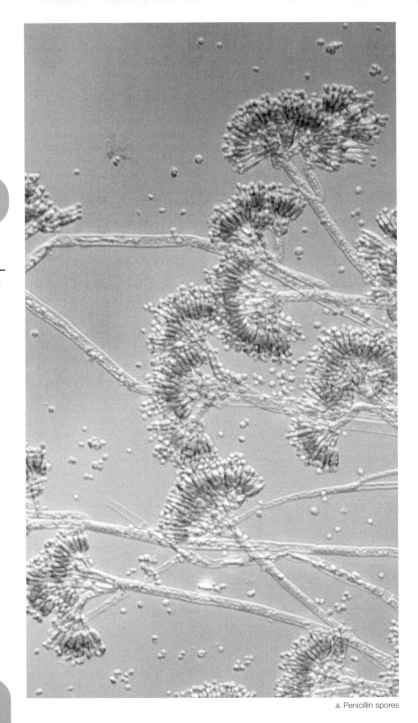

▲ Penicillin spores

Strongyloidiasis

Like hookworms, **strongyloidiasis** (known as **threadworms** in the US) is more common in the tropics and subtropics, but sporadic cases can occur in temperate climates (especially in mines). Through a complicated cycle of autoinfection, the parasite can remain in the body for many years – it's still being picked up in veterans of Vietnam and World War II.

Strongyloidiasis affects humans only, with the adult worms lodging in the small intestine. Their eggs escape in the faeces, after which the next generation of non-parasitic worms hatch in the soil within a week, mature, and produce offspring. This generation of larvae reinfect humans by direct **penetration** of the skin, usually via unshod feet. However once established in the human gut, the larvae are also able to reinfect the host by direct penetration of the intestinal mucosa or peri-anal skin. Like hookworm larvae, they make their way to the lungs before eventually settling in the gut.

Symptoms

It takes about four weeks from initial penetration for the worm to reach maturity in the gut. The vast majority of strongyloidiasis infections show no symptoms, but sometimes there is an itchy **lesion** at the point of entry and a meandering, intensely itchy **rash** occurs transiently as the larvae migrate through the skin. Occasionally **coughs** and **wheezes** occur as the larvae pass through the lungs, after which upper **abdominal pain** and **diarrhoea** can occur as the adult worms mature in the gut. There may also be **weight loss**.

Diagnosis and treatment

Larvae can be seen in the **stool** under a microscope. There are several suitable **drugs** to eradicate the worms, such as tiabendazole (25mg/kg body weight twice daily for three days) and albendazole (400mg twice daily for three days), neither of which should be taken in pregnancy.

Enterobiasis

Occurring worldwide, **enterobiasis** (**threadworms**, **pinworms** or **seat worms** in the US) are the most common of the worm infections to affect humans, and are particularly common in young children living in cool, temperate climates.

The eggs of this thread-like worm can survive for a long time outside the body, but their true home is the human gut, which they reach by the **faecal–oral route** – usually the unwashed fingers of little children handling food. They can also be transferred by bed linen, clothing, toys and the like. The adult worms survive in the gut for only six weeks and therefore ongoing enterobiasis tends to be a cyclical self-reinfection via fingernails.

Symptoms, diagnosis and treatment

Symptoms are usually mild and restricted to anal itching, most prominently at night when the female worm is laying eggs. The vagina can also be affected.

Resembling short threads of cotton, the worms and their eggs can often be seen around the anus. Mebendazole (a single 100mg dose) is the preferred **treatment** option (not recommended for pregnant women or children under 2 – seek advice from your doctor). As reinfection is common, a further dose two to three weeks later is often necessary. All members of a household should take a course of medication regardless of whether or not they are experiencing symptoms, and all clothes and bedding should be washed in tandem with the drug treatment. Regular bathing and scrubbing of fingernails (particularly first thing in the morning) is an essential element in preventing the reinfection cycle during treatment.

Ascariasis

Commonly known as **roundworms**, **ascariasis** are found worldwide but are particularly common in poor, rural communities where local faecal contamination of the soil is highest, perhaps because of agricultural methods. It's estimated that around a quarter of the world's population is affected by roundworms, with a preponderance of cases among children.

The roundworm is large (between 15 and 40cm long), and looks very like the common earthworm. It inhabits the human small **intestine**, feeding from its contents, and only rarely causing blood loss or damage to the bowel.

The mode of transmission is via the **faecal–oral route**. The worm eggs pass out of the body via the stool and can remain infective outside the body for months or even years. After eggs are swallowed (on soil-covered fingers or unwashed raw vegetables), they hatch larvae into the small intestine. The larvae migrate through the gut wall, into the bloodstream and lodge in the lungs to mature further. They then move out of the lungs into the gullet where they are swallowed, ultimately lodging themselves in the small intestine.

Symptoms

Because of the complex life cycle, it takes up to ten weeks for a worm to mature in the gut after an egg is swallowed. Often the infection is entirely without **symptoms**, although occasionally there may be a cough and shortness of breath as the larvae move through the lungs. Heavy infestation can cause nausea, vomiting, loss of appetite, crampy abdominal pain and, in extreme circumstances, an obstructed bowel which in turn leads to complications such as peritonitis and liver or pancreatic damage. In the longer term, untreated, significant worm infection can lead to **malnourishment**. Occasionally, if numerous larvae are involved, the lung phase of the disease can cause cough, wheezing, shortness of breath and fever.

Diagnosis and treatment

The eggs are usually identifiable by microscopic examination of the **stool**. Mebendazole (100mg twice daily for three days; see p.226 for restrictions) or piperazine (single dose of one 4g sachet – may need to be repeated after one month) are effective **treatments**. Piperazine should be avoided in epilepsy, pregnancy and in those with severe kidney or liver problems. It causes mainly gastrointestinal side effects (nausea, diarrhoea etc) but also occasional allergic reactions and neurological symptoms (drowsiness, vertigo, blurred vision, confusion).

Trichuriasis

Trichuriasis (**whipworms**) are found worldwide but, like ascariasis, predominate in warm, wet climates within poor communities with inadequate sanitation. The eggs are found in soil, and the infection is spread through inadequate personal hygiene or eating contaminated unwashed vegetables. Ingested eggs hatch in the small intestine, releasing larvae which embed directly into the lining of the lower gut. The maturing worms, which feed on tissue fluids rather than blood, may cause ulceration leading to significant **blood** and **protein loss** from the body. They reach maturity two to three months later, growing to lengths of up to 5cm. Their eggs are released in the stools and mature in the soil before being ingested once again.

Infection can be **prevented** by simple hygiene measures and avoiding raw fruit or vegetables that haven't been thoroughly washed. Always wash earth-soiled hands before you eat.

▶▶ See Food and drink, p.21–24.

Symptoms, diagnosis and treatment

Symptoms are uncommon and usually only apparent in children. Heavy infestation can lead to diarrhoea, which may contain blood and mucus. In cases of longstanding or heavy infestation, **anaemia** may develop.

Microscopic **stool** examination reveals the worm eggs. Mebendazole (100mg twice daily for three days; see p.226 for restrictions) is an effective **treatment** but it is probably not worth treating light infections.

Trichinosis

Cases of **trichinosis** (trichinellosis) are uncommon but have been reported throughout the world, particularly in Europe and the USA, as well as amongst the hill tribes of northern Thailand. Cysts containing the infective larvae are ingested via undercooked **contaminated meat** (usually pork). The stomach's digestive juices dissolve the cysts and release the larvae into the intestine, where they mature into adult worms and reproduce, discharging larvae into the blood. This generation of larvae form cysts in the muscles and are responsible for most of the symptoms.

The larval cysts in meat are killed by cooking all parts of the meat above 65°C, by freezing to −27°C for 36 hours, or by microwaving. They are unaffected by pickling, smoking, salting or other methods of preserving.

Symptoms

The large majority of infections show no signs of illness. **Abdominal pain** and **vomiting** may occur within 72 hours after eating the contaminated meat. The illness is not usually severe, although the **release of the larvae** into the blood circulation (between two and eight weeks after initial infection) can cause a number of symptoms: fever with rigors, conjunctivitis, sensitivity to light and swelling around the eyes, an itchy rash, diarrhoea, shortness of breath, chest pain, and muscular pain and spasm. Although rare, involvement of the heart or central nervous system can be fatal.

The symptoms gradually resolve spontaneously but the muscle pain, weakness and spasms can continue for several months.

Diagnosis and treatment

Diagnosis can usually be made from blood tests, but sometimes a muscle biopsy is required.

Pain relief, antihistamines for the itch, muscle pain and spasm and bed rest are the basis of **treatment**. Severe symptoms involving the heart or brain need medical supervision and may require high-dose steroids. Treatment against the worms themselves is only useful in the first few weeks to prevent them from multiplying and producing the migratory larvae. Tiabendazole (see strongy-loidiasis, p.229) can be used to eliminate the adult worms from the intestine (25mg per kilo of body weight, twice daily for seven days).

Tapeworms

There are three common types of **tapeworm** affecting humans, all of which are related to the worm causing hydatid disease (see p.146). **Beef tapeworm** is common in Mexico, South America, eastern Europe, the Middle East and Africa (Ethiopia has the highest infection rate in the world). **Pork tapeworm** is common in South America, Africa, Asia, eastern Europe and former Soviet Union republics. **Fish tapeworm** infection (called diphyllobothriasis) can occur worldwide but tends to be more common in Scandinavia, former Soviet Union countries, lakeland regions of Switzerland and the Far East.

The cow, pig or fish ingests the worm eggs during feeding. The eggs hatch in the gut and migrate to the muscles, forming **cysts** (similar to trichinosis; see p.231). If inadequately cooked, the cysts in the meat remain viable and mature into adult worms in the human gut, where they produce more eggs. The only migration outside the human gut takes place with pork tapeworm, when the eggs (eg from poorly washed vegetables) rather than the larval cysts in meat are eaten (see below).

Symptoms

Beef tapeworms are transmitted by eating raw, undercooked or smoked beef, and inhabit the upper gut of humans, where they can grow up to 10m long. **Symptoms**, if any, are usually mild, with vague abdominal discomfort being the most common. Occasionally diarrhoea, vomiting and weight loss can occur, while rarely more serious problems can arise as a result of the physical obstruction caused by the growing worm (eg appendicitis or liver and pancreas inflammation).

Pork tapeworm infections are much less common than beef and often go unnoticed. Symptoms, if they occur, are mild and similar to those of beef tapeworm. A more serious illness, called **human cysticercosis**, can result from swallowing the eggs of the worm (as opposed to the larvae in raw meat). This occurs either by autoinfection (the human host ingesting eggs excreted from their own gut), or by ingesting eggs in contaminated soil through inadequate handwashing. Like trichinosis (see p.231), the eggs hatch in the gut, invade the gut wall, gain access to the blood and are trans-ported to other parts of the body, where they form cysts. The effects of cys-ticercosis may not become apparent for many years – the most commonly affected parts of the body are the brain (where the cysts can cause serious complications such as fits, paralysis and behavioural changes), the eye (caus-ing local inflammation, sometimes leading to blindness) and the skin (with the formation of small, hard, pea-sized nodules).

Fish tapeworm infection results from eating raw freshwater fish, and usual-ly causes only mild symptoms similar to those caused by beef and pork tape-worms. Because the worm interferes with the body's absorption of vitamin B12, a condition known as **pernicious anaemia** (caused by B12 deficiency) can develop, with symptoms similar to that of ordinary anaemia: tiredness, lethargy and easy fatigability.

Diagnosis and treatment

Segments of **beef and pork tapeworms** are often visible to the naked eye in the stool, although microscopic examination of the stools will confirm the presence of eggs. Biopsy of skin nodules, x-rays and blood tests can all help to diagnose cysticercosis caused by pork tapeworm. Eggs of the **fish tapeworm** can usually be found by microscopic examination of the stool.

Niclosamide (single dose of 2g for beef and fish tapeworms, 2g per day for seven days for pork tapeworms) is effective against the gut stage of all tapeworm infections, although the drug's side effects include nausea, vomiting, abdominal pain, itching and lightheadedness. A dose of niclosamide is usually followed by a strong laxative to expel the worms from the gut. Praziquantel is an alternative.

Yellow fever

The WHO estimate that around 200,000 cases of **yellow fever** occur worldwide each year, resulting in 30,000 deaths. Ninety-one percent of reported cases occur in Africa, although the disease is also endemic in South and Central America. Hotspots of the illness are between the latitudes 15° north and 15° south of the equator, with recent epidemics in Senegal, Liberia, Ghana, Benin, Cameroon, Gabon and Kenya. In South America, the majority of cases occur in the Amazon region. Yellow fever is principally a disease of tropical, forested areas but sporadic urban outbreaks do occur.

The virus causing yellow fever is related to dengue fever and Japanese encephalitis. Its natural host is the monkey but it is spread to humans by **mosquitoes**. The disease can reach epidemic proportions in a relatively short space of time and the past twenty years have seen a rise in the number of reported epidemics and the countries affected. Urban outbreaks can be dealt with successfully by public health measures, including insecticide fogging to kill the adult mosquitoes and the elimination of breeding sites such as water butts.

Symptoms

Symptoms appear after an incubation period of three to six days, but are often mild, self-limiting and unrecognizable as yellow fever. The **classical picture of yellow fever** is of a severe illness with an initial sudden high fever and disabling weakness and lethargy, accompanied by headache, generalized muscle pains, abdominal pain and vomiting. A relatively slow pulse rate may be present from the second day of the illness. The majority of those affected will improve over a period of about a week and the symptoms will disappear without treatment. However, around fifteen percent of infected people will develop a second and **more dangerous phase** of the illness after a lull of a day or two. The vomiting returns, together with jaundice (thus the name), a reduced urine output (a sign of failing kidneys), convulsions, signs of bleeding (nosebleeds, bruising under the skin, bleeding gums etc) and shock. The fatality rate is high in those with complications (up to fifty percent), and usually occurs as a result of liver or kidney failure.

Diagnosis and treatment

Blood tests can identify the virus itself in the early stages, or antibodies to the virus later on.

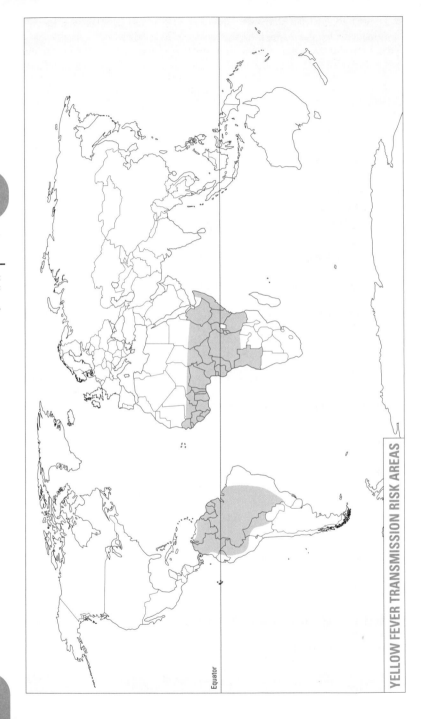

YELLOW FEVER TRANSMISSION RISK AREAS

Equator

There is no specific **treatment** other than life support, symptomatic measures and nursing care. The majority of those infected will recover spontaneously with no long-term effects. Given that the illness is potentially fatal and the vaccine produces a high level of immunity, it would be very unwise to enter a yellow fever zone without being immunized. If you've visited an area where yellow fever is endemic, a **vaccination** (and consequent certification) may be compulsory for entry into some countries; for more information, visit the CDC website (see p.249).

3

First aid

First aid

Equipping yourself with some basic knowledge of **first aid** is essentially preparing yourself for the unexpected, but it's a necessary skill as there's no way of knowing whether you'll need to put such skills to the test whilst away. If you do find yourself in an emergency situation that requires first aid, the first step to take is to call for properly trained **help**. The instructions on the next few pages should be regarded as **urgent temporary measures** while you wait for medical help to arrive.

A book can provide only basic guidelines, and there is no substitute for the hands-on experience of a **first-aid course** before you leave, especially if you're planning outdoor pursuits or you are going to be a long way from medical help for any period.

Unconsciousness

▶▶ See also Fainting and shock, p.242.

Before diving in with a heroic flurry of resuscitation, it's worth remembering that the majority of unrousable people have simply fainted. Look for clues as to why the person may be **unconscious**:

✚ Signs of trauma, eg head injury, electric shock, snake or insect bite etc.

✚ Medicalert bracelets or medallions worn by diabetics, epileptics etc.

✚ Signs of illness such as high fever, meningitis or convulsions.

✚ Signs of drug or alcohol use (opiate overdose is a common cause of respiratory arrest).

Once you're satisfied that there is no personal danger, shake or call to the victim to see if you are able to rouse them. If not, you'll need to check the casualty's **a**irway, **b**reathing and **c**irculation (**ABC**).

Check the casualty's **airway** is not blocked (eg by dentures or their tongue). Look for signs of obstruction or a bluish tinge to the skin indicative of oxygen starvation (cyanosis). You may need to physically clear the obstruction from the mouth or throat. If the patient is lying on their back, then holding their jaw forward and tilting their head backwards will clear their airway, but if you suspect a neck injury, avoid the head tilt and simply support their jaw forward. Once you are happy that there is nothing preventing air from reaching their lungs, check for **breathing** by watching for chest movement and listening to or feeling for inhaled breath from their mouth (if they're not breathing you will need to give mouth-to-mouth resuscitation – see opposite). Check the casualty's **circulation** by feeling for a pulse. The easiest place to feel for a **pulse** is 2–3cm on either side of the windpipe (in women, feel for the notch halfway down the neck; in men, feel just to the side of the Adam's apple). Do not feel both sides together or else you may restrict the blood flow to the brain. If no pulse is felt you will need to start cardiac massage (**CPR**); see opposite.

Once you're satisfied the patient's airway is clear and their breathing and circulation are normal, put them in the **recovery position** (see opposite) and stay with them until they regain consciousness. If after five minutes they show no signs of recovery, reassess and call for help.

Cardiopulmonary resuscitation

Cardiopulmonary resuscitation, or **CPR**, is a temporary measure to maintain oxygen flow to the brain (avoiding brain damage) until medical help arrives. *Never* practise these procedures on anyone whose heart is beating or who is breathing spontaneously.

If the casualty shows no signs of breathing or circulation, roll them on their back and **call for help**. It is usually necessary to perform **mouth-to-mouth resuscitation** and cardiac massage consecutively, and although this is possible to do on your own, it's much easier with two people. To perform mouth-to-mouth resuscitation, first tilt the head backwards. Use one hand to support the jaw and maintain the airway, and with the other squeeze the nostrils to prevent air leaking when you breathe into the mouth. Take a normal breath and blow firmly (not too hard) and steadily into the casualty's mouth while forming an airtight seal with your lips. Watch for the rise and fall in the patient's chest to ensure that the air is reaching their lungs. You should aim for approximately **ten breaths a minute**. If the patient's mouth or jaw is damaged, it is also possible to give mouth to nose ventilation.

To perform **CPR**, kneel beside the casualty and place the heel of your left hand on the lower third of their breastbone (sternum). Cover this hand with the heel of your other hand and lock your fingers together. Lean over the patient, with your shoulders positioned directly over their breastbone. With straight arms, depress the sternum about 4–5cm with each movement before releasing the pressure (don't remove your hands). Try to achieve a steady swaying rhythm. If you press too hard, you risk breaking their ribs; press too softly and you won't maintain circulation. Give **fifteen compressions before two breaths of mouth-to-mouth ventilation**, as a recurring cycle, aiming at a rate of sixty compressions a minute. If the patient is showing signs of recovery, check their ABC again (see opposite). Keep going until help arrives.

The recovery position

The casualty who is unconscious but breathing and maintaining circulation should be put in the **recovery position**. This protects their airway and prevents them from choking in the event of vomiting.

Before manipulating a casualty into the recovery position, consider the possibility of neck or spinal injury. If such an injury is suspected, do not attempt to move the casualty. Holding the jaw forward to maintain the airway is a better option until help arrives.

If spinal injury is not suspected, the procedure is a follows: kneeling beside the patient, who should be lying on his or her back, place the hand of the patient that's nearest you palm upwards under the thigh nearest to you (this will

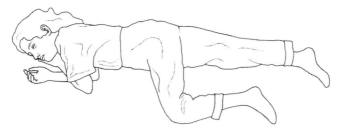

▲ The recovery position

act as a pivot for rotation). Bring their far hand across their chest and hold it palm outwards against their near cheek as you draw the thigh furthest from you towards you, bending the leg at the knee. This has the effect of rotating the patient towards you. Tilt their head backwards to maintain the airway and bend the knee that was previously furthest from you (now the top leg) to an angle of 90° to stabilize the position.

Head injury

If the casualty is unconscious, follow the recommendations above under "Unconsciousness". Before placing them in the recovery position, remember that if someone has suffered a head injury and is unconscious, it is possible that their **neck** may also have been injured (see below).

Caused by the shock of a blow shaking the brain inside the skull, **concussion** can occur with or without a period of unconsciousness and the signs are confusion, bewilderment, nausea, vomiting and short-term memory loss. Concussion may last for a few hours, but is usually followed by complete recovery. However, any head injury must be closely observed for signs of deterioration over the subsequent 24 hours.

In any of the following situations, seek urgent medical help:

✚ If the casualty is unconscious after the initial injury or lapses into delayed unconsciousness.

✚ If blood or blood-stained fluid runs from their nose or ears.

✚ If double vision or speech difficulties become apparent after the first five minutes.

✚ If the patient continues to vomit after the first two hours (vomiting is not uncommon within the first two hours, especially in children).

✚ If the casualty becomes confused or disoriented after having apparently recovered from the initial trauma.

✚ If any weakness or numbness occurs.

✚ If convulsions (fits) occur.

✚ If the pupils become unequal, breathing becomes noisy, body temperature rises or the pulse becomes abnormally slow.

✚ If a fractured skull is suspected.

Neck and spinal injuries

A **neck or spinal injury** should be suspected in anyone who has fallen awkwardly or from a height. If conscious, sufferers may complain of numbness, pins and needles, or the inability to move.

Don't move the casualty unless you absolutely have to; it's imperative that their neck and spine are not bent or twisted. You will need to enlist several helpers and plan carefully before attempting to move them, and should do so only if it's absolutely necessary.

Support their head and neck in the so-called "neutral position" (looking straight ahead), and use clothing or towels as splinting support for their head and neck. If the casualty is unconscious, their airway can be protected by lifting and supporting their jaw. Only attempt to turn the casualty once you are confident of keeping their neck and spine aligned.

Do not attempt to move the casualty unless they are in immediate danger. Check their pulse and more generally for other signs of shock (fracture of a large bone like the femur or pelvis can result in significant blood loss). If a limb is affected, **support and cushion the area**, taking care to keep the bone in a fixed position to avoid further damage. Only attempt to move the casualty when you are confident the fracture is sufficiently immobilized.

For open, or compound, fractures, cover the area with a sterile dressing to minimize the risk of infection. These types of injuries need urgent medical attention.

Broken bones

Sometimes the diagnosis of **broken bones** (fractures) is obvious, with visible deformity, or even bones protruding through the skin (known as a **compound fracture**). More often than not, however, the damage is less easy to assess. Sometimes the casualty will report hearing or feeling a crack, but breakage symptoms such as pain, bruising, swelling and loss of limb function can also occur with soft-tissue injuries (see below). Injuries to the surrounding structures, such as blood vessels and nerves, need to be assessed alongside damage to the bone itself. Check for pulses beyond the suspected fracture on the limbs.

If a fracture is suspected, always seek **medical advice**. The **diagnosis** and the further **treatment** of a broken bone is dependent on x-ray findings and a thorough examination.

Soft-tissue injuries

Soft-tissue injuries are those affecting muscles, tendons and ligaments. Bruising follows damage to the blood vessels in the skin and underlying tissues, usually as a result of direct trauma; the leakage of blood causes pain, swelling and discolouration.

In **treating** a soft-tissue injury, your main aims are firstly to exclude an obvious fracture, and then limit the swelling and relieve the associated pain. Raise and support the affected area and apply ice or a cold compress as soon as possible. For **pain relief**, take paracetamol or ibuprofen as required. Bruising may be a sign of underlying bone damage, and if this is suspected, you will need an x-ray.

A range of homeopathic remedies can be used to treat soft-tissue injuries. **Arnica** is great in cases of overexertion, such as walking too far or carrying a heavy pack, when muscles feel sore and bruised, and for surface bruising (take one 30c tablet every four hours, for one or two days). Arnica ointment is also widely available and is an excellent treatment for bruising – don't apply it to broken skin, as it can cause a rash. In addition to Arnica tablets, taking **Rhus tox** 30c at the end of the day for the first few days will help to relieve stiffness after overexertion – typically you'll benefit from this remedy if you feel very stiff when getting up in the morning but loosen up as you go going. Rhus tox is also excellent for muscle injuries, while **Ruta grav** is helpful in tendon and ligament injuries; take both in a 30c potency, four times a day. **Hypericum** (dosage as for Arnica) is the best remedy for jolting of the spine – backache after horse or camel riding, bumpy journeys and the like. A **combined ointment** containing Arnica, Rhus tox and Ruta grav is particularly useful on any activity holiday, while **cabbage** or **dark lettuce** leaves applied to local inflammations can be soothing and reduce redness and swelling – hold them in place with a sock, scarf or elasticated bandage.

Sprains

Sprains usually describe a strained or **overstretched** muscle, tendon or ligament, and are a frequent problem among travellers carrying heavy luggage. Ankles, wrists, knees, the groin, the back and the neck are the most commonly affected areas – sprains can result from a definite injury or may creep up insidiously. The main **symptoms** are pain that tends to be dull or throbbing and worse on movement, as well as local swelling and, occasionally, bruising. Rest, followed by gentle mobilization, is the best **treatment**, while ice or cold compresses will help to relieve pain. If possible, raise the affected area to reduce swelling. **NSAIDs** (ibuprofen etc) may be used to reduce inflammation and for pain relief (see p.33). Sprained ligaments can take up to two weeks to heal, and a previously injured ligament is likely to be weakened and therefore easily sprained again. Elasticated bandages can help as a physical support.

 Rhus tox is a good homeopathic remedy for sprains and torn ligaments – take a 30c tablet four times a day until improvement.

Choking

Choking is caused by an object lodging itself in the windpipe and obstructing the airway. The person affected experiences sudden difficulty in breathing, is unable to talk and becomes red in the face. Prompt action is needed to prevent them from suffocating. Sometimes it is enough to bend the casualty forwards and slap them sharply between their shoulder blades – children can literally be tipped upside down. If this fails, then perform the **Heimlich manoeuvre**: stand behind the casualty and place your right fist in the solar plexus (the top part of the abdomen in the inverted "V" of the ribs). With your other hand, grasp your fist and sharply thrust inwards and upwards five times. This should be enough to dislodge the blockage from the windpipe but if it fails first time, repeat the procedure or, with help, tip the casualty upside down holding them by the legs, and let gravity do the work.

Fainting and shock

Fainting is caused by a sudden, transient drop in blood pressure, usually brought about by stress, emotion, fear, pain or overheating. If suspected, check the sufferer's airway and breathing, loosen tight clothing and raise their legs. The blood pressure drop is transient, and recovery is usually quick.

Shock, in the medical sense, also occurs when there is a significant drop in blood pressure, and is dangerous in that the drop can impair blood supply to vital organs such as the brain and heart. Common causes are blood loss, septicaemia, heart failure, severe vomiting or diarrhoea, anaphylaxis and burns. The **signs** of shock are feeling faint or loss of consciousness; pale, cold, clammy skin; nausea; a rapid, weak pulse; and involuntary shaking. If shock is suspected, call for help and try to **treat** the underlying cause if it is obvious. Maximize the blood pressure to the brain by lying the casualty down and raising the legs. Keep the casualty warm by covering their body with a blanket. Closely monitor their airway, breathing and pulse rate, and start CPR if necessary.

Fits

The steps below should enable you to safely assist someone who's having a fit:

➕ Stay calm.

➕ Loosen any clothing from around the casualty's neck and, if possible, roll them onto their side or into the recovery position to protect the airway. Otherwise, do not attempt to move someone who is fitting unless they are in immediate danger.

➕ Move potentially hazardous objects away from the casualty.

➕ Do not attempt to restrain the casualty and do not attempt to force open their mouth.

➕ Cushion the head and, as the fitting subsides, keep their airway clear by placing them in the recovery position, if you were unable to do so earlier.

➕ Stay with the casualty until the fitting stops.

➕ Most fits are self-limiting and over by the time help arrives, but if the fit continues for more than five minutes, call for medical help or use rectal diazepam if it's available.

Bleeding

In most wounds, **bleeding** comes from tiny capillary **vessels** which link the arterial system (carrying blood away from the heart) to the venous system (carrying blood towards the heart). The blood tends to ooze and loss is self-limiting. Bleeding from a **vein** tends to flow, the blood is darker and loss can be significant but is rarely life-threatening (depending on the size of the vein). **Arterial bleeding** is the most dangerous and even if a relatively small artery is damaged, blood loss can be serious. The blood in an artery is pumped at high pressure and tends to spurt in pulses with each contraction of the heart.

When someone is losing blood:

➕ Lie them down and assess the degree of bleeding. If significant, call for help immediately.

➕ If you have gloves or other means of protecting yourself from direct blood contact, use them.

➕ If there is an obvious foreign body in the wound, do not try and remove it because it might be acting as a plug, and removal will cause further bleeding.

➕ Apply direct pressure to the wound site, preferably using sterile gauze or a dressing of some kind. Apply pressure to either side of a wound with a foreign body in it.

➕ If the wound is to a limb, raise and support it above the level of the heart. This reduces the blood pressure at the wound site and aids the body's clotting system. In an emergency, when blood loss from a limb wound is severe, applying pressure to the arterial pressure points at the groin or elbow may slow down the blood loss. Tourniquets should be avoided unless the situation is life-threatening. If required, apply the tourniquet as close to the wound as possible and tighten using a twisting motion – you must loosen the tourniquet every twenty minutes to allow blood flow to the limb beyond and to assess whether it's still needed.

➕ Once the bleeding has settled, clean the wound using antiseptic, apply a sterile dressing and, if possible, keep the limb raised.

➕ Seek help if bleeding continues, if the casualty becomes shocked or if a foreign body is present in the wound.

Bleeding from a **head injury** tends to be heavy, even if the wound is relatively small, because of the copious network of blood vessels covering the scalp. If the casualty is conscious and lucid, sit them down (don't lie them down) and apply direct pressure to the wound (do not apply pressure if a skull fracture is suspected). An ice pack or anything cold applied to the wound site may slow the bleeding. If bleeding continues unabated, it may be necessary to **suture** the wound – you'll need to seek medical help for this. Tape, sticking plaster or, better still, Steristrips may be used as a temporary means of drawing the wound together. Do not attempt to suture a dirty wound, one that has been caused by a bite or any wound in which foreign material is visible but cannot be removed.

It's difficult to give specific advice for **superficial cuts and lacerations** because much depends on the nature and situation of the injury. Here are a few guidelines.

✚ Ensure that your tetanus cover is up to date. A booster currently lasts for ten years, although for dirty wounds or high-risk situations, a further booster may be necessary; seek medical advice.

✚ Cuts and abrasions in tropical climates, those which involve foreign bodies (splinters, coral), as well as deep, penetrating injuries and bites (cats and humans in particular) are more likely to become infected. Cleanse the wound thoroughly as soon as possible using lots of clean water or weak antiseptic solution. Alcohol can be used in emergencies. If foreign material is evident in the wound, try to remove it (unless it is large and preventing heavier bleeding) prior to dressing because it will otherwise act as a focus for infection. Cover the wound with a sterile dressing and watch for signs of infection (see p.201). In cases of deep, penetrating wounds, a prophylactic course of antibiotics – flucloxacillin, co-amoxiclav, amoxicillin or erythromycin (see pp.31–37) – will be necessary.

✚ For animal bites, consider the possibility of rabies (see p.182) and, if in doubt, seek urgent medical advice.

▲ First aid station, Cheyenne Rodeo

Calendula, widely available as a cream, ointment, tincture, tea and oil, is an excellent natural antiseptic which heals cuts and grazes, soothes chafing, and helps eczema, nappy (diaper) rash and the like. Use the tincture or lotion (both

of which can be diluted in clean water) or the cream externally as a dressing on wounds, infections, ulcers and septic bites. Avoid calendula for deep or penetrating wounds, as it tends to heal things over quickly and could "seal" infection into the wound. However, used in combination with **hypericum tincture** or **lotion**, its action is retarded slightly, making it more suitable for deep or dirty wounds. A homeopathic remedy of **Hypericum** is useful for injuries to areas rich in nerves – fingers, toes, lips, tongue, genitals. It's ideal after cutting the sole of your foot or tip of your finger, after dental work where nerve pain remains, or after falling over and putting your teeth through your lip. It's also good for what used to be called "railway spine" – the effects of a very jolting journey – or after landing on your tailbone in a fall. It can also help stave off sciatica and neuralgia. Characteristically, pains are sharp and electric, and extend along nerve pathways from the site of the injury. Start with a 30c taken hourly for three or four hours, and then twice a day for a couple more days, as needed.

Nosebleeds

Nosebleeds affecting young, fit people usually come from a part of the nose with a high concentration of blood vessels, located at the front and called Little's Area. The cause is usually direct trauma or nasal congestion after a cold. The dry air at high altitude also desiccates the nasal lining, which often leads to bleeding. Older people can suffer from heavier bleeds from the large blood vessels at the back of the nose – "posterior bleeds" – and these are more difficult to control.

Bleeding from Little's Area is usually identifiable as dripping or a steady flow from one nostril. The bleeding is usually light and easily quelled by direct pressure over the area for five to ten minutes. Applying pressure over the lower part of the nose compresses the offending vessel against the nasal septum and stems the blood flow. Pressure over the upper, bony part (bridge) of the nose is totally ineffective, although an ice pack over the bridge causes contraction of the vessels and may reduce or stop bleeding. Bleeding from Little's Area often recurs, and if frequent nosebleeds are a problem, it may be worth having the area cauterized by a doctor.

Bleeding from the back of the nose is rare in young people. Blood flows heavily, or even gushes, from one or both nostrils. This type of bleed is difficult to stop. Don't underestimate these posterior nosebleeds – fatalities can occur through blood loss. Furthermore, without the right equipment, they can be difficult to treat and may need referral to a hospital with a specialist department. In the meantime, keep calm, sit forward and apply pressure to the front of the nose and ice packs to the bridge (some blood will be swallowed but the

flow will be slowed). Watch for signs of shock (see p.242). Bed rest is recommended for 24 to 48 hours after a posterior bleed.

Homeopathically, **Phosphorus** 30c, taken half-hourly, will help to stop both types of nosebleed.

Burns

From a medical perspective, **burns** are divided into superficial (first degree), partial thickness (second degree) and full thickness (third degree), depending

+ Cool the burn as quickly as possible under cold running water. This reduces pain and swelling and minimizes tissue damage; if the burn is caused by contact with a chemical, the water washes the substance away. In the case of chemical burns, remove contaminated clothing promptly (though note that with severe non-chemical burns, clothing should not be removed if it's stuck to the skin).

+ Assess the severity and extent of the burns. Smoke inhalation and toxic fumes can lead to respiratory failure, so check the casualty's airway, breathing and circulation (see p.238). Resuscitate, treat shock (see p.242), and call for help as necessary.

+ Cover the burn with a sterile dressing. Infection is a real danger because the body's main defence – the skin – has been compromised. Do not use lotions or ointments on the affected area and do not dress with fluffy dressings – a clean polythene bag or kitchen film can be used instead.

+ Burns can be very painful, so always give the casualty adequate pain relief. Calamine lotion may be soothing for superficial burns.

+ Do not burst blisters; allow them to heal by themselves.

+ Antibiotics (flucloxacillin, co-amoxiclav or erythromycin) may be required to stave off infection.

on the depth of the tissue layers affected. **Superficial burns** affect only the outer skin layer. Pain, swelling and redness occur, but with prompt and adequate treatment the burn will heal within a few days without scarring. **Partial thickness burns** result in the formation of blisters, which, when extensive, may result in shock and a loss of blood plasma. Small areas of partial-thickness burns, however, respond well to first-aid measures, and scarring is rare.

Full-thickness burns affect all layers of the skin and sometimes the tissues underneath. The burn may be pale or charred and hard to the touch. Full-thickness burns may be painless because of damage to the nerves. Urgent medical assessment is required, and scarring is likely.

Drowning

Drowning occurs when the lungs are flooded with water, leading to asphyxiation and subsequent respiratory and cardiac arrest. In the event, it is important to check the victim's ABC (see p.238) and start resuscitation as soon as possible, even before you're out of the water.

Resuscitation has been successful with people who, having been pulled from the water, show no initial signs of life. This is because cold water slows the body's metabolic rate, prolonging survival. The effect is particularly pronounced in children. For this reason, you should continue resuscitation for up to 45 minutes after a drowning accident even if initial signs are pessimistic.

Once the casualty starts to breathe again, they should be placed in the recovery position (see p.239). Even after apparently successful resuscitation, the lungs may become swollen and cause delayed breathing difficulties. Remember that **hypothermia** (see p.105) is also a real danger. Medical assessment after a near-drowning is therefore important.

4

Where in
the world

"**Risk**" is a difficult concept to quantify in terms of travel health, as there are so many variables. You are obviously less likely to come into contact with infectious diseases if you stay in hermetically sealed five-star hotels and spend your days lounging by the pool than if you're backpacking on a tight budget off the beaten track, coming into close contact with local people. However, remember that it only takes one infected mosquito bite to give you malaria and one bad prawn to contract dysentery.

The purpose of this section is to provide some guidance on the kinds of health risks you may encounter at your destination. It's important to recognize, however, that the nature of disease, and of disease spread, mean that this kind of information can never be concrete. Every effort has been made to ensure the text is up to date at the time of writing, but **things change** – sometimes quite rapidly – in response to extremes of climate, political unrest or epidemic outbreaks (and if an outbreak occurs in one country, there's always a chance that it could erupt within its neighbours, even in places where it's never been reported before). Additionally, the way in which you travel, the food you eat, the degree to which you come into contact with the indigenous population and the regions you visit within a country all help to determine how likely you are to get ill. Because of these factors, the advice in this section is deliberately generalized, and should be treated as a **guideline only**, to be used in conjunction with the websites listed in the box opposite as well as advice from your doctor or travel clinic.

For the sake of simplicity, we've divided the world into **nine geographically related groups**: Africa; Australia and the South Pacific; Eastern Europe and the former Soviet Union; the Far East; the Indian subcontinent; the Middle East; North America; Central America and the Caribbean; South America; and Western Europe. Large and medically complex areas such as Africa have been further subdivided. For each group (or subsection thereof), there's a fairly broad introduction detailing the most serious disease risks of the area, followed by a table detailing **suggested travellers' vaccinations**; keys in these indicate the following:

M = **mandatory**
R = **recommended**
C = **recommended under certain circumstances**

For most diseases, "certain circumstances" refers to individualized risks such as occupation, length of stay, level of contact with local people, possibility of disease epidemic and high-risk activities such as unsafe sex, freshwater swimming or venturing well off the beaten track – you'll need to decide if any of these apply to you or your destination. In the case of **yellow fever**, we've used the categories slightly differently: there's a "C" rating for countries that require proof of immunization from travellers entering from infected or endemic areas; an "R" rating for countries where immunization is not an obligatory condition of entry but where travellers are at risk of contracting the disease; and an "M" rating for countries where immunization is a mandatory entry requirement. The yellow fever entries in the tables are merely a summary of the county-by-country vaccination requirements that appear in each of the regional sections, and should be used in conjunction with this text. Lastly, there's a **list of other diseases** and conditions that are present in the area, some of which may be quite rare. To find the current extent of infection in the country you're travelling to, check the websites listed in the box opposite, or ask your doctor or travel clinic.

Internet resources

For up-to-date advice on health risks in your destination:
- ⓦ**www.fitfortravel.scot.nhs.uk**
- ⓦ**www.tripprep.com**
- ⓦ**www.mdtravelhealth.com**

For advice on whether or not it's safe to travel to certain areas in terms of war, terrorist threat etc:
- ⓦ**www.fco.gov.uk**
- ⓦ**travel.state.gov**
- ⓦ**www.dfat.goc.au**

For the latest disease outbreak news, particularly useful for information on epidemics of infectious diseases such as malaria, yellow fever, meningitis, dengue fever and cholera:
- ⓦ**www.who.int/csr/don/en**

All travellers, particularly those visiting rural areas or on long trips to developing countries, should ensure that **normal childhood vaccinations are up to date** (particularly polio, tetanus and diphtheria), and check their BCG (TB) status; as protection against these diseases is necessary worldwide, they have not been included in the immunization tables.

Africa

Of all the continents, Africa is perhaps the one that presents the most health hazards to the traveller. **Malaria**, **yellow fever**, **schistosomiasis**, **meningitis** and **African trypanosomiasis** are common, particularly in West, Central and East Africa. **HIV** infection and AIDS are rising to alarming levels; as with **sexually transmitted diseases** and **hepatitis B**, infection rates in sub-Saharan countries are among the highest in the world. Note also that health risks are usually highest in countries where there has been recent political unrest and fighting, leading to a breakdown in immunization campaigns and public health measures; it's a good idea to check the latest situation before you travel (see the box above).

To avoid using local equipment should you require a blood transfusion, carry a sterilized pack of syringes, needles, drip sets and the like. **Blood products** in many countries in Africa may be insufficiently screened for diseases; for details of the Blood Care Foundation, which sends screened blood worldwide, see p.98. As the heat can cause **wounds** to become infected quickly, all abrasions need to be cleansed and dressed with particular care. In rural Africa, general hazards include **snakes** and **scorpions**, while **sandstorms** can make walking and driving treacherous. In some areas, the dry and dusty climate can increase the risk of **respiratory problems** in susceptible individuals. Epidemics of **dengue fever** are common throughout Africa (particularly in Central African countries), and can affect large numbers of people; for details of current outbreaks, visit the WHO website (see the box on p.249). Finally, note that although certification of immunization against **cholera** is no longer an international requirement, you may be asked for it at remote border outposts in some West, Central and East African countries; for more on this, see Part 1 (p.8).

North Africa

Algeria, Egypt, Libya, Morocco, Tunisia

The type and extent of diseases found in North Africa differ from the rest of the continent, mainly because of the geographical separation provided by the Sahara desert. **Malaria risk** is generally very low, so **prophylaxis** is rarely recommended; when it is required, chloroquine alone is usually adequate (get the latest info from the websites listed on p.249, or from your doctor or travel clinic). Areas of low or sporadic localized risk are Ihrir in the Illizi department of **Algeria**; El Faiyum in **Egypt** (June–Oct); southwest **Libya** (Feb–Aug); and eastern **Morocco** (May–Oct).

Although **yellow fever** does not occur in the region, an international **certificate of immunization** against the disease is mandatory for anyone over 1 year old travelling from an infected area to Algeria, Libya, Egypt or Tunisia. **Influenza** outbreaks in North Africa tend to occur seasonally (Nov–April); for details of current outbreaks, visit the websites on p.249 or ask your doctor or travel clinic. See Influenza in Part 1 for some background on influenza vaccinations.

North Africa: vaccinations and malaria prophylaxis

	Algeria	Egypt	Libya	Morocco	Tunisia
Hepatitis A	R	R	R	R	R
Hepatitis B	C	C	C	C	C
Malaria	C	C	C	C	–
Rabies	C	C	C	C	C
Tuberculosis	C	C	C	C	C
Typhoid	R	R	R	R	R
Yellow fever	C	C	C	–	C

Other possible risks

- Cholera
- Filariasis
- Gastrointestinal illness
- Giardiasis
- Hydatid disease
- Intestinal worm infections
- Leishmaniasis (cutaneous)
- Onchocerciasis
- Plague

- Relapsing fever
- Rift Valley fever
- Sandfly fever
- Schistosomiasis
- Trachoma
- Tungiasis
- Typhus
- West Nile fever

West Africa

Benin, Burkina Faso, Cape Verde Islands, Côte d'Ivoire, Gambia, Ghana, Guinea Republic, Guinea-Bissau, Liberia, Mali, Mauritania, Niger, Nigeria, São Tome and Principe, Senegal, Sierra Leone, Togo

Chloroquine-resistant **falciparum malaria** exists throughout the year in all the above countries except Mauritania, where chloroquine resistance remains scarce (hence recommended prophylaxis here is a combination of chloroquine and proguanil), and in the Cape Verde Islands, where risk is seasonal (roughly Sept–Nov) on São Tiago Island only, and where prophylaxis is not normally needed. For all other countries listed above, the recommended **prophylaxis** options are mefloquine, doxycycline or malarone. The table on p.252 indicates the countries where prophylaxis may be necessary. For up-to-date advice on malaria risk in the region, check the websites listed on p.249 or ask your doctor or travel clinic.

Although not always active, **yellow fever** poses a significant risk in rural areas. **Immunization and certification** requirements are as follows: for all travellers entering Ghana; for all travellers over 1 entering Benin, Burkina Faso, Côte d'Ivoire, Liberia, Mali, Mauritania, Niger, São Tome and Principe, and Togo; for all travellers from infected or endemic areas entering Guinea Bissau; for all travellers from endemic areas entering Senegal; for all travellers from infected areas entering Sierra Leone; and for all those over 1 year old travelling from infected areas to Cape Verde Islands, Gambia, Guinea Republic and Nigeria. Note that in Mauritania, vaccination is not required from those travelling from uninfected areas and staying less than two weeks.

Meningitis occurs seasonally in West Africa; risks tend to be greatest during the following months: Oct–April in Mali; Sept–May in Burkina Faso, Côte d'Ivoire, Ghana, Mauritania, Nigeria and Togo; Oct–June in Senegal; Nov–May in Benin and Niger; Nov–June in Gambia and Guinea Republic; Dec–April in Sierra Leone; Dec–May in Guinea-Bissau; Jan–April in Liberia; May–Sept in São Tome and Principe. Bear in mind that these guidelines are by no means concrete; for the latest information on current outbreaks, visit the websites listed on p.249 or ask your doctor or travel clinic. The table on p.252 details countries where vaccination may be advisable.

Influenza risk isn't seasonal in West Africa, so outbreaks can occur at any time of the year; for details of current patterns, visit the websites on p.249 or ask your doctor or travel clinic. See Influenza in Part 1 for some background on influenza vaccinations.

West Africa: vaccinations and malaria prophylaxis

	Benin	Burkina Faso	Cape Verde Islands	Côte d'Ivoire	Gambia	Ghana	Guinea-Bissau	Guinea Republic	Liberia	Mali	Mauritania	Niger	Nigeria	São Tomé & Principe	Senegal	Sierra Leone	Togo
Hepatitis A	R	R	R	R	R	R	R	R	R	R	R	R	R	R	R	R	R
Hepatitis B	C	C	C	C	C	C	C	C	C	C	C	C	C	C	C	C	C
Malaria	R	R	C	R	R	R	R	R	R	R	R	R	R	R	R	R	R
Meningitis	C	C	-	C	C	C	C	C	C	C	C	C	C	C	C	C	C
Rabies	C	C	C	C	C	C	C	C	C	C	C	C	C	C	C	C	C
Tuberculosis	C	C	C	C	C	C	C	C	C	C	C	C	C	C	C	C	C
Typhoid	R	R	R	R	R	R	R	R	R	R	R	R	R	R	R	R	R
Yellow fever	M*	M*	C	M*	C	M	C	C	M*	M*	M*	M*	C	M*	C	C	M*

M* = mandatory only for travellers over 1 year old; see p.251 for details.

Other possible risks

+ African trypanosomiasis
+ Anthrax
+ Buruli ulcer
+ Chikungunya fever
+ Crimean-Congo haemorrhagic fever
+ Dracunculiasis
+ Ebola virus
+ Gastrointestinal illness
+ Giardiasis
+ Hepatitis E
+ Hydatid disease
+ Lassa fever
+ Leishmaniasis (cutaneous and visceral)
+ Leptospirosis
+ Loiasis
+ Lymphatic filariasis
+ Marburg virus
+ Mycetoma
+ Myiasis
+ O'nyong nyong virus
+ Onchocerciasis
+ Paragonimiasis
+ Plague
+ Relapsing fever
+ Rift Valley fever
+ Schistosomiasis
+ Trachoma
+ Tropical sprue
+ Tungiasis
+ Typhus
+ Worm infections

Central Africa

Angola, Cameroon, Central African Republic, Chad, Congo, Democratic Republic of the Congo (Zaire), Equatorial Guinea, Gabon, Sudan, Zambia

There is a high risk of chloroquine-resistant falciparum **malaria** throughout the year in all the countries above. Mefloquine, doxycycline or malarone are the recommended **prophylaxis** options; the table below details countries where prophylaxis may be necessary. For the latest information on malaria in the region, see the websites listed on p.249, or ask your doctor or travel clinic.

Yellow fever immunization and certification requirements are as follows: for all travellers over 1 year old entering Cameroon, the Central African Republic, the Congo, the Democratic Republic of Congo and Gabon; and for all those travelling from an infected area into Angola, Chad, Equatorial Guinea and Sudan. Although a yellow fever vaccination certificate is not required for entry into Zambia, outbreaks do occur in the country so vaccination is recommended.

Meningitis occurs seasonally in Central Africa; risks tend to be greatest during the following months: May–Sep in the Gabon and the Congo; May–Oct in southern Democratic Republic of Congo; May–Nov in Angola and Zambia; Oct–May in Central African Republic and Chad; Oct–June in Cameroon; Nov–July in Sudan; Dec–March in northern Democratic Republic of Congo; Dec–May in Equatorial Guinea. Bear in mind that these guidelines are by no means concrete; for the latest information on current outbreaks, visit the websites listed on p.249 or ask your doctor or travel clinic. The table below details countries where vaccination may be advisable.

Influenza risk isn't seasonal in Central Africa, so outbreaks can occur at any time of the year; for details of current patterns, visit the websites on p.249 or ask your doctor or travel clinic. See Part 1 for some background on influenza vaccinations.

Central Africa: vaccinations and malaria prophylaxis

	Angola	Cameroon	Central African Republic	Chad	Congo	Democratic Republic of the Congo (Zaire)	Equatorial Guinea	Gabon	Sudan	Zambia
Hepatitis A	R	R	R	R	R	R	R	R	R	R
Hepatitis B	C	C	C	C	C	C	C	C	C	C
Malaria	R	R	R	R	R	R	R	R	R	R
Meningitis	C	C	C	C	C	C	C	C	C	C
Rabies	C	C	C	C	C	C	C	C	C	C
Tuberculosis	C	C	C	C	C	C	C	C	C	C
Typhoid	R	R	R	R	R	R	R	R	R	R
Yellow fever	C	M*	M*	C	M*	M*	C	M*	C	R

M* = mandatory only for travellers over 1 year old; see above for details.

Other possible risks

- African trypanosomiasis
- Anthrax
- Buruli ulcer
- Chikungunya fever
- Crimean-Congo haemorrhagic fever
- Dracunculiasis
- Ebola viruses
- Filariasis
- Gastrointestinal illness
- Hepatitis E
- Hydatid disease
- Lassa fever
- Leishmaniasis (cutaneous and visceral)
- Loiasis
- Marburg virus
- Mycetoma
- Myiasis
- O'nyong nyong virus
- Onchocerciasis
- Paragonimiasis
- Plague
- Relapsing fever
- Rift Valley fever
- Schistosomiasis
- Trachoma
- Tropical sprue
- Tungiasis
- Typhus

East Africa

Burundi, The Comoros, Djibouti, Eritrea, Ethiopia, Kenya, Madagascar, Malawi, Mauritius, Mayotte, Mozambique, Réunion, Rwanda, Seychelles, Somalia, Uganda, United Republic of Tanzania

There is a high risk of chloroquine-resistant **falciparum malaria** year-round in Burundi, the Comoros, Djibouti, Eritrea, Ethiopia, Kenya, Madagascar, Malawi, Mayotte, Mozambique, Rwanda, Somalia, Tanzania and Uganda.

East Africa: vaccinations and malaria prophylaxis

	Burundi	The Comoros	Djibouti	Eritrea	Ethiopia	Kenya	Madagascar	Malawi	Mauritius	Mayotte	Mozambique	Réunion	Rwanda	Seychelles	Somalia	Uganda	United Rep. of Tanzania
Hepatitis A	R	R	R	R	R	R	R	R	R	R	R	R	R	R	R	R	R
Hepatitis B	C	C	C	C	C	C	C	C	C	C	C	C	C	C	C	C	C
Malaria	R	R	R	R	R	R	R	R	C	R	R	–	R	–	R	R	R
Meningitis	C	C	C	C	C	C	–	C	–	–	C	–	C	–	C	C	C
Rabies	C	C	C	C	C	C	C	C	C	C	C	–	C	C	C	C	C
Tuberculosis	C	C	C	C	C	C	C	C	C	C	C	C	C	C	C	C	C
Typhoid	R	R	R	R	R	R	R	R	R	R	R	R	R	R	R	R	R
Yellow fever	M*	–	C	C	C	C	–	C	C	–	C	C	M*	C	C	C	C

M* = mandatory only for travellers over 1 year old; see opposite for details.

Mefloquine, doxycycline and malarone are the recommended **prophylaxis** options (the table on p.254 details countries where prophylaxis may be necessary). Vivax malaria is present in some rural areas of Mauritius. For the latest information on malaria in the region, see the websites on p.249, or ask your doctor or travel clinic.

Outbreaks of **yellow fever** can occur in all of the mainland countries listed above and, regardless of official requirements, immunization is recommended, particularly for travel outside urban centres. There is no risk of yellow fever on Comoros, Mayotte or the Seychelles. **Vaccination and certification requirements** are as follows: for all travellers over 1 year old entering Burundi and Rwanda; for all travellers from infected areas entering Eritrea, Malawi and Somalia; from all travellers from endemic areas entering Uganda; and from all those over 1 year old travelling from infected areas to Djibouti, Ethiopia, Kenya and Mauritius, Mozambique, Réunion, the Seychelles and the United Republic of Tanzania. Certification is also required for travellers who have passed through endemic areas within six days of entry to the Seychelles. For those travelling to Mauritius from an uninfected area, vaccination is not required if staying less than two weeks.

Meningitis occurs seasonally in East Africa; risks tend to be greatest during the following months: April–Nov in Mozambique; May–Sept in Burundi; May–Oct in Djibouti; April–Nov in Malawi; May–Oct in Rwanda; June–Nov in the United Republic of Tanzania; July–Nov in Kenya; Sept–April in Eritrea; Oct–June in Ethiopia; Oct–May in Somalia. Outbreaks in Uganda don't tend to follow a seasonal pattern, and can occur at any time of the year, while in the Comoros, they tend to occur towards the end of the dry season. Bear in mind that these guidelines are by no means concrete; for the latest information on current outbreaks, visit the websites listed on p.249 or ask your doctor or travel clinic. The table on p.254 details countries where vaccination may be advisable.

Influenza is a risk throughout the year in all the countries listed above; for details of current outbreaks, visit the websites on p.249 or ask your doctor or travel clinic. See Influenza in Part 1 (p.9) for some background on influenza vaccinations.

Other possible risks

- African trypanosomiasis
- Anthrax
- Buruli ulcer
- Chikungunya fever
- Crimean-Congo haemorrhagic fever
- Dracunculiasis
- Dysentery
- Ebola virus
- Filariasis
- Gastrointestinal illness
- Giardiasis
- Hepatitis E
- Hydatid disease
- Lassa fever
- Leishmaniasis (cutaneous and visceral)

- Leprosy
- Loiasis
- Marburg virus
- Mycetoma
- Myiasis
- O'nyong nyong virus
- Onchocerciasis
- Plague
- Relapsing fever
- Rift Valley fever
- Schistosomiasis
- Trachoma
- Tropical sprue
- Tungiasis
- Typhus
- Worm infections

Southern Africa

Botswana, Lesotho, Namibia, St Helena, South Africa, Swaziland, Zimbabwe

Malaria, predominantly the dangerous falciparum strain, exists in most of the above countries, the exceptions being Lesotho and St Helena. The table below details countries where prophylaxis may be necessary. However as seasonal and regional risk are too varied and changeable to detail here, the table cannot be conclusive, and to ensure you have the most up-to-date information, you should check the websites listed on p.249, or ask your doctor or travel clinic.

Yellow fever is not endemic in the region. **Vaccination and certification requirements** are as follows: for all travellers from infected areas entering Lesotho, Namibia, Swaziland and Zimbabwe; for all those over 1 year old coming from or having passed through infected areas entering Botswana, St Helena, and South Africa.

Meningitis outbreaks occur in Namibia towards the end of the dry season. It is not a significant risk in any of the other countries in the region. For the latest information on current outbreaks, visit the websites listed on p.249 or ask your doctor or travel clinic.

Influenza risk exists throughout the year in northern Botswana and northern Namibia, and tends to occur seasonally (May–Oct) in Lesotho, Namibia (south of the Tropic of Capricorn), South Africa and Swaziland. For details of current outbreaks, visit the websites on p.249 or ask your doctor or travel clinic. See Influenza in Part 1 (p.9) for some background on influenza vaccinations.

Southern Africa: vaccinations and malaria prophylaxis

	Botswana	Lesotho	Namibia	St Helena	South Africa	Swaziland	Zimbabwe
Hepatitis A	R	R	R	R	R	R	R
Hepatitis B	C	C	C	C	C	C	C
Malaria	C	–	C	–	C	R	C
Meningitis	–	–	C	–	–	–	–
Rabies	C	C	C	–	C	C	C
Tuberculosis	C	C	C	–	C	C	C
Typhoid	R	R	R	C	R	R	R
Yellow fever	C	C	C	C	C	C	C

Other possible risks

- African trypanosomiasis
- Anthrax
- Chikungunya fever
- Cholera
- Filariasis
- Gastrointestinal illness
- Hepatitis E
- Hydatid disease
- Leishmaniasis
- Leptospirosis
- O'nyong nyong virus
- Onchocerciasis
- Plague
- Relapsing fever
- Rift Valley fever
- Schistosomiasis
- Trachoma
- Tropical sprue
- Tungiasis
- Typhus (mainly tick-borne)
- Viral haemorrhagic fevers (eg Crimean-Congo haemorrhagic fever)
- Worm infections

Australia and the South Pacific

American Samoa, Australia, Christmas Island, Cook Islands, Federated States of Micronesia, Fiji, French Polynesia, Guam, Kiribati, Marshall Islands, Nauru, New Caledonia, New Zealand, Niue, Northern Mariana Islands, Palau, Papua New Guinea, Pitcairn Island, Samoa, Solomon Islands, Tokelau, Tonga, Tuvalu, Vanuatu, Wake Island, Wallis and Futuna

Malaria (predominantly falciparum) risk exists throughout the year in Vanuatu, Papua New Guinea and in the Solomon Islands; infection rates in the latter are among the highest in the world. Advised **prophylaxis** is mefloquine, doxycycline or malarone. In Australia, occasional localized outbreaks have been reported around Cairns, Cape York and the Torres Strait Islands, but prophylaxis isn't normally necessary unless an outbreak is in progress; for details of the current situation in your destination, see the websites on p.249 or ask your doctor or travel clinic. The table on p.258 details countries where prophylaxis may be necessary.

There is no **yellow fever** risk in any of the countries listed above. For people travelling from an infected area, **vaccination and certification entry requirements** are as follows: for all those over 1 year travelling from infected areas to American Samoa, French Polynesia, Kiribati, Nauru, New Caledonia, Niue, Palau, Papua New Guinea, Pitcairn Islands, Samoa, the Solomon Islands

Australia and South Pacific: vaccinations and malaria prophylaxis

	American Samoa	Australia	Christmas Island	Cook Islands	Federated States of Micronesia	Fiji	French Polynesia	Guam	Kiribati	Marshall Islands	Nauru	New Caledonia	New Zealand	Niue	N. Mariana Islands	Palau	Papua New Guinea	Pitcairn Island	Samoa	Solomon Islands	Tokelau	Tonga	Tuvalu	Vanuatu	Wake Islands	Wallis and Fortuna
Hepatitis A	R	C	R	R	R	R	R	R	R	R	R	I	R	R	R	R	R	C	R	R	R	R	R	C	R	R
Hepatitis B	C	C	C	C	C	C	C	C	C	C	C	C	C	C	C	C	C	C	C	C	C	C	C	C	C	C
Japanese encephalitis	I	I	I	I	I	I	I	I	I	I	I	I	I	I	I	I	C	I	I	I	I	I	I	I	I	I
Malaria	I	C	I	I	I	I	I	I	I	I	I	I	I	I	I	I	R	I	R	I	I	I	I	R	I	I
Rabies	I	I	I	I	I	I	I	I	I	I	I	I	I	I	I	I	C	I	I	I	I	I	I	I	I	I
Tuberculosis	C	I	C	C	C	C	C	C	C	C	C	I	C	C	C	C	C	C	C	C	C	C	C	C	C	C
Typhoid	R	C	R	R	R	R	R	R	R	R	R	I	R	R	R	R	C	C	R	R	R	R	R	R	R	R
Yellow fever	M*	C	C	I	I	C	M*	I	M*	I	M*	M*	I	M*	I	M*	M*	M*	M*	M*	I	M*	I	I	I	I

M* = mandatory only for travellers over 1 year old; see p.257 for details.

and Tonga; for all those over 1 year old entering Fiji within ten days of staying overnight in infected areas; and for those entering Australia and the Christmas Islands within six days of visiting an infected area.

With the exception of the southern, temperate regions of Australia, New Zealand and Pitcairn Island, where outbreaks tend to occur seasonally (May–Oct), **influenza** exists throughout the year in all countries listed above. For details of current outbreaks, visit the websites on p.249 or ask your doctor or travel clinic. See Influenza in Part 1 (p.9) for some background on influenza vaccinations.

Note that epidemics of **dengue fever** are common throughout the region, and can affect large numbers of people; for details of current outbreaks, visit the WHO website (see the box on p.249).

The hot, tropical climate in much of the region leads to an increased incidence of **skin** and **wound infections**; all cuts should be cleaned thoroughly. **Snakes and spiders** can be a hazard – Australia has a high percentage of the worlds most dangerous varieties of both species. **Sharks** are present off many of the coastlines and, although attacks are rare, they do occur. Other maritime hazards include **sea snakes**, **jellyfish** (including the potentially fatal box jellyfish), **poisonous fish**, **dangerous currents** and **coral**. **Ciguatera** and **scombroid poisoning** have been reported from many parts of the region, although occurrences are rare.

Other possible risks

- ✚ Balantidiasis
- ✚ Barmah Forest virus
- ✚ Filariasis
- ✚ Gastrointestinal illness
- ✚ Hydatid disease
- ✚ Leptospirosis
- ✚ Onchocerciasis
- ✚ Paragonimiasis
- ✚ Ross River virus
- ✚ Schistosomiasis
- ✚ Trachoma
- ✚ Typhus
- ✚ Worm infections

Eastern Europe and the former Soviet Union

Albania, Armenia, Azerbaijan, Belarus, Bosnia/Herzegovina, Bulgaria, Croatia, Czech Republic, Estonia, Georgia, Hungary, Kazakhstan, Kyrgyzstan, Latvia, Lithuania, Moldova, Poland, Romania, Russia, Serbia/Montenegro, Slovak Republic, Slovenia, Tajikistan, Turkmenistan, Ukraine, Uzbekistan

There is a limited **malaria** risk in Armenia, Azerbaijan, Georgia, Kyrgyzstan, Russia, Tajikistan, Turkmenistan and Uzbekistan, predominantly of the vivax strain. Chloroquine alone is the recommended prophylaxis except in Tajikistan,

Eastern Europe & former Soviet Union: vaccinations and malaria prophylaxis

	Hepatitis A	Hepatitis B	Malaria	Meningitis	Rabies	Tick-borne encephalitis	Tuberculosis	Typhoid	Yellow fever
Albania	R	C	–	–	C	C	C	C	C
Armenia	R	C	C	–	C	C	C	C	–
Azerbaijan	R	C	C	–	C	C	C	R	–
Belarus	R	C	–	–	C	C	C	C	–
Bosnia/Herzegovina	R	C	–	–	C	C	C	C	–
Bulgaria	R	C	–	–	C	C	C	C	–
Croatia	R	C	–	–	C	C	C	C	–
Czech Republic	C	C	–	–	C	C	C	C	–
Estonia	R	C	–	–	C	C	C	C	–
Georgia	R	C	C	–	C	C	C	C	–
Hungary	C	C	–	–	C	C	C	–	–
Kazakhstan	R	C	–	–	C	C	C	R	C
Kyrgyzstan	R	C	C	C	C	C	C	R	–
Latvia	R	C	–	–	C	C	C	C	–
Lithuania	R	C	–	–	C	C	C	C	–
Moldova	R	C	–	–	C	C	C	C	–
Poland	C	C	–	–	C	C	C	C	–
Romania	R	C	–	–	C	C	C	C	–
Russia	R	C	C	C	C	C	C	R	–
Serbia/Montenegro	R	C	–	–	C	C	C	C	–
Slovak Republic	C	C	–	–	C	C	C	C	–
Slovenia	R	C	–	–	C	C	C	C	–
Tajikistan	R	C	C	–	C	C	C	R	–
Turkmenistan	R	C	C	–	C	C	C	R	–
Ukraine	R	C	–	–	C	C	C	C	–
Uzbekistan	R	C	C	–	C	C	C	R	–

where additional proguanil should be used. The table on p.260 details countries where prophylaxis may be necessary. However as seasonal and regional risk are too varied and changeable to detail here, the table cannot be conclusive, and to ensure you have the most up-to-date information, you should check the websites listed on p.249, or ask your doctor or travel clinic.

Yellow fever vaccination and certification is required for anyone over the age of 1 travelling from infected areas to Albania, and people of any age travelling from infected areas to Kazakhstan.

Meningitis vaccination is not normally recommended for travellers to the region, though you might want to consider it if travelling to the Moscow area, where outbreaks are not uncommon; discuss with your doctor or travel clinic.

Epidemics of **influenza** are seasonal (Nov–April) throughout the region. For details of current outbreaks, visit the websites on p.249 or ask your doctor or travel clinic. See Influenza in Part 1 (p.9) for some background on influenza vaccinations.

Following the collapse of the former Soviet Union, a breakdown in normal public health measures, shortages of drugs and immunizations, and a general deterioration in sanitary standards have led to an increase in the overall level of disease risk. The situation is slowly improving, but **water-borne infections** are a particular problem, whilst outbreaks of **diphtheria** became commonplace in the 1990s due to the breakdown of the standard childhood immunization programmes (these have now been reinstated to good effect). **Respiratory tract infections** are prevalent in autumn and winter, and **gastrointestinal infections** are common in spring and summer. Winter temperatures can be extremely low so **cold exposure** can be a significant hazard to health.

Other possible risks

- Anthrax
- Brucellosis
- Cholera
- Diphyllobothriasis (fish tapeworm)
- Hydatid disease
- Influenza
- Japanese encephalitis
- Leishmaniasis
- Leptospirosis
- Liver flukes (opisthorchiasis)

- Lyme disease
- Plague
- Rodent-borne hantavirus infection
- Sandfly fever
- Trichinosis
- Tularaemia
- Viral haemorrhagic fevers (eg Crimean-Congo haemorrhagic fever)
- West Nile fever

The Far East

Brunei Darussalam, Cambodia, China, Hong Kong, Indonesia, Japan, Laos, Macau, Malaysia, Mongolia, Myanmar (Burma), North Korea, the Philippines, Singapore, South Korea, Taiwan, Thailand, Vietnam

Malaria is present in all the countries other than Brunei Darussalam, Japan, Macau, Mongolia, and Taiwan. The main strains are falciparum and vivax, and mefloquine, doxycycline or malarone are the usual recommended **prophylaxis** regimes. Mefloquine resistance has been reported in northern border areas of Thailand, where doxycycline or malarone are the recommended prophylaxis. Chloroquine is still useful in parts of China and the Philippines. The table on

Far East: vaccinations and malaria prophylaxis

Country	Yellow fever	Typhoid	Tuberculosis	Rabies	Malaria	Japanese encephalitis	Hepatitis B	Hepatitis A
Brunei Darussalam	C	R	C	C	I	C	C	R
Cambodia	C	R	C	C	R	C	C	R
China	C	R	C	C	C	C	C	R
Hong Kong	C	C	C	C	C	C	C	C
Indonesia	C	R	C	C	C	C	C	R
Japan	I	I	I	I	I	C	C	I
Laos	C	R	C	C	R	C	C	R
Macau	C	R	C	C	I	C	C	R
Malaysia	C	R	C	C	C	C	C	R
Mongolia	I	R	C	C	I	C	C	R
Myanmar (Burma)	C	R	C	C	R	C	C	R
North Korea	I	R	C	C	C	C	C	R
The Philippines	C	R	C	C	C	C	C	R
Singapore	C	I	C	C	I	I	C	C
South Korea	I	C	C	C	C	C	C	C
Taiwan	C	C	C	C	I	C	C	R
Thailand	C	R	C	C	C	C	C	R
Vietnam	C	R	C	C	C	C	C	R

p.262 details countries where prophylaxis may be necessary. However as seasonal and regional risk are too varied and changeable to detail here, the table cannot be conclusive, and to ensure you have the most up-to-date information, you should check the websites listed on p.249, or ask your doctor or travel clinic.

There is no risk of contracting **yellow fever** in any of the countries listed above. **Vaccination and certification entry requirements** are as follows: for all those travelling from infected areas to Cambodia, China, Hong Kong, Indonesia, Laos, Macau, Myanmar and Taiwan; for all those over 1 year old travelling from infected areas to the Philippines, Thailand and Vietnam; for all those over 1 year old who have been in an infected or endemic area within six days of entry to Brunei Darussalam, Malaysia and Singapore.

Note that epidemics of **dengue fever** are common in many of the above countries, and can affect large numbers of people; for details of current outbreaks, visit the WHO website (see the box on p.249).

Influenza risk extends throughout the year in Brunei Darussalam, Cambodia, Hong Kong, Indonesia, Laos, Macau, Malaysia, Myanmar, the Philippines, Singapore, Thailand and Vietnam, and from November to April in China, Japan, Mongolia, North Korea, South Korea and Taiwan. For details of current outbreaks, visit the websites on p.249 or ask your doctor or travel clinic. See Influenza in Part 1 (p.9) for some background on influenza vaccinations.

Though **SARS** had been eradicated in the region at the time of writing, it's possible that it might re-emerge; check the websites on p.249 for an update. **Altitude sickness** is a risk in the Himalayas in western China, and in parts of Mongolia. There are a number of **marine hazards** (jellyfish, sea snakes and sharks etc) in the waters surrounding the region, while **snakes** can be a hazard in rural areas of all the countries listed above. Avoid close contact with **monkeys,** as their bites can transmit rabies. Finally, note that **rhesus negative blood type** is rare in the Far East.

Other possible risks

- Anthrax
- Balantidiasis
- Brucellosis
- Chikungunya fever
- Cholera
- Dysentery
- Fasciolopsiasis
- Filariasis
- Gastrointestinal illness
- Giardiasis
- Gnathostomiasis
- Hepatitis C and E
- Human ehrlichiosis
- Hydatid disease
- Leishmaniasis (visceral and cutaneous)
- Leprosy
- Leptospirosis
- Liver flukes (clonorchiasis)
- Melioidosis
- Paragonimiasis
- Plague
- Relapsing fever
- Sandfly fever
- Schistosomiasis
- Trachoma
- Typhus
- Viral haemorrhagic fevers (eg Crimean-Congo haemorrhagic fever)
- Worm infections

The Indian subcontinent

Afghanistan, Bangladesh, Bhutan, India, the Maldives, Nepal, Pakistan, Sri Lanka

With the exception of the Maldives, **malaria** is present throughout the region, often of the falciparum variety. Chloroquine resistance is common, and the recommended **prophylaxis** is a combination of chloroquine and proguanil, except in Bhutan where the choice is between mefloquine, doxycycline and malarone. The table below details countries where prophylaxis may be necessary. However as seasonal and regional risk are too varied and changeable to detail here, the table cannot be conclusive, and to ensure you have the most up-to-date information, you should check the websites listed on p.249, or ask your doctor or travel clinic.

Yellow fever does not occur in the countries listed above. For people travelling from an infected area, **vaccination and certification entry requirements** are as follows: for all travellers entering Afghanistan, Bhutan, Nepal and the Maldives; for all those over 6 months old travelling from endemic areas to Pakistan; for all those over 1 year old travelling from infected areas to Sri Lanka; for all those over 6 months old who have left or passed through an infected area within six days of entering Bangladesh and India (note that India also requires certification from all travellers who have left an infected area by boat within thirty days of arrival).

Note that epidemics of **dengue fever** are common throughout the region, and can affect large numbers of people; for details of current outbreaks, visit the WHO website (see the box on p.249).

Influenza epidemics occur seasonally (Nov–April) in Afghanistan, Bhutan,

Indian subcontinent: vaccinations and malaria prophylaxis

	Afghanistan	Bangladesh	Bhutan	India	Maldives	Nepal	Pakistan	Sri Lanka
Hepatitis A	R	R	R	R	R	R	R	R
Hepatitis B	C	C	C	C	C	C	C	C
Japanese encephalitis	–	C	C	C	–	C	C	C
Malaria	C	R	C	R	–	R	C	R
Rabies	C	R	C	C	C	C	C	C
Tuberculosis	C	C	C	C	C	C	C	C
Typhoid	R	R	R	R	R	R	R	R
Yellow fever	C	C	C	C	C	C	C	C

India (areas north of the Tropic of Cancer), Nepal and Pakistan, and throughout the year in Bangladesh, India (areas south of the Tropic of Cancer), the Maldives and Sri Lanka. For details of current outbreaks, visit the websites on p.249 or ask your doctor or travel clinic. See Influenza in Part 1 (p.9) for some background on influenza vaccinations.

Cholera outbreaks have been reported in most of the countries listed above, with cases of the new, virulent Bengal strain occurring in Bangladesh, India, Nepal, Pakistan and Sri Lanka. Of more general risks, **altitude sickness** and **sunburn** are potential problems in the Himalayas, while venomous **snakes** and **scorpions** are present throughout the region.

Other possible risks

- Anthrax
- Brucellosis
- Chikungunya fever
- Cholera
- Dysentery
- Echinococcosis
- Fasciolopsiasis
- Filariasis
- Gastrointestinal illness
- Giardiasis
- Hepatitis E
- Japanese encephalitis
- Leishmaniasis (visceral and cutaneous)
- Leprosy
- Leptospirosis
- Meningococcal meningitis
- Mycetoma
- Paragonimiasis
- Relapsing fever
- Sandfly fever
- Schistosomiasis
- Trachoma
- Tropical sprue
- Tungiasis
- Typhus
- Viral haemorrhagic fevers (eg Crimean-Congo haemorrhagic fever)
- West Nile fever

The Middle East

Bahrain, Cyprus, Iran, Iraq, Israel, Jordan, Kuwait, Lebanon, Oman, Qatar, Saudi Arabia, Syria, Turkey, United Arab Emirates (including Abu Dhabi), Yemen

Of the countries listed above, **malaria** is present only in Iran, Iraq, Oman, Saudi Arabia, Syria, Turkey, United Arab Emirates and Yemen. The predominant strain in the region is vivax, although infection rates are generally low. Chloroquine alone is the most commonly recommended **prophylaxis**, though there is resistance in some countries. The table on p.266 details countries where prophylaxis may be necessary. However as seasonal and regional risk are too varied and changeable to detail here, the table cannot be conclusive, and to ensure you have the most up-to-date information, you should check the websites listed on p.249, or ask your doctor or travel clinic.

There is no **yellow fever** in the region. **Vaccination and certification entry requirements** are as follows: for all those travelling from infected areas to Iraq, Lebanon, Oman, Saudi Arabia and Syria; for all those over 1 year old travelling from infected areas to Jordan and Yemen.

Note that epidemics of **dengue fever** occur throughout the region, and can affect large numbers of people; for details of current outbreaks, visit the WHO website (see the box on p.249).

Influenza epidemics tend to occur seasonally (Nov–April) in Bahrain, Cyprus, Iraq, Israel, Jordan, Kuwait, Qatar, Saudi Arabia (north of the Tropic of Cancer), Syria, Turkey and the United Arab Emirates; and throughout the year in Iran, Oman, Saudi Arabia (south of the Tropic of Cancer) and Yemen. For details of current outbreaks, visit the websites on p.249 or ask your doctor or travel clinic. See Influenza in Part 1 (p.9) for some background on influenza vaccinations.

Of more general risks, **snakes** and **scorpions** may be a hazard in some rural areas. Dry and dusty conditions may exacerbate **respiratory** and **sinus** problems, as well as causing problems to contact-lens wearers. Those entering Saudi Arabia for the Umra (Hajj pilgrimage) or for related seasonal work require certification of vaccination against the A, C and W135Y **meningococcal infections**; vaccinations must be given between three years and ten days before arrival.

Other possible risks

- Anthrax
- Balantidiasis
- Brucellosis
- Cholera
- Dracunculiasis
- Dysentery
- Filariasis
- Gastrointestinal illness
- Giardiasis
- Hydatid disease

Middle East: vaccinations and malaria prophylaxis

	Bahrain	Cyprus	Iran	Iraq	Israel	Jordan	Kuwait	Lebanon	Oman	Qatar	Saudi Arabia	Syria	Turkey	United Arab Emirates (including Abu Dhabi)	Yemen
Hepatitis A	R	C	R	R	R	R	R	R	R	R	R	R	R	R	R
Hepatitis B	C	–	C	C	C	C	C	C	C	C	C	C	C	C	C
Malaria	–	–	C	C	–	–	–	–	C	–	C	C	C	C	C
Meningitis	–	–	–	–	–	–	–	–	–	–	C	–	–	–	–
Rabies	C	–	C	C	C	C	C	C	C	C	C	C	C	C	C
Tuberculosis	C	–	C	C	C	C	C	C	C	C	C	C	C	C	C
Typhoid	C	–	R	R	C	R	C	R	R	C	R	C	C	C	R
Yellow fever	–	–	–	C	–	C	–	C	C	–	C	C	–	–	C

- Leishmaniasis (cutaneous and visceral)
- Leptospirosis
- Onchocerciasis
- Plague
- Q fever
- Rabies
- Relapsing fever
- Rift Valley fever
- Sandfly fever
- Schistosomiasis
- Trachoma
- Tropical sprue
- Typhus
- Viral haemorrhagic fevers (eg Crimean-Congo haemorrhagic fever)
- West Nile fever

North America

Canada, Greenland, St Pierre and Miquelon, USA (including Hawaii)

Generally speaking, the risk of contracting a significant infectious disease in North America is very low, and there are no routine vaccinations for travel to the region. Air pollution in the large cities and heavily industrialized areas may cause **respiratory problems** in susceptible individuals. The climate in the northern regions can be extremely **cold** in the winter months and conversely very **hot** in the south in the summer months. **Street crime** is common, and tourists have been particularly targeted in some areas (e.g. Florida).

Rabies is on the increase in some area of the US, particularly the mid-Atlantic states; avoid direct contact with raccoons, foxes, skunks, groundhogs and bats. **Influenza** epidemics occur seasonally (Nov–April). For details of current outbreaks, visit the websites on p.249 or ask your doctor or travel clinic. See Influenza in Part 1 (p.9) for some background on influenza vaccinations.

Other possible risks

- Dengue fever
- Eastern and western equine encephalitis
- Human babesiosis
- Human ehrlichiosis
- Lyme disease
- Monkeypox
- Plague
- Rabies
- Relapsing fever
- Rocky Mountain spotted fever
- Rodent-borne hantavirus
- St Louis virus
- Tularaemia
- West Nile fever

Mexico and Central America

Belize, Costa Rica, El Salvador, Guatemala, Honduras, Mexico, Nicaragua, Panama

Malaria, predominantly of the vivax strain, is present throughout the year in all of the above countries, and risk tends to be highest in low-lying, rural areas. Chloroquine generally provides adequate prophylaxis, and the table below details countries where prophylaxis may be necessary. However as seasonal and regional risk are too varied and changeable to detail here, the table cannot be conclusive, and to ensure you have the most up-to-date information, you should check the websites listed on p.249, or ask your doctor or travel clinic.

The Darien province of Panama is the only place in the region where yellow fever is present; vaccination is recommended for those visiting this area. Otherwise, **vaccination and certification entry requirements** are as follows: for all those travelling from infected areas to Belize and Honduras; for those over 6 months old travelling from infected areas to El Salvador; for those over 1 year old travelling from infected areas to Guatemala and Nicaragua.

Note that epidemics of **dengue fever** are common throughout the region, and can affect large numbers of people; for details of current outbreaks, visit the WHO website (see the box on p.249).

The risk of **influenza** occurs throughout the year in all the countries above except Mexico, where the risk is seasonal (Nov–April) to the north of the Tropic of Cancer. For details of current outbreaks, visit the websites on p.249

Mexico & Central America: vaccinations and malaria prophylaxis

	Belize	Costa Rica	El Salvador	Guatemala	Honduras	Mexico	Nicaragua	Panama
Hepatitis A	R	R	R	R	R	R	R	R
Hepatitis B	C	C	C	C	C	C	C	C
Malaria	R	R	C	C	R	C	R	R
Rabies	C	C	C	C	C	C	C	C
Tuberculosis	C	C	C	C	C	C	C	C
Typhoid	R	R	R	R	R	R	R	R
Yellow fever	C	–	C	C	C	–	C	R

or ask your doctor or travel clinic. See Influenza in Part 1 (p.9) for some background on influenza vaccinations.

Of more general risks, **snakes** and **scorpions** may be hazards in rural areas, while air pollution and altitude may lead to **respiratory problems** in Mexico City.

Other possible risks

+ American trypanosomiasis
+ Balantidiasis
+ Brucellosis
+ Cholera
+ Dysentery (amoebic and bacillary)
+ Filariasis
+ Gastrointestinal illness
+ Gnathostomiasis
+ Leishmaniasis (cutaneous and visceral)
+ Leptospirosis

+ Myiasis
+ Onchocerciasis
+ Paragonimiasis
+ Plague
+ Sandfly fever
+ Schistosomiasis
+ Tropical sprue
+ Tungiasis
+ Typhus
+ Venezuelan equine encephalitis

The Caribbean

Anguilla, Antigua and Barbuda, Aruba, the Bahamas, Barbados, Bermuda, Bonaire, the Turks and Caicos Islands, the Cayman Islands, Cuba, Curacao, Dominica, the Dominican Republic, Grenada, Guadeloupe, Haiti, Jamaica, Martinique, Montserrat, Puerto Rico, Saba, St Kitts and Nevis, St Eustatius, St Lucia, St Maarten, St Vincent and the Grenadines, Trinidad and Tobago, the Virgin Islands

Malaria is present year-round in just two Caribbean countries; the falciparum variety has been confirmed in both, but as resistance hasn't been identified, chloroquine alone is regarded as sufficient prophylaxis. There is a low risk of infection throughout the year in the **Dominican Republic**; risk is highest in the western provinces bordering Haiti (Castanuelas, Hondo Valley and Pepilla Salcedo). In **Haiti** itself, malaria is present throughout the country. Prophylaxis may be necessary, depending on where and when you visit; see the table on p.270, and get the latest information from the websites on p.249 or your doctor or travel clinic.

Rare outbreaks of **yellow fever** have occurred in Trinidad (the last human cases were diagnosed in 1980); the rest of the region is free of the disease. **Vaccination and certification entry requirements** are as follows: for all those travelling from infected areas to Haiti; for those over 6 months old

Caribbean: vaccinations and malaria prophylaxis

Note that in the table below, the islands of the Netherlands Antilles (Aruba, Bonaire, Curacao, Saba, St Eustatius and St Maarten) are dealt with under one general heading.

	Hepatitis A	Hepatitis B	Malaria	Rabies	Tuberculosis	Typhoid	Yellow fever
Anguilla	C	C	I	I	C	C	R
Antigua and Barbuda	C	C	I	I	C	C	R
Bahamas	C	C	I	I	C	C	R
Barbados	C	C	I	I	C	C	R
Bermuda	C	C	I	I	C	C	I
Cayman Islands	C	C	I	I	C	C	I
Cuba	C	R	C	I	C	R	I
Dominica	C	R	C	I	C	R	C
Dominican Republic	C	R	C	R	C	R	I
Grenada	C	C	C	I	C	C	C
Guadeloupe	C	C	I	I	C	C	C
Haiti	C	R	C	R	C	R	C
Jamaica	C	C	I	I	C	C	C
Martinique	C	C	I	I	C	C	I
Montserrat	C	C	I	I	C	C	C
Netherlands Antilles	C	C	C	I	C	C	C
Puerto Rico	C	R	C	I	C	R	I
St Kitts and Nevis	C	C	I	I	C	C	C
St Lucia	C	C	I	I	C	C	C
St Vincent and the Grenadines	C	C	I	I	C	C	C
Trinidad and Tobago	C	C	C	I	C	C	C
Turks and Caicos	C	C	I	I	C	C	I
Virgin Islands	C	C	I	I	C	C	I

travelling from infected areas to the Netherlands Antilles (Aruba, Bonaire, Curacao, Saba, St Eustatius and St Maarten); and for those over 1 year old travelling from infected areas to Anguilla, Antigua and Barbuda, the Bahamas, Barbados, Dominica, Grenada, Guadeloupe, Jamaica, Montserrat, St Kitts and Nevis, St Lucia, St Vincent and the Grenadines, and Trinidad and Tobago.

Note that epidemics of **dengue fever** are common throughout the region, and can affect large numbers of people; for details of current outbreaks, visit the WHO website (see the box on p.249).

Influenza risk extends throughout the year on most Caribbean islands; in the Bahamas and Bermuda, epidemics tend to be seasonal (Nov–April). For details of current outbreaks, visit the websites on p.249 or ask your doctor or travel clinic. See Influenza in Part 1 (p.9) for some background on influenza vaccinations.

Of general health risks in the Caribbean, the sea holds a variety of potential hazards, including **spiny sea urchins**, **jellyfish** and **coral**. **Snakes**, **poisonous spiders** and **scorpions** may be hazards in some areas. **Ciguatera** poisoning occurs sporadically throughout the Caribbean.

Other possible risks

+ American trypanosomiasis
+ Filariasis
+ Gastrointestinal illness
+ Leishmaniasis
+ Leptospirosis

+ Myiasis
+ Schistosomiasis
+ Tropical sprue
+ Venezuelan equine encephalitis

South America

Argentina, Bolivia, Brazil, Chile, Colombia, Ecuador, the Falkland Islands, French Guiana, Guyana, Paraguay, Peru, Surinam, Uruguay, Venezuela

In terms of health hazards, South America can be divided into the northern tropical countries (Bolivia, Brazil, Colombia, Ecuador, French Guiana, Guyana, Paraguay, Peru, Surinam, Venezuela), where many diseases are endemic and indeed common, and the southern temperate countries (Argentina, Chile, the Falkland Islands, Uruguay), where risks to the traveller are significantly less in volume and variety.

With the exceptions of Chile, the Falkland Islands and Uruguay, **malaria** (of both the falciparum and vivax varieties) occurs in all the countries listed above. The table on p.272 details countries where prophylaxis may be necessary. However as seasonal and regional risk are too varied and changeable to detail here, the table cannot be conclusive, and to ensure you have the most up-to-date information, you should check the websites listed on p.249, or ask your doctor or travel clinic.

Yellow fever epidemics occur in all the South American countries listed above except for Chile, the Falkland Islands, Paraguay and Uruguay (note that there have been occasional outbreaks along Argentina's northern borders). Regional and seasonal risk are too varied and changeable to list here; the countries where vaccination may be necessary appear in the table below, but as disease patterns vary from year to year, it's also advisable to get the latest advice from the websites listed on p.249, or from your doctor or travel clinic. **Vaccination and certification entry requirements** are as follows: for all those over 6 months old travelling to French Guiana; for all those travelling from endemic areas to Paraguay; for all those travelling from infected areas to Bolivia, Guyana, Surinam and Chile (when visiting Easter Island only); for all those over 6 months old travelling from infected areas to Peru; for those over 9 months old travelling from infected areas to Brazil.

Note that epidemics of **dengue fever** are common in most tropical South American countries, and can affect large numbers of people; for details of current outbreaks, visit the WHO website (see the box on p.249).

In all areas north of the Tropic of Capricorn, **influenza** epidemics can occur throughout the year. South of the Tropic of Capricorn (in Argentina, Chile, southern Paraguay and Uruguay), they tend to occur seasonally (May–Oct). For details of current outbreaks, visit the websites on p.249 or ask your doctor or travel clinic. See Influenza in Part 1 (p.9) for some background on influenza vaccinations.

In terms of general risks, **snakes** and **poisonous spiders** can be a hazard, particularly in jungle areas. **Worm infections** are common throughout the continent. **Altitude** may pose a health threat in the Andes, particularly if you fly in to a high-altitude destination such as La Paz, Bogota or Cusco.

South America: vaccinations and malaria prophylaxis

	Argentina	Bolivia	Brazil	Chile	Colombia	Ecuador	Falkland Islands	French Guiana	Guyana	Paraguay	Peru	Surinam	Uruguay	Venezuela
Hepatitis A	R	R	R	R	R	R	–	R	R	R	R	R	R	R
Hepatitis B	C	C	C	C	C	C	–	C	C	C	C	C	C	C
Malaria	C	R	C	–	C	C	–	R	R	C	C	C	–	C
Rabies	C	C	C	C	C	C	–	C	C	C	C	C	C	C
Tuberculosis	C	C	C	C	C	C	–	C	C	C	C	C	C	C
Typhoid	C	R	C	C	R	R	–	R	R	R	R	R	C	R
Yellow fever	–	C	C	C*	R	C	–	M*	C	C	C	C	–	R

C* = Easter Island only
M* = mandatory only for travellers over 1 year old; see above for details.

Other possible risks

- American trypanosomiasis
- Anthrax
- Balantidiasis
- Bartonellosis
- Brazilian purpuric fever
- Brucellosis
- Cholera
- Eastern equine encephalitis
- Gastrointestinal illness
- Gnathostomiasis
- Hepatitis D
- Hydatid disease
- Leishmaniasis (cutaneous, mucocutaneous and visceral)
- Leptospirosis
- Lymphatic filariasis
- Myiasis
- Onchocerciasis
- Oropouche virus
- Paragonimiasis
- Plague
- Rocky Mountain spotted fever
- Rodent-borne hantavirus
- Schistosomiasis
- Trachoma
- Tropical sprue
- Tungiasis
- Typhus
- Venezuelan equine encephalitis

Western Europe

Andorra, Austria, Azores, Balearic islands, Belgium, Canary Islands, Denmark, Faroe Islands, Finland, France, Germany, Gibraltar, Greece, Iceland, Ireland, Italy, Liechtenstein, Luxembourg, Madeira, Malta, Monaco, Netherlands, Norway, Portugal, San Marino, Sardinia, Sicily, Spain, Sweden, Switzerland, United Kingdom

Generally, serious health risks are rare in Western Europe. **Yellow fever** is not present in any of the above countries. For people travelling from an infected area, **vaccination and certification entry requirements** are as follows: for those over 9 months old travelling from an infected area to Malta; for anyone over 1 year old travelling from infected areas to the Azores and Madeira (certification is not required for those in transit at Funchal, Porto Santo and Santa Maria). **Influenza** epidemics tend to be seasonal (Nov–April. For details of current outbreaks, visit the websites on p.249 or ask your doctor or travel clinic. See Influenza in Part 1 (p.9) for some background on influenza vaccinations.

Of more general risks, **altitude sickness** is a potential problem in the Alps, while the cold and damp climate of Western Europe's northern and central lowlands encourages **respiratory tract infections**, particularly in winter. The **lesser weever fish** can be a hazard off some beaches in the region.

Western Europe: vaccinations

	Yellow fever	Tick-borne encephalitis	Hepatitis A
Andorra	–	–	○
Austria	–	○	–
Azores	○	–	○
Belgium	–	–	–
Denmark (inc. the Faroe Islands)	–	○	–
Finland	–	○	–
France	–	–	–
Germany	–	○	–
Gibraltar	–	–	–
Greece	–	–	○
Iceland	–	–	–
Ireland	–	–	–
Italy (inc. Sardinia and Sicily)	–	–	○
Liechtenstein	–	–	–
Luxembourg	–	–	–
Madeira	○	–	○
Malta	○	–	–
Monaco	–	–	–
Netherlands	–	–	–
Norway	–	○	–
Portugal	○*	–	○
San Marino	–	–	–
Spain (inc. Balearics and Canary Islands)	–	–	○
Sweden	–	○	–
Switzerland	–	○	–
UK	–	–	–

* applies only to the Azores and Madeira

Other possible risks

+ Brucellosis
+ Crimean-Congo haemorrhagic fever
+ Diphyllobothriasis (fish tapeworm)
+ Echinococcosis
+ Fascioliasis
+ Hepatitis B
+ Human babesiosis
+ Legionnaires' disease
+ Leishmaniasis (cutaneous and visceral)
+ Lyme disease
+ Mediterranean spotted fever
+ Rabies
+ Sandfly fever
+ Typhoid
+ Typhus
+ West Nile fever

5

Directory

There are a great many sources of information on travel health. Although it's a good idea to discuss holiday plans face to face with a health professional, there is also much that you can do yourself in terms of preparation. The most accessible and up-to-date resource is the **Internet**, with a huge number of websites dedicated to health in general, and to travel health in particular. The best of the bunch are listed in this section – none of which, unlike many medical sites, charge for access. The selection is divided into dedicated travel health sites, general health sites and those which list travel clinics worldwide. We've also included details of online travel equipment and medical supplies stores and a list of useful publications.

Websites giving disease outbreak information are listed in Part 4 (p.249).

Travel health websites

UK

Ⓦ www.masta.org

Well-established all-round travel health resource from the London School of Tropical Medicine. The Health Library has information for travellers with special needs as well as

Top 5 travel health websites

Ⓦwww.fitfortravel.scot.nhs.uk

Outstanding site, compiled by the Scottish Centre for Infection and Environmental Health. Easy to navigate and brimming with detailed, up-to-date information on diseases, as well as general and specialized travel health advice, country-by-country guides (the malaria maps are very useful) and good links.

Ⓦwww.cdc.gov

The website of the US Center for Disease Control, this is about as good as online health information gets, with a comprehensive travel health section and a general health A–Z among the most useful resources. There's also a Spanish-language version.

Ⓦwww.tripprep.com

Very detailed country-by-country health advice and disease information, as well as a directory of travel clinics in the US and elsewhere in the world. You have to register to use the site, but it's free to do so.

Ⓦwww.who.int

With English, Spanish and French versions, the World Health Organization website is an invaluable resource, albeit somewhat cumbersome in terms of navigation. Content includes an online version of their excellent International Travel and Health book, as well as disease outbreak news, detailed information on infectious diseases and outbreaks, and an A–Z of medical conditions.

Ⓦwww.wtgonline.com

Produced by the American Columbus Publishing Company, and available in English, German, French and Spanish, this is a very easy-access source of country-by-country disease info. Click on the country of your choice, then on "health" to the left for travel advisories and general health information.

outbreak news and sections on environmental and disease risks; there's also travel clinic lists, a chatroom and a travel equipment shop. A customized "Health Brief" for your destination is available online for a small fee.

Ⓦ www.netdoctor.co.uk/travel/index.shtml

General medical site, with a very comprehensive travel health section written primarily by family doctors.

Ⓦ www.bbc.co.uk/health/travel/index.shtml

The health section of the BBC website, with lots of interesting articles relating to travel health as well as useful links.

Ⓦ www.nathnac.org

Backed by the UK Department of Health, this is a relatively new site, with a growing list of travel health factsheets as well as news, clinic lists and links.

Ⓦ www.traveldoctor.co.uk

Maintained and run by a GP/pharmacist team, with lots of general travel health information as well as an interactive section offering customized lists of medicines appropriate for your destinations (for a small fee). The pictures can make it slow to load.

Ⓦ www.travelhealth.co.uk

A well-ordered and comprehensive specialist website, with contributions from experts in the field. Good links and an online shop, too.

US and Canada

Ⓦ www.mdtravelhealth.com

Privately run travel health site, with detailed information on destinations, diseases and travel clinics, as well as links and tips on travel for people with special needs.

Ⓦ www.healthlink.mcw.edu/travel-medicine

Wide-ranging selection of travel health articles from the Medical College of Wisconsin, mercifully free from medical jargon.

Ⓦ www.thetraveldoctor.com

Run by a Dallas-based travel medicine consultancy, with sound, no-nonsense general travel health advice, and personalized destination-based risk profiles for $25.

Ⓦ www.hc-sc.gc.ca

Canadian equivalent of the US CDC website, in French and English, with travel advisories, disease information and lists of travel clinics in Canada.

Australia and New Zealand

Ⓦ www.mydr.com.au

Busy general health website; the travel health section (click on the link on the left of the main page) has information on sun safety, food and drink hygiene, holiday hazards (with particular concentration on Australian spiders, snakes etc) as well as useful articles on a wide variety of updated subjects.

Ⓦ www.everybody.co.nz

Click on the travel link for disease alerts, disease information, research news and travel clinic listings.

General medical websites

Ⓦ www.vnh.org

The US Virtual Naval Hospital offers a wealth of advice on a broad spectrum of health problems, from "Anthrax Prevention" to "Stress Management".

Ⓦ www.healthtouch.com

American website providing information on a wide range of health-related issues. The "Medication Guide" is very useful, with an A–Z of available medicines (using American names), their uses, cautions, side effects, interactions and the like, as well as sections on supplements and natural medicine.

Ⓦ www.drkoop.com

A well-established American site with a huge variety of medical content, from medications to foot care, as well as useful sections designed for men, women, the elderly, children etc.

Ⓦ www.stopgettingsick.com

Exhaustive general health site with an emphasis on preventative measures: everything from Norwegian fish medicine to alternative therapies. Forums and news articles, too.

Ⓦ www.state.sd.us/doh/Pubs/fctindex.htm

Detailed disease factsheets.

Ⓦ www.ama-assn.org/ama/pub/category/7140.html

Online anatomy atlas.

Ⓦ www.hpa.org.uk

The website of the UK Health Information Agency, with content on topical subjects such as SARS as well as comprehensive details on infectious diseases.

Ⓦ www.patient.co.uk

Easy to navigate, this is a very useful resource, with a huge range of links that cover all medical topics.

Travel clinics

The Hospital for Tropical Diseases, London

Mortimer Market, Capper Street, London WC1E 6AU ☎020/7387 9300, travel clinic ☎020/7388 9600, Ⓦwww.thehtd.org
Premium-rate helpline ☎09061/337733

Liverpool School of Tropical Medicine

Pembroke Place, Liverpool L3 5QA ☎0151/708 9393, Ⓦwww.liv.ac.uk/lstm.
Premium-rate helpline ☎09067/010095

Ⓦ www.istm.org

The website of the International Society for Travel Medicine, with a global list of clinics specializing in international travel health alongside outbreak warnings, suggested inoculations, precautions and other background information for travellers.

Ⓦ www.astmh.org

Alongside more general content for its members, the American Society of Tropical Medicine and Hygiene website includes an international database of travel clinics.

Online consultations

ⓦ www.e-med.co.uk

Consultations by email and phone for members; registration costs £20 per annum, and there's a £15 fee per consultation.

Equipment and medical kits

UK

ⓦ www.lifesystems.co.uk

The website of this long-established UK chain of travel equipment shops has a wide range of stock, with serious survival gear alongside all the usual medical kits and water purifiers.

ⓦ nomadtravel.co.uk

UK-based site selling a huge range of travel gear, from medical supplies (including kits), water purifying equipment, mosquito nets and repellents to clothing, boots and shoes, maps, compasses, rucksacks and sleeping bags.

US and Canada

ⓦ www.travmed.com

US-based online store with everything you'll need to keep you healthy, from the mundane (insect-avoidance gear, water purifiers and medical kits) to the somewhat unusual (blood-clotting spray and "Evac U8" smoke-hoods).

ⓦ www.equiptrip.com

US-based online store dedicated to travel medicine and supplies and hence with a really comprehensive range.

ⓦ www.safetravel.com

US-based specialist in travel medical kits.

Australia and New Zealand

ⓦ www.menda.com.au

General travel accessories store, but with a decent range of medically related gear.

Publications

Where There is No Doctor, David Werner, Carol Thurman and Jane Maxwell

Regarded as something of a bible for missionary and relief workers over the years, and fair to say that the book is very much focused on more general health-related issues of the developing world rather than those directly affecting the traveller. Nevertheless it offers a simple, practical, hands-on approach to all sorts of medical problems for the non-medically minded and is worth seeking out if you're planning a prolonged trip off the beaten track.

Travellers' Health, Dr Richard Dawood

First published in 1986, this well-respected book has long been regarded as the last word in travel health. Thoroughly researched and boasting a number of eminent contributors, the text can be hard going in places and may not be ideal if you're intent on travelling light.

Health Advice for Travellers (known as the "T6" leaflet)

Published annually by the UK Department of Health, this booklet contains general information on vaccinations, travel insurance and reciprocal health-care arrangements between countries. It's free, and available from UK post offices.

Everyday Homeopathy, Dr David Gemmell

Accessibly written and easy to use, this is an excellent guide to treating minor ailments with homeopathy.

First Aid Manual, St John Ambulance

The best of the many first aid manuals on the market: well organized and with lots of clear illustrations and pictures.

Mosquito: The Story of Man's Deadliest Foe, Andrew Spielman and Michael D'Antonio

An eye-opening account on how much of a threat this small, seemingly innocuous creature poses to humans.

SAS Survival Guide, John Wiseman

Inexpensive, compact and comprehensive, covering everything from how to fell a tree properly and what parts of animals are safe to eat to how to survive an earthquake.

6

Glossary

Glossary

abscess	a localized collection of pus
allopathic	reference to orthodox medical treatment
anaemia	a deficiency of haemoglobin in the blood
analgesics	painkillers
anaphylaxis	an extreme, hypersensitive allergic reaction which can be life-threatening
antiemetics	drugs used to prevent vomiting
antivenin	an antitoxin which counteracts venom
autoinfection	infection caused by an organism already present in another part of the body or by the larval reproduction of a parasite already present in the body
asymptomatic	without symptoms
balanitis	inflammation of the glans (head) of the penis
BCG	Bacillus Calmette-Guérin: a vaccination against TB
biliary tract	common word for the liver, gall bladder and bile ducts
cardiac	pertaining to the heart
cardiovascular	pertaining to the heart and blood vessels
carrier	a person or animal harbouring disease-producing organisms without exhibiting symptoms
chancre	a red, hard, painless skin lesion associated with syphilis
CNS	Central Nervous System
conjunctiva	thin layer of cells covering the front of the eyeball and the inner surface of the lids
contraindicated	a condition in which a drug must not be given
cyanosis	a blue tinge to the lips and skin resulting from lack of oxygen
cystitis	bladder inflammation
diagnosis	determination of a disease by assessment of the symptoms
diuretic	a drug that promotes fluid loss through the kidneys, causing increased urine output
dysparaenia	pain during sexual intercourse
encephalitis	inflammation of the brain
endemic	prevalent, common or frequently occurring in a particular area
endoscopy	a flexible fibreoptic tube passed down the throat to examine the stomach
envenomation	the transfer of poisonous venom
enzymes	naturally produced proteins which act as catalysts for chemical reactions between other substances
epidemic	a rapid, geographically localized spread of infectious disease
faecal-oral	the method by which most gut microbes are passed on, ie faeces to hands to mouth
fluke	a flatworm, usually parasitic
fracture	a broken bone
glaucoma	a build-up of pressure within the eye producing visual problems
haematemesis	vomiting blood
haematuria	blood in the urine
haemoglobin	the oxygen-carrying molecule of the blood
haemorrhagic fever	a viral infection which results in increased bleeding tendency
hypoglycaemia	low blood sugar
immunoglobulins	antibodies used by the body to fight infection

immunosuppressed	an inability to fight off infection
impetigo	a bacterial infection of the skin which results in honey-coloured crusting
intravenous	drugs or fluids given directly into a vein via a drip or injection
jaundice	yellow discolouration of the skin and conjunctiva resulting from a build-up of bile pigments in the blood and with a variety of causes
lumbar puncture	a large needle passed into the space around the spinal cord to tap off cerebrospinal fluid for lab analysis
lymphangitis	inflammation of the lymphatic system
lymphatic system	the anatomical system connecting the lymph glands to the venous system of the blood
malaise	non-specifically unwell, "out of sorts"
meningism	the physical signs that suggest meningitis
meningitis	swelling of the meninges, the membranes covering the brain
microfilariae	embryos of filariae, a parasitic worm family transmitted to vertebrates by insects
morbidity	the state of being diseased
myasthenia gravis	progressive disorder causing muscle weakness
nodule	a knob-like growth
NSAIDs	Non-Steroidal Anti-Inflamatory Drugs
oedema	(edema in US) – swelling caused by accumulation of fluid in the tissues
pancreatitis	inflammation of the pancreas
perineum	the area of the body between the genitals and anus
peritonitis	inflammation of the peritoneum, the lining of the abdominal cavity
pessary	a drug placed in the vagina
photophobia	intolerance to bright light
pneumothorax	a punctured lung, causing air to escape into the chest cavity
porphyria	a rare, inherited disorder which affects the production of haemoglobin in the red blood cells
prognosis	the likely overall outcome of an illness
prophylactic	preventative
prostate gland	a gland surrounding the urethra (the bladder outflow) in men
protozoa	a single-cell organism
pulmonary	pertaining to the lungs
purgative	a drug that promotes bowel clearance
purulent	the presence of pus
pyrexia	fever
renal	pertaining to the kidneys
reservoir	where disease-causing organisms are maintained in the wild
rickettsia	a virulent sub-group of bacteria responsible for a number of potentially serious illnesses, eg Rocky Mountain spotted fever, Q fever and typhus
RIG	Rabies Immunoglobulin; part of the post-exposure treatment for rabies
rigor	uncontrollable shaking and a sensation of cold caused by fever
sciatica	back pain which radiates down the back of the leg
septicaemia	blood poisoning
sigmoidoscopy	an examination of the large bowel using a fibreoptic instrument
suppository	a drug in tablet form which is placed in the rectum
symptom	a departure of normal body function, appearance or sensation usually indicative of disease
tinnitus	a buzzing or ringing sound in the ear
topical	usually referring to the application of creams or tinctures to the skin

tourniquet	a tight constriction wrapped around a limb to restrict blood flow
URTI	Upper Respiratory Tract Infection; medical speak for a "cold"
vesicle	a fluid-filled skin lesion; "water blisters"
weal	a pale, raised patch of skin caused by allergy or irritation
WHO	World Health Organization
zoonosis	a disease acquired by contact with animals

GLOSSARY

Advertiser

Rough Guides travel...

UK & Ireland
Britain
Devon & Cornwall
Dublin
Edinburgh
England
Ireland
Lake District
London
London mini guide
London Restaurants
London & SE England,
  Walks in
Scotland
Scottish Highlands &
  Islands
Wales

Europe
Algarve
Amsterdam
Andalucía
Austria
Baltic States
Barcelona
Belgium & Luxembourg
Berlin
Brittany & Normandy
Bruges & Ghent
Brussels
Budapest
Bulgaria
Copenhagen
Corfu
Corsica
Costa Brava
Crete
Croatia
Cyprus
Czech & Slovak
  Republics
Dodecanese & East
  Aegean
Dordogne & The Lot
Europe
First-Time Europe
Florence
France

Germany
Greece
Greek Islands
Hungary
Ibiza & Formentera
Iceland
Ionian Islands
Italy
Languedoc & Roussillon
Lisbon
The Loire
Madeira
Madrid
Mallorca
Malta & Gozo
Menorca
Moscow
Netherlands
Norway
Paris
Paris Mini Guide
Poland
Portugal
Prague
Provence & the Côte
  d'Azur
Pyrenees
Romania
Rome
Sardinia
Scandinavia
Sicily
Slovenia
Spain
St Petersburg
Sweden
Switzerland
Tenerife & La Gomera
Turkey
Tuscany & Umbria
Venice & The Veneto
Vienna

Asia
Bali & Lombok
Bangkok
Beijing

Cambodia
China
First-Time Asia
Goa
Hong Kong & Macau
India
Indonesia
Japan
Laos
Malaysia, Singapore &
  Brunei
Nepal
Philippines
Singapore
South India
Southeast Asia
Thailand
Thailand Beaches &
  Islands
Tokyo
Vietnam

Australasia
Australia
Gay & Lesbian Australia
Melbourne
New Zealand
Sydney

North America
Alaska
Big Island of Hawaii
Boston
California
Canada
Chicago
Florida
Grand Canyon
Hawaii
Honolulu
Las Vegas
Los Angeles
Maui
Miami & the Florida
  Keys
Montréal
New England

New Orleans
New York City
New York City Mini
  Guide
New York Restaurants
Pacific Northwest
Rocky Mountains
San Francisco
San Francisco
  Restaurants
Seattle
Skiing & Snowboarding
  in North America
Southwest USA
Toronto
USA
Vancouver
Washington DC
Yosemite

Caribbean
& Latin America
Antigua & Barbuda
Argentina
Bahamas
Barbados
Belize
Bolivia
Brazil
Caribbean
Central America
Chile
Costa Rica
Cuba
Dominican Republic
Ecuador
First-Time Latin
  America
Guatemala
Jamaica
Maya World
Mexico
Peru
St Lucia
South America
Trinidad & Tobago

Rough Guides are available from good bookstores worldwide. New titles are
published every month. Check www.roughguides.com for the latest news.

...music & reference

Africa & Middle East
Cape Town
Egypt
The Gambia
Jordan
Kenya
Morocco
South Africa, Lesotho & Swaziland
Syria
Tanzania
Tunisia
West Africa
Zanzibar
Zimbabwe

Travel Theme guides
First-Time Around the World
First-Time Asia
First-Time Europe
First-Time Latin America
Skiing & Snowboarding in North America
Travel Online
Travel Health
Walks in London & SE England
Women Travel

Restaurant guides
French Hotels & Restaurants
London
New York
San Francisco

Maps
Algarve
Amsterdam
Andalucia & Costa del Sol
Argentina
Athens
Australia
Baja California
Barcelona

Boston
Brittany
Brussels
Chicago
Crete
Croatia
Cuba
Cyprus
Czech Republic
Dominican Republic
Dublin
Egypt
Florence & Siena
Frankfurt
Greece
Guatemala & Belize
Iceland
Ireland
Lisbon
London
Los Angeles
Mexico
Miami & Key West
Morocco
New York City
New Zealand
Northern Spain
Paris
Portugal
Prague
Rome
San Francisco
Sicily
South Africa
Sri Lanka
Tenerife
Thailand
Toronto
Trinidad & Tobago
Tuscany
Venice
Washington DC
Yucatán Peninsula

Dictionary Phrasebooks
Czech
Dutch
Egyptian Arabic
European
French
German
Greek
Hindi & Urdu
Hungarian
Indonesian
Italian
Japanese
Mandarin Chinese
Mexican Spanish
Polish
Portuguese
Russian
Spanish
Swahili
Thai
Turkish
Vietnamese

Music Guides
The Beatles
Cult Pop
Classical Music
Country Music
Cuban Music
Drum'n'bass
Elvis
House
Irish Music
Jazz
Music USA
Opera
Reggae
Rock
Techno
World Music (2 vols)

100 Essential CDs series
Country
Latin
Opera
Rock
Soul
World Music

History Guides
China
Egypt
England
France
India
Islam
Italy
Spain
USA

Reference Guides
Books for Teenagers
Children's Books, 0–5
Children's Books, 5–11
Cult Football
Cult Movies
Cult TV
Digital Stuff
Formula 1
The Internet
Internet Radio
James Bond
Lord of the Rings
Man Utd
Personal Computers
Pregnancy & Birth
Shopping Online
Travel Health
Travel Online
Unexplained Phenomena
The Universe
Videogaming
Weather
Website Directory

Also! More than 120 Rough Guide music CDs are available from all good book and record stores. Listen in at www.worldmusic.net

Number One
Health group
Number One
for Travel Health
Number One
Harley Street
London W1G 9QD

www.travelscreening.co.uk
Tel: 0207 307 8756
info@travelscreening.co.uk
Adult and Child
Vaccinations
Malaria medication and advice
Travel health products

Visa Medicals
Returned traveller
Health checks

7

Index and
small print

A Rough Guide to Rough Guides

In the summer of 1981, Mark Ellingham, a recent graduate from Bristol University, was travelling round Greece and couldn't find a guidebook that really met his needs. On the one hand there were the student guides, insistent on saving every last cent, and on the other the heavyweight cultural tomes whose authors seemed to have spent more time in a research library than lounging away the afternoon at a taverna or on the beach.

In a bid to avoid getting a job, Mark and a small group of writers set about creating their own guidebook. It was a guide to Greece that aimed to combine a journalistic approach to description with a thoroughly practical approach to travellers' needs – a guide that would incorporate culture, history and contemporary insights with a critical edge, together with up-to-date, value-for-money listings. Back in London, Mark and the team finished their Rough Guide, as they called it, and talked Routledge into publishing the book.

That first *Rough Guide to Greece*, published in 1982, was a student scheme that became a publishing phenomenon. The immediate success of the book – with numerous reprints and a Thomas Cook prize shortlisting – spawned a series that rapidly covered dozens of destinations. Rough Guides had a ready market among low-budget backpackers, but soon also acquired a much broader and older readership that relished Rough Guides' wit and inquisitiveness as much as their enthusiastic, critical approach. Everyone wants value for money, but not at any price.

Rough Guides soon began supplementing the "rougher" information about hostels and low-budget listings with the kind of detail on restaurants and quality hotels that independent-minded visitors on any budget might expect, whether on business in New York or trekking in Thailand.

These days the guides – distributed worldwide by the Penguin group – offer recommendations from shoestring to luxury and cover more than 200 destinations around the globe, including almost every country in the Americas and Europe, more than half of Africa and most of Asia and Australasia. Our ever-growing team of authors and photographers is spread all over the world, particularly in Europe, the USA and Australia.

In 1994, we published the *Rough Guide to World Music* and *Rough Guide to Classical Music*; and a year later the *Rough Guide to the Internet*. All three books have become benchmark titles in their fields – which encouraged us to expand into other areas of publishing, mainly around popular culture. Rough Guides now publish:

- Travel guides to more than 200 worldwide destinations
- Dictionary phrasebooks to 22 major languages
- History guides ranging from Ireland to Islam
- Maps printed on rip-proof and waterproof Polyart™ paper
- Music guides running the gamut from Opera to Elvis
- Restaurant guides to London, New York and San Francisco
- Reference books on topics as diverse as the Weather and Shakespeare
- Sports guides from Formula 1 to Man Utd
- Pop culture books from *Lord of the Rings* to Cult TV
- World Music CDs in association with World Music Network

Visit www.roughguides.com to see our latest publications.

Rough Guide Credits

Text editor: Polly Thomas
Design & Layout: Diana Jarvis
Cartography: Ed Wright
Picture research: Sharon Martins
Proofreader: David Price

....

Editorial: **London** Martin Dunford, Kate
Berens, Helena Smith, Claire Saunders, Geoff
Howard, Ruth Blackmore, Gavin Thomas,
Polly Thomas, Richard Lim, Lucy Ratcliffe,
Clifton Wilkinson, Alison Murchie, Fran
Sandham, Sally Schafer, Alexander Mark
Rogers, Karoline Densley, Andy Turner, Ella
O'Donnell, Keith Drew, Andrew Lockett, Joe
Staines, Duncan Clark, Peter Buckley,
Matthew Milton; **New York** Andrew
Rosenberg, Richard Koss, Yuki Takagaki,
Hunter Slaton, Chris Barsanti, Steven Horak
Design & Pictures: **London** Simon Bracken,
Dan May, Diana Jarvis, Mark Thomas, Jj
Luck, Harriet Mills; **Delhi** Madhulita
Mohapatra, Umesh Aggarwal, Ajay Verma,
Jessica Subramanian

Publishing Information

Production: Julia Bovis, John McKay,
Sophie Hewat
Cartography: **London** Maxine Repath, Ed
Wright, Katie Lloyd-Jones, Miles Irving; **Delhi**
Manish Chandra, Rajesh Chhibber, Jai
Prakesh Mishra, Ashutosh Bharti, Rajesh
Mishra, Animesh Pathak, Jasbir Sandhu,
Karobi Gogoi
Cover art direction: Louise Boulton
Online: **New York** Jennifer Gold, Cree
Lawson, Suzanne Welles, Benjamin Ross;
Delhi Manik Chauhan, Narender Kumar,
Shekhar Jha, Rakesh Kumar
Marketing & Publicity: **London** Richard
Trillo, Niki Smith, David Wearn, Chloë
Roberts, Demelza Dallow, Kristina Pentland;
New York Geoff Colquitt, Megan Kennedy
Finance: Gary Singh
Manager India: Punita Singh
Series editor: Mark Ellingham
PA to Managing Director: Julie Sanderson
Managing Director: Kevin Fitzgerald

This 2nd edition published August 2004 by
Rough Guides Ltd,
80 Strand, London WC2R 0RL.
345 Hudson St, 4th Floor,
New York, NY 10014, USA.
Distributed by the Penguin Group
Penguin Books Ltd,
80 Strand, London WC2R 0RL
Penguin Putnam, Inc.
375 Hudson Street, NY 10014, USA
Penguin Books Australia Ltd,
487 Maroondah Highway, PO Box 257,
Ringwood, Victoria 3134, Australia
Penguin Books Canada Ltd,
10 Alcorn Avenue, Toronto, Ontario,
Canada M4V 1E4
Penguin Books (NZ) Ltd,
182–190 Wairau Road, Auckland 10,
New Zealand
Typeset in Bembo and Helvetica to an original
design by Henry Iles.

3   5   7   9   8   6   4   2

Printed in Italy by LegoPrint S.p.A

© Nick Jones

No part of this book may be reproduced in any
form without permission from the publisher
except for the quotation of brief passages in
reviews.

304pp includes index
A catalogue record for this book is available from
the British Library

ISBN 1-84353-324-3

The publishers and authors have done their best
to ensure the accuracy and currency of all the
information in **The Rough Guide to Travel
Health**, however, they can accept no
responsibility for any loss, injury, or
inconvenience sustained by any traveller as a
result of information or advice contained in the
guide.

Help us update

We've gone to a lot of effort to ensure that
the 2nd edition of **The Rough Guide to
Travel Health** is accurate and up-to-date.
However, things change. If you feel we've got
it wrong or left something out, we'd like to
know.

We'll credit all contributions, and send a
copy of the next edition (or any other Rough
Guide if you prefer) for the best letters.
Everyone who writes to us and isn't already a

subscriber will receive a copy of our full-
colour thrice-yearly newsletter. Please mark
letters: "**Rough Guide Travel Health
Update**" and send to: Rough Guides, 80
Strand, London WC2R 0RL, or Rough
Guides, 4th Floor, 345 Hudson St, New York,
NY 10014. Or send an email to
mail@roughguides.com
Have your questions answered and tell
others about your trip at
www.roughguides.atinfopop.com

Acknowledgements

Nick Jones: I would like to dedicate this book to my uncle, Tom Jones, and my daughter, Phoebe, who have reminded me in very different ways that there is a lot more about determination than simply writing a book. Both have been a great inspiration.

As ever it is my family who I must thank most for putting up with the occasional black mood and the inordinate of time I have spent on this project and away from them. My sincere love and thanks to Jo, Wizz and P.

Grateful thanks once again to all at Rough Guides for support, advice and helping to bring it all together, capably led on this occasion by Polly Thomas. I would also like to particularly thank Dr Janet Gray (homeopathy), Bevin Clare (herbalism), Janet Hope-Brown (American translator!) and Dr Charlie Easmon (expert in tropical diseases) for their invaluable contributions, and to all the authors and poor victims of the travellers' tales for adding a sense of grim reality to it all. I am indebted to my friends and colleagues at St Chad's Surgery for their support and encouragement throughout.

Photo Credits

Main front cover picture: Pharmacy sign © Getty
Small front cover right picture: Hikers © Getty
Small front cover left picture: Mosquito © Science Photo Library
Back top cover picture: Climbers © Robert Harding
Back lower cover picture: Scuba diving © Robert Harding

Aspirin © Randy Faris/Corbis
Thai anti-AIDS poster © Eye Ubiquitous/Corbis
Medicinal herbs © Adam Woolfitt/Corbis
Spectactle and denture stall, India © Enzo & Paolo Ragazzini/Corbis
Eye examination ©Liba Taylor/Corbis
Cell cultures in petri dishes © Bill Varie/Corbis
No swimming sign © Joseph Sohm, ChromoSohm Inc/Corbis
Purple jellyfish © Brandon D. Cole/Corbis
Snake venom © Jeffrey L. Rotman/Corbis
Doctor signs © Nik Wheeler/Corbis
Penicillin © Science Pictures Limited/Corbis
Cowboy First Aid © Henry Diltz/Corbis.

A

J

K

L

M

N

O

P

ultraviolet light 210
unconsciousness 238, 242